KB035615

주한미군지위협정(SOFA)

서명 및 발효 6

주한미군지위협정(SOFA)

서명 및 발효 6

한국학술정보

| 머리말

미국은 오래전부터 우리나라 외교에 있어서 가장 긴밀하고 실질적인 우호 · 협력관계를 맺어 온 나라다. 6 · 25전쟁 정전 협정이 체결된 후 북한의 재침을 막기 위한 대책으로서 1953년 11월 한미 상호방위조약이 체결되었다. 이는 미군이 한국에 주둔하는 법적 근거였고, 그렇게 주둔하게 된 미군의 시설, 구역, 사업, 용역, 출입국, 통관과 관세, 재판권 등 포괄적인 법적 지위를 규정하는 것이 바로 주한미군지위협정(SOFA)이다. 그러나 이와 관련한 협상은 계속된 난항을 겪으며 한미 상호방위조약이 체결로부터 10년이 훌쩍 넘은 1967년이 돼서야 정식 발효에 이를 수 있었다. 그럼에도 당시 미군 범죄에 대한 한국의 재판권은 심한 제약을 받았으며, 1980년대 후반 민주화 운동과 함께 미군 범죄 문제가 사회적 이슈로 떠오르자 협정을 개정해야 한다는 목소리가 커지게 되었다. 이에 1991년 2월 주한미군지위협정 1차 개정이 진행되었고, 이후에도 여러 사건이 발생하며 2001년 4월 2차 개정이 진행되어 현재에 이르고 있다.

본 총서는 외교부에서 작성하여 최근 공개한 주한미군지위협정(SOFA) 관련 자료를 담고 있다. 1953년 한미 상호방위조약 체결 이후부터 1967년 발효가 이뤄지기까지의 자료와 더불어, 이후 한미 합동위원회를 비롯해 민 · 형사재판권, 시설, 노무, 교통 등 각 분과위원회의 회의록과 운영 자료, 한국인 고용인 문제와 관련한 자료, 기타 관련 분쟁 자료 등을 포함해 총 42권으로 구성되었다. 전체 분량은 약 2만 2천여 쪽에 이른다.

2024년 3월

한국학술정보(주)

| 일러두기

· 본 총서에 실린 자료는 2022년 4월과 2023년 4월에 각각 공개한 외교문서 4,827권, 76만 여 쪽 가운데 일부를 발췌한 것이다.

· 각 권의 제목과 순서는 공개된 원본을 최대한 반영하였으나, 주제에 따라 일부는 적절히 변경하였다.

· 원본 자료는 A4 판형에 맞게 축소하거나 원본 비율을 유지한 채 A4 페이지 안에 삽입하였다. 또한 현재 시점에선 공개되지 않아 '공란'이란 표기만 있는 페이지 역시 그대로 실었다.

· 외교부가 공개한 문서 각 권의 첫 페이지에는 '정리 보존 문서 목록'이란 이름으로 기록물 종류, 일자, 명칭, 간단한 내용 등의 정보가 수록되어 있으며, 이를 기준으로 0001번부터 번호가 매겨져 있다. 이는 삭제하지 않고 총서에 그대로 수록하였다.

· 보고서 내용에 관한 더 자세한 정보가 필요하다면, 외교부가 온라인상에 제공하는 『대한민국 외교사료요약집』 1991년과 1992년 자료를 참조할 수 있다.

| 차례

정/리/보/존/문/서/목/록

<table>
<tr><td>기록물종류</td><td>문서-일반공문서철</td><td>등록번호</td><td>916
9589</td><td>등록일자</td><td>2006-07-27</td></tr>
<tr><td>분류번호</td><td>741.12</td><td>국가코드</td><td>US</td><td>주제</td><td></td></tr>
<tr><td>문서철명</td><td colspan="5">한.미국 간의 상호방위조약 제4조에 의한 시설과 구역 및 한국에서의 미국군대의 지위에 관한 협정 (SOFA) 전59권. 1966.7.9 서울에서 서명 : 1967.2.9 발효 (조약 232호) *원본</td></tr>
<tr><td>생산과</td><td>미주과/조약과</td><td>생산년도</td><td>1952 - 1967</td><td>보존기간</td><td>영구</td></tr>
<tr><td>담당과(그룹)</td><td>조약</td><td>조약</td><td>서가번호</td><td colspan="2">--</td></tr>
<tr><td>참조분류</td><td colspan="5"></td></tr>
<tr><td>권차명</td><td colspan="5">V.18 실무교섭회의, 제21-27차, 1963.5.-7월</td></tr>
<tr><td>내용목차</td><td colspan="5">1. 제21차 회의, 5.3 (p.2~44)
2. 제22차 회의, 5.17 (p.45~77)
3. 제23차 회의, 5.31 (p.78~110)
4. 제24차 회의, 6.12 (p.111~152)
5. 제25차 회의, 6.26 (p.153~189)
6. 제26차 회의, 7.10 (p.190~217)
7. 제27차 회의, 7.25 (p.218~254)

* 일지 :
1953.8.7 이승만 대통령-Dulles 미국 국무장관 공동성명
- 상호방위조약 발효 후 군대지위협정 교섭 약속
1954.12.2 정부, 주한 UN군의 관세업무협정 체결 제의
1955.1월, 5월 미국, 제의 거절
1955.4.28 정부, 군대지위협정 제의 (한국측 초안 제시)
1957.9.10 Hurter 미국 국무차관 방한 시 각서 수교 (한국측 제의 수락 요구)
1957.11.13, 26 정부, 개별 협정의 단계적 체결 제의
1958.9.18 Dawling 주한미국대사, 형사재판관할권 협정 제외 조건으로 행정협정 체결 의사 전달
1960.3.10 정부, 토지, 시설협정의 우선적 체결 강력 요구
1961.4.10 장면 국무총리-McConaughy 주한미국대사 공동성명으로 교섭 개시 합의
1961.4.15, 4.25 제1, 2차 한.미국 교섭회의 (서울)
1962.3.12 정부, 교섭 재개 촉구 공한 송부
1962.5.14 Burger 주한미국대사, 최규하 장관 면담 시 형사재판관할권 문제 제기 않는 조건으로 교섭 재개 통고
1962.9.6 한.미국 간 공동성명 발표 (9월 중 교섭 재개 합의)
1962.9.20~1965.6.7 제1-81차 실무 교섭회의 (서울)
1966.7.8 제82차 실무 교섭회의 (서울)
1966.7.9 서명
1967.2.9 발효 (조약 232호)</td></tr>
</table>

마/이/크/로/필/름/사/항

촬영연도	*롤 번호	화일 번호	후레임 번호	보관함 번호
2006-11-22	I-06-0068	03	1-254	

0001

1. 제2차 회의, 5.3

0002

기 안 용 지

자 체 통 제		기안처	미주과 이 경 훈	전화번호	근거서류접수일자

	과장	국장	보좌관	차관	장관
	5/2	5/2		3.	

관 계 관 서 명	기획조정관

기 안 년 월 일	63. 5. 2.	시 행 년월일		보존 년한		정 서	기 장
분 류 기 호	외정미	전 체 통 제		종결			

경 유 수 신 참 조	건 의	발 신	

제 목	미주둔군 지위협정 체결 교섭회의 수석대표 임명

정무국장 황호을 이사관을 다음과같은 이유로 진필식 기획조정관을 대신하여 미주둔군지위협정 체결 교섭회의 대표단 수석대표로 임명할것을 건의하나이다.

- 기 -

1. 원래 우리측은 미주둔군지위협정 체결 교섭회의의 수석대표로서 한국측은 외무부차관으로 하고 미국측은 "매지스트레티" 부대사로 할것을 제의하였든바 미국측은 주한미대사관 정치담당 "하비브" 참사관을 수석대표로 임명할것을 주장하여 왔기 이에 부합시키기 위하여 정무국장을 우리측 수석대표로 임명하였던 것임.
2. 정무국장은 미주둔군 지위협정 체결 교섭회의의 주무국장인 동시에 전술 1.에서 언급한것등에 비추어당연직으로서 미주둔군 지위협정체결 교섭회의 수석대표가 된다고 사료됨. 끝

승인양식 1—1—3 (1112—040—016—018) (190mm×260mm16절지)

21-1 0003

SOFA NEGOTIATION

Agenda for 21st Session

14:00 May 2, 1963

1. Continuation of Discussion on:

   a. Armed Forces Contractors Article

   b. Non-appropriated Fund Organizations Article

2. Other Business

3. Agenda and Date of Next Meeting

4. Press Release

0004

기 안 용 지

자 체 통 제		기안처	미주과 이경훈	전화번호	근거서류접수일자

	과장	국장	보좌관	차관	장관
	5/3	5/3		5/3	

관계관 서명	조약과장 기획조정관

기안 년월일	63. 5. 2.	시행 년월일		보존 년한		정서기장
분류 기호	외정미	전체 통제		종결		
경유 수신 참조	건 의			발신		
제목	제21차 및제22차 주둔군지위협정 체결교섭회의에 임할 우리측 입장					

5월 3일에 개최될 제21차 주둔군지위협정 체결 한미간 교섭 회의에서는 군계약자 및 비세출기관 문제에 관하여 토의될 예정이온바 이에관련하여 우리측 교섭 실무자는 5월 1일 회합을 갖고 제21차 회의에서 취할 우리측 태도를 별첨과 같이 결정하였아오니 재가하여 주시기 바랍니다.

유첨 : 제21차 주둔군지위협정 체결교섭회의에 임할 우리측 태도.

1966.12.31 1967.9.30 직권으로 예고문

1966.12.31 에 의거 일반문서로 재분류됨

26-1

승인양식 1-1-3 (1112-040-016-018) (190mm×260mm16절지)

0005

1. 군계약자

(1) 군계약자의 한국법에 대한 복속원칙에 관한 미국측 초안 1항 (이는 우리측 초안 1항에 해당함)에 있어서 (가) 동 미국측 초안은 한국측 초안에 삽입되어 있는 "organized under the laws of the United States" 라는 구절과 who are ordinarily resident in the United States" 라는 용어를 삭제하고 있는데 이는 미국측이 군계약을 체결할수 있는 법인이나, 군계약자가 채용할 고용원을 미국인에 국한시키지 않고 제3국인에게까지 확대시키기 위한 규정으로 사료되는바 우리측은 동 구절을 삭제한 이유를 미국측에 문의한후 우리측 안의 수락을 요구토록 한다. (나) 또한 미국측 초안 제1항에는 우리측 초안에는 없는 "other armed forces in Korea under the Unified Command receiving logistical support from the United States armed forces" 라는 구절이 있는바 현재 한국에는 안전보장이사회의 결의에 의거하여 통합군사령부 하에 주둔하고 있는 미국 이외의 군대가 한국에 주둔하고 있으므로 동구절은 수락해주기로 한다.

(2) 군계약자의 지정 및 지정철회에 관한 미국측 초안 제2항 (이는 우리측 초안 2항에 해당함)은 우리측 초안과 실질적인 차이가 없으므로 미국측안을 수락하기로 한다.

(3) 군계약자가 향유할 이익에관한 미국측 초안 3항 (이는 우리측 초안 3항에 해당함)에 있어서 (가) 미국측은 3(a)항에 우리측 안에없는 토지시설 간의 이동권을 규정하고 있으며, 3(h)항에는 우리측안에 없는 공익물 및 용역에관련한 미국군대에게 부여된 권리규정을 두고있으며 또한 3(i)항에는 우리측안에 없는 운전면허 및 차량등록에 관련된 권리 규정을 두고있는바

26-2

0006

3(a)항을 제외한 3(h) 및 3(i)항은 우리측안대로 삭제하자고 주장한다. (나) 또한 동3항에 있어서 미국측은 3(e)항에 외환관리 규정에 관련하여 부여된 권리 (rights) 라고 규정하고 있는데 동 "권리"라는 용어를 삭제토록 주장하고, (다) 3(b) 및 3(c)항은 관계조항의 합의를 조건으로 수락하고, (다) 기타 항에 대하여는 수락하기로 한다.

(4) 군계약자가 소지할 여권 및 그들의 도착, 출발 및 거주에관한 통고 규정에 관한 미국측 초안 4항 (이는 우리측 초안 4항에 해당함)에 있어서 미국측은 우리측 초안 4항 전단에 있는 여권에관한 규정이 삭제되고 있는데 이규정은 출입국관리의 관계규정과 관련하여있고 또한 군계약자의 신분을 명백히 하는데 필요한것이므로 우리측안대로 동규정은 삽입토록 주장한다.

(5) 감가상각 재산에 대한 면세 규정에관한 미국측 초안 5항은 우리측 초안에는 없는것인바 미국측의 이에관한 설명을 들은후 다시 우리측 태도를 결정토록 한다.

(6) 군계약자에 대한 재산의 보유, 사용 및 이전에관련한 조세면제 규정에관한 미국측 초안 6항 (이는 우리측 초안 5항에 해당함) 에 있어서 "other business" 라는 용어는 우리측안에서 말하는바와 같이 "other business than those executing contracts as described in paragraph 1 of this Article in the Republic of Korea " 로 대치토록하고 미국측안을 수락토록 한다.

(7) 소득세 및 법인세에 관한 미국측초안 7항 (우리측 초안 6항에 해당함)에 있어서 미국측 초안은우리측 안과 실질적 차이가 없으므로 이를 수락하되 다만 미국측 초안 둘째문장의 전단 "Persons in Korea in connection with the execution of such a contract with the United States shall not be liable to pay any Korean taxes to the Government

26-3

0007

of Korea or to any taxing agency in Korea on income derived from sources outside of Korea"

라는 구절은 미국측 초안 셋째문장 전단과 중복되는 것이므로 이의 삭제를 요구하는 동시에 미국측 초안 둘째문장 후단

"nor shall periods during which such persons are in Korea be considered periods of residence or domicile in Korea for the purposes of Korean taxation "

라는 구절은 다음과같은 완전한 1개 문장으로 수정하여 제7항 말미에 삽입토록 제의한다.

"Periods during which such persons are in Korea solely in connection with the execution of a contract with the Government of the United States shall not be considered periods of residence or domicile in Korea for the purpose of such taxation."

(8) 군계약자에 대한 재판 관할권에 관한 규정인 우리측 초안 제7항은 미국측 초안에는 규정되어 있지않으나 우리측은 우리측 안의 수락을 주장한다.

(9) 미국측은 합의의사록에 1개항목을 제시하였는데이에 관하여 미국측의 설명을 요구한후 우리측 태도를 결정토록 한다.

2. 비세출기관

(1) 비세출기관의 설치 허여에관한 미국측 초안 1항 (이는 우리측 초안 1항에 해당함)에 있어서 (가) 미국측은 우리측안에 규정되어있는 "within the facilities and areas" 라는 구절과 "exclusive" 라는 언어가 삭제되어 있는데 우리측은 이의 삽입을 주장토록 하고, (나) 미국측은 신문도 일반 비세출 기관과 마찬가지로 일괄적으로 규정하여 한국 규정에 복종치 않도록 규정하고 있는데 대하여 우리측 안에서는 신문은

26-4

0008

다른 비세출 기관과 구별하여 별도로 규정하여 한국 규정에 복속토록 규정하고 있는바 우리측은 우리측안의 수락을 요구토록 한다.

(2) 조세면제에 관한 미국측 초안 2항 (이는 우리측 초안 2항에 해당함)은 우리측안과 실질적 차이가 없으므로 미국측안을 수락하되 동 미국측 안의 2항 첫재문장 말미에 "except as provided in paragraph 1 (b)"라는 구절을 삽입토록 주장한다.

(3) 비세출기관에 의하여 판매되는 상품에관한 미국측 초안 제3항 (이는 우리측초안 3항에 해당함)은 우리측 초안과 실질적 큰차가 없으므로 미국측안을 수락토록 한다. 다만 미국측 초안에서 사용되고 있는 "permitted" 라는 용어는 다음에 규정된 용어가 "persons not authorized" 로 되어있는것에 비추어 보아 이용어도 "authorized" 로 수정토록 주장한다.

(4) 비세출기관에 의하여 수입되는 상품수량의 제한에 관한 우리측 초안 4항은 미국측안에는 규정되어 있지않는바 이러한 제한은 필요한것이므로 이의 삽입을 주장토록 한다.

(5) 비세출기관에 관련된 정보제공에 관한 미국측 초안 제4항 (이는 우리측 초안 제5항에 해당함)은 우리측 초안과 실질적 차이가 없으므로 미국측 안을 수락하기로 하되 미국측안에서 규정한 "after consultation between the representatives of the two governments in the Joint Committee " 라는 구절은 삭제토록 주장한다.

(6) 비세출기관의 사용자에 대한 예외적 규정에관한 미국측 초안 제5항은 우리측 초안에는 없는것으로 이러한 예외적 규정은 꼭 필요한 경우라면 그성질상 합의의사록에 규정할것이지 조약원문에 규정할것이 아님으로 이를 합의의사록에 규정토록

26-5

0009

제의하되 미국측 안에서 규정한 "by non-Korean persons whose presence ...." 이하는 삭제토록 주장한다.

(7) 비세출기관에 관한 용어문제에 있어서 미국측은 "non-Appropriated Fund Activities"를 주장하고 있는데대하여 우리측은 "Non-Appropriated Fund Organizations " 라는 용어를 주장하고 있는바 이에 관련하여, (가) 우리측은 "organization"의 사용을 주장하도록 하고 이를 미국측이 거부할 경우에는 (나) "Activities" 라는 용어를 수락하되 미국측 초안 1항에서 말한고있는 "other non-appropriated fund Activities " 라는 용어에 해당되는 "activities" 를 명시하여 제한시키자고 주장토록 한다. 만일 미국측이 이것도 거부할시에는 (다) "other non-appropriated fund Activities" 라는 용어를 "such other non-appropriated fund activities as mutually agreed upon between the two governments through the Joint Committee" 라는 구절로 대치토록 제의한다.

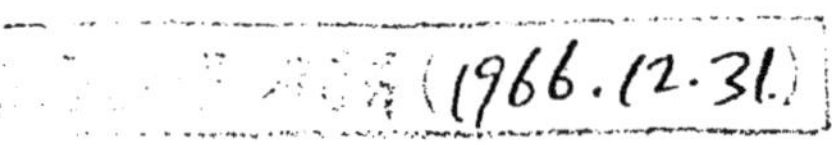

1966.12.31.에 예고문에 의거 일반문서로 재분류됨

26-6

0010

기 안 용 지

자체 통제		기안처	미주과 이경훈	전화번호	근거서류접수일자

	과장	국장	보좌관	차관	장관

관계관 서명: 조약과장

기안 년월일	63. 5. 4.	시행 년월일		보존 년한		정서	기장
분류 기호	외정미 722.2	전체 통제		종결			

경유 수신 참조	국가재건최고회의 의장 (참조: 외무국방위원장) 내각수반	발신	장관

제목: 주둔군지위협정 체결을위한 제21차 교섭회의 보고

1963. 5. 3. 하오 2시부터 동 4시 10분까지 외무부장관 회의실에서 개최된 제21차 주둔군지위협정 체결 교섭회의에서 토의된 내용을 별첨과같이 보고합니다.

유첨 : 제21차 교섭회의 보고서 부. 끝

보통문서로 재분류(1966. 12. 31)

발송 외무부 1963. 5. 6.

1964년 9월30일 직권으로 예고문 ...

1966. 12. 31 에 예고문에 의거 일반문서로 재분류됨

승인양식 1-1-3 (1112-040-016-018) (190mm×260mm16절지)

0011

외 무 부

외정미 722.2 1963. 5. 6.

수 신 : 국가재건 최고회의 의장

참 조 : 외무국방 위원장

제 목 : 주둔군 지위 협정 체결을 위한 제 21차 교섭 회의 보고

1963. 5. 3. 하오 2 시부터 동 4시 10분 까지 외무부 장관 회의실에서 개최된 제 21차 주둔군 지위 협정 체결 교섭 회의에서 토의된 내용을 별첨과 같이 보고 합니다.

유첨 : 제 21차 교섭 회의 보고서 2 부. 끝.

외 무 부 장 관 김 용 식

0012

17-5

외 무 부

외정미 722.2 1963. 5. 6.

수 신 : 내각수반

제 목 : 주둔군 지위 협정 체결을 위한 제 21차 교섭 회의 보고

1963. 5. 3. 하오 2시 부터 동 4시 10분 까지 외무부 장관 회의실에서 개최된 제 21차 주둔군 지위 협정 체결 교섭 회의에서 토의된 내용을 별첨과 같이 보고 합니다.

유첨 : 제 21차 교섭회의 보고서 1부. 끝.

외 무 부 장 관 김 용 식

0013

17-6

제 21 차

한미간 주둔군지위협정 체결 실무자회의

보 고 서

1. 일 시 : 1963. 5. 3. 하오 2시부터 4시 10분 가지

2. 장 소 : 외무부장관 회의실

3. 참석자 : 한국측 : 황 호 을 (외무부 정무국장)

신 관 섭 (재무부 세관국장)

윤 하 정 (외무부 1등서기관)

구 충 회 (외무부 미주과장)

신 정 섭 (외무부 조약과장)

이 남 구 (국방부 군무과장)

주 문 기 (법무부 법무과장)

노 재 원 (외무부 2등서기관)

이 경 훈 (")

조 광 제 (")

강 석 재 (외무부 3등서기관)

미국측 : 교섭대표단 전원 ("로마"장군 제외)

4. 토의사항 :

(1) 비세출기관에 관한 조항을 축조 토의함.

(2) 비세출기관의 설치에 여 규정에있어서, (가) 우리측은 비세출 기관의 설치를 "시설 및 토지내에" 한정시키는 동시에 이러한 기관은 미국군대 구성원, 군속 및 그들의 가족의 "전속적" 사용을 위하여서만 설치될수 있다고 주장한데 대하여 미국측은 비세출기관은 임시적으로 사용하거나 또는 가동적인 성격을 가진경우가 있으므로 토지 및 시설밖에서도 운영 되는것이므로 "시설 및 토지내에" 국한시킬수 없다고 주장한

0014

0015

동시에 비세출기관은 미국군대 구성원, 군속 및 그들의 가족 뿐만아니라 군계약자, 외교사절등에 의하여도 사용되는 것이니 우리측안에서 주장하는 바와같은 "전속적" 이라는 용어는 불필요하다고 주장하였으며, 이에다시 우리측은 비세출기관을 시설 및 토지밖에 설치할 경우에는 합동위원회에서 결정된 장소에 한하도록 하자고 주장하였으며, (나) 미국측은 그의 안에서 신문도 일반 비세출기관과 마찬가지로 일괄적으로 규정하여 한국 규정에 복종치 않도록 규정하고 있는데 대하여 우리측은 신문은 다른 비세출기관과 구별하여 별도로 규정하는 동시에 한국 규정에 복속토록 하자고 주장하였음. 이에대하여 미국측은 우리측안에 원칙적으로 찬동하나 어구를 수정한 미국측 대안을 다음회의에서 제시하겠다고 하였으며, (다) 우리측은 비세출 "기관"이라는 용어를 사용하자고 주장한데 대하여 미국측은 비세출 "활동" 이라는 용어를 사용하자고 주장하여 이에다시 우리측은 "비세출 활동" 이라는 용어를 사용할 경우에는 비세출활동에 해당하는 기관을 합동위원회에서 결정토록 하자고 주장하였으며, (라) 미국측은 또한 자국안에서 "콤미사리"를 삭제한것은 "콤미사리"는 세출기관이기 때문이라고 말하여 결국 비세출 기관의 설치 허여규정에 대하여는 다음에 다시 토의키로 함.

(3) 조세면제에 관한 규정에 있어서 미국측은 비세출기관에 의한 상품 및 용역의 판매에대하여 과세하지 않는다라고 주장한데 대하여 우리측은 신문의 판매에 관한 "1(b)항에 규정된 경우를 제외하고" 비세출기관에 의한 상품 및 용역의 판매에 대하여 과세하지 않는다라고 예외규정의 삽입을 주장한데 대하여 미국측은 원칙적으로만 이에 동의하면서 다음에 다시 토의키로 함.

0016

17-3

63-1-13

미원 89-5

0017

(4) 비세출기관에 의하여 판매되는 상품에관한 한국내에서의 처분 문제에관한 미국측 안은 우리측 안과 실질적 차이가 없으므로 미국측안을 수락하여 주었음.

(5) 비세출기관에 의하여 수입되는 상품수량의 제한에 관한 규정에 있어서 우리측은 이러한 상품은 합리적으로 소요되는 수량에 한하여야할 것이며 합리적인 양에대한 측정은 사회 통염으로서 파악 측정될수 있는것이라고 주장한데 대하여 미국측은 이러한 제한 규정은 실질적 효과를 초래하는 의미가 없는 구절이며 이러한 이유로 다른 나라와의 행정 협정에도 규정되어 있지않는 것이니 삭제하자고 주장하여 이문제는 다음에 다시 토의키로 함.

(6) 비세출기관에 관련된 정보제공에 관한 규정에 있어서 미국측은 그의 안에서 이러한 정보제공은 "합동위원회에서 양정부 대표간의 협의후에" 제공토록 규정하고 있는데 대하여 우리측은 이러한 협의규정은 불필요하다고 주장하여 이문제는 다음에 다시 토의키로 함.

(7) 비세출기관의 사용자에 대한 예외규정에 있어서 미국측은 미국군대 구성원, 군속 및 그들의 가족이외에도 기타 미국 정부의 관리 및 직원, 군계약자 그리고 주로 미국군대의 이익을 위하여 한국에 현존하는 기관등도 비세출기관을 사용할수 있도록 하자고 주장한데 대하여 우리측은 이러한 예외적 규정은 불필요한것이니 삭제하자고 주장하여 이문제는 다음에 다시 토의키로 함.

5. 기타사항

63-1-10

(1) 차기회의 일자 : 1963. 5. 17. 하오 2시

(2) 차기회의 의제 : 차기회의까지 양측 수석대표간에 합의된 사항

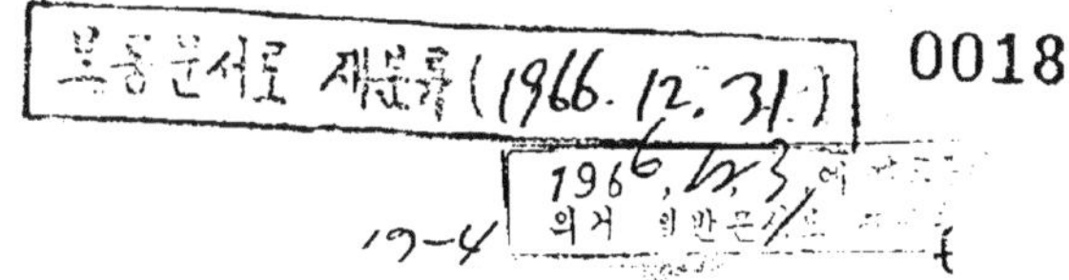
보통문서로 재분류(1966. 12. 31.)
1966, 12, 3, 에
의거 일반문서로
19-4

0018

0013

Mr. Shin said that if the word "activities" were adopted, it would impose difficulties on the Korean side. Therefore, he suggested that in case the word "activities" was used in the text of the Articles, every specific non-appropriated fund activity falling under the phrase "other non-appropriated fund activities" in paragraph 1 of the U.S. draft should be designated and listed by agreement between the two Governments through the Joint Committee.

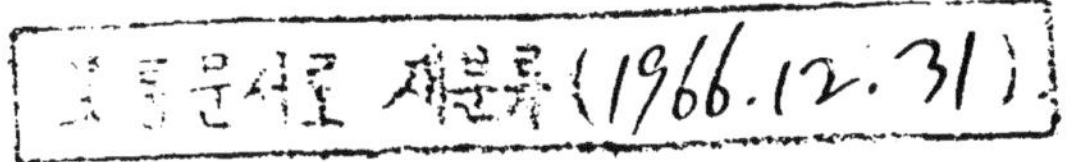

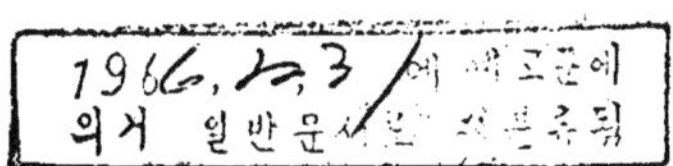

0020

Mr. Robert Kinney

st Meeting, May 3, 1963

1. Mr. Whang opened the meeting by welcoming back to the negotiating table Mr. Shin Chung Sup, who had just returned from a diplomatic mission abroad, and Mr. Kang Suk Jae, who had just returned from his honeymoon. On behalf of the U.S. side, Mr. Habib extended congratulations to both gentlemen upon the successful completion of their assignments and welcomed them back to the SOFA negotiations. Mr. Whang then introduced Mr. Roh Jae Won, Second Secretary in the America Section of the Ministry of Foreign Affairs, as a new member of the Korean negotiating team.

Non-Appropriated Fund Activities/Organizations

2. Turning to the drafts of the article dealing with Non-Appropriated Fund Activities/Organizations, both sides agreed to a paragraph by paragraph discussion in order to clarify the views of each side on the differences of language.

3. Speaking for the Korean side, Mr. Shin Kwan Sop pointed out that the Korean draft used the word "organizations" throughout whereas the U.S. draft used the word "activities". He referred to the use in the first paragraph of the Korean draft of the phrase "within the facilities and areas in use by the United States armed forces" and the words "exclusive use". Referring to that portion of the U.S. draft which provides that "such activities shall not be subject to Korean regulations", he requested clarification of the word "regulations". Specifically, he asked whether this would include Korean customs regulations. He reminded the negotiators that the article dealing with Korean customs regulations had not yet been agreed upon.

4. Following Mr. Shin's opening remarks, Mr. Habib began a review of the first paragraph. He stated that the words "military exchanges" were used in the U.S. draft because this was an all-inclusive term which embraced Navy exchanges, post exchanges, and base exchanges. Mr. Shin stated that the term "military exchanges" was acceptable to the Korean side.

5. Continuing his review of paragraph one, Mr. Habib stated that commissaries had not been mentioned in the U.S. draft (although included in the Korean draft)

0021

because they are official U.S. Government agencies financed by appropriated funds. Therefore, they do not fall within the category of non-appropriated fund activities. The U.S. draft did list newspapers, Mr. Habib continued, because they are non-appropriated fund activities. Regarding the question of whether to use the word "activities" or the word "organizations", Mr. Habib said that the U.S. side had frequently pointed out that the word "activities" was a more accurate description of the entities concerned, since they are not organizations in the real sense of the word. With regard to the phrase in the Korean draft "within the facilities and areas in use by the United States armed forces", Mr. Habib pointed out that it was customary to use temporary or mobile exchanges during maneuvers outside established facilities and areas. He said it might also be desirable to establish exchange facilities in tourist hotels. For these reasons, the phrase had not been included in the U.S. draft. With regard to the phrase "exclusive use" in the Korean draft, Mr. Habib said that this would not permit the extension of the use of non-appropriated fund activities to invited contractors. It also would not be consistent with paragraph 5 of the U.S. draft, which extends the use of these activities to certain designated groups of persons. In response to Mr. Shin's question whether the last sentence of the 1st paragraph of the U.S. draft included Korean customs regulations, Mr. Habib pointed out that the phrase "except as otherwise provided in this Agreement" was a key phrase in that sentence. The answer to Mr. Shin's question, therefore, was that Korean customs regulations would be included among those regulations to which non-appropriated fund activities would not be subject, except as this exemption might be modified by the provisions of the customs article.

6. Turning to paragraph 1(b) of the Korean draft, regarding the regulation of newspapers on sale to the general public, Mr. Habib remarked that the U.S. side considered this question to be relatively unimportant. The public sale of "The Pacific Stars and Stripes" was carried on at hotels as a service to troops who might be

0022

there as transients. He said the U.S. side would like to exempt such sales from taxation but would not strongly object to the inclusion of the Korean paragraph 1(b) in the article. He pointed out that the result of any such taxation would probably be that all sales of the newspaper outside of established facilities and areas would cease. In reply, Mr. Whang stated that the Korean side believed that the SOFA should establish the principle that when newspapers regulated by the U.S. armed forces are sold to the general public, they should be subject to the same regulations and procedures as other publicly sold newspapers. He said the manner in which such a SOFA provision would be implemented was another matter. What the Korean side wished to do was to establish the principle. Mr. Habib said that the U.S. side agreed in principle to the inclusion of the Korean paragraph 1(b); however the U.S. side was not entirely happy with the wording and punctuation of the Korean draft and would suggest alternative language at a subsequent meeting.

7. In response to a question by Mr. Shin, Mr. Habib stated that the phrase "other non-appropriated fund activities" in the first sentence of the U.S. draft included such activities as sports activities, craft shops, and schools. Mr. Shin stated that the reason for his question was that the word "activities" was so indefinite as to make it difficult to know which activities are meant to be included. The Korean side preferred the word "organizations" which carries a conception of structure and duration. Mr. Habib pointed out that the phrase "authorized and regulated by the United States military authorities" provides the assurance of the official nature of activities to be covered by this article. At this point, Mr. Habib read into the record the definitions of "organization" and "activity" given in Webster's International Dictionary, as follows:

0023

"Activity - an instance of being active, as in an occupation, recreation, or the like; as business or social activities. Education: an extracurricular activity.

"Organization - Any systematic whole, as the organization of an army or a government."

8. Mr. Habib stated that the procedure for authorization of a non-appropriated fund activity is specifically laid out in the military regulations. He said such an activity was just as much a part of the U.S. armed forces as any supply room which issues equipment to the troops. Mr. Shin replied that the Korean side knew that such activities are carefully regulated; however, it appeared difficult to make a definitive listing of all the activities which would be covered by this article. Therefore, the Korean side suggested that the question of what activities would be covered should be decided by the Joint Commission. Mr. Habib replied that the question could properly be a subject of discussion by the Joint Committee.

9. Mr. Shin remarked that the Korean side believed that the phrase "exclusive use" in the Korean draft conflicted with the proposed provisions of paragraph 5 of the U.S. draft. Mr. Habib agreed and pointed out that by excluding contractors it also conflicted with both the U.S. and Korean drafts of the article dealing with contractors (para. 3(d), U.S. draft and para. 3(c), Korean draft). It was agreed to discuss this question more thoroughly in connection with subsequent discussion of paragraph 5 of the U.S. draft.

10. Regarding the phrase "within the facilities and areas in use by the United States armed forces", Mr. Shin remarked that activities conducted outside such areas, as proposed by the U.S. side, would be difficult to control. If restrictions were not provided for, confusion might result. Mr. Habib replied that this need not be the case. He said it is normal procedure to provide mobile exchanges during field maneuvers. Such exchanges provide cigarettes, candy, tobacco and similar items and are a major factor in maintaining the morale of the troops. He pointed out that although they are not located within a facility or established area, they are regulated in the normal fashion. Mr. Shin suggested that whenever it is necessary to operate such a temporary exchange outside the facilities and areas, such exchange should be established at the place agreed upon with the Joint Committee. Mr. Habib stated that the U.S. side would consider this suggestion but believed that it would

0024

create an unnecessary set of consultations for members of the Joint Committee.

11. Turning to paragraph 2 of the U.S. draft, Mr. Shin stated that the paragraph was generally acceptable to the Korean side. However, the Korean side wondered if the words "other purchasers" referred to general purchasers. Mr. Habib replied that this was a correct interpretation and that the draft was intended to avoid the imposition of discriminatory taxes on the non-apprppriated fund activities. Mr. Whang suggested that the phrase "except as provided in paragraph 1(b)" be added to the first sentence. Mr. Habib said the U.S. side agreed in substance to this addition, with the final wording to be worked out later.

12. Mr. Shin stated that the Korean side accepted paragraph 3 of the U.S. draft. He then asked whether the word "goods" included newspapers. Mr. Habib replied that paragraph 1(b), which had just been agreed upon in substance, established an exception to the provisions of paragraph 3 by providing for the sale of newspapers to the general public. Paragraph 1(b), therefore, came within the scope of the phrase "except as such disposal may be permitted by the United States and Korean authorities in accordance with mutually agreed conditions". Therefore, the term "goods" does include newspapers, which are not to be sold to unauthorized purchasers except under the provisions of paragraph 1(b).

13. Turning to paragraph 4 of the Korean draft (which has no counterpart in the U.S. draft), Mr. Shin noted that the paragraph provided for a limitation on the quantity of goods to be imported "to the extent reasonably required". Mr. Habib stated that this would be very difficult to define and for that reason such a limitation was not to be found in any other Status of Forces Agreement. The goods imported were for the consumption and use of the people utilizing the particular activity; the amount required for such use at any one time would not be subject to any reasonable

0025

definition. Previous paragraphs in this article specify that these ~~xxxxx~~ activities are for the use of authorized persons and that there shall be no disposal of goods to unauthorized persons, except as mutually agreed upon. Mr. Habib pointed out that one man's consumption is not necessarily the same as that of other men. We cannot define, he continued, the limits of individual consumption. He pointed out that abuses were taken care of in other articles, which define the measures to be taken. There is no need, he concluded, for a vague redefinition, such as that proposed for ~~xxxxxxxx~~ inclusion in this paragraph.

14. Mr. Shin stated that the reasonable amount of consumption by a group of 3,000 men or 20,000 men could be through common sense ~~roughly~~ calculated. Mr. Habib replied that this was the basis on which buyers for these activities place their orders. He said it was quite clearly a question of rational ordering, purchase, and import. What is reasonably required is what is used within the limits imposed. He pointed out that if the Korean side's proposal were accepted, there would be no change in present procedures, nor any improvement in the methods currently used to prevent abuse, such as the rationing system in the exchanges regarding purchases of cigarettes, cosmetics and similar items.

15. Mr. Shin stated that ~~xxxxxxx~~ Korean law prohibits the use ~~xxxxxx~~ by Korean nationals of goods imported through military channels. He stated that the Government of the Republic of Korea was endeavoring to restrict consumption and was receiving much aid from the United States. He asked the U.S. side to consider the Korean draft in the light of aiding the growth of the Korean economy. Mr. Habib replied that the U.S. side was fully aware of the Korean efforts to develop the national economy. He said that the only effect (on the economy) of goods imported by non-appropriated fund activities occurred as a result of abuse or black market operations. He said that the U.S. armed forces maintained full cooperation with the Korean police and there existed a remarkably good measure of prevention against such ~~xxx~~ abuses. He said the black market has ~~nothing to do~~ with the quantity of goods imported but

0026

was the result of the breaking of Korean and U.S. laws and regulations. He pointed out that the latter was an entirely different subject. Mr It was agreed to defer further discussion on this question.

16. Turning to paragraph 4 in the U.S. draft and its counterpart, paragraph 5 in the Korean draft, Mr. Shin noted that the U.S. draft provided for the passing of information to the Korean tax authorities "after consultation ... in the Joint Committee". He said discussion by the Joint Committee would be unnecessary, inasmuch as this was a matter involving customs. Mr. Habib replied that the purpose of the U.S. language is to forestall unreasonable requests upon the authorities administering the activities. He said such requests could become an excessive administrative burden and the Joint Committee could serve a useful function by screening out the more unreasonable ones. He pointed out that consultation does not necessarily mean agreement. In the absence of this provision, he said any agency of the ROK Government could make a request, which the U.S. armed forces would feel obliged to answer. He pointed out that the armed forces are obviously prepared to provide that information which is necessary and the U.S. draft so states. Mr. Shin stated that the Korean side was willing to accept the U.S. draft of paragraph 4, except for the phrase "after consultation between the representatives of the two governments in the Joint Committee."

17. Mr. Habib pointed out that paragraph 5 of the U.S. draft had no counterpart in the Korean draft. He said this paragraph had appeared as an Agreed Minute in the SOFA with Japan. He said the U.S. side preferred to include it in the body of the Agreement in order to keep the number of Agreed Minutes to a minimum. He said the paragraph was intended to regularize the normal practice, wherever non-appropriated fund activities exist. He said it would not provide privileges which the persons covered by the paragraph would not normally have. The U.S. side believed it to be necessary to spell out specifically and with clarity the categories of persons who will be entitled to use the activities. He pointed out that the binding

0027

phrase was "ordinarily accorded such privileges". He said persons covered under this phrase included U.S. Government personnel, retired military personnel, and contract personnel. He pointed out that the latter group was also provided for in the article dealing with contractors.

18. Mr. Shin stated that the sale of certain prohibited foreign goods was forbidden in the Republic of Korea. However, for the convenience of foreigners, special shops had been established where foreigners could purchase such articles. These could be expanded, if necessary. He said the Korean side believed that contractors and USO personnel were not qualified for the privileges extended to the U.S. armed forces. Mr. Habib replied that USO personnel are present in Korea "primarily for the benefit and service of the United States armed forces personnel". They are not in the same position as U.S. businessmen. As a part of their normal perquisites, they usually enjoy the use of non-appropriated fund activities. They are part of the armed services in a practical sense, although not legally. The same applies to contractors, he continued.

19. Mr. Shin replied that if such a line of reasoning were adopted, the number of persons entitled to use these activities would be too large. The persons such as contractors and USO personnel were not qualified. Maintenance of control over the contractors by either the U.S. armed forces or the ROK Government would be difficult, and prevention of abuses. Mr. Habib stated that contractors are subject to the same regulations as any other user of these activities. Therefore, it is not correct to say that they are not under control of the U.S. armed forces. Mr. Shin asked what action on the part of the U.S. side if contractors sold goods on the black market. Mr. Habib replied that their privileges would be removed and the guilty party could be shipped out of Korea. He pointed out that contractors are not exempt from the administrative provisions or from any other relevant article of the SOFA. In effect, he continued, they are a support arm of the U.S. armed forces. If they are not permitted to use the facilities

0028

of the non-appropriated fund activities, it would become much more difficult to get them to come to Korea.

20. It was agreed to hold the next meeting on May 17 at 2 p.m.

0029

JOINT SUMMARY RECORD OF THE 21ST SESSION
STATUS FORCES NEGOTIATIONS

May 3, 1963

I. Time and Place : 2:00 to 4:10 p.m. May 3, 1963 at the Foreign Minister's Conference Room

II. Attendants:

ROK Side:

Mr. Whang, Ho Eul	Director Bureau of Political Affairs Ministry of Foreign Affairs
Mr. Shin, Kwan Sup	Director Bureau of Costums Duty Ministry of Finance
Mr. Yoon, Ha Jong	1st Secretary Ministry of Foreign Affairs
Mr. Koo, Choong Whay	Chief, America Section Ministry of Foreign Affairs
Mr. Shin, Jung Sup	Chief, Treaty Section Ministry of Foreign Affairs
Mr. Lee, Nam Koo	Chief, Military Affairs Section Ministry of National Defense
Mr. Chu, Mun Ki	Chief, Legal Affairs Section Ministry of Justice
Mr. Roh Jae Won	2nd Secretary Ministry of Foreign Affairs
Mr. Lee, Kyung Hoon	2nd Secretary Ministry of Foreign Affairs
Mr. Cho, Kwang Je	2nd Secretary Ministry of Foreign Affairs
Mr. Kang, Suk Jae	3rd Secretary Ministry of Foreign Affairs

U.S Side:

Mr. Philip C. Habib	Counselor of the Embassy for Political Affairs
Mr. William J. Ford	First Secretary of the Embassy
Col. G.G. O'Connor	Deputy Chief of Staff 8th Army

미주과	안고	담 당	과 장	국 장	특별보좌관	차 관	장 관

0030

Capt. R.M. Brownlie	Assistant Chief of Staff USN/K
Mr. L.J. Fuller	Staff Judge Advocate United Nations Command
Mr. Benjamin A. Fleck (Rapporteur and Press Officer)	First Secretary of the Embassy
Mr. Robert A. Lewis	Second Secretary and Consul of the Embassy
Lt. Col. R.E. Miller	Staff Officer, JAG 8th Army
Lt. Col. W.A. Burt	J-5
Kenneth Campen	Interpreter

1. Mr. Whang opened the meeting by welcoming back to the negotiating table Mr. Shin Chung Sup, who had just returned from a diplomatic mission abroad, and Mr. Kang Suk Jae, who had just returned from his honeymoon. On behalf of the U.S. side, Mr. Habib extended congratulations to both gentlement upon the successful completion of their assignments and welcomed them back to the SOFA negotiations. Mr. Whang then introduced Mr. Roh Jae Won, Second Secretary in the America Section of the Ministry of Foreign Affairs, as a new member of the Korean negotiating team.

Non-Appropriated Fund Activities/Organizations

2. Turning to the drafts of the article dealing with Non-Appropriated Fund Activities/Organizations, both sides agreed to a pargraph by paragraph discussion in order to clarify the views of each side on the differences of language.

3. Speaking for the Korean side, Mr. Shin Kwan Sup pointed out that the Korean draft used the word

0031

"organizations" throughout whereas the U.S. draft used the word "activities". He referred to the use in the first paragraph of the Korean draft of the phrase "withih the facilities and areas in use by the United States armed forces" and the words "exclusive use". Referring to that portion of the U.S. draft which provides that "such activities shall not be subject to Korean regulations", he requested clarification of the word "regulations". Specifically, he asked whether this word would include Korean customs regulations. He reminded the negotiators that the article dealing with Korean customs regulatinns had not yet been agreed upon.

4. Following Mr. Shin's opening remarks, Mr. Habib began a review of the first paragraph. He stated that the words "military exchanges" were used in the U.S. draft because this was an all-inclusive term which embraced Navy exchanges, post exchanges, and base exchanges. Mr. Shin stated that the term "military exchanges" was acceptable to the Korean side.

5. Continuing his review of paragraph one, Mr. Habib stated that commissaries had not been mentioned in the U.S. draft (although included in the Korean draft) because they are official U.S. Government agencies financed by appropriated funds. Therefore, they do not fall within thecategory of non-appropriated fund activities. The U.S. draft did list newspapers, Mr. Habib continued, becaase they are non-appropriated fund activities. Regarding the question of whether to use the word "activities" of the word "organizations",

0032

Mr. Habib said that the U.S. side had frequently pointed out that the word "activities" was a more accurate description of the entities concerned, since they are not organizations in the real seanse of the word. With regard to the phrase in the Korean draft "within the facilities and areas in use by the United States armed forces", Mr. Habib pointed out that it was customary to use temporary or mobile exchanges during maneuvers outside established facilities and areas. He said it might also be desirable to establish exchange facilities in tourist hotels. For these reasons, the phrase had not been included in the U.S. draft. With regard to the phrase "exclusive use" in the Korean draft, Mr. Habib said that this ~~With~~ would not permit the extension of the use of non-appropriated fund activities to invited contractors. It also would not be consistent with paragraph 5 of the U.S. draft, which extends the use of these activities to certain designated groups of persons. In response to Mr. Shin's question whether the last sentence of the 1st paragraph of the U.S. draft included Korean customs regulations, Mr. Habib pointed out that the phrase "except as otherwise provided in this Agreement" was a key phrase in that sentence. The answer to Mr. Shin's question, therefore, was that Korean customs regulations would be included among those regulations to which non-appropriated fund activities would not be subject, except as this exemption might be modified by the provisions of the customs article.

6. Turning to paragraph 1(b) of the Korean draft, regarding the regulation of newspapers on sale to the

general public, Mr. Habib remarked that the U.S. side considered this question to be relatively unimportant. The public sale of "The Pacific Stars and Stripes" was carried on at hotels as a service to troops who might be there as transients. He said the U.S. side would like to exempt such sales from taxation but would not strongly object to the inclusion of the Korean paragraph 1(b) in the article. He pointed out that the result of any such taxation would probably be that all sales of the newspaper outside of established facilities and areas would ~~ease~~ cease. In reply, Mr. Whang stated that the Korean side believed that the SOFA should establish the principle that when newspapers regulated by the U.S. armed forces are sold to the general public, they should be subject to the same regulations and procedures as other publicly sold newspapers. He said the manner in which such a SOFA provision would be implemented was another matter. What the Korean side wished to do was to establish the principle. Mr. Habib said that the U.S. side agreed in principle to the inclusion of the Korean paragraph 1(b); however the U.S. side was not entirely happy with the wording and punctuation of the Korean draft and would suggest alternative language at a subsequent meeting.

7. In response to a question by Mr. Shin, Mr. Habib stated that the phrase "other non-appropriated fund activities" in the first sentence of the U.S. draft included such activities as sports activities, craft

0034

shops, and schools. Mr. Shin stated that the reason for his question was that the word "activities" was so indefinite as to make it difficult to know which activities are meant to be included. To make these ambiguous points clear and incontrovertible and in view of U.S. side's original proposal in which it put forward the word "organizations", the Korean side preferred the word "organizations" which carries a conception of structure and duration. Mr. Habib pointed out that the phrase "authorized and regulated by the United States military authorities" provides the assurance of the official nature of activities to be covered by this article. At this point, to the further question raised by Mr. Shin as to wether or not, for instance a baseball team invited by the U.S. armed forces in Korea would be a non-appropriated fund activity, Mr. Habib replied in the negative. In this connection, Mr. Habib read into the record the definitions of "organization" and "activity" given in Webster's International Dictionary, as follows:

> "Activity - an instance of being active, as in an occupation, recreation, or the like; as business or social activities. Education: an extracurricular activity.
>
> "Organization - Any systematic whole, as the organization of an army or a government."

8. Mr. Habib stated that the procedure for authorization of a non-appropriated fund activity is specifically laid out in the military regulations. He said such an activity was just as much a part of the U.S. armed forces as any supply room which issues equipment to the troops. Mr. Shin said that if the

word "activities" were adopted, it would impose difficulties on the Korean side. Therefore, he suggested that in case the word "activities" was used in the text of the Articles, every specific non-appropriated fund activity falling under the phrase "other non-appropriated fund activities" in paragraph 1 of the U.S. draft should be designated and listed by agreement between the two Governments through the Joint Committee. Mr. Habib replied that the question could properly be a subject of discussion by the Joint Committee.

9. Mr. Shin remarked that the Korean side believed that the provisions of paragraph 5 of the U.S. draft were outside the scope of the SOFA. He further stated that the phrase "exclusive use" in the Korean draft conflicted with the proposed provisions of paragraph 5 of the U.S. draft. Mr. Habib agreed and pointed out that by excluding contractors it also conflicted with both the U.S. and Korean drafts of the article dealing with contractors (para. 3(d), U.S. draft and para. 3(c), Korean draft). It was agreed to discuss this question more thoroughly in connection with subsequent discussion of paragraph 5 of the U.S. draft.

10. Regarding the phrase "within the facilities and areas in use by the United States armed forces", Mr. Shin remarked that activities conducted outside such areas, as proposed by the U.S. side, would be difficult to control. If restrictions were not provided for, confusion might result. Mr. Habib replied that this need not be the case. He said it

0036

is normal procedure to provide mobile exchanges during field maneuvers. Such exchanges provide cigarettes, candy, tobacco and similar items and are a major factor in maintaining the morale of the troops. He pointed out that although they are not located within a facility or established area, they are regulated in the normal fashion. Mr. Shin suggested that whenever it is necessary to operate such a temporary exchange outside the facilities and areas such an exchange should be established at the place agreed upon between the two governments through the Joint Committee. Mr. Habib stated that the U.S. side would consider this suggestion but believed that it would create an unnecessary set of consultations for members of the Joint Committee.

11. Turning to paragraph 2 of the U.S. draft, Mr. Shin stated that the paragraph was generally acceptable to the Korean side. However, the Korean side wondered if the words "other purchasers" referred to general purchasers. Mr. Habib replied that this was a correct interpretation and that the draft was intended to avoid the imposition of discriminatory taxes on the non-appropriated fund activities. Mr. Whang suggested that the phrase "except as provided in paragraph 1(b)" be added to the first sentence. Mr. Habib said the U.S. side agreed in substance to this addition, with the final wording to be worked out later.

12. Mr. Shin stated that the Korean side accepted paragraph 3 of the U.S. draft. He then asked whether the word "goods" included newspapers. Mr. Habib replied

that paragraph 1(b), which had just been agreed upon in substance, established an exception to the provisions of paragraph 3 by providing for the sale of newspapers to the general pŭblic. Paragraph 1(b), therefore, came within the scope of the phrase "except as such disposal may be permitted by the United States and Korean authorities in accordance with mutually agreed conditions". Therefore, the term "goods" does include newspapers, which are not to be sold to unauthorized purchasers except under the provisions of paragraph 1(b).

13. Turning to paragraph 4 of the Korean draft (which has no counterpart in the U.S. draft), Mr. Shin noted that the paragraph provided for a limitation on the quantity of goods to be imported "to the extent reasonably required". Mr. Habib stated that this would be very difficult to define and for that reason such a limitation was not to be found in any other Status of Forces Agreement. The goods imported were for the consumption and use of the peoplè utilizing the particular activity; the amount required for such use at any one time would not be subject to any reasonable definition. Previous paragraphs in this article specify that these activities are for the use of authorized persons and that there shall be no disposal of goods to unauthorized persons, except as mutually agreed upon. Mr. Habib pointed out that one man's consumption is not necessarily the same as that of other men. We cannot define, he continued, the limits of individual consumption. He pointed out that abuses were taken

0038

care of in other articles, which define the measures to be taken. There is no need, he concluded, for a vague redefinition, such as that proposed for inclusion in this paragraph.

14. Mr. Shin stated that the reasonable amount of consumption by a group of 3,000 men or 20,000 men could be calculated through common sense. Mr. Habib replied that this was the basis on which buyers for these activities place their orders. He said it was quite clearly a question of rational ordering, purchase, and import. What is reasonalby required is what is used within the limits imposed. He pointed out that if the Korean side's proposal were accepted, there would be no change in present procedures, nor any improvement in the methods currently used to prevent abuse, such as the rationing system in the exchanges regarding purchases of cigarettes, cosmetics and similar items.

15. Mr. Shin stated that Korean law prohibits the use by Korean nationals of goods imported through military channels. He stated that the Government of the Republic of Korea was endeavoring to restrict consumption and was receiving much aid from the United States. He asked the U.S. side to consider the Korean draft in the light of aiding the growth of the Korean economy. Mr. Habib replied that the U.S. side was fully aware of the Korean efforts to develop the national economy. He said that the only effect on the economy of goods imported by non-appropriated fund activities occufred as a result of abuse or black

market operations. He said that the U.S. armed forces maintained full cooperation with the Korean police and there existed a remarkably good measure of prevention against such abuses. He said the black market has nothing to do with the quantity of goods imported but was the result of the breaking of Korean and U.S. laws and regulations. He pointed out that the latter was an entirely different subject. It was agreed to defer further discussion on this question.

16. Turning to paragraph 4 in the U.S. draft and its counterpart, paragraph 5 in the Korean draft, Mr. Shin noted that the U.S. draft provided for the passing of information to the Korean tax authorities after consultation ... in the Joint Committee". He said discussion by the Joint Committee would be unnecessary, inasmuch as this was a matter involving customs. Mr. Habib replied that the purpose of the U.S. language is to forestall unreasonable requests upon the authorities administering the activities. He said such requests could become an excessive administrative burden and the Joint Committee could serve a useful function by screening out the more unreasonable ones. He pointed out that consultation does not necessarily mean agreement. In the absence of this provision, he said any agency of the ROK Government could make a request, which the U.S. armed forces would feel obliged to answer. He pointed out that the armed forces are obviously prepared to provide that information which is necessary and the U.S. draft so states. Mr. Shin stated that the Korean side was willing to accept the U.S. draft

0040

of paragraph 4, except for the phrase "after consultation between the representatives of the two governments in the Joint Committee".

17. Mr. Habib pointed out that paragraph 5 of the U.S. draft had no counterpart in the Korean draft. He said this paragraph had appeared as an Agreed Minute in the SOFA with Japan. He said the U.S. side preferred to include it in the body of the Agreement in order to keep the number of Agreed Minutes to a minimum. He said the paragraph was intended to regularize the normal practice, wherever non-appropriated fund activities exist. He said it would not provide privileges which the persons covered by the paragraph would not normally have. The U.S. side believed it to be necessary to spell out specifically and with clarity the categories of persons who will be entitled to use the activities. He pointed out that the binding phrase was "ordinarily accorded such privileges". He said persons covered under this phrase included U.S. Government personnel, retired military personnel, and contract personnel. He pointed out that the latter group was also provided for in the article dealing with contractors.

18. Mr. Shin stated that the sale of certain prohibited foreign goods was forbidden in the Republic of Korea. However, for the convenience of foreigners, special shops had been established where foreigners could purchase such articles. These could be expanded, if necessary. He said the Korean side believed that contractors and USO personnel were not qualified for the privileges extended to the U.S. armed forces.

Mr. Habib replied that USO personnel are present in Korea "primarily for the benefit and service of the United States armed forces personnel". They are not in the same position as U.S. businessmen. As a part of their normal perquisites, they usually enjoy the use of non-appropriated fund activities. They are part of the armed services in a practical sense, although not legally. The same applies to contractors, he continued.

19. Mr. Shin replied that if such a line of r reasoning were adopted, the number of persons entitled to use these activities would be too large. The persons such as contractors and USO personnel, etc. were not qualified. Maintenance of control over the contractors by either the U.S. armed forces or the ROK Government and preventin of abuses would be difficult. Mr. Habib stated that contractors are subject to the same regulations as any other user of these activities. Therefore, it is not correct to say that they are not under control of the U.S. armed forces. Mr. Shin asked what action could be taken on the part of the U.S. side if contractors sold goods on the black market. Mr. Habib replied that their privileges would be removed and the guilty party could be shipped out of Korea. He pointed out that contractors are not exempt from the administrative provisions or from any other relevant article of the SOFA. In effect, he continued, they are a support arm of the U.S. armed forces. If they are not permitted to use the facilities of the non-appropriated fund activities, it would become much more difficult to get them to come to Korea.

20. It was agreed to hold the next meeting on May 17 at 2 p.m.

1966,12,31에 예고문에 의거 일반문서로 재분류됨
1966.9.30일 미주과장 직권으로 예고문 로 재분류
일반문서로 재분류(1966.12.31.)

0042

18-13

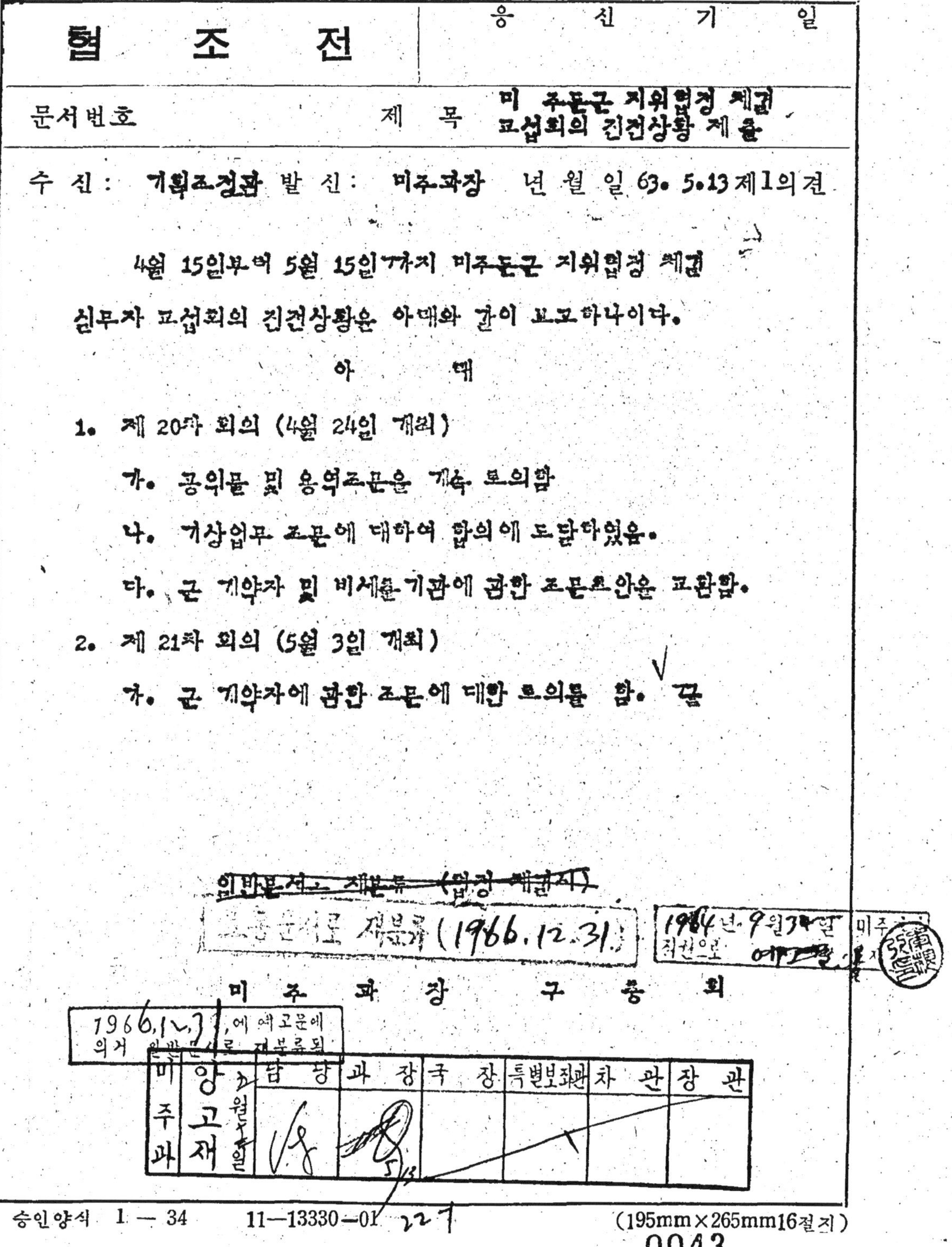
협 조 전

응 신 기 일

문서번호 제 목 미 주둔군 지위협정 체결 교섭회의 진전상황 제출

수 신: 기획조정관 발 신: 미주과장 년 월 일 63. 5.13 제1의견

4월 15일부터 5월 15일까지 미주둔군 지위협정 체결 실무자 교섭회의의 진전상황을 아래와 같이 보고하나이다.

아 래

1. 제 20차 회의 (4월 24일 개최)

가. 공익물 및 용역조문을 계속 토의함

나. 기상업무 조문에 대하여 합의에 도달하였음.

다. 군 계약자 및 비세출기관에 관한 조문초안을 교환함.

2. 제 21차 회의 (5월 3일 개최)

가. 군 계약자에 관한 조문에 대한 토의를 함. 끝

일반문서로 재분류 (협정 체결시)

일반문서로 재분류 (1966.12.31.)

1964년 9월 7일 미주과 직권으로 예고문 [illegible]

미 주 과 장 구 충 회

1966.12.31.에 예고문에 의거 일반문서로 재분류됨

미주과	양고재	5월 13일	담 당	과 장	국 장	특별보좌관	차 관	장 관
			[illegible]	[illegible] 5/13				

승인양식 1 — 34 11—13330—01 (195mm×265mm16절지)

0043

주한 미국군대의 지위에 관한 협정체결 교섭

(지금까지 완전합의된 조항의 주요내용)

1963. 7. 30.

1. 서 문

미국군대가 한국에 주둔하게된 근거가 국제연합안전보장이사회의 결의와 한미상호방위조약 제4조에 있으며 한미 양국간의 상호 이익의 밀접한 유대를 강화하기 위하여 토지, 시설 및 주한미국 군대지위에 관한 협정을 체결한다는 것이다.

2. 용어의 정의

본 조항은 미국군대의 구성원, 군속 및 그들의 가족에 대한 정의를 규정하고 있으며 미국군대의 구성원이라함은 주한 미국군사고문단 및 주한 미국대사관 무관을 제외한 대한민국 영역에 있는 동안에 미국의 육군, 해군 또는 공군에 속하는 현역 복무자를 말하며, 군속이라 함은 주로 미국국적을 소유하고 있는 민간인(제 3국인인 경우도 있음)으로서 대한민국에 있는 미국군대에 고용되어 이에 근무하고 또는 이에 수반하는 자를 말하며, 그들의 가족이라 함은 배우자 및 21세 미만의 자녀 그리고 부모, 21세 이상의 자녀 그리고 기타 친척으로서 그들의 생계비의 반액이상을 미국군대의 구성원 또는 군속에게 의존하고 있는 자를 말한다.

3. 합동 위원회

본 문제에 대한 조문은 3개항으로 되어 있으며 각항의 내용은 대략 다음과 같다.

(가) 제 1항은 합동위원회는 행정협정의 시행에 관하여 상호협의를 필요로 하는 모든 문제에 대한 한미간 협의체이며 특히 토지, 시설결정을 위한 협의체이라는 것을 규정하고 있다.

0044

(나) 제 2 항은 합동위원회는 한미간 대표로서 구성되며 그의 자신의 절차를 결정하고 보조기관을 설치할수 있다는 등을 규정하고 있다.

(다) 제 3 항은 만일 합동위원회가 어느 문제를 해결할수 없을 시는 동위원회는 그러한 문제를 적절한 경로를 통하여 각기 정부에 회부한다는 규정을 하고 있다.

. 출입국 관리

출입국 관리에 관한 조항은 6개항으로 되어 있으며 각항의 내용은 대략 다음과 같다.

(가) 제 1 항은 미군대구성원, 군속 및 그들의 가족은 한국영역에 출입할수 있으며 미국당국은 이들의 인원수를 정기적으로 한국정부에 통고할것을 규정하고 있다.

(나) 제 2 항은 미군대구성원은 한국의 여권 및 사증에 관한 규정에 따르지 않으며 미군대구성원, 군속 및 그들의 가족은 한국 외국인등록법의 대상에서 제외되나, 영주권을 취득하는 것이 아님을 규정하고 있다.

(다) 제 3 항은 미국군인이 한국영역에 입국시 또는 체재시 신분증명서와 여행명령서를 소지할 것을 규정하고 있다.

(라) 제 4 항은 군속 및 그 가족과 미군인 가족은 그들의 신분을 확인할수 있는 적절한 문서를 소지할 것을 규정하고 있다.

(마) 제 5 항은 미국은 협약 규제대상 인원의 신분이 변경된 경우 이를 한국정부에 통고할 것과, 한국정부가 그러한 인원의 퇴거를 요구할 경우 미국측이 이에 응할 것을 규정하고 있다.

(바) 제 6 항은 한국정부가 미군대구성원, 군속의 퇴거를 요구하였을 시, 또는 전 미군인, 군속 및 그들의 가족의 강제퇴거명령을 내렸을 시, 미국은 이들의 퇴거에 책임을 질것을 규정하고 있다

0045

5. 선박 및 항공기의 기착

본 문제에 관한 조문은 3개항으로 되어 있으며 각항의 내용은 대략 다음과 같다.

(가) 제1항은 미국소유 또는 미국의 관리하에 운임되는 외국 선박 및 항공기는 한국항구와 공항에 입항료를 지불하지 않고 출입할수 있다는 것과 이러한 선박 또는 항공기에 적재된 물품과 인원으로서 본 협정의 대상이 되지 않는 것은 한국의 법에 따라서 규제된다고 규정하고 있다.

(나) 제2항은 전기 제1항의 선박 및 항공기와 미국소유차량이 통행료를 부과받지 않고 한국에 출입하고 한국내 토지, 시설간을 왕래할 것을 규정하고 있다.

(다) 제3항은 선박의 입항시에는 한국당국에의 적절한 통고의무를 규정하고 있다.

6. 예비병의 소집 및 훈련

이 문제에 관한 조문은 제1항으로 되어 있으며 그내용은 미국은 대한민국에 입국하는 해당 미국시민을 한국에서 미국의 예비군대에 소집하고 훈련시킬수 있다는 것이다.

7. 기상업무

본 조항은 한국정부가 양정부의 적절한 당국자 간의 협정에 따라서 기상관측, 기상자료, 전기통신업무 및 지진관측자료 등을 미국군대에 제공한다는 것을 규정하고 있음.

8. 접수국법의 존중

본 조항은 한국에 있어서 한국의 법규를 존중하고 본 협정의 정신에 위배되는 활동, 특히 정치적 활동을 하지 않는다는 것이 미국군대 구성원, 군속, 군계약자 및 그들의 가족의 의무이라고 규정하고 있음.

9. 보건 및 위생

본 조항은 미국군대구성원, 군속 및 그들의 가족에 대하여 의료 지원을 제공하는 미국의 권리에 부합하여, 전염병의 예방 또는 기타 공중보건, 의료, 위생 및 수의업무의 조정에 관한 상호간의 문제는 합동위원회에서 양국정부 당국에 의하여 해결되도록 규정하고 있음.

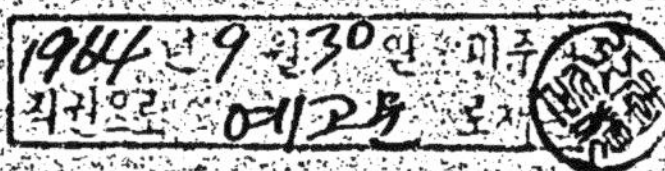

보통문서로 재분류(1966.12.31.)

1966.12.31.에 예고문에 의거 일반문서로 재분류됨

2. 제22차 회의, 5. 17

0048

SOFA NEGOTIATION

Agenda for 22nd Session

14:00 May 17, 1963

1. Continuation of Discussion on:

   a. Non-Appropriated Fund Organizations/ Activities Article

   b. Armed Forces Contractors Article

2. Other Business

3. Agenda and Date of Next Meeting

4. Press Release

0049

기 안 용 지

자 체 통 제		기안처	미주과 이 경 훈	전화번호	근거서류접수일자
	과장	국장	보좌관	차관	장관
관계관 서명	조약과장	1등서기관			
기안 년월일	63. 5. 18.	시행 년월일		검열 1963. 통제관	정서기장
분류 기호	외정미 722.2	전체 통제		종	
경유 수신 참조	국가재건최고회의 의장 (참조: 외무국방위원장) 내각수반	발신	장 관		
제목	주둔군지위협정 체결을위한 제22차 교섭회의 보고				

1963. 5. 17. 하오 2시부터 동 4시 10분 까지 외무부장관 회의실에서 개최된 제22차 주둔군지위협정 체결 교섭회의에서 토의된 내용을 별첨과 같이 보고합니다.

유첨 : 제22차 교섭회의 보고서 부. 끝

보통문서로 재분류(1966. 12. 31.)

1964 년 9 월 30 일 미주과장 직권으로 예고문 재분류

1966. 12. 31 에 예고문에 의거 일반문서로 재분류

접수 1963. 5. 20 외무부

승인양식 1-1-3 (1112-040-016-018) (190mm×260mm16절지)

0050

외 무 부

외정미 722.2　　　　　　　　　　　　1963. 5. 20.

수 신　국가재건최고회의 의장

참 조　외무국방위원장

제 목　주둔군지위협정 체결을위한 제22차 교섭회의 보고

1963. 5. 17. 하오 2시부터 동 4시 10분까지 외무부장관 회의실에서 개최된 제22차 주둔군지위협정 체결 교섭 회의에서 토의된 내용을 별첨과같이 보고합니다.

유첨 : 제 22 차 교섭회의 보고서 2부. 끝

외 무 부 장 관　　김 용 식

19-7

0051

외 무 부

외정미 722.2 1963. 5. 20.

수 신 내각수반

제 목 주둔군지위협정 체결을위한 제22차 교섭회의 보고

1963. 5. 17. 하오 2시부터 동 4시 10분까지 외무부장관회의실에서 개최된 제22차 주둔군지위협정 체결 교섭회의에서 토의된 내용을 별첨과같이 보고합니다.

유첨 : 제22차 교섭회의 보고서 1부. 끝

외 무 부 장 관 김 용 식

19-8

0052

제 22 차

한미간 주둔군지위협정 체결 실무자회의

보 고 서

1. 일 시 : 1963. 5. 17. 하오 2시부터 4시 10분까지

2. 장 소 : 외무부장관 회의실

3. 참석자 : 한국측 : 황 호 을 (외무부 정무국장)

신 관 섭 (재무부 세관국장)

구 충 회 (외무부 미주과장)

신 정 섭 (외무부 조약과장)

박 도 준 (국방부 군무과)

노 재 원 (외무부 2등서기관)

이 경 훈 (")

조 광 재 (")

강 석 재 (외무부 3등서기관)

미국측 : 교섭대표단 전원 ("하비브"참사관 및 "오로나"대령 제외)

4. 토의사항:

(1) 비세출기관 및 군계약자에 관한 문제를 순차적으로 토의함.

(2) 비세출기관에 관한 조항의 토의에 있어서 우리측은 미국군 당국이 공인하고 규제하는 신문이 일반인에게 판매될때에는 동신문은 그배포에 관한한 우리나라의 규제, 면허, 수수료, 조세 또는 유사한 관리에 복속해야 한다라는 요지의 구정을 할것을 제의한데 대하여 미국측은 이와 비등한 대안을 제시하였기 우리측은 이를 수락하여 주었음.

(3) 군계약자의 한국법에 대한 복속원칙에 관한 구정에 있어서 (가) 우리측은 ~~비세출기관~~ 군계약자의 규제대상이될 인원중 법인에 대해서는 "미국 법률하에서 조직된" 법인을 포함시키자고

0053

0054

주장한데 대하여 미국측은 제3국법인도 포함시켜야 하므로 우리측이 주장하는 "미국의 법률하에서 조직된" 이라는 구절은 삭제하자고 주장하였고, (나) 우리측은 또한 군계약자가 채용할 고용원은 "통상 미국에 거주하는" 자로하자고 주장한데 대하여 미국측은 제3국인의 고용자도 필요하므로 우리측이 주장하는 "통상미국에 거주하는" 이라는 용어는 삭제하자고 주장하여 이문제들은 다음에 다시토의키로 하였고, (다) 군계약자는 미국군대의 이익을 위하여서뿐만 아니라 "미국군대로부터 병참지원을 받는 통합군사령부하의 주한 기타군대"의 이익을 위하여서도 미국과 계약할수 있다라고 미국측이 주장한데 대하여 원래 우리측 안에는 "미국군대로부터 병참지원을 받는 통합군사령부 하의 주한미타 군대"라는 구절이 없었으나 현재● 우리나라에는 안전보장이사회의 결의에 의거하여 통합군사령부 하에 주둔하고있는 미국이외의 다른나라 군대도 주둔하고 있으므로 우리측은 동구절을 수락해주었음.

(4) 군계약자의 지정 및 지정철회에 관한 규정에 있어서 미국측이 제시한 초안의 규정은 우리측의 규정과 실질적차이가 없으므로 우리측은 원칙적으로 이를 수락하였으며 다만 군계약자의 지정은 "대한민국 정부와 협의하여" 행한다는 점에 관하여 동협의의 범위와 한계가 어느정도이냐에 대해서는 추후에 다시 토의키로 함.

63-1-7

(5) 군계약자가 향유할 이익에관한 규정에 있어서 (가) 군계약자들이 토지시설간을 왕래할수 있다는것을 "권리"로규정하자고 미국측이 주장한데 대하여 우리측은 본항은 군계약자가 향유할 이익에관한 규정이므로 "권리"라는 용어는 삭제하자고 주장하였고, (나) 군계약자는 출입국관리 조항에 의거하여 한국에 입국

0055

13-1-1U

미분 89-4

0056

할수 있다라는 규정은 우리측안과 동일하므로 이를 수락하였고, (다) 개인용 사용을위한 물품의 세관면제 규정에 대하여 우리측은 동관계조항이 완전합의 되는것을 조건으로 원칙적으로 합의해주었으며, (라) 군계약자의 비세출기관 사용문제도 우리측안과 차이가 없으므로 동관계조항이 완전 합의되는것을 조건으로 원칙적인 합의를하였으며, (마) 외환관리 규정에 관련하여 동조항에서 허여된 범위내에서 외환을 이전할수 있다는 규정에 대하여 미국측인 이를 "권리"로서 인정하자고 주장한데 대하여 우리측은 전기 (5)의 (가)에서 언급한바와 같은 이유로 "권리"라는 용어의 삭제를 주장하였으며, (바) 군표사용에 관한 규정은 우리측 조안과 차이가 없으므로 원칙적으로 이를 수락하였으며, (사) 군사우편에관한 규정도 우리측 조안과 상이가 없으므로 원칙적으로 이를 수락하였으며, (아), 미국측은 공익물 및 용역에관련되어 부여된 권리도 군계약자에게 부여하자고 주장한데 대하여 우리측은 군계약자가 공익물 및 용역을 사용할 혜택을 가질수는 있으나 이들에게 공익물 및 용역을 운영할 권리까지 부여할수는 없으므로 미국측이 제시한 이러한 규정은 삭제하자고 주장하였으며, (자) 운전면허 및 차량등록에 관한 규정에 대하여도 우리측은 원칙적으로 이러한 규정의 삭제를 주장하였으며, (차) 고용조건 및 법인 등록등에 관한 규정은 우리측안과 실질적 차이가 없으므로 이를 수락하였음. 63-1-8

(6) 군계약자가 소지할 여권 및 그들의 도착, 출발 및 거주에관한 통고규정에 있어서 우리측은 군계약자와 그들이 채용한 고용원은 한국의 여권 및 사증규정에 복속하여야 하며 그들은 또한 그들의 신분을 밝힌 여권을 소지하여야 한다라는 규정을 삽입하자고 주장한데 대하여 미국측은 이러한 규정은 그의 조안에 규정하고 있지않아 이문제는 다음에 다시 토의키로 함.

0057

63-1-14

0058

5. 기타사항:

(1) 차기회의 일자 : 1963. 5. 31. 하오 2시

(2) 차기회의 의제 : 차기회의까지 양측 수석대표간에 합의된 사항

6. 참고자료 : 미국측이 제의한 수정안(비세출기관) 별첨참조

63-1-140

1P-5 0059

63-1-14

미북 89-4

0060

Non-Appropriated Fund Activities Article

Suggested Paragraph 1 (b):

(b) When a newspaper authorized and regulated by the United States military authorities is sold to the general public, it shall be subject to Korean regulations, licenses, fees, taxes or similar controls so far as such circulation is concerned.

보통문서로 재분류(1966. 12. 31.)

1966. 12. 31에 예고문에 의거 일반문서로 재분류됨

19-6

0061

63-1-14 (5)

마이크로 89-4 (5)

0062

1. Before beginning substantive discussion, Mr. Whang introduced Lt. Col. Pak Do Joon, attending in place of Colonel Lee. Lt. Col. Pak was welcomed by the U.S. side.

Non-Appropriated Fund Activities/Organizations

2. Opening substantive discussion, Mr. Whang recalled that at the previous meeting, the U.S. side had said that it would submit alternative language for sub-paragraph 1(b) of the draft article dealing with non-appropriated fund activities. General Lawlor replied that the U.S. side wished to submit such alternative language and tabled the following suggested sub-paragraph:

> "When a newspaper authorized and regulated by the United States military authorities is sold to the general public, it shall be subject to Korean regulations, licenses, fees, taxes or similar controls so far as such circulation is concerned."

Mr. Whang stated that the Korean side accepted the language proposed by the U.S. side.

Contractors

3. The negotiators then turned their attention to the drafts of the article dealing with contractors. General Lawlor stated that Lt. Colonel Miller would negotiate this article for the U.S. side. Lt. Colonel Miller suggested that the article be taken up paragraph by paragraph. Mr. Whang agreed.

Paragraph 1

4. Mr. Whang remarked that the two drafts of paragraph 1 more or less differed both in expression and in substance. He said it was the view of the Korean side that the contractors working for the armed forces differed in nature from the civilian components employees of the armed forces. Since the contractors were in business to make profits, they should be accorded treatment with regard to privileges and immunities which was different than the treatment accorded to the civilian component ~~employees~~. He said the Korean

side was prepared to agree to particularly favorable treatment of corporations, organized under the laws of the United States, contractors and their employees ordinarily resident in the United States.

5. Lt. Colonel Miller replied that the contractors working for the U.S. armed forces were contributing to the successful completion of the mission of the armed forces just as much as were the civilian component. However, the contractors were contributing in a different manner. There are times when it is more economical for the armed forces to deal with contractors rather than hiring civilian employees. He added that it is not always possible to secure contractors in the United States. Therefore, the U.S. draft of this article makes provision for contracting with third-country corporations and personnel. Lt. Colonel Miller pointed out that there is little difference between a corporation operating in order to make a profit and an individual working for wages. He said that the contractors should receive the same treatment as the civilian component of the armed forces. He pointed out that both drafts applied only to those corporations and persons who are present in Korea "solely for the purpose of executing contracts with the United States for the benefit of the United States armed forces". He said that the word "solely" was a key word and that the only exception to this provision was to be found in the proposed Agreed Minute of the U.S. draft.

6. Mr. Whang said that the U.S. side might be laboring under the misapprehension that the terms of the Korean draft would rule out the possibility of entering into contracts with third-country corporations or personnel. He said the Korean draft did not prevent this from being done when necessary. However, the privileges and immunities conferred by the SOFA would be given only to United States corporations and residents of the United States. Third-country nationals not resident in the United States would be treated by the Government of the Republic of Korea as ordinary aliens.

7. Lt. Colonel Miller pointed out that the U.S. armed forces had to pay for

0064

the services of the contractors. If the U.S. armed forces could accomplish their mission in Korea most economically by hiring third-country contractors, they wanted the SOFA to confer on them the right to do so. He pointed out that the third-country national employees of the contractors were in Korea solely to perform services for the accomplishment of the mission of the U.S. armed forces. If they were present in Korea for any other purpose, they would not be subject to the provisions of this article. He pointed out that if they were declared ineligible for the benefits of this article, they would be most reluctant to come to Korea.

8. Mr. Whang said that the Korean draft was similar to the corresponding article of the Status of Forces Agreement between the United States Government and the Government of Japan. Lt. Colonel Miller replied that the SOFA currently under negotiation was intended to fit the needs of the situation in Korea. He said that both sides had been negotiating consistently on that basis and had been seeking an agreement that would meet the unique circumstances existing in Korea. He reiterated the belief of the U.S. side that in order to accomplish their mission most economically, the U.S. armed forces from time to time would need to use third-country contractors.

9. Mr. Whang reiterated the view of the Korean side that inasmuch as the SOFA would be an agreement between the United States Government and the ROK Government, this article should cover only United States corporations and residents of the United States. Although quite willing to extend the suggested privileges and immunities to such corporations and residents, the ROK Government would find it difficult to extend the same treatment to third-country nationals. He said if the U.S. side would agree to the ROK position, the Korean side was prepared to consider favorably the inclusion of dependents of residents of the United States under the provisions of this article.

0065

10. Lt. Colonel Miller replied that agreement had been reached previously with regard to the Definitions Article, which provides for the direct hire by the U.S. armed forces of third-country nationals. The U.S. side believed that the same principle should apply to contractors. He said the U.S. side appreciated the statement of the Korean side with regard to dependents. Mr. Whang remarked that the ROK draft was similar to the provisions of the SOFA with Japan, which made no mention of third-country nationals. He said if the U.S. side would accept the Korean side's language regarding this point, the Korean side would accept the U.S. side's language regarding dependents and "other armed forces in Korea under the Unified Command". Lt. Colonel Miller remarked that the latter phrase was almost identical to language already agreed upon in the Customs Article.

Paragraph 2

11. Turning to paragraph 2, Lt. Colonel Miller called the attention of the Korean side to an apparent typographical error in the first sentence of the Korean draft. He said the word "contracts" apparently should be "contractors". Mr. Whang agreed and the correction was made. Lt. Colonel Miller also suggested that the word "or" immediately following the word "involved" in the Korean draft could be omitted in order to make a smoother sentence. Mr. Whang agreed. Lt. Colonel Miller then stated that the word "consultation" in both drafts should not be interpreted as meaning agreement. He pointed out that there would be instances in which decisions would have to be made concerning the technical qualifications which would have to be met by the contractor in order to carry out a specific task. Only the U.S. armed forces would be able to make such decisions, he said. Mr. Whang stated that the Korean side would give further consideration to this point. Lt. Colonel Miller then suggested that the introductory portion of paragraph 2 of the U.S. draft be agreed to, subject to further study by the Korean side of the implications of the word "consultation". Mr. Whang pointed out that the U.S. draft read

0066

"Korea" instead of "Republic of Korea". Lt. Colonel Miller replied that this was the type of stylistic question which it had been agreed would be settled at the close of the negotiations during final review of the entire Agreement.

12. Mr. Whang stated that the Korean side accepted subparagraphs (a) and (b) of the U.S. draft of Paragraph 2.

13. Mr. Whang stated that the wording of the two drafts of subparagraph (c) was different, although the substance was the same. Lt. Colonel Miller replied that the U.S. draft, in using the phrase "upon proof that", states a definite point in time at which the requisite action can be taken. The details could be worked out by the Joint Committee. He said the U.S. draft, while not differing in substance, was more precise than the Korean draft. Mr. Whang then asked for clarification of the phrase "upon proof that". Did it mean only after a court verdict of guilty had been handed down, or did it mean simply after the presentation of material evidence of guilt? Lt. Colonel Miller replied that the U.S. draft did not contemplate the necessity for a court conviction but only the presentation of such material evidence of guilt as may be agreed upon by the two governments through the Joint Committee. General Lawlor confirmed this interpretation and Mr. Whang said the Korean side accepted the U.S. draft of subparagraph (c) with that understanding.

Paragraph 3

14. Turning to paragraph 3, Mr. Whang stated that the U.S. draft omitted mention of employees. He requested an explanation of this omission. Lt. Colonel Miller replied that the phrase "such persons" referred to the contractors, their employees, and their dependents, as identified in paragraph 1 of the U.S. draft. Mr. Whang then stated that the problem here was the same as that with paragraph 1. If the U.S. side would agree to limiting the provision to corporations organized under the laws of the United States and to residents of the United States, the Korean side would agree to the inclusion of dependents, throughout the article with regard to such definition of contractors.

~~and to the U.S. draft of paragraph 3. He said the Korean side was prepared to agree~~

0067

~~to such a definition of contractors throughout the article.~~

15. Mr. Whang pointed out that subparagraph (a) of paragraph 3 of the U.S. draft had no counterpart in the Korean draft. He said the Korean side had no objection in principle to the inclusion of this subparagraph. However, in view of the use of the word "benefits" which appeared in the introductory part of Paragraph 3 ~~in order to make the language of the various subparagraphs consistent,~~ he suggested the deletion from subparagraph (a) of the phrase "rights of". Lt. Colonel Miller replied that the U.S. side did not understand the objection to the use of the word "rights" in this subparagraph, particularly in view of the fact that both sides had used the word in other sections of this paragraph - the Korean side in subparagraphs (c) and (e) and the U.S. side in subparagraphs (d), (e), (f), (h), and (i). ~~Mr. Whang replied that to be consistent, the U.S. side should also include the word in subparagraphs (b) and (c).~~ In reply, Mr. Whang ~~He~~ pointed out that the "rights" referred to in subparagraphs (c) and (e) of the Korean draft and subparagraphs (d) and (f) of the U.S. draft were rights conferred by the U.S. armed forces on the contractors, whereas the other rights referred to in the U.S. draft were benefits ~~rights~~ conferred on the U.S. armed forces. Lt. Colonel Miller said the U.S. side would consider this question.

16. Mr. Whang stated that the Korean side accepted subparagraph (b) of the U.S. draft.

17. Mr. Whang stated that subparagraph (c) of the U.S. draft and subparagraph (b) of the Korean draft were almost identical. He said the Korean side accepted the U.S. draft, with the understanding that no agreement had yet been reached on paragraph 3 of the Customs Article, to which this subparagraph refers.

18. Mr. Whang stated that the Korean side accepted subparagraph (d) of the U.S. draft, with the understanding that the unresolved question of using the word "activities" or the word "organizations" would be settled at a later date and subject to agreement on the non-appropriated Fund Organization Article.

19. With regard to subparagraph (e) of the U.S. draft and its counterpart, subparagraph (d) of the Korean draft, Mr. Whang suggested acceptanne of the

0068

Korean language, for the sake of consistency with the introductory language of the paragraph and the other subparagraphs. Lt. Colonel Miller stated that this was the same question that had been raised in connection with subparagraph (a) of the U.S. draft. He said the U.S. side would consider it.

20. Mr. Whang stated that the Korean side accepted subparagraph (f) of the U. S. draft, subject to subsequent agreement on the MPC Article.

21. Mr. Whang stated that the Korean side accepted subparagraph (g) of the U.S. draft, subject to subsequent agreement on the Military Post Offices Article.

22. Mr. Whang suggested deletion from the U.S. draft of subparagraph (h), which had no counterpart in the Korean draft. He said that contractors working for the U.S. armed forces would be given the use of utilities and services to the fullest extent within the capability of the ROK Government. Lt. Colonel Miller pointed out that this subparagraph was intended to guarantee the contractors the same rates and treatment as those accorded the U.S. armed forces. Mr. Whang then suggested the deletion of the subparagraph to use the utilities and services which were accorded to the U.S. armed forces would be granted to the contractors. He explained that the draft Utilities and Services Article includes not only the right to use utilities and services but also the right to operate them. He said the Korean side was unwilling to agree to giving the contractors the right to operate utilities involving electric supply, water supply or transportation facilities. He said the Korean side had no objection to the U.S. armed forces being given the right of operation but the Korean side did not believe the SOFA should give the same right directly to the contractors. The contractors could be permitted by the U.S. armed forces to operate some of these utilities on behalf of the armed forces, but the right to do so would be the right of the armed forces and not the right of the contractors. In sum, the SOFA should not give the contractors

0063

the right to operate utilities and services in their own name. Lt. Colonel Miller replied that the U.S. side would study the Korean position.

23. Mr. Whang stated that subparagraph (i) of the U.S. draft also had no counterpart in the Korean draft. He said that the Korean side anticipated that contractors would follow the same procedure with regard to registration of vehicles and procurement of driving permits as other aliens and Korean nationals. Lt. Colonel Miller replied that the contractors would be (in Korea) for the purpose of contributing to the accomplishment of the mission of the U.S. armed forces. Therefore, the U.S. side believed that they should be treated in the same manner as members of the (armed forces,) the civilian component, and their dependents. Mr. Whang replied that the importation of vehicles free of duty is one thing but the registration of those vehicles is quite another matter. He said there was no objection to the importation of vehicles by the contractors but the Korean side believed that the registration procedures covering those vehicles should be the same as those which applied to the vehicles of other aliens and Korean nationals. The Korean side believed this should also be the case with regard to the vehicles imported by the members of the civilian component and dependents. Lt. Colonel Miller suggested that further discussion of this subject be deferred until after the draft article dealing with the registration of vehicles was tabled. The Korean side agreed.

24. Mr. Whang stated that the Korean side accepted subparagraph (j) of the U.S. draft.

Paragraph 4

25. Turning to the two drafts of paragraph 4, Mr. Whang stated that this paragraph was relevant to the Entry and Exit Article. He said the Korean side believed the contractors should possess passports which would enable the ROK authorities to verify their status. Lt. Colonel Miller pointed out that the Korean side had just agreed to paragraph 3(b), which stated that entry of contractors into

0070

Korea should be effected in accordance with the provisions of the Entry and Exit Article. Turning to paragraph 4 of the latter article, Lt. Colonel Miller reminded the negotiators that it called for the issuance of "appropriate documentation" by the United States authorities to permit verification of the status of the bearers. He said it thus appeared that paragraph 3(b) of the Contractors Article covered the points raised in the Korean draft of paragraph 4 of the latter article. Mr. Whang replied that contractors are different from civilian employees because the former are in business to make profits. They should be subject to Korean entry and exit regulations and their status should be verified by the Korean authorities upon entry or exit. Therefore, they should possess passports in which their status is clearly described. Lt. Colonel Miller remarked that paragraph 3(b) and the Korean draft of paragraph 4 appeared to be contradictory.

26. Mr. Whang stated that the Korean side had agreed to paragraph 3(b). However, in paragraph 4, the Korean side wished to define clearly the fact that contractors should be subject to Korean passport and visa regulations. Paragraph 3(b), therefore, was within the scope of the proposed paragraph 4. Mr. Whang added that when the Korean side had agreed to the Entry and Exit Article, it had agreed to appropriate documentation in addition to passports. Members of the U.S. side objected to this interpretation of the Entry and Exit Article. Mr. Fleck was asked to read paragraph 7 of the Agreed Joint Summary Record of the 6th meeting, which records that Mr. Habib had stated that "persons of U.S. nationality falling under the provisions of paragraph 4 (of the Entry and Exit Article) would ordinarily carry documentation including passports and other identifying papers", sufficiently detailed to permit verification of their status. The record shows that the Korean side then agreed to the use of "appropriate documentation" with the understanding that it would include sufficient information to permit verification.

27. Mr. Whang stated that the Korean side desired the contractors to have passports and additional identifying documents. He pointed out that paragraph 2 of the Entry and Exit Article specifically exempts members of the U.S. armed

0071

forces from Korean passport and visa laws and regulations but does not so exempt the civilian component and ~~their~~ dependents, except for the Korean laws and regulations on the registration and control of aliens. At this point, it was decided to adjourn the meeting and continue discussion of this article at the next meeting.

28. The next meeting was scheduled for May 31 at 2:00 p.m.

보통문서로 재분류(1966. 12. 31.)

1966. 12. 31. 예고문에 의거 일반문서로 재분류됨

0072

JOINT SUMMARY RECORD OF THE 22ND SESSION
STATUS FORCES NEGOTIATIONS

May 17, 1963

I. Time and Place : 2:00 to 4:10 p.m. May 17, 1963 at the Foreign Minister's Conference Room

II. Attendants:

ROK Side:

Mr. Whang, Ho Eul	Director Bureau of Political Affairs Ministry of Foreign Affairs
Mr. Shin, Kwan Sup	Director Bureau of Costums Duty Ministry of Finance
Mr. Koo, Choong Whay	Chief, America Section Ministry of Foreign Affairs
Mr. Shin, Jung Sup	Chief, Treaty Section Ministry of Foreign Affairs
Mr. Pak, Do Joon	Lt. Col. Ministry of National Defense
Mr. Roh, Jae Won	2nd Secretary Ministry of Foreign Affairs
Mr. Lee, Kyung Hoon	2nd Secretary Ministry of Foreign Affairs
Mr. Cho, Kwang Je	2nd Sedretary Ministry of Foreign Affairs
Mr. Kang, Suk Jae	3rd Secretary Ministry of Foreign Affairs

US Side:

Brig. Gen. J. D. Lawlor	Deputy Chief of Staff 8th Army
Mr. William J. Ford	First Secretary of the Embassy
Capt. R.M. Brownlie	Assistant Chief of Staff USN/K
Mr. L.J. Fuller	Staff Judge Advocate United Nations Command

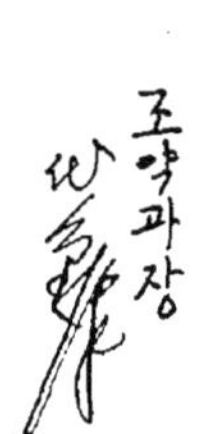

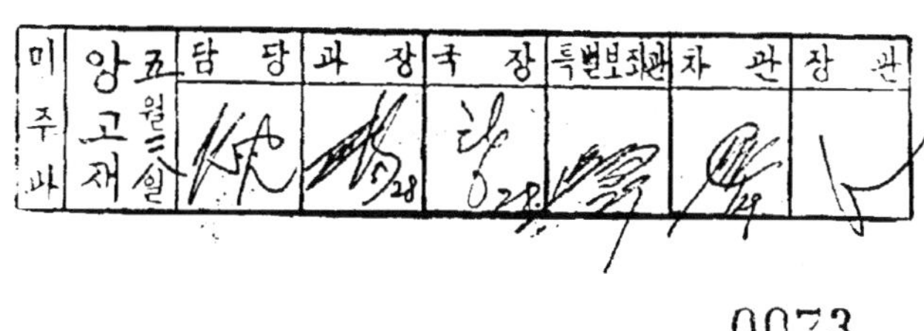

0073

Mr. Benjamin A. Fleck (Rapporteur and Press Officer)	First Secretary of the Embassy
Mr. Robert A. Lewis	Second Secretary and Consul of the Embassy
Lt. Col. R.E, Miller	Staff Officer, JAG 8th Army
Lt. Col. W.A. Burt	J-5

1. Before beginning substantive discussion, Mr. Whang introduced Lt. Col. Pak Do Jooh, attending in place of Colonel Lee. Lt. Col. Pak was welcomed by the U.S. side.

Non-Appropriated Fund Activities/Organizations

2. Opening substantive discussion, Mr. Whang recalled that at the previous meeting, the U.S. side had said that it would submit alternative language for subparagraph 1(b) of the draft article dealing with non-appropriated fund activities. General Lawlor replied that the U.S. side wished to submit such alternative language and tabled the following suggested sub-paragraph:

> "When a newspaper authorized and regulated by the United States military authorities is sold to the general public, it shall be subject to Korean regulations, licenses, fees, taxes or similar controls so far as such circulation is concerned."

Mr. Whang stated that the Korean side accepted the language proposed by the U.S. side.

Contractors

3. The negotiators then turned their attention to the drafts of the article dealing with contractors. General Lawlor stated that Lt. Colonel Miller would negotiate this article for the U.S. side. Lt. Colonel Miller suggested that the article be taken up paragraph by paragraph. Mr. Whang agreed.

0074

Paragraph 1

4. Mr. Whang remarked that the two drafts of paragraph 1 more or loss differed both in expression and in substance. He said it was the view of the Korean side that the contractors working for the armed forces differed in nature from the civilian component of the armed forces. Since the contractors were in business to make profits, they should be accorded treatment with regard to privileges and immunities which was different than the treatment accorded to the civilian component. He said the Korean side was prepared to agree to favorable treatment of corporations, organized under the laws of the United States, contractors and their employees ordinarily resident in the United States.

5. Lt. Colonel Miller replied that the contractors working for the U.S. armed forces were contributing to the successful completion of the mission of the armed forces just as much as were the civilian component. However, the contractors were contributing in a different manner. There are times when it is more economical for the armed forces to deal with contractors rather than hiring civilian employees. He added that it is not always possible to secure contractors in the United States. Therefore, the U.S. draft of this article makes provision for contracting with third-country corporations and personnel. Lt. Colonel Miller pointed out that there is little difference between a corporation operating in order to make a profit and an individual working for wages. He said that the contractors should receive the same treatment as the civilian component of the armed forces. He pointed out that both drafts applied only to those corporations and persons who are present in Korea "solely for the purpose

of executing contracts with the United States for the benefit of the United States armed forces". He said that the word "solely" was a key word and that the only exception to this provision was to be found in the proposed Agreed Minute of the U.S. draft.

6. Mr. Whang said that the U.S. side might be laboring under the misapprehension that the terms of the Korean draft would rule out the possibility of entering into contracts with third-country corporations or personnel. He said the Korean draft did not prevent this from being done when necessary. However, the privileges and immunities conferred by the SOFA would be given only to United States corporations and residents of the United States. Third-country nationals not resident in the United States would be treated by the Government of the Republic of Korea as ordinary aliens.

7, Lt. Colonel Miller pointed out that the U.S. armed forces had to pay for the services of the contractors. If the U.S. armed forces could accomplish their mission in Korea most economically by hiring third-country contractors, they wanted the SOFA to confer on them the right to do so. He pointed out that the third-country national employees of the contractors were in Korea solely to perform services for the accomplishment of the mission of the U.S. armed forces. If they were present in Korea for any other purpose, they would not be subject to the provisions of this article. He pointed out that if they were declared ineligible for the benefits of this article, they would be most reluctant to come to Korea.

0076

8. Mr. Whang said that the Korean draft was similar to the corresponding article of the Status of Forces Agreement between the United States Government and the Government of Japan. Lt. Colonel Miller replied that the SOFA currently under negotiation was intended to fit the needs of the situation in Korea. He said that both sides had been negotiating consistently on that basis and had been seeking an agreement that would meet the unique circumstances existing in Korea. He reiterated the belief of the U.S. side that in order to accomplish their mission most economically, the U.S. armed forces from time to time would need to use third-country contractors.

9. Mr. Whang reiterated the view of the Korean side that inasmuch as the SOFA would be an agreement between the United States Government and the ROK Government, this article should cover only United States corporations and residents of the United States. Although quite willing to extend the suggested privileges and immunities to such corporations and residents, the ROK Government would find it difficult to extend the same treatment to third-country nationals. He said if the U.S. side would agree to the ROK position, the Korean side was prepared to consider favorably the inclusion of dependents of residents of the United States under the provisions of this article.

10. Lt, Colonel Miller replied that agreement had been reached previously with regard to the Definitions Article, which provides for the direct hire by the U.S. armed forces of third-country nationals. The U.S. side

believed that the same principle should apply to contractors. He said the U.S. side appreciated the statement of the Korean side with regard to dependents. Mr. Whang remarked that the ROK draft was similar to the provisions of the SOFA with Japan, which made no mention of third-country nationals. He said if the U.S. side would accept the Korean side's language regarding this point, the Korean side would accept the U.S. side's language regarding dependents and "other armed forces in Korea under the Unified Command". Lt. Colonel Miller remarked that the latter phrase was almost identical to language already agreed upon in the Customs Article.

Paragraph 2

11. Turning to paragraph 2, Lt. Colonel Miller called the attention of the Korean side to an apparent typographical error in the first sentence of the Korean draft. He said the word "contracts" apparently should be "contractors". Mr. Whang agreed and the correction was made. Lt. Colonel Miller also suggested that the word "or" immediately following the word "involved" in the Korean draft could be omitted in order to make a smoother sentence. Mr. Whang agreed. Lt. Colonel Miller then stated that the word "consultation" in both drafts should not be interpreted as meaning agreement. He pointed out that there would be instances in which decisions would have to be made concerning the technical qualifications which would have to be met by the contractor in order to carry out a specific task. Only the U.S. armed forces would be able to make such decisions, he said. Mr. Whang stated that the Korean side would give further consideration

0078

to this point. Lt. Colonel Miller then suggested that the introductory portion of paragraph 2 of the U.S. draft be agreed to, subject to further study by the Korean side of the implications of the word "consultation". Mr. Whang pointed out that the U.S. draft read "Korea" instead of "Republic of Korea". Lt. Colonel Miller replied that this was the type of stylistic question which it had been agreed would be settled at the close of the negotiations during final review of the entire Agreement.

12. Mr. Whang stated that the Korean side accepted subparagraphs (a) and (b) of the U.S. draft of paragraph 2.

13. Mr. Whang stated that the wording of the two drafts of subparagraph (c) was different, although the substance was the same. Lt. Colonel Miller replied that the U.S. draft, in using the phrase "upon proof that", states a definite point in time at which the requisite action can be taken. The details could be worked out by the Joint Committee. He said the U.S. draft, while not differing in substance, was more precise than the Korean draft. Mr. Whang then asked for clarification of the phrase "upon proof that". Did it mean only after a court verdict of guilty had been handed down, or did it mean simply after the presentation of material evidence of guilt? Lt. Colonel Miller replied that the U.S. draft did not contemplate the necessity for a court conviction but only the presentation of such material evidence of guilt as may be agreed upon by the two governments through the Joint Committee. ~~Material evidence of guilt~~ General Lawlor confirmed this interpretation and Mr. Whang said the Korean side accepted the U.S. draft of subparagraph (c) with that understanding.

0079

Paragraph 3

14. Turning to paragraph 3, Mr. Whang stated that the U.S. draft ommitted mention of employees. He requested an explanation of this omission. Lt. Colonel Miller replied that the phrase "such persons" referred to the contractors, their employees, and their dependents, as identified in paragraph 1 of the U.S. draft. Mr. Whang then stated that the problem here was the same as that with paragraph 1. If the U.S. side would agree to limiting the provision to corporations organized under the laws of the United States and to residents of the United States, the Korean side would agree to the inclusion of dependents throughout the article with regard to such definitions of contractors.

15. Mr. Whang pointed out that subparagraph (a) of paragraph 3 of the U.S. draft had no counterpart in the Korean draft. He said the Korean side had no objection in principle to the inclusion of this subparagraph. However, in view of the use of the word "benefits" which appeared in the introductory part of Paragraph 3, he suggested the deletion from subparagraph (a) of the phrase "rights of". Lt. Colonel Miller replied that the U.S. side did not understand the objection to the use of the word "rights" in this sub-paragraph, particularly in view of the fact that both sides had used the word in other sections of this paragraph - the Korean side in subparagraphs (c) and (e) and the U.S. side in subparagraph (d), (e), (f), (h), and (i). In reply, Mr. Whang pointed out that the "rights" referred to in subparagraphs (c) and (e) of the Korean draft and subparagraphs (d) and (f)

0080

of the U.S. draft were rights conferred by the U.S. armed forces on the contractors, whereas the other rights referred to in the U.S. draft were benefits conferred on the U.S. armed forces. Lt. Colonel Miller said the U.S. side would consider this question.

16. Mr. Whang stated that the Korean side accepted subparagraph (b) of the U.S. draft.

17. Mr. Whang stated that subparagraph (c) of the U.S. draft and subparagraph (b) of the Korean draft were almost identical. He said the Korean side accepted the U.S. draft, with the understanding that no agreement had yet been reached on paragraph 3 of the Customs Article, to which this subparagraph refers.

18. Mr. Whang stated that the Korean side accepted subparagraph (d) of the U.S. draft, with the understanding that the unresolved question of using the word "activities" or the word "organizations" would be settled at a later date and subject to agreement on the non-appropriated fund organization article.

19. With regard to subparagraph (e) of the U.S. draft and its counterpart, subparagraph (d) of the Korean draft, Mr. Whang suggested acceptance of the Korean language, for the sake of consistency with the introductory language of the paragraph and the other subparagraphs. Lt. Colonel Miller stated that this was the same question that had been raised in connection with subparagraph (a) of the U.S. draft. He said the U.S. side would consider it.

20. Mr. Whang stated that the Korean side accepted subparagraph (f) of the U.S. draft, subject to subsequent agreement on the MPC Article.

0081

21. Mr. Whang stated that the Korean side accepted subparagraph (g) of the U.S. draft, subject to subsequent agreement on the Military Post Offices Article.

22. Mr. Whang suggested deletion from the U.S. draft of subparagraph (h), which had no counterpart in the Korean draft. He said that contractors working for the U.S. armed forces would be given the use of utilities and services to the fullest extent within the capability of the ROK Government. Lt. Colonel Miller pointed out that this subparagraph was intended to guarantee the contractors the same rates and treatment as those accorded the U.S. armed forces. Mr. Whang then suggested the deletion of the subparagraph with the understand that the right to use the utilities and services which were accorded to the U.S. armed forces would be granted to the contractors. He explained that the draft Utilities and Services Article includes not only the right to use utilities and services but also the right to operate them. He said the Korean side was unwilling to agree to giving the contractors the right to operate utilities involving electric supply, water supply or transportation facilities. He said the Korean side had no objection to the U.S. armed forces being given the right of operation but the Korean side did not believe the SOFA should give the same right directly to the contractors. The contractors could be permitted by the U.S. armed forces to operate some of these utilities on behalf of the armed forces, but the right to do so would be the right of the armed forces and not the right of the contractors. In sum, the SOFA should not give the contractors the right to operate utilities and services in their own name.

0082

Lt. Colonel Miller replied that the U.S. side would study the Korean position.

23. Mr. Whang stated that subparagraph (i) of the U.S. draft also had no counterpart in the Korean draft. He said that the Korean side anticipated that contractors would follow the same procedure with regard to registration of vehicles and procurement of driving permits as other aliens and Korean nationals. Lt. Colonel Miller replied that the contractors would be in Korea for the purpose of contributing to the accomplishment of the mission of the U.S. armed forces. Therefore, the U.S. side believed that they should be treated in the same manner as members of the armed forces, the civilian component, and their dependents. Mr. Whang replied that the importation of vehicles free of duty is one thing but the registration of those vehicles is quite another matter. He said there was no objection to the importation of vehicles by the contractors but the Korean side believed that the registration procedures covering those vehicles should be the same as those which applied to the vehicles of other aliens and Korean nationals. The Korean side believed this should also be the case with regard to the vehicles imported by the members of the civilian component and dependents. Lt. Colonel Miller suggested that further discussion of this subject be deferred until after the draft article dealing with the registration of vehicles was tabled. The Korean side agreed.

24. Mr. Whang stated that the Korean side accepted subparagraph (j) of the U.S. draft.

0083

Paragraph 4

25. Turning to the two drafts of paragraph 4, Mr. Whang stated that this paragraph was relevant to the Entry and Exit Article. He said the Korean side believed the contractors should possess passports which would enable the ROK authorities verify their status. Lt. Colonel Miller pointed out that the Korean side had just agreed to paragraph 3(b), which stated that entry of contractors into Korea should be effected in accordance with the provisions of the Entry and Exit Article. Turning to paragraph 4 of the latter article, Lt. Colonel Miller reminded the negotiators that it called for the issuance of "appropriate documentation" by the United States authorities to permit verification of the status of the bearers. He said it thus appeared that paragraph 3(b) of the Contractors Article covered the points raised in the Korean draft of paragraph 4 of the latter artcle. Mr. Whang replied that contractors are different from civilian employees because the former are in business to make profits. They should be subject to Korean entry and exit regulations and their status should be verified by the Korean authorities upon entry or exit. Therefore, they should possess passports in which their status is clearly described. Lt. Colonel Miller remarked that paragraph 3(b) and the Korean draft of paragraph 4 appeared to be contradictory.

26. Mr. Whang stated that the Korean side had agreed to paragraph 3(b). However, in paragraph 4, the Korean side wished to define clearly the fact that contractors should be subject to Korean passport and visa regulations. Paragraph 3(b), therefore, was within the scope of the proposed paragraph 4. Mr. Whang added that

0084

when the Korean side had agreed to the Entry and Exit Article, it had agreed to appropriate documentation in addition to passports. Members of the U.S. side objected to this interpretation of the Entry and Exit Article. Mr. Fleck was asked to read paragraph 7 of the Agreed Joint Summary Record of the 6th meeting, which records that Mr. Habib had stated that "persons of U.S. nationality falling under the provisions of paragraph 4, (of the Entry and Exit Article) would ordinarily carry documentation including passports and other identifying papers",sufficiently detailed to permit verification of their status. The record shows that the Korean side then agreed to the use of "appropriate documentation" with the understanding that it would include sufficient information to permit verification.

27. Mr. Whang stated that the Korean side desired the contractors to have passports and additional identifying documents. He pointed out that paragraph 2 of the Entry and Exit Article specifically exempts members of the U.S. armed forces from Korean passport and visa laws and regulations but does not so exempt the civilian component and dependents, except for the Korean laws and regulations on the registration and control of aliens. At this point, it was decided to adjourn the meeting and continue discussion of this article at the next meeting.

28. The next meeting was scheduled for May 31 at 2:00 p.m.

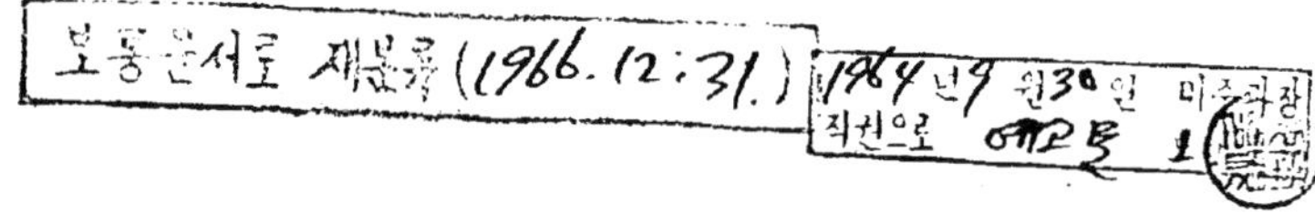

0085

3. 제23차 회의, 5.31

0086

기 안 용 지

자 체 통 제		기안처	미 주 과 강 석 재	전화번호	근거서류접수일자

	과장	국장	보좌관	차관	장관
	5/28	28		28	

관계관 서 명	의전장
기안 년월일	63. 5. 28
시행 년월일	
보존 년한	
정서기장	
분류 기호	의정미
전체 통제	
종결	
경유 수신 참조	건 의
발 신	
제 목	미주둔군 지위협정 미국측실무교섭자 환송및 환영 오찬 회

미주둔군 지위협정 체결 미국측 실무교섭자의 인사이동으로 인한 J.D. Lawlor 준장 환송과 L.J. Fuller 대령 환영을 위한 오찬회를 아래와 같이 갖고저 하오니 재가하여 주시기 바랍니다.

아 래

1. 초 청: 외무부 차관 명의로 초청함
2. 인 원: 미국측대표 8명 한국측 대표 8명 계 16명
   (명단 별첨 참조)
3. 시 일: 1963년 6월 5일 정오 12시
4. 장 소: 조선 호텔
5. 경 비: 16명 X 800 원 = 12,800원 끝

승인양식 1-1-3 (1112-040-016-018) (190mm×260mm16절지)

0087

오찬회 참석자 명단

미국측	한국측
Mr. Philip C. Habib (미대사관 참사관)	외무부차관
Brig. Gen. J.D. Lawlor (미8군 참모차장)	보좌관
Mr. William J. Ford (미대사관 1등서기관)	기획조정관
Col. G.G. O'Conner (미8군 참모차장)	정무국장
Capt. R.M. Brownlie (주한미해군 참모부장)	미주과장
Col. L.J. Fuller (유엔사령부 법무관)	조약과장
Mr. Benjamin A. Fleck (미대사관 1등서기관)	이경훈 2등서기관
Mr. Robert A. Lewis (미대사관 2등서기관겸 영사)	강석재 2등서기관

0088

기 안 용 지

자체 통제		기안처	미주과 이경훈	전화번호	근거서류접수일자

	과장	국장	보좌관	차관	장관
	30	30	30	30	

관계관 서명	조약과장 5/30 / 동서기관 5.30

기안 년월일	63. 5. 29.	시행 년월일		보존 년한		정서기장
분류 기호	외정미	전체 통제		종결		
경유 수신 참조	건 의			발신		
제목	제23차 주둔군지위협정 체결교섭회의에 임할 우리측 입장					

5월 31일에 개최될 제23차 주둔군지위협정 체결 한미간 교섭회의에서는 군계약자, 그리고 운전면허 및 차량등록 접수국법의 존중 문제에 관하여 토의될 예정이온바 이에 관련하여 우리측 교섭 실무자는 5월 28일 회합을 갖고 제23차 회의에서 취할 우리측 태도를 별첨과 같이 결정하였아오니 재가하여 주시기 바랍니다.

유첨 : 제23차 주둔군지위협정 체결교섭회의에 임할 우리측 태도

(1966. 12. 31) 1964년 9월 30일 예고문 제1호

1966. 12. 31.에 예고문에 의거 일반문서로 재분류됨

승인양식 1-1-3 (1112-040-016-018) (190mm×260mm16절지)

0083

1. 군계약자

(1) 군계약자의 한국법에 대한 복속원칙에 관한 미국측 초안 1항 (이는 우리측 초안 1항에 해당함)에 있어서 (가) 동 미국측 초안은 한국측 초안에 삽입되어 있는 "organized under the laws of the United States " 라는 구절과 who are ordinarily resident in the United States" 라는 용어를 삭제하고 있는데 이는 미국측이 군계약을 체결할수 있는 법인이나 군계약자나 또는 그가 채용할 고용원을 미국인에 국한시키지 않고 제3국인에게까지 확대시키기 위한 규정인바 우리측은 동 구절의 삽입을 계속 주장한다.

(2) 군계약자의 지정 및 지정철회에 관한 미국측 초안 제2항 (이는 우리측 초안 2항에 해당함)은 우리측 초안과 실질적인 차이가 없으므로 미국측안을 수락하되 " consultation " 이라는 용어의 해석에 있어서는 대한민국 정부의 견해가 상당히 반영된다는 협의로서 해석된다는 양해사항을 공동회의록에 남겨두도록 한다.

(3) 군계약자가 향유할 이익에관한 미국측 초안 3항 (이는 우리측 초안 3항에 해당함)에 있어서 (가) 미국측은 3(a)항에 우리측 안에없는 토지시설 간의이동권을 규정하고 있으며, 3(h)항에는 우리측안에 없는 공익물 및 용역에관련한 미국군대에게 부여된 권리규정을 두고있으며 또한 3(i)항에는 우리측안에 없는 운전면허 및 차량등록에 관련된 권리 규정을 두고있는바 3(a)항을 제외한 3(h) 및 3(i)항은 우리측안대로 삭제하자고 계속 주장한다. (나) 또한 동3항에 있어서 미국측은 3(e)항에 외환관리 규정에 관련하여 부여된 권리(rights) 라고 규정하고 있는데 동 "권리"라는 용어를 삭제토록 계속 주장하고, (다) 3(b) 및 3(c)항은 관계조항의 합의를 조건으로 수락하고, (다) 기타항에 대하여는 수락하기로한다.

0090

(4) 군계약자가 소지할 여권 및 그들의 도착, 출발 및 거주에관한 통고 규정에 관한 미국측 초안 4항 (이는 우리측 초안 4항에 해당함)에 있어서 미국측은 우리측 초안 4항 전단에 있는 여권에관한 규정이 삭제되고 있는데 이규정은 출입국관리의 관계규정과 관련하여있고 또한 군계약자의 신분을 명백히 하는데 필요한것이므로 우리측안대로 동규정은 삽입토록 주장한다.

(5) 감가상각 재산에 대한 면세 규정에관한 미국측 초안 5항은 우리측 초안에는 없는것인바 미국측의 이에관한 설명을 들은후 다시 우리측 태도를 결정토록 한다.

(6) 군계약자에 대한 재산의 보유, 사용 및 이전에관련한 조세면제 규정에관한 미국측 초안 6항 (이는 우리측 초안 5항에 해당함) 에 있어서 "other business" 라는 용어는 우리측안에서 말하는바와 같이 "other business than those excuting contracts as described in paragraph 1 of this Article in the Republic of Korea" 로 대치토록 하고 미국측안을 수락토록 한다.

(7) 소득세 및 법인세에 관한 미국측초안 7항 (우리측 초안 6항에 해당함)에 있어서 미국측 초안 둘째문장의 전단

"Persons in Korea in connection with the execution of such a contract with the United States shall not be liable to pay any Korean taxes to the Government of Korea or to any taxing agency in Korea on income derived from sources outside of Korea"

라는 구절은 미국측 초안 셋째문장 전단과 중복되는 것이므로 이의 삭제를 요구하는 동시에 미국측 초안 둘째문장 후단 "Nor shall periods during which such persons are in Korea be considered periods of residence or domicile in Korea for the purposes of Korean taxation "

0091

라는 구절은 다음과같이 완전한 1개 문장으로 수정하여 제7항 말미에 삽입토록 제의한다.

"Periods during which such persons are in Korea solely in connection with the execution of a contract with the Government of the United States shall not be considered periods of residence or domicile in Korea for the purpose of such taxation".

따라서 미국측 초안 7항 (우리측 초안 6항에 해당함)에 대하여 우리측은 별첨과같은 대안을 제시한다.

(8) 군계약자에 대한 재판 관할권에 관한 규정인 우리측 초안 제7항은 미국측 초안에는 규정되어 있지않으나 우리측은 우리측안의 수락을 주장한다.

(9) 미국측은 합의의사록에 1개항목을 제시하였는데 이에 관하여 미국측의 설명을 요구한후 우리측 태도를 결정토록 한다.

2. <u>접수국법의 존중</u>

(1) 미국측 초안은 접수국법이 존중대상 인원에 군계약자도 포함시키고 있는바 우리측은 이에관하여 동규정이 다른조항과도 관련이 있는지의 여부를 미국측에 문의한후 우리측 태도를 결정하기로 한다.

3. <u>운전면허 및 차량등록</u>

(1) 미국의 운전면허 허여원측, 공용차량의 표식 그리고 사유차량의 표식 등에관한 규정을 내용으로하는 별첨과같은 우리측 조문초안을 제시한다.

(2) 미국측이 제시하는 안이 우리측안과 비등할때에는 우리측안을 수락해달라고 요구한다.

0092

ARTICLE (Contractors)

6. The persons referred to in paragraph 1 shall not be liable to pay income or corporation taxes to the Government of the Republic of Korea or to any other taxing agency in Korea on any income derived under a contract with the Government of the United States in connection with the construction, maintenance or operation of any of the facilities or areas covered by this Agreement. The provisions of this paragraph do not exempt such persons from payment of income or corporation taxes on income derived from Korean sources, other than those sources referred to in the first sentence of this paragraph, nor do they exempt such persons who claim Korean residence for United States income tax purposes from payment of Korean taxes on income. Periods during which such persons are in Korea solely in connection with the execution of a contract with the Government of the United States shall not be considered periods of residence or domicile in Korea for the purpose of such taxation."

0093

ARTICLE

1. The Republic of Korea shall accept as valid, without a driving test or fee, the driving permit or license or military driving permit issued by the United States to a member of the United States armed forces, the civilian component, and their dependents.

2. (a) Official vehicles of the United States armed forces and the civilian component shall carry a distinctive numbered plate or individual marking which will readily identify them.

(b) Privately owned vehicles of the members of the United States armed forces, the civilian component, and their dependents shall carry Korean number plates to be acquired under the same conditions as those applicable to the nationals of the Republic of Korea.

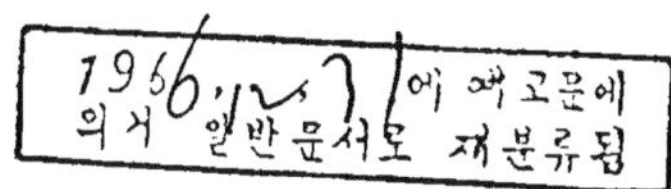

0094

기 안 용 지

자체 통제	(서명)	기안처	미주과 이경훈	전화번호	근거서류접수일자
	과장	국장	보좌관	차관	장관
	(서명)	(서명) 6.3	(서명)	(서명) 6.3	(서명)
관계관 서명	조약과장 (서명)		-동서기관 (서명)		
기안 년월일	63. 6. 1.	시행 년월일	검열 1963.6.4. 통제관	보존 년한	정서 / 기장
분류 기호	외정미 722.2	전체 통제		종결 (서명)	(서명)
경유 수신 참조	국가재건최고회의 의장 (참조: 외무국방위원장) 내각수반			발신	장관
제목	주둔군지위협정 체결을위한 제23차 교섭회의 보고				

1963. 5. 31. 하오 2시부터 동 4시까지 외무부장관 회의실에서 개최된 제23차 주둔군지위협정 체결 교섭회의에서 토의된 내용을 별첨과같이 보고합니다.

유첨 : 제23차 교섭회의 보고서 부, 끝

보통문서로 재분류(1966. 12. 31.)

1964년 9월 30일 미주과 기안으로 예고문 재분류

0095

승인양식 1—1—3 (1112—040—016—018) (190mm×260mm16절지)

1966, 12, 31 에 예고문에 의거 일반문서로 재분류됨

외 무 부

외정미 722.2 1963. 6. 3.

수 신 국가재건최고회의 의장

참 조 외무국방위원장

제 목 주둔군지위협정 체결을위한 제23차 교섭회의 보고

1963. 5. 31. 하오 2시부터 동 4시까지 외무부장관 회의실에서 개최된 제23차 주둔군지위협정 체결 교섭회의에서 토의된 내용을 별첨과같이 보고합니다.

유첨 : 제23차 교섭회의 보고서 2부. 끝

외 무 부 장 관 김 용 식

0096

외 무 부

외정미 722.2 1963. 6. 3.

수 신 내각수반

제 목 주둔군지위협정 체결을위한 제23차 교섭회의 보고

1963. 5. 31. 하오 2시부터 동 4시까지 외무부장관 회의실에서 개최된 제23차 주둔군지위협정 체결 교섭회의에서 토의된 내용을 별첨과같이 보고합니다.

유첨 : 제23차 교섭회의 보고서 1부. 끝

외 무 부 장 관 김 용 식

0097

제 23 차

한미간 주둔군지위협정 체결 실무자회의

보 고 서

1. 일 시 : 1963. 5. 31. 하오 2시부터 4시7까지

2. 장 소 : 외무부장관 회의실

3. 참석자 : 한국측 : 황 호 을 (외무부 정무국장)

신 관 섭 (재무부 세관국장)

구 충 회 (외무부 미주과장)

신 정 섭 (외무부 조약과장)

이 남 구 (국방부 군무과장)

주 문 기 (법무부 법무과장)

이 경 훈 (외무부 2등서기관)

조 광 제 (")

강 석 재 (")

미국측 : 교섭대표단 전원

4. 토의사항 :

(1) 군계약자 및 접수국법의 존중에관한 문제를 순차적으로 토의하고 윤전면허 및 차량등록에 관한 양측 조문초안을 교환함.

(2) 군계약자가 소지할 여권 및 그들의 도착, 출발 및 거주에관한 통고규정에 있어서 미국측은 출입국 관리의 관계조항의 해석상의 문제 ~~해석~~에 관련하여 미군인가족, 군속 및 그들의 가족은 여권을 소지하는 동시에 그들의 신분을 증명하는 적절한 문서도 가져야한다는 우리측 해석론에 동의하여 왔으므로 우리측은 군계약자가 소지할 여권에관한 부분은 삭제하고 다만 그들의 도착, 출발 및 거주에 관한 통고 의무만을 규정한 미국측안에 합의하여 주었음.

0098

63-1-15 (4)

마이크로 89-3 (4)

0093

(3) 감가상각 재산에대한 면세규정에 있어서 미국측은 동 규정은 부동산에 대하여 규제하고 있는것이며 군계약자에 대한 재산의 소지, 사용 및 이전에 관련한 조세면제 규정은 동산에 대하여 규제하고 있는것이라고 설명한데 대하여 우리측은 군계약자에 대한 재산의 소지, 사용 및 이전에 관련한 조세면제 규정의 단서로서 본항의 면세는 투자를 위하여 또는 "기타사업"을 행하기 위하여 한국에 있어서 보유되는 재산 또는 한국에 있어서 등록된 무체재산에는 적용되지 않는다라는 규정중 "기타사업"이라는 용어는 불명확한 것이니 좀더 구체적으로 "본조 제1항에서 기술한 대한민국내에서 이행중인 계약 이외의 기타사업" 이라는 용어로 대치하자고 주장하여 이문제는 다음에 다시 토의키로 함.

(4) 소득세 및 법인세에 관한 규정에 있어서 미국측안과 우리측안은 실질적인 면에 있어서 큰차이가 없으나 조문의 체제에 있어서 다소 차이가 있으므로 우리측은 새로이 미국측안에 대한 대안을 제시하여 이문제는 다음에 다시토의키로 함.

(5) 군계약자에 대한 재판관할권에 관한 규정은 우리측 초안에만 있고 미국측 초안에는 없으므로 우리측은 이에관한 미국측안을 제시하도록 촉구하자 미국측은 이를 다음에제시할것이라고 하여 이문제는 추후 다시 토의키로 함.

(6) 미국측은 합의의사록에 있어서 동합의의사록에서 말하는 조항은 군계약자에 관한 조항을 의미한다고 설명하면서, 본조항은 예를들면 군계약자가 미국군대 이외에 "유솜"등과도 계약할때에 본조항의 규정을 적용시키고저 한것이라고하여 이문제는 다음에 다시 토의키로 함.

0100

63-1-15

미문 89-3

0101

(7) 접수국법의 존중문제에 있어서 미국측은 법존중의 인적대상에 미국군대 구성원, 군속 및 그들의 가족 이외에 군계약자로 포함시키자고 주장한데 대하여 우리측은 본조항은 군계약자의 재판관할권에 관한 규정과 밀접한 관련이 있는것으로 사료되니 미국측이 동조항 초안을 제시할때 까지 보류하자고 하여 이문제는 추후 다시 토의키로 함.

(8) 양측은 운전면허 및 차량등록에 관한 조문을 교환하고 이에관한 토의를 다음 회기에서 행하기로 함.

5. 기타사항 :

(1) 차기회의 일자 : 1963. 6. 12. 하오 2시

(2) 차기회의 의제 : 차기회의 까지 양측 수석대표간에 합의된 사항

6. 참고자료 :

미국측이 제의한 조문초안 (운전면허 및 차량등록) 별첨참조.

끝

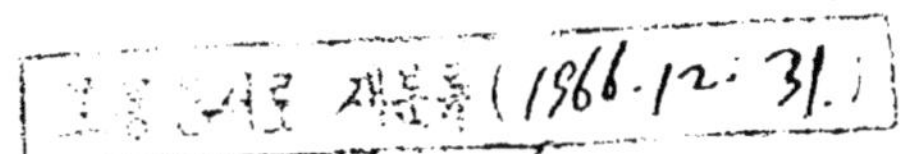

1966.12.31.에 예고문에 의거 일반문서로 재분류됨

0102

63-1-15

미원 89-3

0103

ARTICLE

LICENSING OF MOTOR VEHICLES

1. Korea shall accept as valid, without a driving test or fee, the driving permit or license or military driving permit issued by the United States, or political subdivision thereof, to a member of the United States armed forces, the civilian component, and their dependents.

2. Official vehicles of the United States armed forces and the civilian component shall carry distinctive numbered plates or individual markings which will readily identify them.

3. Privately owned vehicles of members of the United States armed forces, the civilian component and their dependents may be licensed or registered, and shall be provided with license plate or other identification as appropriate, by the United States. The authorities of the United States shall take adequate safety measures for, and shall assure the technical supervision of, the vehicles licensed by them and shall, where necessary, and at the request of the Government of the Republic of Korea, furnish the name and address of the owner of a vehicle licensed by them.

보통문서로 재분류(1966.12.31.)

1966.12.31.에 예고문에 의거 일반문서로 재분류됨

0104

63-1-15(4)

[illegible] 89-3(4)

0105

23rd meeting, May 31

1. Mr. Habib opened the meeting by announcing regretfully that this would be the last meeting attended by General Lawlor and Lt. Col. Miller, who were both being reassigned. He then introduced Mr. Robert A. Kinney, a civilian employee of the Department of the Army, working in the J-5 section of the UNC, who was taking Lt. Col. Burt's place on the negotiating team, and Major Robert D. Peckham, who would be replacing Lt. Col. Miller. Mr. Whang welcomed Mr. Kinney and Major Peckham, expressed great regret at the imminent departure of General Lawlor and Lt. Col. Miller, and wished them good fortune in their next assignments.

Contractors Article

2. Turning to substantive matters, Mr. Whang reminded the negotiators that at the previous meeting, discussion of the contractors article had been interrupted at paragraph 4. He inquired whether the U.S. side wished to resume discussion at that point or to begin discussion again at the beginning of the article. Lt. Col. Miller replied that the U.S. side wished to resume the discussion at the point at which it had been broken off at the last meeting.

3. Lt. Col. Miller then read the following statement:

"Just prior to adjournment of our last meeting we were discussing paragraphs 4 of our respective draft Invited Contractor articles. We had considered the effect of your draft first sentence of your paragraph 4 on paragraph 3(b) of our draft and 3(a) of your draft. The first sentence of paragraph 4 of your draft provides that invited contractors and their dependents shall be subject to Korean passport and visa regulations and shall possess passports with their status described therein.

"In the course of this discussion, we also referred to paragraph 4 of the exit and entry article which provides for appropriate documentation. I believe that there was some misunderstanding at that point. I would like to clarify our views at this time.

"It is our understanding that civilian employees of our armed forces and the dependents of our armed forces personnel and civilian employees will possess passports. In addition, they will possess 'Appropriate documentation' issued by U.S. authorities, so that their status may be verified by Korean officials.

"We also expect that our invited contractors, their employees, and their dependents, will be in possession of passports. However, our passport regulations do not provide for all of the other data which may be re-

0106

quired to show their status. This is no different than in the case of armed forces civilian employees and dependents. We believe that the additional requirement for 'appropriate documentation', ~~[struck out]~~ which supplements passports, meets your requirements. Inasmuch as we would expect the 'appropriate documentation' provisions to apply to invited contractors, their employees, and dependents, we suggest that the first sentence of paragraph 4 of your draft article is not sufficient. I suggest that you consider accepting our draft in view of the above explanation."

4. Mr. Whang thanked the U.S. side for the explanation given by Lt. Colonel Miller. He said that according to paragraph 2 of the Entry and Exit Article, members of the armed forces would be exempt from Korean visa and passport laws and regulations, whereas the civilian component and dependents would only be exempt from Korean laws and regulations on the registration and control of aliens. In addition, Mr. Whang continued, the Entry and Exit article calls for "appropriate documentation" in addition to passports. If invited contractors also carry passports and appropriate documentation, they would be subject to the same control as the ~~members of the~~ civilian component and dependents. ~~Therefore, he said, the Korean side would take this matter under consideration.~~ Mr. Habib remarked that this was exactly what the U.S. side had in mind.

5. Mr. Whang said that the Korean side was willing to delete the first sentence from the Korean draft of paragraph 4, with the understanding that the contractors should carry passports and appropriate documentation in the same manner as the dependents of members of the U.S. armed forces, the civilian component and their dependents in accordance with paragraphs 2 and 4 of the Entry and Exit Article. He noted that the U.S. draft contained the phrase "from time to time". He requested clarification of this phrase. Lt. Colonel Miller replied that the interpretation of this phrase would be mutually agreed upon by the two governments through the Joint Committee. He pointed out that the ROK Government officials would know of the arrival of contractors almost immediately because of the requirements involving the possession of passports and appropriate documentation. Mr. Habib added that the phrase in question referred to lists of arrivals, which lists presumably would be compiled on other than a daily basis.

0107

6. Mr. Whang commented that the ROKG authorities would issue visas beforehand to contractors intending ~~to come to Korea.~~ He asked, however, about

departure procedures. Mr. Habib replied that the U.S. side considered the issuance of visas to be insufficient notification of arrival. He pointed out that the date of arrival and the temporary residence address would be notified to the ROK Government by the U.S. armed forces. With regard to departure, he said departure rosters would be kept up to date and passed to the ROK Government through the Joint Committee.

7. Mr. Whang stated that he presumed there would be cases in which the ROKG authorities might feel it necessary to ~~contact~~ get in touch with a contractor before his departure from Korea. He asked if this would be possible. Mr. Habib said that this could be done through the Joint Committee. He said that any inquiry of this nature would be accepted at face value. Mr. Whang then stated that, with that understanding, the Korean side accepted including the words "from time to time" paragraph 4 of the U.S. draft.

~~Paragraph 5~~

8. Mr. Whang pointed out that there was no paragraph in the Korean draft comparable with paragraph 5 of the U.S. draft. He asked what was meant by the phrase "depreciable assets". Lt. Col. Miller replied that paragraphs 5 and 6 of the U.S. draft go together. Paragraph 5 is concerned with land, whereas paragraph 6 is concerned with private and personal property. As an example of depreciable assets, he mentioned a contractor excavating a gravel pit, with the value of the gravel remaining in the pit steadily depreciating. Another example would be a lease held on a building. As the period of the lease is gradually used up, the value of the lease declines proportionately. He pointed out that the only property referred to in paragraph 5 is property held exclusively for the execution of the contract held by the contractor. Mr. Whang stated that the Korean side would consider paragraph 5, ~~on the basis of~~ making reference to Lt. Colonel Miller's explanation.

0108

~~Paragraph 6~~

9. Mr. Whang stated that there did not appear to be much difference between

paragraph 6 of the U.S. draft and paragraph 5 of the Korean draft. Referring to phrases in the U.S. draft such as "tangible or intangible" and "other business in Korea", he said that the Korean draft spelled out the substance of the paragraphs more clearly and left no room for misunderstanding. Lt. Col. Miller stated that the U. S. side would consider the proposal but that ~~it did not appear as though~~ the extra wording ~~was~~ did not appear to be necessary.

~~Paragraph 7~~

10. Mr. Whang noted that the first sentence of paragraph ~~five~~ 5 in the U. S. draft provided for certification by an "authorized representative" while the Korean draft provided for certification by an "authorized officer". Mr. Whang stated that the number of persons authorized to certify should be small and that the Korean draft used "officer" to mean a high ranking official. Mr. Whang then asked what was the meaning of "representative". He suggested that the individual should be designated through the Joint Committee. Mr. Habib replied that the designation would be made through the Joint Committee and that the "representative" would be notified through the Joint Committee. Mr. Habib further explained that it would be an appropriate person or persons. Mr. Whang stated that he accepted the word "representative" in view of Mr. Habib's explanation.

~~Paragraph 7~~

11. Turning to paragraph 7 of the U.S. draft and its counterparts paragraph 6 of the Korean draft, Mr. Whang stated that the Korean draft did not include corporation taxes but that the Korean side agreed that they should be included. Mr. Whang stated that the U. S. paragraph ~~seven~~ 7 was somewhat redundant and for that reason the Korean side was submitting a revised paragraph ~~six~~ 6. Mr. Whang said that the Korean side had no ~~quarrel~~ difficulty with the first sentence of the U. S. draft but some with the second sentence. ~~was different.~~ Mr. Habib noted that the second sentence of U.S. draft paragraph 7 provided a specific

0109

exemption for income of contractors from sources outside Korea, whereas the Korean draft did not provide this exemption. Mr. Whang stated that ~~the meaning of~~ the Korean draft ~~was~~ meant to provide the exemption. Mr. Habib replied that the exemption was somewhat obscure in the Korean draft but that the U. S. side would consider the draft. Mr. Habib stated that he thought the Korean side would find the U.S. wording a little clearer. Mr. Whang stated that the exemption was provided by implication, but if the U.S. side insisted on a specific exemption the Korean side would study the matter further and give their views at a subsequent meeting. Mr. Whang asked if it was the intention of the U. S. side to allow the exemption only during the term of the contract. Mr. Habib stated that the U.S. side would consider the matter.

~~Paragraph 8~~

12. Mr. Whang asked if the U.S. side had a paragraph eight (criminal jurisdiction) for consideration. Mr. Habib stated that ~~we~~ the U.S. side would like to defer on this paragraph. Mr. Whang then asked if the U.S. side had considered paragraph seven of the Korean draft. Mr. Habib replied that we would reserve our opinion.

~~Paragraph 10~~ ~~Respect for Local Law~~

~~13. Turning to the next agenda item, the article~~ on Respect for Local Law Mr. Whang stated that, as contractors were mentioned in the article, consideration of the paragraph on the jurisdiction in the contractors article might well precede discussion of the Respect for Local Law article. ~~the article should wait until agreement was reached on the contractor article.~~ Mr. Habib stated that the Respect for Local Law article was not dependent on the contractors article and that the article stood on its own merits. Mr. Whang stated that the article includes persons covered in other articles and without agreement on articles covering these persons the Respect for Local Law article would have little meaning. Mr. Habib stated the obligation to respect local law is imposed on these people ~~xxx~~ regardless of the exact terms of other articles on jurisdiction

0110

which are to be negotiated covering these people, but if the Korean side preferred to postpone discussion on this article, that would be agreeable, although the U.S. side did not see the necessity. Mr. Whang said that he was not insisting on postponing discussion until the jurisdiction article was presented but that there was a relationship with the contractors article as contractors are named in the Respect for Local Law article. Mr. Habib agreed to postponement of further discussion. Mr. Habib then asked if the Korean side had any comment to make on the agreed minute.

Agreed Minute to Contractors Article

13. Mr. Whang asked what was the meaning of this agreed minute. Lt. Col. Miller replied that the purpose of this minute was to provide coverage under the SOFA to contractors who might also have a contract with another U.S. Government agency as well as the U.S. armed forces in Korea. The U.S. side did not wish to exclude contractors from coverage by reason of their having a contract with another U.S. Government agency. Mr. Habib suggested that the Korean side examine the principle that the U.S. side is trying to establish. Mr. Whang agreed to examine the principle.

Jurisdiction Article

14. Mr. Whang stated that he was not insisting on postponing discussion of the Respect for Local Law article but that he was suggesting that the jurisdiction article should be tabled as soon as possible to give sufficient time for detailed consideration. Mr. Habib replied that at the opening of these negotiations it was agreed to discuss less complex matters first and that in due time the negotiators would come to the jurisdiction article. He further stated that the U.S. side is not prepared to table a jurisdiction article at this time but that we will take the Korean request under consideration. Mr. Habib reminded the Korean negotiators that there is still much work to be done on less complex articles. Mr. Whang said that his understanding was the same but that he hoped that each side would have as much time as possible to study proposals on jurisdiction. Mr. Habib replied that there

0111

Respect for Local Law

would be sufficient time to study the proposals. Mr. Whang stated that with that understanding the Korean side would like to discuss the Respect for Local Law article. 15. Turning to the Respect for Local Law article, Mr. Whang noted that contractors were included in the U.S. draft. Mr. Habib stated that it was appropriate to include contractors. Mr. Whang asked if it was appropriate to include contractors in the Respect for Local Law Article, in view of the fact that there are separate articles on civilian component and contractors. Mr. Habib replied that there was no conflict and that for the sake of completeness contractors were included. Mr. Habib pointed out that contractors are not named in the Japanese SOFA, but that they should be to make the article complete. Mr. Whang stated that he was seeking assurance that contractors and the civilian component are different. Mr. Habib replied that the Korean side could be assured that there is a difference and that reference to the definitions article would show the difference. Mr. Whang thanked Mr. Habib and stated that the Korean side would consider the article further and give its views at a later meeting.

Motor Vehicles

16. Drafts of the article on Licensing and Registration of Motor Vehicles were then tabled by each side. Mr. Habib noted that there were substantial differences in the two drafts and suggested that detailed discussion be delayed. Mr. Whang agreed.

17. The next meeting was scheduled for June 12, 1963 at 2:00 P.m.

보통문서로 재분류(1963. 12. 31.)

0112

JOINT SUMMARY RECORD OF THE 23RD SESSION
STATUS OF FORCES NEGOTIATIONS

May 31, 1963

I. Time and Place: 2;00 to 4;00 p.m. May 31, 1963 at the Foreign Minister's Conference Room

II. Attendants:

ROK Side:

Mr. Whang, Ho Eul	Director Bureau of Political Affairs Ministry of Foreign Affairs
Mr. Shin, Kwan Sup	Director Bureau of Customs Duty Ministry of Finance
Mr. Koo, Choong Whay	Chief, America Section Ministry of Foreign Affairs
Mr. Shin, Jung Sup	Chief, Treaty Section Ministry of Foreign Affairs
Col. Nam Koo Lee	Chief, Military Affairs Section Ministry of National Defense
Mr. Chu, Mun Ki	Chief, Legal Affairs Section, Ministry of Justice
Mr. Lee, Kyung Hoon	2nd Secretary Ministry of Foreign Affairs
Mr. Cho, Kwang Je	2nd Secretary Ministry of Foreign Affairs
Mr. Kang, Suk Jae	2nd Secretary Ministry of Foreign Affairs

U.S. Side:

Mr. Philip C. Habib	Counselor of the Embassy for Political Affairs
Brig. Gen. J. D. Lawlor	Deputy Chief of Staff 8th Army
Mr. William J. Ford	First Secretary of the Embassy
Capt. R. M. Brownlie	Assistant Chief of Staff USN/K
Col. G. G. O'Connor	Deputy Chief of Staff 8th Army
Col. L. J. Fuller	Staff Judge Advocate United Nations Command

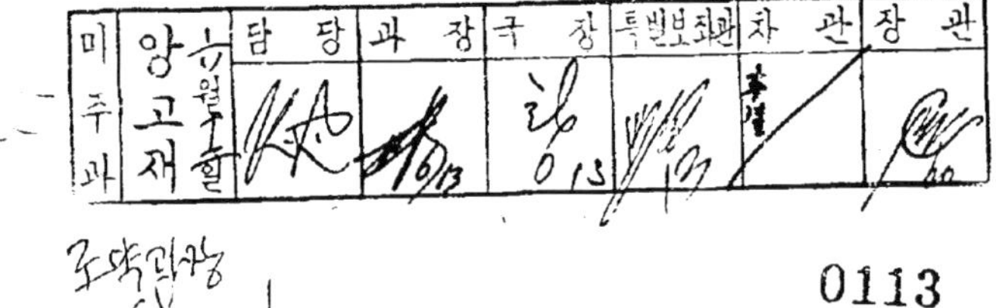

조약과장

0113

Mr. Robert A. Lewis	Second Secretary and Consul of the Embassy
Lt. Col. R. E. Miller	Staff Officer, JAG 8th Army
Robert A. Kinney	J-5 United Nations Command
Major Robert D. Peckham	Staff Officer, JAG 8th Army

1. Mr. Habib opened the meeting by announcing regretfully that this would be the last meeting attended by General Lawlor and Lt. Col. Miller, who were both being reassigned. He then introduced Mr. Robert A. Kinney, a civilian employee of the Department of the Army, working in the J-5 section of the UNC, who was taking Lt. Col. Burt's place on the negotiating team, and Major Robert D. Peckham, who would be replacing Lt. Col. Miller. Mr. Whang welcomed Mr. Kinney and Major Peckham, expressed great regret at the imminent departure of General Lawlor and Lt. Col. Miller, and wished them good fortune in their next assignments.

Contractors Article

2. Turning to substantive matters, Mr. Whang reminded the negotiators that at the previous meeting, discussion of the contractors article had been interrupted at paragraph 4. He inquired whether the U.S. side wished to resume discussion at that point or to begin discussion again at the beginning of the article. Lt. Col. Miller replied that the U.S. side wished to resume the discussion at the point at which it had been broken off at the last meeting.

3. Lt. Col. Miller then read the following statement:

"Just prior to adjournment of our last meeting we were discussing paragraphs 4 of our respective draft Invited Contractor articles. We had considered the effect of your draft first sentence of your paragraph 4

0114

on paragraph 3(b) of our draft and 3(a) of your draft. The first sentence of paragraph 4 of your draft provides that invited contractors and their dependents shall be subject to Korean passport and visa regulations and shall possess passports with their status described therein.

"In the course of this discussion, we also referred to paragraph 4 of the exit and entry article which provides for appropriate documentation. I believe that there was some misunderstanding at that point. I would like to clarify our views at this time.

"It is our understanding that civilian employees of our armed forces and the dependents of our armed forces personnel and civilian employees will possess passports. In addition, they will possess 'Appropriate documentation' issued by U.S. authorities, so that their status may be varified by Korean officials.

"We also expect that our invited contractors, their employees, and their dependents, will be in possesstion of passports. However, our passport regulations do not provide for all of the other data which may be required to show their status. This is no different than in the case of armed forces civilian employees and dependents. We believe that the additional requirement for "appropriate documentation' which supplements passports, meets your requirements. Inasmuch as we would expect the 'appropriate documentation' provisions to apply to invited contractors, their employees, and dependents, we suggest that the first sentence of paragraph 4 of your draft article is not sufficient. I suggest that you consider accepting our draft in view of the above explanation."

4. Mr. Whang thanked the U.S. side for the explanation given Lt. Colonel Miller. He said that according to paragraph 2 of the Entry and Exit Article, members of the armed forces would be exempt for Korean visa and passport laws and regulations, whereas the civilian component and dependents would only be exempt from Korean laws and regulations on the registration and control of aliens. In addition, Mr. Whang continued, the Entry and Exit article calls for "appropriate documentation" in addition to passports. If invited contractors also carry passports and appropriate documentation, they would be subject to the same control as the civilian component and dependents. Mr. Habib remarked that this was exactly what the U.S. side had in mind.

5. Mr. Whang said that the Korean side was willing to delete the first sentence from the Korean draft of paragraph 4,

0115

with the understanding that the contractors should carry passports and appropriate documentation in the same manner as the dependents of members of the U. S. armed forces, the civilian component and their dependents in accordance with paragraphs 2 and 4 of the Entry and Exit article. He noted that the U.S. draft contained the phrase "from time to time". He requested clarification of this phrase. Lt. Colonel Miller replied that the interpretation of this phrase would be mutually agreed upon by the two governments through the Joint Committee. He pointed out that the ROK Government officials would know of the arrival of contractors almost immediately because of the requirements involving the possession of passports and appropriate documentation. Mr. Habib added that the phrase in question referred to lists of arrivals, which lists presumably would be compiled on other than a daily basis.

6. Mr. Whang commented that the ROKG authorities would issue visas beforehand to contractors intending to come to Korea. He asked, however, about departure procedures. Mr. Habib replied that the U.S. side considered the issuance of visas to be insufficient notification of arrival. He pointed out that the date of arrival and temporary residence address would be notified to the ROK Government by the U.S. armed forces. With regard to departure, he said departure rosters would be kept up to date and passed to the ROK Government through the Joint Committee.

7. Mr. Whang stated that he presumed there would be cases in which the ROKG authorities might feel it necessary to get in touch with a contractor before his departure from Korea. He asked if this would be possible. Mr. Habib said

0116

this could be done through the Joint Committee. He said that that any inquiry of this nature would be accepted at face value. Mr. Whang then stated that, with that understanding, the Korean side accepted paragraph 4 of the U.S. draft including the words "from time to time".

8. Mr. Whang pointed out that there was no para-graph in the Korean draft comparable with paragraph 5 of the U.S. draft. He asked what was meant by the phrase "depreciable assest". Lt. Col. Miller replied that paragraphs 5 and 6 of the U.S. draft go together. Paragraph 5 is concerned with land, whereas paragraph 6 is concerned with private and personal property. As an example of depreciable assests, he mentioned a contractor excavating a gravel pit, with the value of the gravel remaining in the pit steadily depreciating. Another example would be a lease held on a building. As the period of the lease is gradually used up, the value of the lease declines proportionately. He pointed out that the only property referred to in paragraph 5 is property held exclusively for the execution of the contract held by the contractor. Mr. Whang stated that the Korean side would consider paragraph 5, making reference to Lt. Colonel Miller's explanation.

9. Mr. Whang stated that there did not appear to be much difference between paragraph 6 of the U.S. draft and paragraph 5 of the Korean draft. Referring to phrases in the U.S. draft such as "tangible or intangible" and "other business in Korea", he said that the Korean draft spelled out the substance of the paragraph more clearly and left no room for misunderstanding. Lt. Col. Miller stated that the U.S. side would consider the proposal but that the extra wording did not appear to be necessary.

10. Mr. Whang noted that the first sentence of paragraph 5 in the U.S. draft provided for certification by

an "authorized representative" while the Korean draft provided for certification by an "authorized officer". Mr. Whang stated that the number of persons authorized to certify should be small and that the Korean draft used "officer" to mean a high ranking official. Mr. Whang then asked what the meaning of "representative". He suggested that the individual should be designated through the Joint Committee. Mr. Habib replied that the designation would be made through the Joint Committee and that the "representative" would be notified through the Joint Committee. Mr. Habib further explained that it would be an appropriate person or persons. Mr. Whang stated that he accepted the word "representative" in view of Mr. Habib's explanation.

11. Turning to paragraph 7 of the U.S. draft and its counterpart, paragraph 6 of the Korean draft, Mr. Whang stated that the Korean draft did not include corporation taxes but that the Korean side agreed that they shoud be included. Mr. Whang stated that the U.S. paragraph 7 was somewhat redundant and for that reason the Korean side was submitting a revised paragraph 6. Mr. Whang said that the Korean side had no difficulty with the first sentence of the U.S. draft but some with the second sentence. Mr. Habib noted that the second sentence of U.S. draft paragraph 7 provided a specific exemption for income of contractors from sources outside Korea, whereas the Korean draft did not provide this exemption. Mr. Whagg stated that the Korean draft was meant to provide the exemption. Mr. Habib replied that the exemption was somewhat obscure in the Korean draft but that the U.S. side would consider the draft. Mr. Habib stated that he thought the Korean

0118

side would find the U.S. wording a little clearer. Mr. Whang stated that the exemption was provided by implication, but if the U.S. side insisted on a specific exemption the Korean side would study the matter further and give their views at a subsequent meeting. Mr. Whang asked if it was the intention of the U.S. side to allow the exemption only during the term of the contract. Mr. Habib stated that the U.S. side would consider the matter.

12. Mr. Whang asked if the U.S. side had a paragraph eight (criminal jurisdiction) for consideration. Mr. Habib stated that ~~we~~ the U.S. side would like to defer on this paragraph. Mr. Whang then asked if the U.S. side had considered paragraph seven of the Korean draft. Mr. Habib replied that we would reserve our opinion. Mr. Whang stated that as contractors were mentioned in the article on Respect for Local Law, consideration of the paragraph on jurisdiction in the contractors article might well precede discussion of the Respect for Local Law article. Mr. Habib stated that the Respect for Local Law article was not dependent on the contractors article and that the article stood on its own merits. Mr. Whang stated that the article includes persons covered in other articles and without agreement on articles covering these persons the Respect for Local Law article would have little meaning. Mr. Habib stated the obligation to respect local law is imposed on these people regardless of the exact terms of other articles on jurisdiction which are to be negotiated covering these people, but if the Korean side preferred to postpone discussion on this article, that would be agreeable, although the

0119

U.S. side did not see the necessity. Mr. Whang said that he was not insisting on postponing discussion until the jurisdiction article was presented but that there was a relationship with the contractors article as contractors are named in the Respect for Local Law article. Mr. Habib agreed to postponement of further discussion.

Agreed Minute to Contractors Article

13. Mr. Habib then asked if the Korean side had any comment to make on the agreed minute. Mr. Whang asked what was the meaning of this agreed minute. Lt. Col. Miller replied that the purpose of this minute was to provide coverage under the SOFA to contractors who might also have a contract with another U.S. Government agency as well as the U.S. armed forces in Korea. The U.S. side did not wish to exclude contractors from coverage by reason of their having a contract with another U.S. Government agency. Mr. Habib suggested that the Korean side examine the principle that the U.S. side is trying to establish. Mr. Whang agreed to examine the principle.

Jurisdiction Article

14. Mr. Whang stated that he was not insisting on postponing discussion of the Respect for Local Law article but that he was suggesting that the jurisdiction article should be tabled as soon as possible to give sufficient time for detailed consideration. Mr. Habib replied that at the opening of these negotiations it was agreed to discuss less complex matters first and that in due time the negotiators would come to the jurisdiction article. He further stated that the U.S. side is not prepared to table a jurisdiction article at this time but that we will

0120

take the Korean request under consideration. Mr. Habib reminded the Korean negotiators that there is still much work to be done on less complex articles. Mr. Whang said that his understanding was the same but that he hoped that each side would have as much time as possible to study proposals on juriddiction. Mr. Habib replied that there would be sufficient time to study the proposals. Mr. Whang stated that with that understanding, the Korean side would like to discuss the Respect for Local Law article.

Respect for Local Law

15. Turning to the Respect for Local Law article, Mr. Whang noted that contractors were included in the U.S. draft. Mr. Habib stated that it was appropriate to include contractors. Mr. Whang stated that the Korean side did not object, but asked if it was appropriate to include contractors in the Respect for Local Law article in view of the fact that there are separate articles on civilian component and contractors. Mr. Habib replied that there was no conflict and that for the sake of completeness contractors were included. Mr. Habib pointed out that contractors are not named in the Japanese SOFA, but that they should be to make the article complete. Mr. Whang stated that he was seeking assurance that contractors and the civilian component are different. Mr. Habib replied that the Korean side could be assured that there is a difference and that reference to the definitions article would show the difference. Mr. Whang thanked Mr. Habib and stated that the Korean side would consider the article further and give its views at a later meeting.

Mortor Vehicles

16. Drafts of the article on Licensing and Regis-

0121

tration of Motor Vehicles were then tabled by each side. Mr. Habib noted that there were substantial differences in the two drafts and suggested that detailed discussion be delayed. Mr. Whang agreed.

17. The next meeting was scheduled for June 12, 1963 at 2:00 p.m.

보통문서로 재분류(협정체결시)

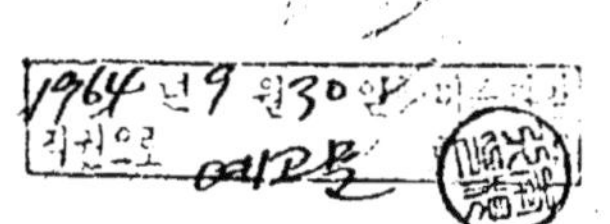

1966.12.31 에 예고문에 의거 일반문서로 재분류됨

0122

4. 제24차 회의, 6.12

0123

기 안 용 지

자체통제		기안처	미주과 이 경 훈	전화번호	근거서류접수일자

	과장	국장	보좌관	차관	장관	

관계관 서명	조약과장

기안 년월일	63. 6.12.	시행 년월일		보존 년한		정서	기장
분류 기호	외정미	전체 통제		종결			
경유 수신 참조	건 의			발신			
제목	제24차 주둔군지위협정 체결 교섭회의에 임할 우리측 입장						

6. 12.에 개최될 제24차 주둔군지위협정 체결 한미간 교섭회의에서는 운전면허 및 차량, 접수국법의 존중, 공익물 및 용역, 조세문제에 관하여 토의될 예정이온바 이에 관련하여 우리측 교섭 실무자는 6. 11. 회합을 갖고 제24차 회의에서 취할 우리측 태도를 별첨과같이 결정하였아오니 재가하여 주시기 바랍니다.

유첨 : 제24차 주둔군지위협정 체결교섭회의에 임할 우리측 태도, 끝

일반문서로 재분류(1966.12.31.)

1966.12.31.에 예고문에 의거 일반문서로 재분류됨

1964년 9월 30일 미주과장 직권으로 비고문 0재분

승인양식 1—1—3 (1112—040—016—018) (190mm×260mm16절지)

0124

1. 운전면허 및 차량

(1) 운전면허 허여원칙에 관한 미국측 초안 1항 (이는 우리측 초안 1항에 해당함)에는 우리측 초안에 없는 "political subdivisions thereof" 라는 구절이 포함되어 있는바 우리측은 동구절에 대한 미국측의 견해를 문의한후 미국측 초안 1항의 수락 여부를 결정한다.

(2) 공용차량의 표식에관한 미국측 초안 2항은 우리측 초안 2 (a) 항에해당 하는바 양측초안은 거의 같으므로 미국측안을 수락토록 한다.

(3) 사유차량의 표식에관한 규정에 있어서 미국측은 그의초안 3항에서 미국군대 구성원, 군속 및 그들의 가족의 개인용 차량은 미국에 의하여 부여되는 표식을 사용토록 하는것 등을 규정한데 반하여 우리측은 우리측 초안 2(b)항에서 이들의 개인용 차량은 한국이 부여한 표식을 사용토록 규정하므로서 양측안은 실질적 차의를 나타내고 있는바 우리측은 우리측안의 수락을 미국측에게 요구토록 한다.

2. 접수국법의 존중

(1) 미국측 안에는 우리측안에 없는 군계약자도 접수국법에 대한 존중 의무자의 대상으로 포함시키고 있는바, 미국측은 군계약자가 이에 포함된것이 다른 조항과 관련이 없다고 설명하였으므로 우리측은 미국측안을 수락키로 한다.

3. 공익물 및 용역

(1) 공익물 및 용역의 사용허여 원칙을 규정한 미국측 초안 3(a)항의 첫째문장은 우리측 초안 1항의 첫째문장에 해당하는바 미국측은 동 첫째문장에 대하여 새로운 대안으로서 " whether publicly or privately owned " 라는 구절을 삭제하는 동시에 "which are"

0125

구절 다음에 "owned," 라는 어구를 삽입하고 "political subdivisions" 대신에 "local administrative subdivisions" 라는 구절을 삽입할것을 제의하여 왔기 이는 우리측안과 비등하므로 수락하기로 한다.

(2) 공익물 및 용역의 정의에관한 미국측 초안 3(a)항의 둘째문장 (이는 우리측 초안 1항 둘째문장에 해당함)에 있어서 본규정은 공익물 및 용역 그자체의 정의에관한 것이니 만큼 " however produced" 라는 구절은 불필요하니 이의 삭제를 주장한다.

(3) 공익물 및 용역의 운영관리에 관한 미국측 초안 3(a)항의 셋째문장에 대하여 우리측은 대안을 제시하였던바 미국측은 우리측 대안에 대한 재수정안을 제시하여 온바,이는 우리측안과 비등하므로 수락토록 한다.

(4) 공익물 및 용역의 사용 우선순위에 관한 미국측 초안 3(b)항의 첫째문장 (이는 우리측 초안 1항 셋째문장에 해당함)에 있어서 " any other user " 라는 구절이 구체적으로 무엇들인가를 문의토록 한다.

(5) 비상시의 운영에관한 미국측 초안 3(b)항의 마지막 문장은 우리측 초안에는 없는것으로 이에대하여 우리측은 "emergency operating needs" 라는 구절이 구체적으로 무엇을 의미하는가를 문의토록 한다.

(6) 세부규정으로서 협약의 유효성에 관한 미국측 초안 4항(이는 우리측 초안 2(a)항에 해당함)은 우리측안과 실질적인 큰차이는 없으나 우리측안이 보다 상세하고 광범하므로 우리측 초안을 받아드리도록 주장한다.

(7) 미국측이 제시한 합의의사록에 있어서 (가) 순위 및 율의 변경에 대한 합동위원회에서의 사전 협의에관한 미국측 초안 1항은 불필요한것이니 이의 삭제를 요구하고 (나) 기존협정의 유효성에

0126

관한 2항은 우리측 초안 2(b)항에 해당하는 것으로 이는 이는 우리측 수정 안과 실질적 차이가 없으나 우리측 안이 보다며 포괄적이므로 우리측안의 수락을 요구한다.

4. 조세문제

(1) 미국군대의 면세원칙, 미국군대 구성원, 군속 및 그들의 가족의 수입에 대한 면세 허여원칙, 그리고 이들의 동산에대한 면세 허여원칙 등을 규정한 별첨과같은 우리측 초안을 제시토록 한다.

(2) 미국측이 제시하는 안이 우리측안과 비등할때에는 우리측안의 수락을 요구토록 한다.

1966.12.31.

0127

ARTICLE ____

1. The United States armed forces shall not be subject to taxes or similar charges on property held, used or transferred by such forces in the Republic of Korea.

2. Members of the United States armed forces, the civilian component, and their dependents shall not be liable to pay Korean taxes to the Government of the Republic of Korea or to any other taxing agency in the Republic of Korea on income received as a result of their service with or employment by the United States armed forces, or by the organizations provided for in Article [illegible]. The provisions of this Article do not exempt such persons from payment of Korean taxes on income derived from sources other than those provided for in this paragraph.

3. Members of the United States armed forces, the civilian component, and their dependents shall be exempt from taxation in the Republic of Korea on the holding, use, transfer <u>inter se</u>, or transfer by death of any movable property, the presence of which in the Republic of Korea is due solely to the temporary presence of these persons in the Republic of Korea provided that such exemption shall not apply to property held for the purpose of investment or the conduct of business in the Republic of Korea.

0128

4. Periods during which the persons referred to in the preceding paragraph are in the Republic of Korea solely by reason of being mebmers of the United States armed forces or of the civilian component, or their dependents shall not be considered as periods of residence or domicile in the Republic of Korea for the purpose of Korean taxation.

보통문서로 재분류(1966.12.31.)

1966.12.31.에 예고문에 의거 일반문서로 재분류됨

기 안 용 지

자체 통제		기안처	미주과 이경훈	전화번호	근거서류접수일자

	과장	국장	보좌관	차관	장관
	6/13	13		후결	20

관계관 서명	1등서기관				
기안 년월일	63. 6. 13.	시행 년월일		보존 년한	정서기장
분류 기호	외정미 722.2	전체 통제	후결		
경유 수신 참조	국가재건최고회의 의장 (참조: 외무국방위원장) 내각수반	발신	장 관		
제목	주둔군지위협정 체결을위한 제24차 교섭회의 보고				

1963. 6. 12. 하오 2시부터 동 4시 20분까지 외무부장관 회의실에서 개최된 제24차 주둔군지위협정 체결 교섭회의에서 토의된 내용을 별첨과 같이 보고합니다.

유첨 : 제24차 교섭회의 보고서 부, 끝

보통문서로 재분류(1966. 12. 31.)

발송 1963. 6. 14 외무부

1964년 9월 30일 미주국장 직권으로 예고문 재분류

0130

승인양식 1-1-3 (1112-040-016-018) (190mm×260mm16절지)

에 예고문에 의거 일반문서로 재분류됨

외 무 부

외정미 722.2 1963. 6. 14.

수 신 국가재건최고회의 의장

참 조 외무국방위원장

제 목 주둔군지위협정 체결을위한 제24차 교섭회의 보고

1963. 6. 12. 하오 2시부터 동 4시 20분까지 외무부 장관 회의실에서 개최된 제24차 주둔군지위협정 체결 교섭회의에서 토의된 내용을 별첨과 같이 보고합니다.

유첨 : 제24차 교섭회의 보고서 2부. 끝

외 무 부 장 관 김 용 식

0131

외 무 부

외정미 722.2 1963. 6. 14.

수 신 내각수반

제 목 주둔군지위협정 체결을위한 제24차 교섭회의 보고

1963. 6.12. 하오 2시부터 동 4시 20분까지 외무부 장관 회의실에서 개최된 제24차 주둔군지위협정 체결 교섭회의에서 토의된 내용을 별첨과같이 보고합니다.

유첨 : 제24차 교섭회의 보고서 1 부. 끝

외 무 부 장 관 김 용 식

0132

제 24 차

한미간 주둔군 지위협정 체결 실무자회의

보 고 서

1. 일 시 : 1963. 6. 12. 하오 2시부터 4시 20분까지

2. 장 소 : 외무부장관 회의실

3. 참석자 : 한국측 : 황호을 (외무부 정무국장)

신관섭 (재무부 세관국장)

구충회 (외무부 미주과장)

신정섭 (외무부 조약과장)

이남구 (국방부 군무과장)

주문기 (법무부 법무과장)

이경훈 (외무부 2등서기관)

강석재 (")

조광제 (")

미국측 : 교섭대표단 전원

4. 토의사항 :

(1) 접수국법의 존중, 운전면허 및 차량 그리고 공의물 및 용역 문제를 순차적으로 토의하고 조세문제에 관한 양측초문 초안을 교환함.

(2) 접수국법의 존중문제에 있어서 미국측 안에는 우리측 안에 없는 군계약자도 접수국법에 대한 존중 의무자의 대상으로 포함시키고 있는바 이에 관련하여 미국측은 군계약자가 동 조항에 포함 되었다고 해서 다른조항과 관련이 있는것이 아니고 군계약자는 완전히 별개의 조항으로 취급되는 것이라고 설명하였으므로 우리측은 미국측 안을 수락하여 완전 합의에 도달함.

63-1-1

0133

63-1-16(5)

미국문 89-2(5)

0134

(3) 운전면허 및 차량등록에 관한 조항의 토의에 있어서 운전면허 허여원칙에 관한 양측 초안은 실질적 차이가 없으므로 미국측 안을 수락하여 주었음.

(4) 공용차량의 표식에관한 양측안은 거의 같으므로 미국측안을 수락하여 주었음.

(5) 사유차량의 표식에 관한 규정에 있어서 미국측은 미국군대 구성원, 군속 및 그들의 가족의 개인용 차량은 미국에 의하여 부여되는 표식을 사용토록 하자고 주장한데 대하여 우리측은 이들의 개인용 차량은 한국이 부여한 표식을 사용토록 하되 차량 감찰을 이들에게 부여함에 있어서 수반되는 과세, 채권 구입은 부과하지 않을것이나 차량감찰의 실비만을 지불하면 족하다고 설명하여 이문제는 다음에 다시 토의키로 함.

(6) 공익물 및 용역조항의 토의에 있어서 공익물 및 용역의 사용 허여 규정에 관하여 미국측은 그의 초안에서 규정한 "공유이건 사유이건" 이라는 구절을 삭제하고 "대한민국 정부 또는 그의 정치상의 예하 기관에의하여 관리되거나 규제되고 있는" 이라는 구절을 "대한민국 정부 또는 그의 지방행정 기관에 의하여 소유되거나, 관리되거나, 제약되고 있는" 이라는 용어로 대치하겠다는 수정안을 제시하여 왔기 우리측은 이를 수락하였음.

(7) 공익물 및 용역의 정의에 관한 규정에 있어서 우리측은 이규정은 공익물 및 용역 그자체의 정의에 관한 것이니 만큼 "어떻게 생산되든지" 라는 생산 방식에 관한 수식어는 불필요하다고 주장한데 대하여 미국측은 해석상의 오해를 없애기위하여 이것이 필요하다고 주장하여 이문제는 다음에 다시 토의키로 함.

0135

63-1-16

미원 89-2

0136

(8) 공의물 및 용역의 운영관리에 관한 규정에 있어서 우리측은 "미국군대에 의한 군용운수, 통신, 전력 그리고 기타 공익물 및 용역의운영은 미국군대의 운영에 필요한 정도와 이러한 공익물 및 용역의 대한민국에 의한 운영과 상치하지 않는 정도 이어야 한다" 라는 수정안을 제시한바 있는데 이에대하여 미국측은 다시 이와 유사한 재수정안을 제시하여 왔기 우리측은 이 재수정안을 수락하여 주었음.

(9) 양측은 조세문제에 관한 초안을 교환하고 이문제를 다음에 토의키로 함.

5. 중요 합의사항 :

접수국법의 존중문제에 관한 조항에 완전 합의함.

6. 기타사항 :

(1) 차기회의일자 : 1963. 6.26. 하오 2시

(2) 차기회의 의제: 차기회의까지 양측수석대표간에 합의된 사항

7. 참고자료 :

미국측이 제의한 조문초안 (조세문제) 별첨참조.

보통문서로 재분류(1966.12.31.)

1966.12.31 ... 의거 일반문서로 재분류

0137

63-1-16

미속 89-2

0138

ARTICLE ____

TAXATION

1. The United States armed forces shall not be subject to taxes or similar charges on property held, used or transferred by such forces in Korea.

2. Members of the United States armed forces, the civilian component, and their dependents shall not be liable to pay any Korean taxes to the Government of Korea or to any other taxing agency in Korea on income received as a result of their service with or employment by the United States armed forces, including the activities provided for in Article   . Persons in Korea solely by reason of being members of the United States armed forces, the civilian component, or their dependents shall not be liable to pay any Korean taxes to the Government of Korea or to any taxing agency in Korea on income derived from sources outside of Korea, nor shall periods during which such persons are in Korea be considered as periods of residence or domicile in Korea for the purpose of Korean taxation. The provisions of this Article do not exempt such persons from payment of Korean taxes on income derived from Korean sources, other than those sources referred to in the first sentence of this paragraph, nor do they exempt United States citizens who claim Korean residence for United States income tax purposes from

0139

43-1-16

미문 89-2

0140

payment of Korean taxes on income.

8. Members of the United States armed forces, the civilian component, and their dependents shall be exempt from taxation in Korea on the holding, use, transfer <u>inter se</u>, or transfer by death of movable property, tangible or intangible, the presence of which in Korea is due solely to the temporary presence of these persons in Korea, provided that such exemption shall not apply to property held for the purpose of investment or the conduct of business in Korea or to any intangible property registered in Korea.

보통문서로 재분류(1966, 12.31.)

1966, 12, 31 에 예고문에 의거 일반문서로 재분류됨

0141

63-1-16 (5)　　　　마이쿤 89-2(5)

0142

June 12, 1963

1. Mr. Habib opened the meeting by introducing Colonel Howard Smigelow, Colonel O'Connor's replacement as Deputy Chief of Staff, United Nations Command. Mr. Habib reminded the negotiators that Colonel O'Connor had succeeded Brigadier General Lawlor as Deputy Chief of Staff, Eighth United States Army and would henceforth be the principal military member of the U.S. negotiating team. Mr. Whang congratulated Colonel O'Connor and welcomed Colonel Smigelow to the negotiations.

Respect for Local Law

2. Turning to substantive matters, Mr. Whang stated that at the previous meeting the U.S. side had given assurances that the status of contractors was different than the status of the civilian component, even though contractors were mentioned in the Respect for Local Law article. With that understanding, he said, the Korean side accepted the U.S. draft of the Respect for Local Law article. Mr. Habib replied that Mr. Whang's statement was correct and that any exception would be specifically stated in the relevant article.

Licensing and Registration of Motor Vehicles

3. Mr. Whang began discussion of the Motor Vehicle article by pointing out a few minor differences in the two drafts of paragraph 1. He said the U.S. draft mentioned "Korea" where the Korean draft read "Republic of Korea"; he assumed that this divergence could be adjusted in the final stage of negotiation. He also pointed out that the U.S. draft spoke of "political subdivision thereof" whereas in the article on Utilities and Services the U.S. side had previously proposed changing the term "political subdivisions" to "local administrative subdivisions". He suggested that, for the sake of consistency, "local administrative subdivisions" be made the language in both articles.

0143

4. Mr. Habib replied that the entities referred to in the two articles

were different. Whereas in the Utilities and Services article, the "local administrative subdivisions" referred to were located in the Republic of Korea, the "political subdivisions" referred to in the Motor Vehicles article were the individual states in the United States. He reminded the Korean side that because it had said that there were no political subdivisions in the Republic of Korea, the U.S. side had proposed to substitute the phrase "local administrative subdivisions". "Political subdivision", however, was the only term which would accurately describe the states under the existing federal system in the United States. Furthermore, automobile licenses and registrations were handled by the individual states and not, as in Korea, by the national government. He said the U.S. side had suggested changing the language in the Utilities and Services article to suit the internal situation described by the ROK side; therefore, he requested the ROK side to accept the terminology used by the U.S. side to describe the internal situation in the United States. Mr. Whang thanked Mr. Habib for the explanation and said that the Korean side accepted the phrase "political subdivision thereof".

5. Mr. Whang noted that the only difference between the U.S. draft of paragraph 2 and paragraph 2(a) of the Korean draft was that the U.S. draft used the plural whereas the ROK draft used the singular. He said the ROK side accepted the U.S. draft. Mr. Habib remarked that the U.S. side believed the plural usage to be more accurate and more appropriate.

6. Mr. Whang noted that there were substantial differences between the U.S. draft of paragraph 3 and its counterpart, paragraph 2(b) of the Korean draft, particularly with regard to privately-owned vehicles. He noted that the U.S. draft called for licensing by the U.S. armed forces, whereas the Korean draft would provide for licensing and registration under the same conditions as those applicable to nationals of the Republic of Korea. Mr. Whang pointed out that a separate provision for the importation of privately owned vehicles free of customs duty was included in the Customs Article. He reminded

0144

the negotiators that there are ROK regulations setting forth certain requirements for the registration of vehicles. In order to permit the ROK Government to keep accurate account of the inflow of vehicles, registration should be the responsibility of the ROK Government under the existing regulations. Mr. Whang added that the ROK side did not wish to cause the U.S. armed forces any inconvenience. He stated that applications for registration would be handled as speedily as possible. He stated further that the members of the U.S. armed forces, civilian component, and their dependents would not be asked to pay the taxes which Korean nationals are required to pay in connection with licensing and registration. On the contrary, they would be asked to pay only the actual costs of issuing licenses.

7. Mr. Habib replied that the U.S. negotiators were not trying to cause the ROK Government any difficulty but were endeavoring to establish an administrative system that would be simple and easy to operate. He said that certain portions of the existing Korean regulations regarding licensing and registration, particularly those requiring the payment of taxes, were inappropriate for application to members of the U.S. armed forces. Although Mr. Whang had stated that the ROKG had no intention to tax members of the armed forces, the civilian component , or their dependents, nevertheless one of the existing requirements under the Korean regulations is the submission of a certificate to the appropriate authority stating that all taxes have been paid. This, of course, would be a useless exercise if, in fact, the taxes were not collected. Moreover, Mr. Habib continued, applicants for licenses and registration are required to purchase a minimum number of national savings bonds. This also is an inappropriate requirement, insofar as the U.S. armed forces are concerned.

8. Mr. Habib stated that under the provisions of the Automobile Tax Law (Law No. 511), the current annual cost of a license for a U.S. made passenger automobile for non-business use is 100,000 Won (or about $769 at the current official exchange rate). In addition, he continued, for the purpose of limiting the number of automobiles as well as providing for tax revenue, a surtax of 60% is imposed in

0145

the Seoul area, which would make the total annual cost of a license approximately $1230.00 for a standard size privately owned automobile. Mr. Habib stated that the U.S. draft reflects the Status of Forces Agreements with the NATO countries, particularly paragraph 4, Article XVII of ~~the SOFA with the Federal Republic of Germany~~. Through experience throughout the world, he said, the U.S. Government has reached the conclusion that the problem under discussion is best handled by allowing the U.S. armed forces to do the actual licensing, with adequate safety measures and technical supervision of the vehicles, with the names and addresses of the owners furnished to the host government. He said this system has worked very well in other parts of the world. He asked if the Korean side had any further suggestions to put forward as ways of expediting the issuance of licenses, meeting the problems faced by both sides, and avoiding the inappropriate aspects of the existing ROKG regulations.

9. Mr. Whang replied that the U.S. side appeared to have given very careful study to the problems under consideration. He assured the U.S. side that taxes, certificates, purchase of national savings bonds, and similar requirements levied on Korean nationals would not be applied to the U.S. armed forces, members of the civilian component, or their dependents. In response to Mr. Habib's statement that such exemption was not spelled out in the Korean draft, Mr. Whang said that ~~as the U.S. armed forces would be exempted from the payment of taxes by the Taxation Article, it is taken for granted that they would be exempted from paying~~ any taxes in connection with licensing and registration of motor vehicles. He said the total cost to each applicant would come only to about $1.10 or $1.20 for the license plates. He said it would be sufficient if the Joint Committee informed the ROK Government of the type of car, make, year, and name and address of the owner. He said the ROK Government would make the procedure as simple as possible. In reply to a further query by Mr. Habib, Mr. Whang said that a system similar to that

0146

now in force with regard to automobiles imported by diplomatic personnel would be satisfactory.

10. Mr. Habib said that Mr. Whang's explanation had made the position of the Korean side much clearer. He asked whether the Korean side envisaged any limitation on the number of licenses to be issued. Mr. Whang replied that if a five-member family applied for registration of five vehicles, the request would not be considered reasonable. The Korean side was thinking in terms of the average needs of the average family in the U.S. He said the ROK Government was concerned with the traffic problem ~~of heavy wear and tear on the roads~~ which would result from ~~a large influx~~ an increasing number of automobiles. He inquired about the number of privately owned automobiles currently in use by the U.S. armed forces. Mr. Habib replied that at present there were about 400 automobiles, which were owned by members of the Military Advisory Group, and that about 50 additional cars are authorized for other personnel on two year tours in the R.O.K.

Utilities and Services

11. Turning to the drafts relating to utilities and services, Mr. Whang summarized the changes proposed by each side at the 20th meeting regarding paragraph 3(a) of the U.S. draft and paragraph 1 of the Korean draft. He said the Korean side was prepared to accept the U.S. proposals to delete "whether publicly or privately owned", to insert "owned" following the words "which are", to substitute the phrase "local administrative subdivisions" for "political subdivisions", as well as to accept the new 3rd and 4th sentences proposed by the U.S. side, provided the U.S. side was willing to delete the phrase "however produced".

12. In reply, Mr. Habib stated that the U.S. side continued to favor the retention of the phrase "however produced" and did not understand the objection to it of the Korean side. He said that this article should not differentiate the sources of production of utilities. Furthermore, the U.S. armed forces did not want to be placed in the position of being refused use of a particular type of utility on the basis of the manner in which it was produced. He said that Mr. Whang's previous

0147

arguments that if "however produced" were retained, the phrases "by whomever produced" and "wherever produced" should also be used were already taken care of in the paragraph. "By whomever produced" was covered by the phrase "owned, controlled or regulated by the Government of Korea" and "wherever produced" was covered by the obvious fact that any such utilities would be produced in Korea. He said the U.S. side appreciated and accepted Mr. Whang's assurances that the U.S. armed forces would be furnished with utilities and services. That being the case, the Korean side should have no objection to inclusion of the phrase. He pointed out that the phrase is included in the text of the Utilities and Claims Settlement Agreement, which will remain in force, and was also included in the first Korean draft of the Utilities and Services Article. Therefore, he urged the Korean side to reconsider its position.

13. Mr. Whang replied that the paragraph under discussion applied only to the scope of the utilities and services to be furnished and not to the manner of their production. Pointing out the phrase "but not be limited to", he continued that the phrase "however produced" was not necessary. He said that the ROK Government intended to such utilities and services to the U.S. armed forces, since Far Eastern ethics required the host to treat his guest well. In reply, Mr. Habib pointed out that the phrase "however produced" applied only to electricity, gas, water, steam, heat, light, and power and did not modify all of the items covered by the phrase "shall include, but not be limited to". He said if ethics were to determine the content of the SOFA, there was no need for an Agreement at all, since each party would feel itself bound to deal with the other party in an ethical manner. He said the U.S. side appreciated the willingness of the ROK Government to furnish utilities. The U.S. side believed that the phrase "however produced" added clarity to the paragraph and therefore should cause the Korean side no difficulty. Mr. Whang stated that the Korean side would be prepared to discuss the matter further at the next meeting.

14. Turning to paragraph 3(b) of the U.S. draft, Mr. Whang asked the U.S.

0148

side to specify whom it meant by the phrase "any other user". Mr. Habib replied that the phrase was meant to include any other user, public or private, in Korea of the utilities in question. He pointed out that Agreed Minute #1 of the U.S. draft was related and would require consultation in the Joint Committee prior to any change in priority or rates. He said the U.S. side was trying to avoid the possibility of discriminatory rates being levied against the U.S. armed forces.

15. Mr. Whang replied that the Korean side fully understood the concern of the U.S. side. However, the rates charged the U.S. armed forces are better than those charged to other users. Mr. Habib remarked that all the U.S. side asked was that the rates be no less favorable than those charged to other users. He said that large users like the U.S. armed forces might justifiably be charged more favorable rates on economic grounds. Mr. Whang said that the U.S. armed forces were receiving discrimination of a favorable nature. He said the Korean side agreed to the deletion of "governmental or private" from the first sentence of paragraph 3(b) of the U.S. draft and the deletion of the entire second sentence.

16. Turning to Agreed Minute #1 of the U.S. draft, which is related to paragraph 3(b), Mr. Habib said the U.S. side agreed to the deletion of the phrase "increase in utility or service". Mr. Whang stated that the Korean side desired the deletion of the entire Agreed Minute. Mr. Habib pointed out that all the U.S. side was asking was that the ROK Government consult with the U.S. armed forces in advance of any changes. He said the U.S. draft would not require the ROK Government to seek agreement of the U.S. armed forces for any such changes. He said the requirement for consultation was not unreasonable in view of the magnitude of the operations involved.

17. Mr. Whang replied that the ROK Government would not drastically change the rates because to do so would cause a great strain on the national economy. Therefore, any change in rates the exercise of utmost prudence. Prior consultation under these circumstances would not be convenient. He suggested

0149

the substitution of the phrase "notification within 15 days" for the phrase "prior consultation". He said that in view of the close friendly relations existing between the ROK Government and the U.S. Government, this matter would normally be discussed in advance with the armed forces. He asked the U.S. side to consider his proposal. Mr. Habib agreed to take the proposal under consideration.

18. Referring to the third sentence of paragraph 3(b) of the U.S. draft, Mr. Whang asked how the existence of emergency operating needs would be determined. He asked whether the reopening of hostilities would be a criterion. Mr. Habib replied that a state of hostilities would be a primary determinant but that the occurrence of natural disasters should also be considered as a source of emergency operating needs. It was then agreed to defer further discussion of this sentence until the tabling of a separate article dealing with emergency situations.

19. Turning to paragraph 4 of the U.S. draft, Mr. Habib reminded the negotiators that at the previous meeting, the U.S. side had promised to give a short explanation of current accounting procedures in use by the U.S. armed forces. He then asked Captain Brownlie to present such an explanation.

20. Captain Brownlie stated that the purpose of paragraph 4 of the U.S. draft is to provide for the establishment of systematic methods of keeping accounts financial transactions arising out of the Status of Forces Agreement, for the mutual benefit of both the ROK Government and the U.S. Government. He pointed out that such a paragraph is normally included in Status of Forces agreements. For example, the wording of paragraph 4 is identical with that of paragraph 3, Article XXIV of the U.S.-Japan SOFA. In general, he continued, the U.S. side is not concerned with the details of how ROK Government agencies or private contractors keep their books. However, it is in the interest of both governments to insure systematic accounting in the financial transactions between the U.S. armed forces and the Korean contractors and/or ROK Government agencies. The present procedures used by the U.S. armed forces in executing contracts and in providing for accounting, proper billings,

0150

and appropriate payments, Captain Brownlie continued, were outlined in a paper, copies of which he then distributed to the Korean side.

21. The paper handed to the Korean side reads as follows:

"Method of Accounting Currently Used by USFK

"1. The appropriate Technical Service has specifications prepared for the type of services or purchases desired and processes these specifications along with fund citations to the U.S. Army Korea Procurement Agency.

"2. The U.S. Army Korea Procurement Agency analyzes the specifications, determines the type of action required, and then either advertises for bids from private Korean contractors or arranges for contract negotiations with Korean government agencies, as in the case of nationalized utility systems. Bids or negotiations are usually on the basis of unit price for the utility or service furnished. Contracts normally specify what is to be shown on billings so that a proper basis of making payments can be established.

"3. Upon completion of successful bidding or negotiations the U.S. Army Korea Procurement Agency awards the contract for the specified services or purchases. Normally service contracts run for one year and indicate that the contractor or Korean government agency will present a bill for the services every 30 days or at least once each quarter. A Contracting Officer Representative from the Technical Service concerned accomplishes inspection duties for the U.S. armed forces and insures that the services rendered are of the quality and amount required by specifications. The appropriate Technical Service certifies to the correctness of the billing received and forwards the certified billing to the U.S. Army Korea Procurement Agency.

"4. The Army Procurement Agency process the billing and prepares appropriate payment documents and processes these to the U.S. Army Finance and Accounting Office.

"5. U.S. Army Finance and Accounting Office makes payment by check to the contractor or Korean agency involved."

22. Mr. Whang thanked Captain Brownlie but stated that paragraph 2(a) of the Korean draft was more comprehensive, since it provided for specific arrangements to be made by the appropriate authorities of the two governments. He pointed out that these arrangements were to include not only payment but also means of requesting the use of additional utilities and services by the U.S. armed forces.

23. Mr. Habib remarked that the intent of the language of the Korean draft appeared to relate to the supply" of utilities and services, rather

0151

their "use", inasmuch as the U.S. armed forces, after receiving the supply of utilities and services, would determine their use. He said that the problem which the Korean side was raising was outside the scope of this article. In effect, the two drafts dealt with two different subjects, since the U.S. draft was intended to establish a (mutually acceptable) system of accounting for financial transactions arising out of the Agreement. It was decided to devote further study to this question and to defer further discussion of this paragraph.

24. The negotiators then turned their attention to Agreed Minute #2 of the U.S. draft. Mr. Whang remarked that this Agreed Minute was similar in intent to paragraph 2(b) of the Korean draft. Mr. Habib demurred, saying that the intent of the Agreed Minute was to specifically establish that the right of the U.S. armed forces to use utilities and services shall not be construed as abrogating the Utilities and Claims Settlement Agreement of December 18, 1958. Pointing out that the 1958 agreement is not duplicated by the SOFA and that the SOFA would not abrogate any of the provisions of the earlier agreement, Mr. Habib stated that unless this was specifically stated in the SOFA, there was a possibility that arguments might arise in the future. He suggested that both sides review the question and defer further discussion until a later meeting. Mr. Whang agreed.

Taxation

25. Each side tabled a draft article on taxation and it was agreed that these should be discussed at the next meeting.

Procedural Question - Tabling of Additional Articles

26. Mr. Habib stated that he would like to discuss a subject which had arisen in informal conversation outside the negotiating room. He said the U.S. side wished to have clearly and firmly established the principle that either side could table for discussion any subject or article which it believed pertinent to the negotiations. This would include articles or subjects not included in the list of subjects

0152

discussed at the second and third negotiating meetings. Mr. Habib emphasized that that list had never been intended to be all-inclusive. He said that either side should feel free to table any pertinent document after appropriate notification to the other side. He stated that the U.S. side was under instructions to table an article on health and sanitation. If the Korean side was in agreement with the general principle he had just mentioned, the U.S. side would table and explain the draft article at the next meeting. Mr. Whang replied that the Korean side had no objection to the principle referred to by Mr. Habib, ~~had no objection,~~ in principle, to the tabling of the article in question by the U.S. side at the next meeting.

27. It was then decided to hold the next meeting on June 26 at 2 p.m.

보통문서로 재분류(1966.12.31.)

0153

JOINT SUMMARY RECORD OF THE 24TH SESSION
STATUS OF FORCE NEGOTIATIONS

June 12, 1963

I. Time and Place : 2:00 to 4:20 p.m. June 12, 1963 at the Foreign Minister's Conference Room

II. Attendants:

ROK Side:

Mr. Whang, Ho Eul	Director Bureau of Political Affairs Ministry of Foreign Affairs
Mr. Shin, Kwan Sup	Director Bureau of Customs Duty Ministry of Finance
Mr. Koo, Choong Whay	Chief, America Section Ministry of Foreign Affairs
Mr. Shin, Jung Sup	Chief, Treaty Section Ministry of Foreign Affairs
Col. Nam Koo Lee,	Chief, Military Affairs Section Ministry of National Defense
Mr. Chu, Mun Ki	Chief, Legal Affairs Section, Ministry of Justice
Mr. Lee, Kyung Hoon	2nd Secretary Ministry of Foreign Affairs
Mr. Kang, Suk Jae	2nd Secretary Ministry of Foreign Affairs
Mr. Cho, Kwang Je	2nd Secretary Ministry of Foreign Affairs

U.S. Side:

Mr. Philip C. Habib	Counselor of the Embassy for Political Affairs
Mr. William J. Ford	First Secretary of the Embassy
Col. G.G. O'Connor	Deputy Chief of Staff 8th Army
Col. Howard Smigelow	Deputy Chief of Staff UNC
Capt. R.M. Brownlie	Assistant Chief of Staff USN/K

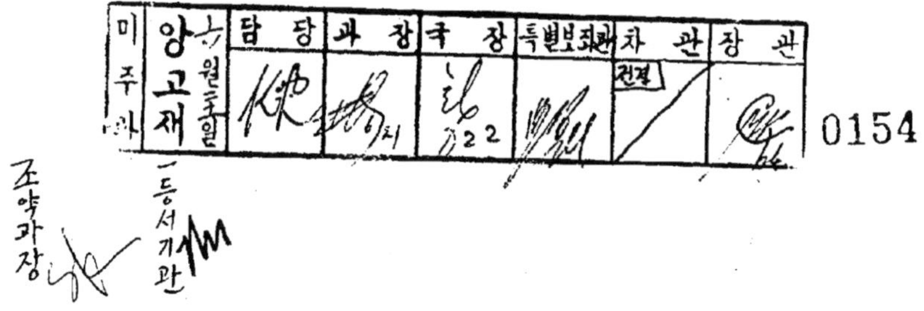

0154

조약과장

一등서기관

Col. L.J. Fuller	Staff Judge Advocate United Nations Command
Mr. Benjamin A. Fleck (Rapporteur and Press Officer)	First Secretary Embassy
Mr. Robert A. Lewis	Second Secretary and Consul of the Embassy
Robert A. Kinney	J-5
Major Robert D. Peckham	Staff Officer, JAG 8th Army

1. Mr. Habib opened the meeting by introducing Colonel Howard Smigelow, Colonel O'Connor's replacement as Deputy Chief of Staff, United Nations Command. Mr. Habib reminded the negotiators that Colonel O'Connor had succeeded Brigadier General Lawlor as Deputy Chief of Staff, Eighth United States Army and would henceforth be the principal military member of the U.S. negotiating team. Mr. Whang congratulated Colonel O'Connor and welcomed Colonel Smigelow to the negotiations.

Respect for Local Law

2. Turning to substantive matters, Mr. Whang stated that at the previous meeting the U.S. side had given assurances that the status of contractors was different than the status of the civilian component, even though contractors were mentioned in the Respect for Local Law article. With that understanding , he said, the Korean side accepted the U.S. draft of the Respect for Local Law article. Mr. Habib replied that Mr. Whang's statement was correct and that any exception would be specifically stated in the relevant article.

0155

Licensing and Registration of Motor Vehicles

3. Mr. Whang began discussion of the Motor Vehicle article by pointing out a few minor differences in the two drafts of paragraph 1. He said the U.S. draft mentioned "Korea" where the Korean draft read "Republic of Korea"; he assumed that this divergence could be adjusted in the final stage of negotiation. He also pointed out that the U.S. draft spoke of "political subdivision thereof" whereas in the article on Utilities and Services the U.S. side had previously proposed changing the term "political subdivisions" to "local administrative subdivisions". He suggested that, for the sake of consistency, "local administrative subdivisions" be made the language in both articles.

4. Mr. Habib replied that the entities referred to in the two articles were different. Whereas in the Utilities and Services article, the "local administrative subdivisions" referred to in the Motor Vehicles article were the individual states in the United States. He reminded the Korean side that because it had said that there were no political subdivisions in the Republic of Korea, the U.S. side had proposed to subsitute the phrase "local administrative subdivisions". "Political subdivision", however, was the only term which would accurately describe the states under the existing federal system in the United States. Furthermore, automobile licenses and registrations were handled by the individual states and not, as in Korea, by the national government.

0156

He said the U.S. side had suggested changing the language in the Utilities and Services article to suit the internal situation described by the ROK side; therefore, he requested the ROK side to accept the terminology used by the U.S. side to describe the internal situation in the United States. Mr. Whang thanked Mr. Habib for the explanation and said that the Korean side accepted the phrase "political subdivision thereof".

5. Mr. Whang noted that the only difference between the U.S. draft of paragraph 2 and paragraph 2(a) of the Korean draft was that the U.S. draft used the plural whereas the ROK draft used the singular. He said the ROK side accepted the U.S. draft. Mr. Habib remarked that the U.S. side believed the plural usage to be more accurate and more appropriate.

6. Mr. Whang noted that there were substantial differences between the U.S. draft paragraph 3 and its counterpart, paragraph 2(b) of the Korean draft, particularly with regard to privately-owned vehicles. He noted that the U.S. draft called for licensing by the U.S. armed forces, whereas the Korean draft would provide for licensing and registration under the same conditions as those applicable to nationals of the Republic of Korea. Mr. Whang pointed out that a separate provision for the importation of privately owned vehicles free of customs duty was included in the Customs Article. He reminded the negotiators that there are ROK regulations setting forth certain requirements for the registration of vehicles.

In order to permit the ROK Government to keep accurate account of the inflow of vehicles, registration should be the responsibility of the ROK Government under the existing regulations. Mr. Whang added that the ROK side did not wish to cause the U.S. armed forces any inconvenience. He stated that applications for registration would be handled as speedily as possible. He stated further that the members of the U.S. armed forces, civilian component, and their dependents would not be asked to pay to taxes which Korean nationals are required to pay in connection with licensing and registration. On the contrary, they would be asked to pay only the actual costs of issuing licenses.

7. Mr. Habib replied that the U.S. negotiators were not trying to cause the ROK Government any difficulty but were endeavoring to establish an administrative system that would be simple and easy to operate. He said that certain portions of the existing Korean regulations regarding licensing and registration, particularly those requiring the payment of taxes, were inappropriate for application to members of the U.S. armed forces. Although Mr. Whang had stated that the ROKG had no intention to tax members of the armed forces, the civilian component, or their dependents, nevertheless one of the existing requirements under the Korean regulations is the submission of a certificate to the appropriate authority stating that all taxes have been paid. This, of course, would be a useless exercise if, in fact, the taxes were not collected. Moreover, Mr. Habib continued, applicants for licenses and registration

0158

are required to purchase a minimum number of national savings bonds. This also is an inappropriate requirement, insofar as the U.S. armed forces are concerned.

8. Mr. Habib stated that under the provisions of the Automobile Tax Law (Law No. 511), the current annual cost of a license for a U.S. made passenger automobile for non-business use is 100,000 Won (or about $769 at the current official exchange rate). In addition, he continued, for the purpose of limiting the number of automobiles as well as providing for tax revenue, a surtax of 60% is imposed in the Seoul area, which would make the total annual cost of a license approximately $1230.00 for a standard size privately owned automobile. Mr. Habib stated that the U.S. draft reflects the Status of Forces Agreements with the NATO countries, particularly paragraph 3, Article IX of the Agreement of August 3, 1959 to supplement the Agreement between the Parties to the North Atlantic Treaty regarding the Status of their Forces with respect to Foreign Forces stationed in the Federal Republic of Germany. Through experience throughout the world, he said, the U.S. Government has reached the conclusion that the problem under disucssion is best handled by allowing the U.S. armed forces to do the actual licensing, with adequate safety measures and technical supervision of the vehicles, with the names and addresses of the owners furnished to the host government. He said this system has worked very well in other parts of the world. He asked if the Korean side had any further suggestions to put forward as ways of expediting

the issuance of licenses, meeting the problems faced by both sides, and avoiding the inappropriate aspects of the existing ROKG regulations.

9. Mr. Whang replied that the U.S. side appeared to have given very careful study to the problems under consideration. He assured the U.S. side that taxes, certificates, purchase of national savings bonds, and similar requirements levied on Korean nationals would not be applied to the U.S. armed forces, members of the civilian component, or their dependents. In response to Mr. Habib's statement that such exemption was not spelled out in the Korean draft, Mr. Whang said that the Korean side had no intention to impose upon the U.S. armed forces any taxes in connection with licensing and registration of motor vehicles with the same spirit as envisaged in the Taxation and customs certicles. He said the total cost to each applicant would come only to about $1.10 or $1.20 for the license plates. He said it would be sufficient if the Joint Committee informed the ROK Government of the type of car, make, year, engine number and name and address of the owner. He said the ROK Government would make the procedure simple as possible. In replay to a further query by Mr. Habib, Mr. Whang said that a system similar to that now in force with regard to automobiles imported by diplomatic personnel would be satisfactory.

10. Mr. Habib said that Mr. Whang's explanation had made the position of the Korean side much clearer. He asked whether the Korean side envisaged any limitation

0160

on the number of licenses to be issued. Mr. Whang replied that if a five-member family applied for registration of five vehicles, the request would not be considered reasonable. The Korean side was thinking in terms of the average needs of the average family in the U.S.. He said the ROK Government was concerned with the traffic problem which would result from an increasing number of automobiles. He inquired about the number of privately owned automobiles currently in use by the U.S. armed forces. Mr. Habib replied that at present there were about 400 automobiles which were owned by members of the Military Advisory Group, and that about 50 additional cars are authorized for other personnel on two year tours in the ROK.

Utilities and Services

11. Turning to the drafts relating to utilities and services, Mr. Whang summarized the changes proposed by each side at the 20th meeting regarding paragraph 3(a) of the U.S. draft and paragraph 1 of the Korean draft. He said the Korean side was prepared to accept the U.S. proposals to delete "whether publicly or privately owned", to insert "owned" following the words "which are", to substitute the phrase "local administrative subdivisions" for "political subdivisions", as well as to accept the new 3rd and 4th sentences proposed by the U.S. side, provided the U.S. side was willing to delete the phrase "however produced".

12. In reply, Mr. Habib stated that the U.S. side continued to favor the retention of the phrase "however

produced" and did not understand the objection to it of the Korean side. He said that this article should not differentiate the sources of production of utilities. Furthermore, the U.S. armed forces did not want to be placed in the position of being refused use of a particular type of utility on the basis of the manner in which it was produced. He said that Mr. Whang's previous arguments that if "however produced" were retained, the phrases "by whomever produced" and "wherever produced" should also be used were already taken care of in the paragraph. "By whomever produced" was covered by the phrase "owned, controlled or regulated by the Governmrnt of Korea" and "wherever produced" was covered by the obvious fact that any such utilities would be produced in Korea. He said the U.S. side appreciated and accepted Mr. Whang's assurances that the U.S. armed forces would be furnished with utilities and services. That being the case, the Korean side should have no objection to inclusion of the phrase. He pointed out that the phrase is included in the text of the Utilities and Claims Settlement Agreement, which will remain in force, and was also included in the first Korean draft of the Utilities and Services Article. Therefore, he urged the Korean side to reconsider its position.

13. Mr. Whang replied that the paragraph under discussion applied only to the scope of the utilities and services to be furnished and not to the manner of their production. Pointing out the phrase "but not be limited to", he continued that the phrase "however produced" was not necessary. He said that the ROK Government intended

0162

to provide such utilities and services to the U.S. armed forces, since Far Eastern ethics required the host to treat his guest well. In reply, Mr. Habib pointed out that the phrase "however produced" applied only to electricity, gas, water, steam, heat, light, and power and did not modify all of the items covered by the phrase "shall include, but not be limited to". He said if ethics were to determine the content of the SOFA, there was no need for an Agreement at all, since each party would feel itself bound to deal with the other party in an ethical manner. He said the U.S. side appreciated the willingness of the ROK Government to furnish utilities. The U.S. side believed that the phrase "however produced" added clarity to the paragraph and therefore should cause the Korean side no difficulty. Mr. Whang stated that the Korean side would be prepared to discuss the matter further at the next meeting.

14. Turning to paragraph 3(b) of the U.S. draft, Mr. Whang asked the U.S. side to specify whom it meant by the phrase "any other user". Mr. Habib replied that the phrase was meant to include any other user, public or private, in Korea of the utilities in question. He pointed out that Agreed Minute #1 of the U.S. draft was related and would require consultation in the Joint Committee prior to any change in priority or rates. He said the U.S. side was trying to avoid the possibility of discriminatory rates being levied against the U.S. armed forces.

15. Mr. Whang replied that the Korean side fully understood the concern of the U.S. side. However, the

rates charged the U.S. armed forces are better than those charged to other users. Mr. Habib remarked that all the U.S. side asked was that the rates be no less favorable than those charged to other users. He said that large users like the U.S. armed forces might justifiably be charged more favorable rates on economic grounds. Mr. Whang said that the U.S. armed forces were receiving discrimination of a favorable nature. He said the Korean side agreed to the deletion of "governmental or private" from the first sentence of paragraph 3(b) of the U.S. draft and the deletion of the entire second sentence.

16. Turning to Agreed Minute #1 of the U.S. draft, which is related to paragraph 3(b), Mr. Habib said the U.S. side agreed to the deletion of the phrase "increase in utility or service". Mr. Whang stated that the Korean side desired the deletion of the entire Agreed Minute. Mr. Habib pointed out that all the U.S. side was asking was that the ROK Government consult with the U.S. armed forces in advance of any changes. He said the U.S. draft would not require the ROK Government to seek agreement of the U.S. armed forces for any such changes. He said the requirement for consultation was not unreasonable in view of the magnitude of the operations involved.

17. Mr. Whang replied that the ROK Government would not drastically change the rates because to do so would cause a great strain on the national economy. Therefore, any change in rates would require the exercise of utmost prudence. Prior consultation under these circumstances would not be convenient. He suggested insertion of the

0164

phrase "shall, at the Joint Committee, be notified within 15 days after the effective date of such a change" in substitution for the phrase "shall be the subject of prior consultation in the Joint Committee". He said that in view of the close friendly relations existing between the ROK Government and the U.S. Government, this matter would normally be discussed in advance with the armed forces. He asked the U.S. side to consider his proposal. Mr. Habib agreed to take the proposal under consideration.

18. Referring to the third sentence of paragraph 3(b) of the U.S. draft, Mr. Whang asked how the existence of emergency operating needs would be determined. He asked whether the reopening of hostilities would be a criterion. Mr. Habib replied that a state of hostilities would be a primary determinant but that the occurance of natural disasters should also be considered as a source of evergency operating needs. It was then agreed to defer further discussion of this sentence until the tabling of a separate article dealing with hostility situations.

19. Turning to paragraph 4 of the U.S. draft, Mr. Habib reminded the negotiators that at the previous meeting, the U.S. side had promised to give a short explanation of current accounting procedures in use by the U.S. armed forces. He then asked Captain Brownlie to present such an explanation.

20. Captain Brownlie stated that the purpose of paragraph 4 of the U.S. draft is to provide for the establishment of systematic methods of keeping accounts

0165

of financial transactions arising out of the Status of Forces Agreement, for the mutual benefit of both the ROK Government and the U.S. Government. He pointed out that such a paragraph is normally included in Status of Forces agreements. For example, the wording of paragraph 4 is identical with that of paragraph 3, Article XXIV of the U.S.-Japan SOFA. In general, he continued, the U.S. side is not concerned with the details of how ROK Government agencies or private contractors keep their books. However, it is in the interest of both governments to insure systematic accounting in the financial transactions between the U.S. armed forces and the Korean contractors and/or ROK Government agencies. the present procedures used by the U.S. armed forces in executing contracts and in providing for accounting, proper billings, and appropriate payments, Captain Brownlie continued, were outlined in a paper, copies of which he then distributed to the Korean side.

21. The paper handed to the Korean side reads as follows:

"<u>Method of Accounting Currently Used by USFK</u>

"1. The appropriate Technical Service has specifications prepared for the type of services or purchases desired and processes these specifications along with fund citations to the U.S. Army Korea Procurement Agency.

"2. The U.S. Army Korea Procurement Agency analyses the specifications, determines the type of action required, and then either advertises for bids from private Korean contractors or arranges for contract negotiations with Korean government agencies, as in the case of nationalized utility systems. Bids or negotiations are usually on the basis of unit price for the utility or service furnished. Contracts normally specify what is to be shown on billings so that a proper basis of

0166

making payments can be established.

"3. Upon completion of successful bidding or negotiations the U.S. Army Korea Procurement Agency awards the contract for the specified services or purchases. Normally service contracts run for one year and indicate that the contractor or Korean government agency will present a bill for the services every 30 days or at least once each quarter. A Contracting Officer Representative from the Technicial Service concerned accomplishes inspection duties for the U.S. armed forces and insures that the services rendered are of the quality and amount required by specifications. The appropriate Technical Service certifies to the correctness of the billing received and forwards the certified billing to the U.S. Army Korea Procurement Agency.

4. "4. The Army Procurement Agency process the billing and prepares appropriate payment documents and processes these to the U.S. Army Finance and Accounting Office.

"5. U.S. Army Finance and Accounting Office makes payment by check to the contractor or Korean agency involved."

22. Mr. Whang thanked Captain Brownlie but stated that paragraph 2(a) of the Korean draft was more comprehensive, since it provided for specific arrangements to be made by the appropriate authorities of the two governments. He pointed out that these arrangements were to include not only payment but also means of requesting the use of additional utilities and services by the U.S. armed forces.

23. Mr. Habib remarked that the intent of the language of the Korean draft appeared to relate to the "supply" of utilities and services, rather their "use", inasmuch as the U.S. armed forces after receiving the supply of utilities and services, would determine their use. He said that the problem which the Korean side was raising was outside the scope of this article. In effect, the two drafts dealt with two different subjects, since

the U.S. draft was intended to establish a mutually acceptable system of accounting for financial transactions arising out of the Agreement. It was decided to devote further study to this question and to defer further discussion of this paragraph.

24. The negotiators then turned their attention to Agreed Minute #2 of the U.S. draft. Mr. Whang remarked that this Agreed Minute was similar in intent to paragraph 2(b) of the Korean draft. Mr. Habib demurred, saying that the intent of the Agreed Minute was to specifically establish that the right of the U.S. armed forces to use utilities and services shall not be construed as abrogating the Utilities and Claims Settlement Agreement of December 18, 1958. Pointing out that the 1958 agreement is not duplicated by the SOFA and that the SOFA would not abrogate any of the provisions of the earlier agreement, Mr. Habib stated that unless this was specifically stated in the SOFA, there was a possibility that arguments might arise in the future. He suggested that both sides review the question and defer further discussion until a later meeting. Mr. Whang agreed.

Taxation

25. Each side tabled a draft article on taxation and it was agreed that these should be discussed at the next meeting.

Procedural Question - Tabling of Additional Articles

26. Mr. Habib stated that he would like to discuss a subject which had arisen in informal conversation

0168

outside the negotiating room. He said the U.S. side wished to have clearly and firmly established the principle that either side could table for discussion any subject or article which it believed pertinent to the negotiations. This would include articles or subjects not included in the list of subjects discussed at the second and third negotiating meetings. Mr. Habib emphasized that list had never been intended to be all-inclusive. He said that either side should feel free to table any pertinent document after appropriate notification to the other side. He stated that the U.S. side was under instructions to table an article on health and sanitation. If the Korean side was in agreement with the general principle he had just mentioned, the U.S. side would table and explain the draft article at the next meeting. Mr. Whang replied that the Korean side in principle had no objection to the principle referred to by Mr. Habib, nor to the tabling of the article in question by the U.S. side at the next meeting.

27. It was then decided to hold the next meeting on June 26 at 2 p.m.

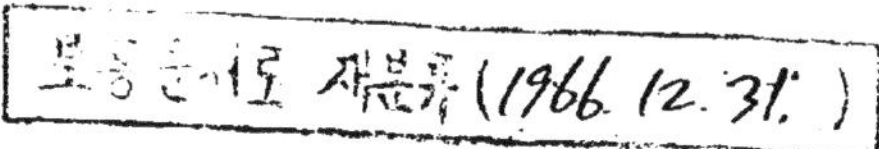

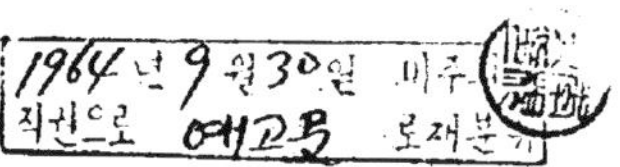

1966 12. 31.에 예고문에

0169

5. 제25차 회의, 6.26

0170

기 안 용 지

자체 통제		기안처	미주과 이경훈	전화번호	근거서류접수일자
	과장	국장	보좌관	차관	장관
	25	28		28	
관계관 서명	조약과장		一등서기관		
기안 년월일	63.6.25.	시행 년월일		보존 년한	정서기장
분류 기호	외정미	전체 통제		종결	
경유 수신 참조	건 의		발신		
제목	제25차 주둔군지위협정 체결 교섭회의에 임할 우리측 입장				

6.26.에 개최될 제25차 주둔군지위협정 체결 한미간 교섭회의에서는 관세문제, 현지조달 및 미국군대 및 재산에대한 안전보장 문제에 관하여 토의될 예정이온바 이에 관련하여 우리측 교섭 실무자는 6.24. 관계부처 실무자와 연석회합을 갖고 제25차 회의에서 취할 우리측 태도를 별첨과같이 결정하였아오니 재가하여 주시기 바랍니다.

유첨 : 제24차 주둔군지위협정 체결교섭회의에 임할 우리측 태도. 끝

1966.12.31.에 예고문에 의거 일반문서로 재분류됨

1966.12.31

1966년 9월 30일 직권으로 예고문

승인양식 1-1-3 (1112-040-016-018) (190mm×260mm16절지)

0171

1. 조세문제

(1) 미국군대의 면세 허여 원칙에관한 미국측 초안 1항 (이는 우리측 초안 1항에 해당함) 은 우리측 안과 같으므로 미국측 안을 수락한다.

(2) 미국군대 구성원, 군속 및 그들의 가족의 소득세 면제 원칙에 관한 미국측초안 제2항 (이는 우리측 초안 제2항에 해당함)에 있어서 (가) 동항 첫째 문장은 비세출 기관에관한 용어를 "activities" 로 하고있는데 대하여 우리측은 "organization" 로 하고 있는점을 제외하고는 서로 같으므로 이문제가 최종적으로 결정되는 것을 보류 하는 조건으로 동항을 수락하기로 하고 (나) 동항 둘째문장의 전단은 우리측 초안에는 없으나 본규정과 동항 둘째 문장의 후단의 period와의 관계에 대하여 이중 과세를위한 것인지를 미국측에 문의하기로 하고 (다) 제2항 셋째문장은 우리측 초안 제2항 둘째문장에 해당하는바 우리측 초안과 실질적 차이가 없으므로 이를 수락하기로 한다.
(라) 따라서 미국측 초안 제2항에 대하여 이상과 같은 우리측 입장을 참작하여 다음과 같은 수정안을 제시토록 한다.
"Members of the United States armed forces, the civilian component, and their dependents shall not be liable to pay Korean taxes to the Government of the Republic of Korea or to any other taxing agency in the Republic of Korea on income received as a result of their service with or employment by the United States armed forces, or by the organizations provided for in Article____. The provisions of this Article do not exempt such persons from payment of Korean taxes on income

0172

derived from Korean sources, nor do they exempt United States citizens who claim Korean residence for United States income tax purposes from payment of Korean taxes on income. Periods during which such persons are in the Republic of Korea solely by reason of being members of the United States armed forces, civilian component, or their dependents shall not be considered as periods of residence or domicile in the Republic of Korea for the purpose of Korean taxation."를 조약원문에 삽입하고, "members of the United States armed forces, the civilian component, or their dependents shall not be liable to pay any Korean taxes to the Government of the Republic of Korea or to any taxing agency in the Republic of Korea on income derived from sources outside of Korea" 를 합의 의사록에 삽입토록 한다.

(3) 동산의 소유, 사용 및 대내이전 등에 대한 면세 허여규정인 미국측 초안 3항 (이는 우리측 초안 3항에 해당함)은 우리측 안과 차의가 없으므로 미국측안을 수락토록 한다.

2. <u>현지 조달</u>

(1) 현지 조달허여 원칙, 이에대한 예외 규정, 미국군대의 조달에 따르는 면세규정, 미국군대 구성원, 군속 및 그들의 가족의 개인용 구입에 대한 과세등을 내용으로 하는 별첨과 같은 우리측 초안을 제시한다.

(2) 미국측이 제시하는 안이 우리측안과 비등할때에는 우리측안의 수락을 주장한다.

0173

3. 미국군대 및 재산에 대한 안전

(1) 미국군대, 미국군대 구성원, 군속 및 그들의 가족에 대한 안전 보장책을 내용으로 하는 법조과 같은 우리측안을 제시한다.

(2) 미국측이 제시하는 안이 우리측안과 비등할때에는 우리측안의 수락을 주장한다.

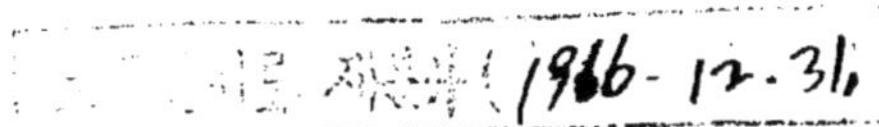

0174

ARTICLE _____

1. The United States may contract for any supplies or construction work to be furnished or undertaken in the Republic of Korea for purposes of, or authorized by, this Agreement, without restriction as to choice of supplier or person who does the construction work. Such supplies or construction work may, upon agreement between the appropriate authorities of the two Governments, also be procured through the Government of the Republic of Korea.

2. Materials, supplies, equipment and services which are required from local sources for the maintenance of the United States armed forces and the proucrement of which may have an adverse effect on the economy of the Republic of Korea shall be procured in coordination with, and, when desirable, through or with the assistance of, the competent authorities of the Republic of Korea.

3. Materials, supplies, equipment and services procured for official purposes in the Republic of Korea by the United States armed forces, or by authorized procurement agencies of the United States armed forces upon appropriate certification shall be exempt from the following Korean taxes:

(a) Commodity tax

~~(b) Travelling tax~~

(b) Gasoline tax

(c) Electricity and gas tax.

0175

Materials, supplies, equipment and services procured for ultimate use by the United States armed forces shall be exempt from commodity and gasoline taxes upon appropriate certification by the United States armed forces. With respect to any present or furture Korean taxes not specifically referred to in this Article which might be found to constitute a significant and readily identifiable part of the gross purchase price of materials, supplies, equipment and services procured by the United States armed forces, or for ultimate use by such forces, the two Governments will agree upon a procedure for granting such exemption or relief therefrom as is consistent with the purposes of this Article.

4. Neither members of the United States armed forces, civilian component, nor their depednents, shall by reason of this Article enjoy any exemmption from taxes or similar charges relating to personal purchases of goods and services in the Republic of Korea chargeable under Korean legislation.

5. Except as such disposal may be authorized by the Korean and United States authorities in accordance with mutually agreed conditions, goods purchased in the Republic of Korea exempt from the taxes referred to in paragraph 3, shall not be disposed of in the Republic of Korea to persons not entitled to purchase such goods exempt from such tax.

0176

ARTICLE ____

The Republic of Korea and the United States will cooperate in taking such steps as may from time to time be necessary to ensure the security of the United States armed forces, the members thereof, the civilian component, their dependents, and their property. The Government of the Republic of Korea agrees to seek such legislation and to take such other action as may be necessary to ensure the adequate security and protection within its territory of installations, equipment, property, records and official information of the United States, and for the punishment of offenders under the applicable laws of the Republic of Korea.

1966.12.31.에 예고문에 의거 일반문서로 재분류됨

0177

SOFA NEGOTIATION

Agenda for 25th Session

14:00 June 26, 1963

1. Continuation of Discussion on:

   Taxation Article

2. Discussion on:

   a. Health and Senitation Article

   b. Local Procurement Article

   c. Safety and Security Measures for U.S. Armed Forces, Its Members, Dependents, Property Article

3. Other Business

4. Agenda and Date of Next Meeting

5. Press Release

0178

기 안 용 지

자 체 통 제	(서명)	기안처	미주과 이경훈	전화번호	근거서류접수일자

	과장	국장	보좌관	차관	장관
	(서명) 27	(서명) 27	(서명)	전결	(서명) 28

관계관 서명	조약과장 (서명) 1등서기관 (서명)

기안 년월일	63. 6.27.	시행 년월일		보존 년한		정서	기장
분류 기호	의정미 722.2—	전체 통제		종결			

경유 수신 참조	국가재건최고회의 의장 (참조 : 외무국방위원장) 내각수반	발신	장관
제목	주둔군지위협정체결을 위한 제25차 교섭회의 보고		

1963. 6. 26. 하오 2시부터 동 3시 10분까지 외무부장관 회의실에서 개최된 제25차 주둔군지위협정 체결 교섭회의에서 토의된 내용을 별첨과 같이 보고합니다.

유첨 : 제24차 교섭회의 보고서 부, 끝

보통문서로 재분류(1966. 12. 31.)

1964년 9월 30일 직권으로 예고문 재분류

1966. 12. 31. 예고문에 의거 일반문서로 재분류됨

승인양식 1-1-3 (1112-040-016-018) (190mm×260mm16절지)

0179

외 무 부

외정미 722.2 1963. 6. 29.

수 신 국가재건최고회의 의장

참 조 외무국방위원장

제 목 주둔군지위협정 체결을 위한 제25차 교섭회의 보고

1963. 6. 26. 하오 2시부터 동 3시 10분까지 외무부 장관 회의실에서 개최된 제25차 주둔군지위협정 체결 교섭회의에서 토의된 내용을 별첨과 같이 보고합니다.

유첨 : 제 25차 교섭회의 보고서 3부. 끝

외 무 부 장 관 김 용 식

0180

외 무 부

외정미 722.2 1963. 6. 29.

수 신 대통령(참조 : 비서실장) 국가재건최고회의의장 (참조 : 외무국방위원장) 내각수반

제 목 주둔군지위협정 체결을 위한 제25차 교섭회의 보고

1963. 6. 26. 하오 2시부터 동 3시 10분 까지 외무부 장관 회의실에서 개최된 제25차 주둔군지위협정 체결 교섭회의에서 토의된 내용을 별첨과 같이 보고합니다.

유첨 : 제 25 차 교섭회의 보고서 1부, 끝

외 무 부 장 관 김 용 식

0181

제 25 차

한미간 주둔군지위협정 체결 실무자회의

보 고 서

1. 일 시 : 1963. 6.26. 하오 2시부터 3시 10분까지

2. 장 소 : 외무부장관 회의실

3. 참석자 : 한국측 : 황 호 을 (외무부 정무국장)

신 관 섭 (재무부 세관국장)

구 충 회 (외무부 미주과장)

신 정 섭 (외무부 조약과장)

이 남 구 (국방부 군무과장)

주 문 기 (법무부 법무과장)

이 경 훈 (외무부 2등서기관)

강 석 재 (")

김 윤 택 (외무부 3등서기관)

미국측 : 교섭대표단 전원 ("하비브", "포드" 및 "루이스" 대표 불참)

4. 토의사항 :

(1) 조세문제를 토의한후 미국측은 보건 및 위생조치에 관한 조문 초안을 제시하였고 또한 현지조달 및 미국군인, 가족 및 재산의 안전조치에 관한 양측 조문초안이 교환되었음.

(2) 조세문제의 토의에 있어서 미국군대가 한국에서 보유하고, 사용하고 또는 이전하는 재산에 대하여는 조세의 면제를 허여한다는 규정에 있어서는 양측안이 거의 같으므로 미국측안을 수락하여 주었음. 63-1-105

0182

0183

(3) 미국군대 구성원, 군속 및 그들의 가족이 미국군대에 근무하거나 또는 미국군대 및 비세출 기관에 고용된 결과 취득하는 소득에 관하여는 한국의 조세로부터 면제를 받는다는 규정에 있어서는 우리측이 "비세출기관" 이라는 용어의 사용을 주장한데 대하여 미국측은 "비세출 활동"이라는 용어의 사용을 주장한것을 제외하고는 양측안이 같으므로 동 문제의 용어가 최종적으로 양측간에 합의되는 것을 조건으로 본 규정에관한 미국측안을 수락하여 주었음.

(4) 한국의 내외로부터 발생되는 소득에 관한 조세의 납부규정에 있어서 우리측은 미국군대 구성원, 군속 및 그들의 가족은 한국의 원천으로부터 발생되는 소득에 대하여는 한국에 대하여 조세를 납부토록 하자고 주장한데 대하여 미국측은 이러한 한국측 주장의 규정이외에 첨가하여 한국이외의 원천으로부터 발생되는 소득에 대하여는 한국 조세의 납부로부터 면제된다는 규정까지도 삽입하자고 주장하여 우리측은 다시 이러한 추가적 규정은 예외적 사항이므로 이를 조약원문에 규정하는 대신 합의의사록에 규정함이 좋을것이라고 제시하자 미국측은 이를 고려해보겠다고 하였음.

(5) 미국군대 구성원, 군속 및 그들의 가족이 미국군대 구성원, 군속 및 그들의 가족이라는 이유만으로서 한국에 있는 기간은 한국의 조세부과 목적을 위하여 한국에 거소 또는 주소를 가지는 기간으로 인정하지 않는다 라는 규정에 있어서는 미국측은 동 규정을 한국외의 원천으로부터 발생되는 소득에 대한 한국 조세 지불면제 규정에 하나의 구절로서 첨부하자고 주장한데 대하여 우리측은 동구절을 완전히 독립된 하나의 문장으로 조약원문에 삽입하자고 주장하자 미국측은 이를 고려해보겠다고 하였음.

63-1-106

0184

63-1-17

미문 89-1

0185

(6) 미국군대 구성원, 군속 및 그들의 가족의 동산의 보유, 사용, 그들간의 이전 또는 사망에 의한 이전에 관한 조세 면제 규정에 있어서 이에관한 미국측안이 우리측안 보다 더 상세하고 포괄적이었으므로 우리측은 미국측안을 수락하여 주었음.

(7) 보건 및 위생조치 문제에 관한 미국측 조문초안이 제시되어 이문제는 다음에 토의키로 함.

(8) 현지조달 및 안전조치에 관한 양측 조문초안이 교환되었고 이문제들은 다음에 토의키로 함.

5. 기타사항 :

(1) 차기회의 일자 : 1963. 7. 10. 하오 2시

(2) 차기회의 의제 : 차기회의까지 양측 수석대표간에 합의된 사항

6. 참고자료 :

미국측이 제의한 조문초안 (보건 및 위생조치, 현지조달 그리고 안전조치) 별첨참조

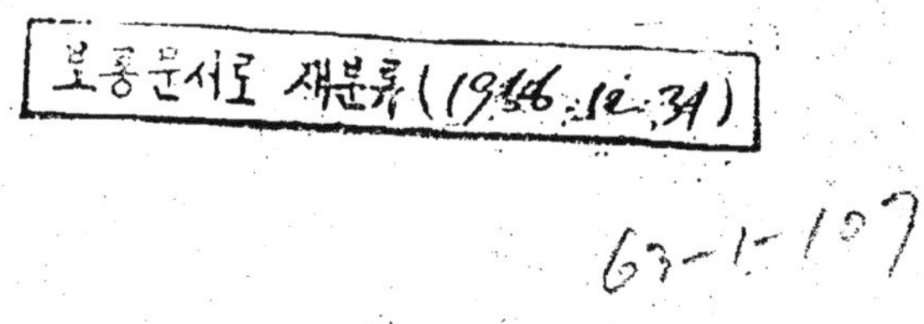

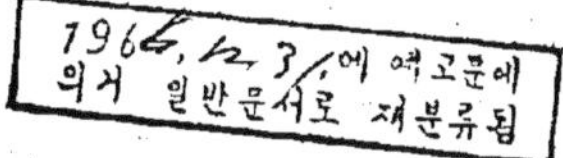

0186

63-1-17

미문 89-1

0187

ARTICLE

Health and Sanitation

Consistent with the right of the United States to furnish medical support for its armed forces, civilian component and their dependents, matters of mutual concern pertaining to the control and prevention of diseases and the coordination of other public health, medical, sanitation, and veterinary services shall be resolved by the authorities of the two Governments in the Joint Committee established under Article______ .

63-1-108

0188

63-1-9

미문 89-1

0189

Article

Local Procurement

1. The United States may contract for any supplies or construction work to be furnished or undertaken in the Republic of Korea for purposes of, or authorized by, this Agreement, without restriction as to choice of supplier or person who does the construction work. Such supplies or construction work may, upon agreement between the appropriate authorities of the two Governments, also be procured through the Government of the Republic of Korea.

2. Materials, supplies, equipment and services which are required from local sources for the maintenance of the United States armed forces and the procurement of which may have an adverse effect on the economy of the Republic of Korea shall be procured in coordination with, and, when desirable, through or with the assistance of, the competent authorities of the Republic of Korea.

3. Materials, supplies, equipment and services procured for official purposes in the Republic of Korea by the United States armed forces, including their authorized procurement agencies, or procured for ultimate use by the United States armed forces shall be exempt from the following Korean taxes upon appropriate certification by the United States armed forces:

(a) Commodity tax;

(b) Traffic tax;

(c) Petroleum tax;

(d) Electricity and gas tax;

(e) Business tax.

63-1-10

0190

63-1-17

미운 89-1

0191

With respect to any present or future Korean taxes not specifically referred to in this Article which might be found to constitute a significant and readily identifiable part of the gross purchase price of materials, supplies, equipment and services procured by the United States armed forces, or for ultimate use by such forces, the two Governments will agree upon a procedure for granting such exemption or relief therefrom as is consistent with the purpose of this Article.

4. Neither members of the United States armed forces, civilian component, nor their dependents, shall by reason of this Article enjoy any exemption from taxes or similar charges relating to personal purchases of goods and services in the Republic of Korea chargeable under Korean legislation.

5. Except as such disposal may be authorized by the United States and Korean authorities in accordance with mutually agreed conditions, goods purchased in the Republic of Korea exempt from taxes referred to in paragraph 3, shall not be disposed of in the Republic of Korea to persons not entitled to purchase such goods exempt from such tax.

AGREED MINUTE

1. The United States armed forces will furnish the Korean authorities with appropriate information as far in advance as practicable on anticipated major changes in their procurement program in the Republic of Korea.

2. The problem of a satisfactory settlement of difficulties with respect to procurement contracts arising out of differences between Korean and United States economic laws and business practices will be studied by the Joint Committee or other appropriate persons. 63-1-110

0192

63-1-15

미문 89-1

0193

3. The procedures for securing exemptions from taxation on purchases of goods for ultimate use by the United States armed forces will be as follows:

(a) Upon appropriate certification by the United States armed forces that materials, supplies and equipment consigned to or destined for such forces, are to be used, or wholly or partially used up, under the supervision of such forces, exclusively in the execution of contracts for the construction, maintenance or operation of the facilities and areas referred to in Article or for the support of the forces therein, or are ultimately to be incorporated into articles or facilities used by such forces, an authorized representative of such forces shall take delivery of such materials, supplies and equipment directly from manufacturers thereof. In such circumstances the collection of taxes referred to in Article , paragraph 3, shall be held in abeyance.

(b) The receipt of such materials, supplies and equipment in the facilities and areas shall be confirmed by an authorized agent of the United States armed forces to the Korean authorities.

(c) Collection of the taxes on such materials, supplies and equipment shall be held in abeyance until

(1) The United States armed forces confirm and certify the quantity or degree of consumption of the above referred to materials, supplies and equipment, or

(2) The United States armed forces confirm and certify the amount of the above referred to materials, supplies, and equipment which have been incorporated into articles or facilities used by the United States armed forces. 63-1-111

0194

63-1-17

미문 89-1

0195

(d) Materials, supplies, and equipment certified under (c) (1) or (2) shall be exempt from taxes referred to in Article , paragraph 3, insofar as the price thereof is paid out of United States Government appropriations or out of funds contributed by the Government of the the Republic of Korea for disbursement by the United States.

63-1-112

0196

63-1-17

미문 89-1

0197

ARTICLE ____

SECURITY MEASURES

"The United States and the Republic of Korea will cooperate in taking such steps as may from time to time be necessary to ensure the security of the United States armed forces, the members thereof, the civilian component, the persons who are present in the Republic of Korea pursuant to Article ______, their dependents and their property. The Government of the Republic of Korea agrees to seek such legislation and to take such other action as may be necessary to ensure the adequate security and protection within its territory of installations, equipment, property, records, and official information of the United States, of the persons referred to in this paragraph, and their property and, consistent with Article ______, to ensure the punishment of offenders under the applicable laws of the Republic of Korea."

63-1-113

보통문서로 재분류(1966.12.31.)

0198

63-1-17(9)

마이문 89-1 (9)

0199

June 26, 1963

1. Mr. Whang opened the meeting by welcoming Colonel O'Connor, who was heading the U.S. side for the first time, and Mr. Rodney Armstrong, an Economic Officer of the Embassy, who was sitting in for Mr. William Ford.

Taxation

2. In taking up the draft articles dealing with taxation, Colonel O'Connor announced that Colonel Fuller would be the U.S. spokesman on this subject and Mr. Whang stated that Mr. Shin Kwan Sop would be the spokesman for the Korean side. In introducing the U.S. draft, Colonel Fuller made the following opening statement:

> "The taxation articles of our various status of forces agreements provide generally that the visiting armed forces are not subject to host-country taxes on property which they hold or use or transfer. They also provide generally that the members and civilian employees and dependents of the visiting forces are not subject to host-country income taxes or property taxes except on such private business income and investment type property they may have in the host country apart from their official presence there.
>
> "The reasons for such exemptions are first that the visiting forces themselves should not be taxed on the property which they must use or hold for mutual defense purposes and second, the members, civilian employees, and dependents, being fully taxed on their income and property by their own country should not be taxed a second time by the host country to which they are invountarily ordered.
>
> "In the United States the income and property of a service member, civilian employee, and dependents are already fully taxed by the federal government, state government, county government, and city government. These taxes continue and must be paid even when the serviceman, employee, or dependent is serving overseas, in Korea or elsewhere. It would not be proper to subject him to additional taxes because of such overseas service."

Colonel Fuller noted that the U.S. and Korean drafts are generally similar and that they both are based on other existing status of forces agreements. He proposed that they be discussed paragraph by paragraph. The Korean side agreed.

3. Colonel Fuller noted that the two drafts of paragraph 1 are identical except for the variation between "Korea" and "the Republic of Korea". He proposed that the paragraph be agreed to, with the adjustment of this difference in language to be made during the final editing of the agreement. Mr. Shin agreed.

4. Turning to paragraph 2, Colonel Fuller pointed out that in the first sentence of the U.S. draft the word "any" appears before the words "Korean taxes". Although it does not appear in the Korean draft, he pointed out that it is included in the taxation articles of other status of forces agreements. He stated that its —esence or absence would not appear to make any substantive difference. He proposed that it be included in the sentence. He pointed to two more instances in the first sentence of the variation between "Korea" and "the Republic of Korea", which he proposed should be handled in the manner already proposed. He also referred to a recurrence in e first sentence of the previously discussed usage of the word "activities" in the U.S. draft and "organizations" in the Korean draft. He proposed that the basic decision in regard to this difference of usage be made in relation to the article on Non-Appropriated Fund Activities/Organizations and that this sentence then be made to conform to that decision. Whichever word is decided upon, he stated that the word "including" in the U.S. draft is more appropriate than the words "or by" in the Korean draft, inasmuch as the nonappropriated fund activities or organizations referred to are official agencies of the United States armed forces.

5. Mr. Shin replied that the first sentence of the U.S. draft was acceptable to the Korean side, with the understanding that the question of "activities" or "organizations" would be settled later.

6. Colonel Fuller pointed out that the second sentence of paragraph 2 of the U.S. draft has two clauses. The first clause, he said, is intended to provide tax exemption on income derived from sources outside Korea. Although this provision does not appear in the Korean draft, Colonel Fuller stated that it should be included here inasmuch as it is not covered elsewhere in the SOFA. The second clause of the second sentence, he continued, is substantially the same as paragraph 4 of the Korean draft. The U.S. side, he said, believes that since it relates to the other provisions of paragraph 2 it should form a part of that paragraph, as it does in other status of forces agreements.

0201

7. Mr. Shin stated that the second sentence of paragraph 2 of the U.S. draft appeared to be similar in construction to the second sentence of paragraph 7 of the U.S. draft of the contractors article. The Korean side wondered, therefore, whether the sentence in the taxation article might not be redundant. If not, was there any particular reason for including it? Colonel Fuller replied that the Korean draft of paragraph 2 and the first and third sentences of the U.S. draft refer only to income derived from sources inside Korea. Therefore, the inclusion of the second sentence was not redundant, since there should be some mention in the article of income from sources outside of Korea.

8. Mr. Shin stated that the ~~first and~~ third sentence of the U.S. draft of paragraph 2 ~~do not~~ does not exempt members of the U.S. armed forces from payment of taxes on income derived from sources within Korea other than those sources refferred to in the first sentence of the Paragraph 2. Therefore, it could be taken for granted that no tax would be imposed on income derived from sources outside Korea. He suggested that it would be more appropriate to place the substance of the second sentence of the U.S. draft in an Agreed Minute.

9. Colonel Fuller pointed out that if this sentence were not included, the SOFA would contain no explicit provisions regarding taxation on income derived from outside sources. The U.S. side, he said, preferred to have an explicit statement in the agreement. Mr. Shin replied that the Korean side interpreted this sentence also to be related to the question of prevention of double taxation, a question which was currently of concern to the authorities of both governments. He suggested that this question be left for settlement outside of the SOFA. To avoid misunderstanding, he reiterated his suggestion that the substance of the second sentence be placed in an Agreed Minute.

10. Colonel Fuller referred to the frequently expressed desire of both sides to hold the number of Agreed Minutes to ~~the~~ a minimum. He also referred to Mr. Shin's previous statement that the ROK Government had no intention to tax income derived from sources outside of Korea. If that is so, he inquired, why was the Korean side so reluctant to spell it out in the SOFA? Mr. Shin replied that the Korean side desired ~~this~~ provision

0202

to be placed in an Agreed Minute because the first and third sentences of the U.S. draft refer to income from sources within Korea. It was then agreed to defer further discussion of this point until after both sides had had the opportunity to give it further study.

11. Mr. Whang reiterated the position of the Korean side that the first clause of the second sentence of the U.S. draft of paragraph 2 should be placed in an agreed minute. He asked whether the second clause of that sentence was relevant to the prevention of double taxation. Colonel Fuller replied that the entire article relates to the prevention of double taxation as well as to escape from all taxation. Mr. Whang stated that the Korean side believed the second clause should appear as a separate sentence, as in paragraph 4 of the ROK draft. It was agreed to give further study to this question.

12. Colonel Fuller then stated that the third sentence of paragraph 2 of the U.S. draft is similar to the last sentence of paragraph 2 of the Korean draft, with three exceptions. First, the U.S. draft, in accordance with the example of other agreements, uses the word "Korean" before the word "sources", whereas the word "Korean" has been omitted from the Korean draft. Inasmuch as the U.S. side presumes that the ROK Government does not intend to tax income derived from non-Korean sources, Colonel Fuller continued, there should be no objection to the inclusion of the word "Korean" before the word "sources". Secondly, he pointed out, the U.S. draft uses the words "other than those sources referred to in the first sentence of this paragraph" while the corresponding words in the Korean draft are "other than those provided for in this paragraph". He said the U.S. side believed the wording of the U.S. draft stated more precisely the substance intended by both sides. Thirdly, Colonel Fuller continued, the U.S. draft ends with the following words not included in the Korean draft: "nor do they exempt United States citizens who claim Korean residence for United States income tax purposes from payment of Korean taxes on income". These words, he said, are designed to prevent a person from escaping from both U.S. and

0203

Korean taxes by providing that if a U.S. citizen covered by this agreement seeks to avoid or reduce his U.S. taxes because he claims residence in Korea, then he loses his exemption from paying Korean taxes. Colonel Fuller pointed out that this wording has precedents in other status of forces agreements and the U.S. side proposed its adoption as beneficial to both governments. Mr. Shin stated that the Korean side appreciated the additional language at the end of the sentence and that the entire final sentence of the U.S. draft of paragraph 2 was acceptable to the Korean side.

13. Turning to paragraph 3 of both drafts, Colonel Fuller stated that they are similar, with three exceptions. First, the U.S. draft includes the words "tangible or intangible" to clarify the intent of the words "movable property". They are not included in the Korean draft, although they are found in other status of forces agreements. Secondly, there was another occurrence of the difference between "Korea" and "the Republic of Korea", which he proposed should be handled in the previsously agreed upon manner. Thirdly, the U.S. draft contains the following words not found in the Korean draft: "or to any intangible property registered in Korea". He said these words had been included in the U.S. draft to make it clear that the ROK Government may tax intangible property if it is registered in Korea. These words also are found in other status of forces agreements, he pointed out. Mr. Shin stated that the third paragraph of the U.S. draft was acceptable to the Korean negotiators.

14. Colonel Fuller stated that paragraph 4 of the Korean draft had already been discussed in connection with paragraph 2 of the U.S. draft and that both paragraphs would be given further study.

Health and Sanitation

15. Mr. Whang reminded the negotiators that at the previous meeting, it had been agreed that either side might table whatever draft articles or documents it considered appropriate. He inquired whether the U.S. side had a draft article to table. Colonel O'Connor replied affirmatively and made the following statement:

"The United States Government proposes that an

0204

article on Health and Sanitation be included in the ROK-U.S. Status of Forces Agreement in order to regularize the current U.S. medical services to the Republic of Korea. We believe that such an Article in the SOFA will provide a sound basis for continued cooperation and coordination in these fields between our respective governments. The United States armed forces have endeavored to work closely with the ROK armed forces and other agencies of the Korean Government in the fields of public health and sanitation. Most of the joint ROK-U.S. cooperation in these fields occurs in the front lines areas in the environs of the forward U.S. military installations, in such fields as preventive medicine and the treatment of Korean personnel in need of emergency medical treatment because of injuries or other causes. Incidental to their performance of their normal services to U.S. personnel, the Medical Services of the United States armed forces have been ready and willing to respond to ROK Government requests for assistance to meet urgent needs in times of natural disasters and other emergencies. Of course this Article does not obligate the U.S. to continue to supply medical services to Korean nationals, but we feel it does provide the basis for continued mutually beneficial joint ROK-U.S. cooperation in these fields."

16. Colonel O'Connor then tabled the U.S. draft of an article dealing with Health and Sanitation. He said the Korean side could see from reading the draft that the U.S. side believed the article should be stated in general terms. He suggested that detailed implementation of matters of mutual concern to the two governments in the fields of health and sanitation could be handled as required through the Joint Committee. He offered to answer any questions by members of the Korean side, either immediately or after they had had a chance to study the draft article.

17. Mr. Whang stated that the Korean side was quite aware of the excellent cooperation and coordination which has existed and continues to exist in this field. He said the Korean side hoped that the U.S. armed forces would continue to provide such aid in times of emergency or disaster. He said the Korean side would study the U.S. draft.

18. Each side then tabled a draft of the article dealing with Local Procurement.

19. Each side then tabled a draft of the article dealing with security measures.

20. The next meeting was scheduled for July 10 at 2:00 p.m.

보통문서로 재분류(1966. 12. 31.) 0205

JOINT SUMMARY RECORD OF THE 25TH SESSION
STATUS OF FORCE NEGOTIATIONS

June 26, 1963

I. Time and Place : 2:00 to 3:10 p.m. June 26, 1963 at the Foreign Minister's Conference Room

II. Attendants:

ROK Side:

Mr. Whang, Ho Eul	Director Bureau of Political Affairs Ministry of Foreign Affairs
Mr. Shin, Kwan Sup	Director Bureau of Customs Duty Ministry of Finance
Mr. Koo, Choong Whay	Chief, America Section Ministry of Foreign Affairs
Mr. Shin, Jung Sup	Chief, Treaty Section Ministry of Foreign Affairs
Col. Lee, Nam Koo	Chief, Military Affairs Section Ministry of National Defense
Mr. Chu, Mun Ki	Chief, Legal Affairs Section Ministry of Justice
Mr. Lee, Kyung Hoon	2nd Secretary Ministry of Foreign Affairs
Mr. Kang, Suk Jae	2nd Secretary Ministry of Foreign Affairs
Mr. Kim, Yu Taik	3rd Secretary Ministry of Foreign Affairs

U.S. Side:

Col. G.G. O'Connor	Deputy Chief of Staff 8th Army
Col. Howard Smigelow	Deputy Chief of Staff UNC
Capt. R.M. Brownlie	Assistant Chief of Staff USN/K
Col. L.J. Fuller	Staff Judge Advocate United Nations Command

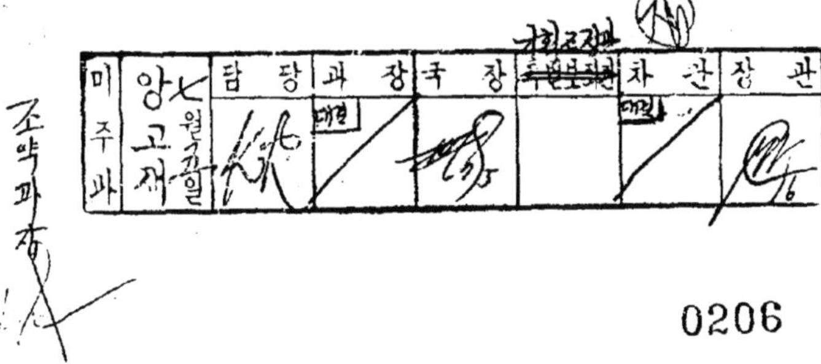

0206

Mr. Benjamin A. Fleck (Rapporteur and Press Officer)	First Secretary Embassy
Mr. Rodney Armstrong,	Economic Officer, American Embassy
Mr. Robert A. Kinney	J-5
Major Robert D. Peckham	Staff Officer, JAG 8th Army

1. Mr. Whang opened the meeting by welcoming Colonel O'Connor, who was heading the U.S. side for the first time, and Mr. Rodney Armstrong, an Economic Officer of the Embassy, who was sitting in for Mr. William Ford.

Taxation

2. In taking up the draft articles dealing with taxation, Colonel O'Connor announced that Colonel Fuller would be the U.S. spokesman on this subject and Mr. Whang stated that Mr. Shin Kwan Sup would be the spokesman for the Korean side. In introducing the U.S. draft, Colonel Fuller made the following opening statement:

"The taxation articles of our various status of forces agreements provide generally that the visiting armed forces are not subject to host-country taxes on property which they hold or use or transfer. They also provide generally that the members and civilian employees and dependents of the visiting forces are not subject to host-country income taxes or property taxes except on such private business income and investment type property they may have in the host country apart from their official presence there.

"The reasons for such exemptions are first that the visiting forces themselves should not be taxed on the property which they must use or hold for mutual defense purposes and second, the members, civilian employees, and dependents, being fully taxed on their income and property by their own country should not be taxed a second time by the host country to which they are invountarily ordered.

"In the United States the income and property of a service member, civilian employee, and dependents are already fully taxed by the federal government, state government, county government, and city government. These taxes continue and must be paid even when the serviceman, employee, or

0207

> dependent is serving overseas, in Korea or elsewhere. It would not be proper to subject him to additional taxes because of such overseas service."

Colonel Fuller noted that the U.S. and Korean drafts are generally similar and that they both are based on other existing status of forces agreements. He proposed that they be discussed paragraph by paragraph. The Korean side agreed.

3. Colonel Fuller noted that the two drafts of paragraph 1 are identical except for the variation between "Korea" and "the Republic of Korea". He proposed that the paragraph be agreed to, with the adjustment of this difference in language to be made during the final editing of the agreement. Mr. Shin agreed.

4. Turning to paragraph 2, Colonel Fuller pointed out that in the first sentence of the U.S. draft the word "any" appears before the words "Korean taxes". Although it does not appear in the Korean draft, he pointed out that it is included in the taxation articles of other status of forces agreements. He stated that its presence or absence would not appear to make any substantive difference. He proposed that it be included in the sentence. He pointed to two more instances in the first sentence of the variation between "Korea" and "the Republic of Korea", which he proposed should be handled in the manner already proposed. He also referred to a recurrence in the first sentence of the previously discussed usage of the word "activities" in the U.S. draft and "organizations" in the Korean draft. He proposed that the basic decision in regard to this difference of usage be made in relation

0208

to the article on Non-Appropriated Fund Activities/ Organizations and that this sentence then be made to conform to that decision. Whichever word is decided upon, he stated that the word "including" in the U.S. draft is more appropriate than the words "or by" in the Korean draft, inasmuch as the nonappropriated fund activities or organizations referred to are official agencies of the United States armed forces.

5. Mr. Shin replied that the first sentence of the U.S. draft was acceptable to the Korean side, with the understanding that the question of "activities" or "organizations" would be settled later.

6. Colonel Fuller pointed out that the second sentence of paragraph 2 of the U.S. draft has two clauses. The first clause, he said, is intended to provide tax exemption on income derived from sources outside Korea. Although this provision does not appear in the Korean draft, Colonel Fuller stated that it should be included here inasmuch as it is not covered elsewhere in the SOFA. The second clause of the second sentence, he continued, is substantially the same as paragraph 4 of the Korean draft. The U.S. side, he said, believes that since it relates to the other provisions of paragraph 2 it should form a part of that paragraph, as it does in other status of forces agreements.

7. Mr. Shin stated that the second sentence of paragraph 2 of the U.S. draft appeared to be similar in construction to the second sentence of paragraph 7 of the U.S. draft of the contractors article. The Korean side

wondered, therefore, whether the sentence in the taxation article might not be redundant. If not, was there any particular reason for including it? Colonel Fuller replied that the Korea draft of paragraph 2 and the first and third sentences of the U.S. draft refer only to income derived from sources inside Korea. Therefore, the inclusion of the second sentence was not redundant, since there should be some mention in the article of income from sources outside of Korea.

8. Mr. Shin stated that the third sentence of the U.S. draft of paragraph 2 does not exempt members of the U.S. armed forces from payment of taxes on income derived from sources within Korea other than those sources refferred to in the first sentence of the paragraph 2. Therefore, it could be taken for granted that no tax would be imposed on income derived from sources outside Korea. He suggested that it would be more appropriate to place the substance of the second sentence of the U.S. draft in an Agreed Minute.

9. Colonel Fuller pointed out that if this sentence were not included, the SOFA would contain no explicit provisions regarding taxation on income derived from outside sources. The U.S. side, he said, preferred to have an explicit statement in the agreement. Mr. Shin replied that the Korean side interpreted this sentence also to be related to the question of prevention of double taxation, a question which was currently of concern to the authorities of both governments. He suggested that this question be left for settlement outside of the SOFA. To avoid misunderstanding, he reiterated his

0210

suggestion that the substance of the second sentence be placed in an Agreed Minute.

10. Colonel Fuller referred to the frequently expressed desire of both sides to hold the number of Agreed Minutes to a minimum. He also referred to Mr. Shin's previous statement that the ROK Government had no intention to tax income derived from sources outside of Korea. If that is so, he inquired, why was the Korean side so reluctant to spell it out in the SOFA? Mr. Shin replied that the Korean side desired this provision to be placed in an Agreed Minute because the first and third sentences of the U.S. draft refer to income from sources within Korea. It was then agreed to defer further discussion of this point until after both sides had the opportunity to give it further study.

11. Mr. Whang reiterated the position of the Korean side that the first clause of the second sentence of the U.S. draft of paragraph 2 should be placed in an agreed minute. He asked whether the second clause of that sentence was relevant to the prevention of double taxation. Colonel Fuller replied that the entire article relates to the prevention of double taxation as well as to escape from all taxation. Mr. Whang stated that the Korean side believed the second clause should appear as a separate sentence, as in paragraph 4 of the ROK draft. It was agreed to give further study to this question.

12. Colonel Fuller then stated that the third sentence of paragraph 2 of the U.S. draft is similar to the last sentence of paragraph 2 of the Korean draft,

0211

with three exceptions. First, the U.S. draft, in accordance with the example of other agreements, uses the word "Korean" before the word "sources", whereas the word "Korean" has been omitted from the Korean draft. Inasmuch as the U.S. side presumes that the ROK Government does not intend to tax income derived from non-Korean sources, Colonel Fuller continued, there should be no objection to the inclusion of the word "Korean" before the word "sources". Secondly, he pointed out, the U.S. draft uses the words "other than those sources referred to in the first sentence of this paragraph" while the corresponding words in the Korean draft are "other than those provided for in this paragraph ". He said the U.S. side believed the wording of the U.S. draft stated more precisely the substance intended by both sides. Thirdly, Colonel Fuller continued, the U.S. draft ends with the following words not included in the Korean draft: "nor do they exempt United States citizens who claim Korean residence for United States income tax purposes from payment of Korean taxes on income". These words, he said, are designed to prevent a person from escaping from both U.S. and Korean taxes by providing that if a U.S. citizen covered by this agreement seeks to avoid or reduce his U.S. taxes because he claims residence in Korea, then he loses his exemption from paying Korean taxes. Colonel Fuller pointed out that this wording has precedents in other status of forces agreements and the U.S. side proposed its adoption as beneficial to both governments. Mr. Shin stated that the Korean side

0212

appreciated the additional language at the end of the sentence and that the entire final sentence of the U.S. draft of paragraph 2 was acceptable to the Korean side.

13. Turning to paragraph 3 of both drafts, Colonel Fuller stated that they were similar, with three exceptions. First, the U.S. draft includes the words "tangible or intangible" to clarify the intent of the words "movable property". They are not included in the Korean draft, although they are found in other status of forces agreements. Secondly, there was another occurrence of the difference between "Korea" and "the Republic of Korea", which he proposed should be handled in the previsously agreed upon manner. Thirdly, the U.S. draft contains the following words not found in the Korean draft: "or to any intangible property registered in Korea". He said these words had been included in the U.S. draft to make it clear that the ROK Government may tax intangible property if it is registered in Korea. These words also are found in other status of forces agreements, he pointed out. Mr. Shin stated that the third paragraph of the U.S. draft was acceptable to the Korean negotiators.

14. Colonel Fuller stated that paragraph 4 of the Korean draft had already been discussed in connection with paragraph 2 of the U.S. draft and that both paragraphs would be given further study.

<u>Health and Sanitation</u>

15. Mr. Whang reminded the negotiators that at the previous meeting, it had been agreed that either side might table whatever draft articles or documents it considered appropriate. He inquired whether the U.S. side

had a draft article to table. Colonel O'Connor replied affirmatively and made the following statement:

> "The United States Government proposes that an article on Health and Sanitation be included in the ROK-U.S. Status of Forces Agreement in order to regularize the current U.S. medical services to the Republic of Korea. We believe that such an article in the SOFA will provide a sound basis for continued cooperation and coordination in these fields between our respective governments. The United States armed forces have endeavored to work closely with the ROK armed forces and other agencies of the Korean Government in the fields of public health and sanitation. Most of the joint ROK-U.S. cooperation in these fields occurs in the front lines areas in the environs of the forward U.S. military installations, in such fields as preventive medicine and the treatment of Korean personnel in need of emergency medical treatment because of injries or other causes. Incidental to their performance of their normal services to U.S. personnel, the Medical Services of the United States armed forces have been ready and willing to respond to ROK Government requests for assistance to meet urgent needs in times of natural disasters and other emergencies. Of course this Article does not obligate the U.S. to continue to supply medical services to Korean nationals, but we feel it does provide the basis for continued mutually beneficial joint ROK-U.S. cooperation in these fields."

16. Colonel O'Connor then tabled the U.S. draft of an article dealing with Health and Sanitation. He said the Korean side could see from reading the draft that the U.S. side believed the article should be stated in general terms. He suggested that detailed implementation of matters of mutual concern to the two governments in the fields of health and sanitation could be handled as required through the Joint Committee. He offered to answer any questions by members of the Korean side, either immediately or after they had a chance to study the draft article.

17. Mr. Whang stated that the Korean side was quite aware of the excellent cooperation and coordination which has existed and continues to exist in this field. He

0214

said the Korean side hoped that the U.S. armed forces would continue to provide such aid in times of emergency or disaster. He said the Korean side would study the U.S. draft.

18. Each side then tabled a draft of the article dealing with Local Procurement.

19. Each side then tabled a draft of the article dealing with security measures.

20. The next meeting was scheduled for July 10 at 2:00 p.m.

407

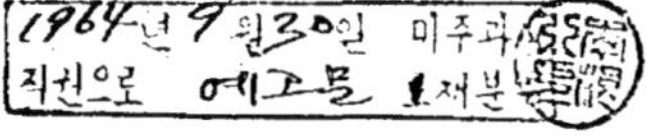

6. 제26차 회의, 7.10

0216

기 안 용 지

자체 통제		기안처	미주과 이경훈	전화번호	근거서류접수일자
	과장	국장	기획조정관	차관	장관
관계관 서명	조약과장				
기안 년월일	63. 7. 9	시행 년월일		보존 년한	정서 기장
분류 기호	외정미	전체 통제		총결	
경유 수신 참조	건의			발신	
제목	제 26 차 주둔군지위협정 체결 교섭회의에 임할 우리측 입장				

7.10.에 개최될 제 26 차 주둔군지위협정체결 한미간 교섭회의에서는 보건 및 위생조치, 안전보장 조치 및 현지 조달 문제에 관하여 토의될 예정이온바 이에 관련하여 우리측 교섭 실무자는 7.8. 관계부처 실무자와 연석회합을 갖고 제 26 차 회의에서 취할 우리측 태도를 별첨과 같이 결정하였아오니 재가하여 주시기 바랍니다.

유 첨: 제 26 차 주둔군 지위협정 체결교섭회의에 임할 우리측태도. 끝

1966.12.31.에 예고문에 의거 일반문서로 재분류됨

0217

1966. 12. 31.

승인양식 1-1-3 (1112-040-016-018) (190mm×260mm 16절지)

1966년 9월 30일 미주국장 직권으로 예고문 로재분류

1. 보건 및 위생조치

(1) 미국측 초안에 있어서 "consistent with the right of the United States to furnish medical support for its armed forces, civilian component and their dependents" 라는 구절이 무엇을 의미하며 특히 "medical support" 가 내포하고 있는 범위와 한계가 어느정도인가를 미국측에 문의하고 미국측 설명을 들은후 상기 구절을 삭제토록 주장한다.

2. 안전보장 조치

(1) 미국측이 제시한 초안에는 안전보장 조치를 받게되는 대상자로서 미국군대, 그들의 구성원, 군속 및 그들의 가족과 재산 이외에 우리측 초안에 없는 군계약자, 그들의 가족 및 재산 까지도 포함시키고 있는데 이에 관하여 우리측은 군계약자는 군속과 같이 취급할수 없으며 또한 군계약자 조항이 별도로 토의되고 있으므로 이의 삭제를 주장토록 한다. (Respect for Local Law)

(2) 미국측 안에는 또한 우리측 안에 없는 형사재판 관할권 조항에 부합시켜 한국법에 의거한 범죄자에 대한 처벌을 보증한다라고 규정하고 있는데, 형사재판관할권 조문 초안은 상금 교환되지 않았을 뿐 아니라 군계약자 조항의 미측안 제 8 항에 군계약자에 대한 관할권문제를 규제할 안이 제시되지 않았으므로 동 조문 초안들이 교환된후 다시 토의토록 주장한다.

3. 현지 조달

(1) 현지 조달 허여원측 및 이에 대한 예외 규정에 관한 미국측 초안 제 1 및 2 항은 우리측안과 꼭 같으므로 미국측안을 수락토록 한다.

(2) 미국군대의 현지 조달에 따르는 물품에 대한 면세규정인 미국측 초안 제 3 항에 있어서,

가. 최종적으로 미국군대에 의하여 사용케되는 물자의 구매에도 보통 일반물자의 구매에 따르는 바와 같은 과세의 면제를 요구하고 있는 결과,

0218

나. 과세의 면제를 받게될 조세로서 물품세, 석유세, 전기 및 까스세 이외에도 통행세 및 사업세를 추가하고 있는 점이 우리측 조안과 차이가 있는바 이에 관련하여 우리측은 통행세는 사람에게 부과하는 것이니 이것을 삭제하자고 주장토록 한다.

(3) 개인용 물품의 구입에 대한 과세규정 및 구입된 물품의 처분에 관한 미국측 조안 제 4, 5 항은 우리측 조안과 꼭 같으므로 미국측안은 수락토록 한다.

(4) 합의 의사록에 있어서,

가. 구매계획의 변경에 따르는 사전 통고 규정 및 구매계약에 관련된 의견차이의 조정에 관한 미국측 조안 제 1 및 제 2 항은 수락토록 하고,

나. 최종적으로 미국군대가 사용케될 물품의 구매에 관한 면세절차에 관한 제 3 항에 있어서는 (b)항의"agent " 라는 용어 대신에"representative "라는 용어로 대치 하자고 제의하고 나머지 조항은 수락토록 한다.

보통문서로 재분류(1966.12.31.

1966.12.31에 예고문에 의거 일반문서로 재분류됨

기 안 용 지

자체 통제		기안처	미주과 이경훈	전화번호	근거서류접수일자
	과장	국장	기획조정관	차관	장관
				대결	
관계관 서명	조약과장 1동서기관				
기안 년월일	1963.7.11	시행 년월일		보존 년한	정서	기장
분류 기호	외정미 722-	전체 통제				
경유 수신 참조	국가재건최고회의 의장 (참조: 외무국방위원장) 내각수반		발신	장관		
제목	주둔군지위협정체결을 위한 제 26차 교섭회의 보고					

1963년 7월 10일 하오 2시부터 4시까지 외무부장관 회의실에서 개최된 제 26차 주둔군지위협정 체결 교섭회의에서 토의된 내용을 별첨과 같이 보고합니다.

유첨: 제 26 차 교섭회의 보고서 부.

1964년 9월 30일 직권으로 예고문

0220

승인양식 1-1-3 (1112-040-016-018) (190mm×260mm16절지)

외 무 부

외정미 1963. 7. 12.

수 신 국가재건최고회의 의장

참 조 외무국방위원장

제 목 주둔군지위협정체결을 위한 제 26 차 교섭회의 보고

1963년 7 월 10 일 하오 2 시부터 4시 7까지 외무부장관 회의실에서 개최된 제 26 차 주둔군지위협정 체결 교섭회의에서 토의된 내용을 별첨과 같이 보고합니다.

유 첨 : 제 26 차 교섭회의 보고서 2 부. 끝

외 무 부 장 관 김 용 식

0221

외 무 부

외정미 1963. 7. 12

수 신 내 각 수 반

제 목 주둔군 지위협정체결을 위한 제 26 차 교섭회의보고

1963년 7 월 10 일 하오 2 시부터 4시까지 외무부장관 회의실에서 개최된 제 26 차 주둔군 지위협정체결 교섭회의에서 토의된 내용을 별첨과 같이 보고합니다.

유 첨 : 제 26 차 교섭회의 보고서 1 부 끝

외 무 부 장 관 김 용 식

0222

제 26 차

한미간 주둔군 지위 협정 체결 실무자회의

보 고 서

1. 일 시 : 1963 년 7 월 10 일 하오 2시부터 4시까지

2. 장 소 : 외무부장관 회의실

3. 참석자 : 한국측 : 신 관 섭 (재무부 세관국장)

구 충 회 (외무부 미주과장)

신 정 섭 (외무부 조약과장)

이 남 구 (국방부 군무과장)

주 문 기 (법무부 법무과장)

이 경 훈 (외무부 2등서기관)

강 석 재 (")

조 광 제 (")

미국측 : 교섭대표단 전원 ("포드" 대표 불참)

4. 토의 사항 :

(1) 보건 및 위생조치, 현지 조달 그리고 안전보장 조치문제를 순차적으로 토의함.

(2) 보건 및 위생조치 문제의 토의에 있어서 미국측은 동 조치에 관하여 상호 관련된 사항은 "미국군대, 군속 및 그들의 가족을 위하여 의료지원을 제공하는 미국의 권리에 부합시켜" 합동위원회에서 양국 정부의 관계당국에 의하여 해결토록 하자고 주장한데 대하여 우리측은 "미국군대, 군속 및 그들의 가족을 위하여 의료지원을 제공하는 미국의 권리에 부합시켜" 라는 구절에 대한 미국측 저의를 질문하고 동 구절은 없어도 무방한 것이 아니냐고 주장하여 이 문제는 다음에 다시 토의키로 함.

0223

(3) 현지 조달 허여원측, 한국경제에 불리한 영향을 끼치게 될 현지 조달은 한국 관계당국을 통하여 구입한다라는 등의 규정은 한미 양측 안이 같으므로 상호 합의를 보았음.

63-1-18 (3)

0223-1

(4) 미국군대의 현지 조달에 따르는 물품에 대한 면세규정에 있어서 최종적으로 미국군대에 의하여 사용케되는 자재, 수급품, 비품 및 용역의 구매에 있어서도 보통 미국군대의 공인 조달기관이 적절한 증명서를 제시하고 한국에서 공용 목적을 위하여 구매되는 자재, 수급품, 비품 및 용역과 동일하게 물품세, 통행세, 석유세, 전기 및 까스세 그리고 사업세를 면제토록 하자고 미국측이 주장한데 대하여 우리측은 현지조달용 물품의 생산에 사용된 전기량과 기타 물품의 생산에 사용된 전기량의 구별은 실질적으로 행하기 곤란하니 전기세의 삭제를 주장하여 미국측은 한국측 안을 고려해 보겠다고 하였음.

(5) 개인용 물품의 구입에 대한 과세규정 및 구입된 물품의 처분에 관한 규정은 한미 양측 초안이 동일하였으므로 동 문제에 대하여는 상호 합의하였음.

(6) 현지 조달조항의 합의의사록에 있어서 (가) 한국 및 미국의 경제관계법률 및 상업관례의 차이로 인하여 발생되는 조달계약에 관한 제 문제 해결은 합동위원회나 또는 기타 "적절한 자"에 의하여 검토되도록 하자고 미국측은 주장한데 대하여 우리측은 "적절한 자"가 법률을 검토한다는 것은 적당치 않으니 "적절한 대표"로 하자고 주장하여 미국측은 한국측 제의를 원칙적으로 수락한다고 하였으며 (나) 현지조달 물품의 수령은 미국군대의 권한있는 "대행자"에 의하여 확인되어야 한다고 미국측은 주장한데 대하여 우리측은 이러한 물품의 수령은 미국군대의 권한있는 "대표"에 의하여 확인되어야 한다고 주장하여 이문제도 미국측은 원칙적으로 수락한다고 하였음.

(7) 안전보장조치문제의 토의에 있어서 미국측은 군계약자도 미국군대, 그들의 구성원, 군속 및 그들의 가족과 같이 안전보장조치를 받게되는 대상자로 포함시키자고 주장한데 대하여 우리측은 군계약자는 영리를 목적으로하는 자이므로 군속과 같이 취급할수 없으며 또한 제3국인의 사업가들을 고려해서 군계약자에게 지나친 특권을 부여할수 없으므로 이를 삭제하자고 주장하여 동 문제는 다음에

0224

63-1-18

미-문-108-12

0224-1

다시 토의키로 함.

(8) 미국측은 또한 한국법에 의거한 안전보장에 위배되는 행위를 한 범죄자의 처벌은 형사재판 관할권 조항에 부합시켜 행하도록 하자고 주장하여 왔기 우리측은 상금 형사재판관할권 조항이 교환되지 않았으므로 동 문제는 형사재판관할권 조항이 교환된 후 다시 토의 하자고 주장하자, 미국측은 우리 제안에 동의하여 동 문제는 형사 재판 관할권 조항이 교환된 후에 다시 토의키로 함.

5. 기타 사항 :

(1) 차기회의 일자 : 1963년 7월 25일 하오 2시

(2) 차기회의 의제 : 차기회의77가지 양측 수석대표간에 합의된 사항

63-1-

0225

63-1-18(3)

108-12 (3)

0225-1

July 10, 1963

1. Mr. Shin Kwan Sop opened the meeting by announcing that in the absence of Mr. Whang Ho Eul on an official trip abroad, Mr. Shin would act as Chief Negotiator for the Korean side. Mr. Habib welcomed Mr. Shin on behalf of the U.S. side.

Health and Sanitation

2. Taking up the Health and Sanitation Article tabled by the U.S. side at the previous meeting, Mr. Shin ~~remarked that this subject had not been included in the original list of items to be included in the SOFA and that therefore the ROK side did not have a draft to table. He~~ requested the U.S. side to explain its draft.

3. Mr. Habib stated that it is a ~~matter of~~ fact that the U.S. medical services, incidental to their normal duties of looking after the health of the U.S. armed forces, civilian component, and dependents, render extensive medical services to Korean personnel and to the Korean community in general, particularly in the areas immediately adjacent to U.S. military installations. He pointed out that in these endeavors, the U.S. medical services enjoy a great deal of cooperation from ROK personnel. Medical facilities and treatment are provided to members of the Korean Service Corps. Efforts are undertaken in the field of preventive medicine in order to control communicable diseases in the areas near U.S. installations. Koreans injured as a result of activities of the U.S. armed forces are given treatment. Instruction and advice are given on public health, sanitation, and other preventive medicine measures. Also, Mr. Habib continued, U.S. military medical authorities are members of the ROK Ministry of Health and Social Welfare's Public Health Coordinating Committee.

4. In effect, Mr. Habib stated, the purpose of this article is to recognize and regularize within the SOFA these activities and services which are currently being carried out, establish a sound basis for their continuance, and place in the hands of the Joint Committee the responsibility for working out details. The article speaks of matters of mutual concern, coordination, and the role of the Joint Committee.

0226

There is nothing in the draft, he continued, which would obligate the U.S. armed forces to extend medical services to the Korean people, nor would the ROK side wish to include such a provision. The article is intended to regularize and authorize the continuance of the medical services which are being provided, particularly in the vicinity of U.S. military camps.

5. Mr. Shin thanked Mr. Habib for his explanation and stated that the ROK side realized the friendly intent of the U.S. side. However, the ROK side did not completely understand the intent of the introductory language and would appreciate a further explanation of the first three lines of the draft.

6. Mr. Habib replied that the primary function of the U.S. medical services is to take care of the members of the U.S. armed forces, the civilian component, and their dependents. Consistent with that primary responsibility, he continued, the U.S. side is prepared to agree that other functions of the medical services will be carried out through mutual agreement in the Joint Committee. He said the U.S. side realizes that the SOFA with the Government of Japan does not contain such an article. However, there are provisions similar to those contained in this draft article in Article 59 of the German Supplementary Agreement, Article VIII of the Philippine SOFA, and Article V of the 1953 Ethippian Base Agreement. He pointed out that these provisions are more or less standard and that experience has shown that it is well to regularize medical activities by means of a SOFA article.

7. Mr. Shin stated that each government should be responsible for furnishing medical services to its own people. The U.S. side had asserted that matters of mutual concern pertaining to medical services would be carried out through mutual agreement in the Joint Committee. Therefore, the ROK side suggested the deletion of the introductory clause. Mr. Habib replied by pointing out that the language in no way commits the U.S. armed forces to providing medical services to the Korean people, nor does it involve ROK medical services to U.S. forces. He presumed that the ROK side was not questioning the right of the U.S. Government to provide medical

0227

support to the U.S. armed forces. Mr. Shin asked what was meant by the phrase "furnish medical support". Mr. Habib replied that it meant the provision of medical services, doctors, hospitals, and other facilities for members of the U.S. armed forces.

8. Mr. Shin remarked that there were two principal methods which could be used in "the prevention of diseases". One was to treat patients who appeared for treatment; the other was to practice preventive medicine. He asked whether the language of the U.S. draft covered both methods. Mr. Habib replied that the operative phrase in this connection was "mutual concern". These matters were to be worked out mutually by the authorities of both governments. He said it was the understanding of the U.S. side that the ROK Government welcomed the various medical services which are now being provided for Koreans by the U.S. armed forces. He referred to the provisions of vaccines during epidemics and the spraying of insecticides to eliminate noxious insects. Was the ROK side implying, he asked, that such services were not wanted? If they are to be continued, he added, they should be recognized and regularized in this SOFA, as has been done in other similar agreements. Mr. Shin replied that the ROK side believed that such services should be continued. He said the ROK side would consider the explanation of the draft article given by the U.S. side and would give its views at the next meeting.

Local Procurement

9. Turning to the Local Procurement Article, Mr. Shin remarked that paragraphs 1 and 2 in both drafts were identical in language and substance. They were thereupon accepted by both sides.

10. Turning to paragraph 3, Mr. Shin stated that the U.S. draft contained the phrase "including their authorized procurement agencies" and Agreed Minute 3(b) proposed by the U.S. side contained the phrase "an authorized agent of the United States armed forces". He asked for an explanation of these phrases. Mr. Habib replied that the first phrase referred to by Mr. Shin was consistent with the phraseology used in

the Customs Article, which had already been discussed. He said this language was more appropriate than the phrase "or by authorized procurement agencies of the United States armed forces" used in the Korean draft, inasmuch as these procurement agencies are actually a part of the armed forces. They are the machinery of the armed forces by which procurement is effected. With regard to the use of the term "agent" rather than "officer", Mr. Habib pointed out that the former term is a broader one which would include a member of the civilian component or a non-commissioned officer. The term "officer", he explained, has a very specific meaning which is too narrow for the purposes of this provision.

11. Mr. Shin then referred to the tax exemptions provided for in the two drafts of paragraph 3. He said the Korean side had included only commodity, gasoline, and electricity and gas taxes because of the ambiguity which would result from the inclusion of any others. He said that the Korean draft did not exempt goods and services procured for ultimate use from the payment of electricity and gas taxes because of the great difficulty in distinguishing those amounts of electricity and gas used for official purposes from those procured for ultimate use.

12. Mr. Habib replied that one of the purposes of the Agreed Minute #3 proposed by the U.S. side was to establish procedures for certification. He said that the ROK side accepted the principle of exemption from payment of taxes. He said the negotiators were now engaged in trying to define the taxes and (to establish) appropriate procedures for claiming exemptions. He said that the proposed Agreed Minute #3 would establish the exemption procedures and would specify the amounts of materials and/or services used. He said that the U.S. draft had placed items procured for ultimate use in the first sentence of paragraph 3 since the U.S. side believed that these items should also be exempted from taxation. He said paragraph 3 and Agreed Minute 3 should be read together.

13. Mr. Shin stated that there should be a clear distinction in paragraph 3

0223

between items procured for official purpose by the U.S. armed forces and items procured for ultimate use. With particular reference to the electricity tax, he said that it would be difficult and impractical to try to identify electricity procured by the U.S. armed forces for ultimate use because of the difficulty of differentiating between electricity used for the manufacture of goods to be ultimately used by the armed forces and goods intended for immediate sale on the Korean market. Mr. Habib stated that the U.S. side would consider the Korean position.

14. Mr. Shin stated that the ROK side agreed to the inclusion of business tax in the list of exemptions but suggested that the term should be "Business Activities Tax". Mr. Habib replied that the terminology in the SOFA should correspond with the terminology of the ROK laws. Mr. Shin agreed and stated that the relevant laws were the Business Tax Law and the Petroleum Tax Law. It was agreed to use the terms "Business Tax" and "Petroleum Tax" in the article.

15. With regard to the desire of the U.S. side to include traffic taxes in the list of exemptions, Mr. Shin remarked that the tax was levied on persons, not on goods. It would be difficult, therefore, to identify how much of an individual bus fare, for instance, would be tax. The amount would be trifling and the difficulty of providing exemption would be great. In reply, Colonel Fuller pointed out that paragraph 3 relates only to bulk procurement by the U.S. armed forces, including their procurement agencies, but not to purchases by individuals. He said that currently the armed forces were making bulk purchases of transportation on an annual basis. He said this system was obviously practical since it is currently in effect. Mr. Habib pointed out that paragraph 4 covers individual purchases and provides that such purchases shall not be exempt from payment of the relevant taxes. Mr. Shin stated that the ROK side had thought that paragraph 3 included individual purchases. He said the ROK side would consider the explanation given by the U.S. side.

16. Mr. Shin pointed out that paragraphs 4 and 5 in both drafts are identical

0230

with the exception of the omission of the word "the" before the word "taxes" in the third line of paragraph 5 in the U.S. draft. It was agreed to leave this difference in wording until the final editing of the agreement and both paragraphs were agreed upon.

Agreed Minute #1

17. Mr. Habib stated that inasmuch as major changes in the procurement program of the U.S. armed forces in the Republic of Korea would have definite effects on the Korean economy, it was only right that the Korean authorities should be notified as far in advance as practicable of any such changes. Such notification is provided for in Agreed Minute #1, which places on the U.S. armed forces the obligation to make such notification. Mr. Shin inquired whether the U.S. armed forces were prepared to provide information also on the current procurement program. In reply, Mr. Armstrong pointed out the existence of the ROK-U.S. Joint Meeting for Military Supply Promotion, a body established for that very purpose which has been meeting on a monthly basis for a little more than a year.

Agreed Minute #2

18. Referring to Agreed Minute #2, Mr. Habib stated that this proposed Minute recognizes that there are differences between the laws and business practices of Korea, where the procurement occurs, and the laws and business practices of the United States, which governs the internal procurement activities of the U.S. armed forces. The Minute provides for the resolution in the Joint Committee of any conflict between the two sets of law or business practices.

19. Mr. Shin stated that the ROK side did not believe that "other appropriate persons" should be concerned with questions of law. ~~which should be considered only by the Joint Committee~~. Mr. Habib said this phrase in the U.S. draft referred to groups as well as individuals. He said there might be in existence bodies more appropriate than the Joint Committee to consider legal questions. Mr. Shin said the ROK side was not suggesting deletion of the phrase. Perhaps

0231

"representatives" would be a better word than "persons". Mr. Habib said the U.S. side agreed in principle to the proposed change but, of course, would have to seek approval from Washington. He pointed out that the key operative word in the phrase was "appropriate".

20. Mr. Shin referred to the use in subparagraph (a) of Agreed Minute #3 of the word "representative" and the use in subparagraph (b) of the word "agent". He suggested that for the sake of uniformity, the wording in both cases should be "representative". Colonel Fuller replied that in each case, the operative word was "authorized". Mr. Habib said the U.S. side accepted the suggestion of the ROK side in principle, subject to approval from Washington.

21. Mr. Shin asked for clarification of the phrase in subparagraph (d) of Agreed Minute #3 "out of funds contributed by the Government of the Republic of Korea for disbursement by the United States". Mr. Habib explained that this wording referred to a percentage of certain counterpart funds which is turned over by the ROK Government to the U.S. Government under the provisions of the Commodity Sales Agreement.

Security Measures

22. Mr. Shin referred to the reference in the first sentence of the U.S. draft to invited contractors and stated that the ROK side believed that the ROK Government should not be obligated to take security measures on behalf of invited contractors, if the ROK government provided the same treatment for invited contractors as that provided for the civilian components, it would bring about discrimination against third country nationals. Therefore, he suggested the deletion of invited contractors from this draft article. ~~particularly since this group might include third country nationals.~~ Mr. Habib replied that to exclude the invited contractors from the provisions of this article would be discriminatory to the contractors. He pointed out that the contractors would be in the Republic of Korea solely for the purpose of providing services to the U.S. armed forces. He reminded the negotiators that they had previously agreed that if a particular benefit were not specifically mentioned in the Invited Contractors Article, it should be included in the relevant article. Since security

0232

measures are not mentioned in the Invited Contractors Article, this benefit should be extended to the contractors in the Security Measures Article.

23. Mr. Shin replied that the invited contractors are in the Republic of Korea for the purpose of making a profit and therefore they should be treated differently from the other groups covered by the provisions of this article. He suggested that inasmuch as the two sides appeared to have differing ideas of the role and functions of the invited contractors, it would be well to defer further discussion on this provision after agreement was reached on the Invited Contractors Article. Mr. Habib said that the status of the contractors was in no way comparable to that of foreign businessmen operating in the Republic of Korea, or to that of other third country nationals. These contractors are here solely for the purpose of providing services to the U.S. armed forces. Mr. Shin agreed.

24. Mr. Shin proposed that discussion of the remainder of the article be deferred until after the Criminal Jurisdiction Article had been tabled. Mr. Habib agreed.

25. The next meeting was scheduled for July 25 at 2:00 p.m.

0233

JOINT SUMMARY RECORD OF THE 26TH SESSION

July 18 , 1963

I. Time and Place : 2:00 to 4:00 p.m. July 10 , 1963 at the Foreign Minister's Conference Room

II. Attendants:

ROK Side:

Mr. Shin, Kwan Sup	Director Bureau of Customs Duty Ministry of Finance
Mr. Koo, Choong Whay	Chief, America Section Ministry of Foreign Affairs
Mr. Shin, Jung Sup	Chief, Treaty Section Ministry of Foreign Affairs
Col. Lee, Nam Koo	Chief, Military Affairs Section Ministry of National Defense
Mr. Chu, Mun Ki	Chief, Legal Affairs Section Ministry of Justice
Mr. Lee, Kyung Hoon	2nd Secretary Ministry of Foreign Affairs
Mr. Kang, Suk Jae	2nd Secretary Ministry of Foreign Affairs
Mr. Cho, Kwang Je	2nd Secretary Ministry of Foreign Affairs

U.S. Side:

Mr. Philip C. Habib	Counselor of the Embassy for Political Affairs
Col. G.G. O'Connor	Deputy Chief of Staff 8th Army
Col. Howard Smigelow	Deputy Chief of Staff UNC
Capt. R.M. Brownlie	Assistant Chief of Staff USN/K
Col. L.J. Fuller	Staff Judge Advocate United Nations Command

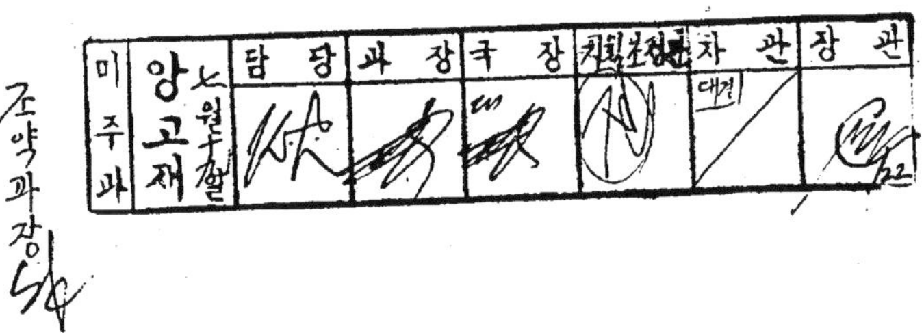

0234

Mr. Benjamin A. Fleck (Rapporteur and Press Officer)	First Secretary
Mr. Rodney Armstrong	Economic Officer, American Embassy
Mr. Robert A. Kinney	J-5
Major Robert D. Peckham	Staff Officer, JAG 8th Army
Mr. Kenneth Campen	Interpreter

1. Mr. Shin Kwan Sup opened the meeting by announcing that in the absence of Mr. Whang Ho Eul on an official trip abroad, Mr. Shin would act as Chief Negotiator for the Korean side. Mr, Habib welcomed Mr. Shin on behalf of the U.S. side.

Health and Sanitation

2. Taking up the Health and Sanitation Article tabled by the U.S. side at the previous meeting, Mr. Shin requested the U.S. side to explain its draft.

3. Mr. Habib stated that it is a fact that the U.S. medical services, incidental to their normal duties of looking after the health of the U.S. armed forces, civilian component, and dependents, render extensive medical services to Korean personnel and to the Korean community in general, particularly in the areas immediately adjacent to U.S. military installations. He pointed out that in these endeavors, the U.S.medical services enjoy a great deal of cooperation from ROK personnel. Medical facilities and treatment are provided to members of the Korean Service Corps. Efforts are undertaken in the field of preventive medicine in order to control communicable diseases in the areas near U.S. installations. Koreans injured as a result of activities of the U.S. armed forces are given treatment. Instruction and advice are given on public health, sanitation, and other preventive medicine measures. Also, Mr. Habib continued, U.S. military medical authorities are members of the ROK Ministry of Health and Social Welfare's Public Health Coordinating Committee.

0235

4. In effect, Mr. Habib stated, the purpose of this article is to recognize and regularize within the SOFA these activities and services which are currently being carried out, establish a sound basis for their continuance, and place in the hands of the Joint Committee the responsibility for working out details. The article speaks of matters of mutual concern, coordination, and the role of the Joint Committee. There is nothing in the draft, he continued, which would obligate the U.S. armed forces to extend medical services to the Korean people, nor would the ROK side wish to include such a provision. The article is intended to regularize and authorize the continuance of the medical services which are being provided, particularly in the vicinity of U.S. military camps.

5. Mr. Shin thanked Mr. Habib for his explanation and stated that the ROK side realized the friendly intent of the U.S. side. However, the ROK side did not completely understand the intent of the introductory language and would appreciate a further explanation of the first three lines of the draft.

6. Mr. Habib replied that the primary function of the U.S. medical services is to take care of the U.S. armed forces, the civilian component, and their dependents. Consistent with that primary responsibility, he continued, the U.S. side is prepared to agree that other functions of the medical services will be carried out through mutual agreement in the Joint Committee. He said the U.S. side realizes that the SOFA with the Government of Japan does not contain such an article. However, there are provisions similar to those contained in this draft article in Article 59 of the German Supplementary Agreement, Article VIII of the Philippine SOFA, and Article V of the 1953 Ethiopian Base Agreement. He pointed out that these provisions are more or less standard and that experience has shown that it is well to regularize medical activities by means of a SOFA article.

0236

7. Mr. Shin stated that each government should be responsible for furnishing medical services to its own people. The U.S. side had asserted that matters of mutual concern pertaining to medical services would be carried out through mutual agreement in the Joint Committee. Therefore, the ROK side suggested the deletion of the introductory clause. Mr. Habib replied by pointing out that the language in no way commits the U.S. armed forces to providing medical services to the Korean people nor does it involve ROK medical services to U.S. forces. He presumed that the ROK side was not questioning the right of the U.S. Government to provide medical support to the U.S. armed forces. Mr. Shin asked what was meant by the phrase "furnish medical support". Mr. Habib replied that it meant the provision of medical services, doctors, hospitals, and other facilities for members of the U.S. armed forces.

8. Mr. Shin remarked that there were two principal methods which could be used in "the prevention of diseases". One was to treat patients who appeared for treatment; the other was to practice preventive medicine. He asked whether the language of the U.S. draft covered both methods. Mr. Habib replied that the operative phrase in this conneciton was "mutual concern". These matters were to be worked out mutually by the authorities of both governments. He said it was the understanding of the U.S. side that the ROK Government welcomed the various medical services which are now being provided for Koreans by the U.S. armed forces. He referred to the provision of vaccines during epidemics and the spraying of insecticides to eliminate noxious insects. Was the ROK side implying, he asked, that such services were not wanted? If they are to be continued, he added, they should be recognized and regularized in this SOFA, as has been done in other similar agreements. Mr. Shin replied that the ROK side believed that such services should be continued. He said the ROK side would consider the explanation of the draft article

0237

given by the U.S. side and would give its views at the next meeting.

Local Procurement

9. Turning to the Local Procurement Article, Mr. Shin remarked that paragraphs 1 and 2 in both drafts were identical in language and substance. They were thereupon accepted by both sides.

10. Turning to paragraph 3, Mr. Shin stated that the U.S. draft contained the phrase "including their authorized procurement agencies" and Agreed Minute 3(b) proposed by the U.S. side contained the phrase "an authorized agent of the United States armed forces". He asked for an explanation of these phrases. Mr. Habib replied that the first phrase referred to by Mr. Shin was consistent with the phraseology used in the Customs Article, which had already been discussed. He said this language was more appropriate than the phrase "or by authorized procurement agencies of the United States armed forces" used in the Korean draft, inasmuch as these procurement agencies are actually a part of the armed forces. They are the machinery of the armed forces by which procurement is effected. With regard to the use of the term " agent" rather than "officer", Mr. Habib pointed out that the former term is a broader one which would include a member of the civilian component or a non-commissioned officer. The term "officer", he explained, has a very specific meaning which is too narrow for the purposes of this provision.

11. Mr. Shin then referred to the tax exemptions provided for in the two drafts of paragraph 3. He said the Korean side had included only commodity, gasoline, and electricity and gas taxes because of the ambiguity which would result from the inclusion of any others. He said that the Korean draft did not exempt goods and services procured for ultimate use from the payment of electricity and gas taxes because of the great difficulty in distinguishing those amounts of electricity and gas

0238

used for official purposes from those procured for ultimate use.

12. Mr. Habib replied that one of the purposes of the Agreed Minute #3 proposed by the U.S. side was to establish procedures for certification. He said that the ROK side accepted the principle of exemption from payment of taxes. He said the negotiators were now engaged in trying to define the taxes and to establish appropriate procedures for claiming exemptions. He said that the proposed Agreed Minute #3 would establish the exemption procedures and would specify the amounts of materials and/or services used. He said that the U.S. draft had placed items procured for ultimate use in the first sentence of paragraph 3 since the U.S. side believed that these items should also be exempted from taxation. He said paragraph 3 and Agreed Minute 3 should be read together.

13. Mr. Shin stated that there should be a clear distinction in paragraph 3 between items procured for official purposes by the U.S. armed forces and items procured for ultimate use. With particular reference to the electricity tax, he said that it would be fifficult and impractical to try to identify electricity procured by the U.S. armed forces for ultimate use because of the difficulty of differentiating between electricity used for the manufacture of goods to be ultimately used by the armed forces and goods intended for immediate sale on the Korean market. Mr. Habib stated that the U.S. side would consider the Korean position.

14. Mr. Shin stated that the ROK side agreed to the inclusion of business tax in the list of exemptions but suggested that the term should be "Business Activities Tax". Mr. Habib replied that the terminology in the SOFA should correspond with the terminology of the ROK laws. Mr. Shin agreed and stated that the relevant laws were the Business Tax Law and the Petroleum Tax Law. It was agreed to use the erms "Business Tax" and "Petroleum Tax" in the article.

15. With regard to the desire of the U.S. side to include

0233

traffic taxes in the list of exemptions, Mr. Shin remarked that the tax was levied on persons, not on goods. It would be diffi- cult, therefore, to identify how much of an individual bus fare, for instance, would be tax. The amount would be trifling and the difficulty of providing exemption would be great. In reply, Colonel Fuller pointed out that paragraph 3 relates only to bulk procurement by the U.S. armed forces, including their procurement agencies, but not to purchases by individuals. He said that currently the armed forces were making bulk purchases of transportation on an annual basis. He said this system was obviously practical since it is currently in effect. Mr. Habib pointed out that paragraph 4 covers individual purchases and provides that such purchases shall not be exempt from payment of the relevant taxes. Mr. Shin stated that the ROK side had thought that paragraph 3 included individual purchases. He said the ROK side would consider the explanation given by the U.S. side.

16. Mr. Shin pointed out that paragraphs 4 and 5 in both drafts are identical with the exception of the omission of the word "the" before the word "taxes" in the third line of paragraph 5 in the U.S. draft. It was agreed to leave this difference in wording until the final editing of the agreement and both paragraphs were agreed upon.

Agreed Minute #1

17. Mr. Habib stated that inasmuch as major changes in the procurement program of the U.S. armed forces in the Republic of Korea would have definite effects on the Korean economy, it was only right that the Korean authorities should be notified as far in advance as practicable of any such changes. Such notification is provided for in Agreed Minute #1, which places on the U.S. armed forces the obligation to make such notifica- tion. Mr. Shin inquired whether the U.S. armed forces were

0240

prepared to provide information also on the current procurement program. In reply, Mr. Armstrong pointed out the existence of the ROK-U.S. Joint Meeting for Military Supply Promotion, a body established for that very purpose which has been meeting on a monthly basis for a little more than a year.

Agreed Minute #2

18. Referring to Agreed Minute #2, Mr. Habib stated that this proposed Minute recognizes that there are differences between the laws and business practices of Korea, where the procurement occures, and the laws and business practices of the United States, which governs the internal procurement activities of the U.S. armed forces. The Minute provides for the resolution in the Joint Committee of any conflict between the two sets of law or business practices.

19. Mr. Shin stated that the ROK side did not believe that "other appropriate persons" should be concerned with questions of law. Mr. Habib said this phrase in the U.S. draft referred to groups as well as individuals. He said there might be in existence bodies more appropriate than the Joint Committee to consider legal questions. Mr. Shin said the ROK side was not suggesting deletion of thephrase. Perhaps "representatives" would be a better word than "persons". Mr. Habib said the U.S. side agreed in principle to the proposed change but, of course, would have to seek approval from Washington. He pointed out that the key operative word in the phrase was "appropriate".

20. Mr. Shin referred to the use in subparagraph (a) of Agreed Minute #3 of the word "representative" and the use in subparagraph (b) of the word "agent". He suggested that for the sake of uniformity, the wording in both cases should be "representative". Colonel Fuller replied that in each case, the operative word was "authorized". Mr. Habib said the U.S. side accepted the suggestion of the ROK side in principle, subject

0241

to approval from Washington.

21. Mr. Shin asked for clarification of the phrase in subparagraph (d) of Agreed Minute #3 "out of funds contributed by the Government of the Republic of Korea for disbursement by the United States". Mr. Habib explained that this wording referred to percentage of certain counterpart funds which is turned over by the ROK Government to the U.S. Government under the provisions of the Commodity Sales Agreement.

Security Measures

22. Mr. Shin referred to the reference in the first sentence of the U.S. draft to invited contractors and stated that if the ROK government provided the same treatment for invited contractors as that provided for the civilian component, it would bring about discrimination against third country nationals. The ROK side believed that the ROK Government should not be obligated to take security measures on behalf of invited contractors. Therefore, he suggested the deletion of invited contractors from this draft article. Mr. Habib replied that to exclude the invited contractors from the provisions of this article would be discriminatory to the contractors. He pointed out that the contractors would be in the Republic of Korea solely for the purpose of providing services to the U.S. armed forces. He reminded the negotiators that they had previously agreed that if a particular benefit were not specifically mentioned in the Invited Contractors Article, it should be included in the relevant article. Since security measures are not mentioned in the Invited Contractors Article, this benefit should be extended to the contractors in the Security Measures Article.

23. Mr. Shin replied that the invited contractors are in the Republic of Korea for the purpose of making a profit and therefore they should be treated differently from the other groups covered by the provisions of this article.

0242

Mr. Habib said that the status of the contractors was in no way comparable to that of foreign businessmen operating in the Republic of Korea, or to that of other third country nationals. These contractors are here solely for the purpose of providing services to the U.S. armed forces. He suggested that inasmuch as the two sides appeared to have differing ideas of the role and functions of the invited contractors, it would be well to defer further discussion on this provision until after agreement was reached on the Invited Contractors Article. Mr. Shin agreed.

24. Mr. Shin proposed that discussion of the remainder of the article be deferred until after the Criminal Jurisdiction Article had been tabled. Mr. Habib agreed.

25. The next meeting was scheduled for July 25 at 2:00 p.m.

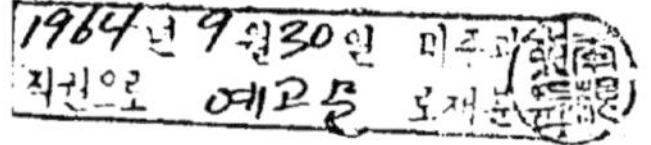

0243

7. 제27차 회의, 7.25

0244

기 안 용 지

자 체 통 제		기안처	미주과 이경훈	전화번호	근거서류접수일자
	과 장	국 장	기획조정관	차 관	장 관
				대결	
관 계 관 서 명	조약과장				
기 안 년 월 일	63. 7.24.	시 행 년월일		보 존 년 한	
분 류 기 호		전 체 통 제		종결	
경 유 수 신 참 조	건 의			발 신	
제 목	제 27 차 주둔군지위협정 체결 교섭회의에 임할 우리측 입장				

정 서 | 기 장

7.25.에 개최될 제27차 주둔군지위협정 체결 한미간 교섭회의에서는 보건 및 위생조치, 현지조달 및 외환관리 문제에 관하여 토의될 예정이온바 이에 관련하여 우리측 교섭 실무자는 7.23. 관계부처 실무자와 연석회합을 갖고 제27차 회의에서 취할 우리측 태도를 별첨과 같이 결정하였아오니 재가하여 주시기 바랍니다.

유첨 .. 제27차 주둔군지위협정 체결교섭회의에 임할 우리측 태도. 끝

27次

1964 년 9 월 30 일 직권으로 예고문

1966. 12. 31.

196 . . . 에 예고문에 의거 일반문서로 재분류

승인양식 1-1-3 (11-00900-03) (195mm×265mm16절지)

0245

1. 보건 및 위생조치

(1) 보건 및 위생에 관한 한미 상호간에 관련된 문제는 합동위원회에서 양국정부 관계당국자에 의하여 결정된다 라는 규정에 관하여 우리측은 보건 및 위생에 관한 대한민국의 관계법령의 규정이 동 위원회에서 상당히 존중되어야 한다는 것을 조건으로 미국측안을 수락해 주도록 한다.

2. 현지조달

(1) 미국군대의 현지조달용 물품에 대한 면세규정인 미국측 초안 제3항 (이는 우리측 초안 제3항에 해당함)에 있어서 미국측은 최종적으로 미국군대에 의하여 사용케되는 물자의 구매에 따르는 면세사항을 보통 미국군대가 사용케되는 물자의 구매에 따르는 면세사항과 일괄하여 같이 규정하고 있는데 반하여 우리측은 이양자를 구별하여 규정하고 있는데 이에관하여(가) 조문의 체제를 우리측 초안대로 하자고 주장하되 (나) 보통 미국군대에 의하여 사용되는 물자의 구매에 따르는 면세사항으로서는 미국측이 제시한대로 물품세, 통행세, 석유세, 전기 및 가스세 그리고 영업세등 미국측이 제시한대로 모두 받아주기로 하고 (나) 최종적으로 미국군대에 의하여 사용케되는 물자의 구매에 따르는 면세 사항으로는 물품세 및 석유세 만을 규정토록 하자고 주장한다.

(2) 합의의사록에 있어서 (가) 제2항에 있어서 미국측은 한국 및 미국의 경제상의법률에 관한 차이로부터 발생하는 구매계약에 관하여 곤란한 문제의 해결이 합동위원회나 또는 기타 적절한자 (other appropriate persons) 에 의하여 심의토록 하자고 주장하고 있는데 법률을 적절한자가 심의한다는 것은 부적당하니 기타 적절한 대표 (other appropriate representative) 로 대치하자고 우리측은 계속 주장토록 하고

0246

(나) 제3항에 있어서 (b)항의 agent라는 용어도 부적당하니 representative라는 용어로 대치하자고 계속 주장한다.

3. <u>외환 관리</u>

(1) 합의의사록에 있어서 (가) 비세출 기관에 관한 용어를 우리측은 "organizations"로 하자고 주장한데 반하여 미국측은 "activities"로 하자고 주장하고 있는데 이문제는 ~~추후~~ 우리측 주장을 미국측이 수락하여줄것을 ~~최종적으로 결정될때까지 보류토록 하자고~~ 주장하고 (나) 원화대 불화의 교환율에 관한 용어의 사용에 있어서 우리측은 "effective official rate"라는 용어를 사용하자고 계속 주장토록하고 미국측이 이를 거부할시에는 "basic rate"로 하자고 주장토록 한다.

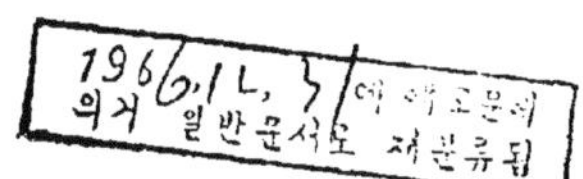

0247

기 안 용 지

자체 통제		기안처	미주과 이경훈	전화번호	근거서류접수일자
	과장	국장	기획조정관	차관	장관
				대결	
관계관 서명	조약과장				
기안 년월일	1963.7.26	시행 년월일		보존 년한	정서 / 기장
분류 기호	외정미722.2	전체 통제		종결	
경유 수신 참조	국가재건최고회의 의장 (참조 : 외무국방위원장) 내각수반	발신	장관		
제목	주둔군지위협정체결을 위한 제27차 교섭회의 보고				

1963년 7월 25일 하오 2시부터 3시30분까지 외무부장관 회의실에서 개최된 제27차 주둔군지위협정 체결교섭 회의에서 토의된 내용을 별첨과 같이 보고합니다.

유첨 : 제27차 교섭회의 보고서 부. 끝.

1964년 9월 30일 직권으로 예고문

승인양식 1-1-3 (1112-040-016-018) (190mm×260mm16절지)

0248

외 무 부

외정미 722.2 1963. 7. 27.

수 신 : 국가재건최고회의 의장

참 조 : 외무국방위원장

제 목 : 주둔군지위협정체결을 위한 제 27 차 교섭회의 보고

1963 년 7 월 25 일 하오 2 시부터 3시30분까지 외무부 장관 회의실에서 개최된 제 27 차 주둔군지위협정 체결교섭회의에서 토의된 내용을 별첨과 같이 보고합니다.

유 첨: 제 27 차 교섭회의 보고서 2 부, 끝.

외 무 부 장 관 김 용 식

0249

외 무 부

외정미 722.2　　　　　　　　　　　　1963. 7. 27.

수 신 : 내각수반

제 목 : 주둔군지위협정체결을 위한 제 27 차 교섭회의 보고

1963 년 7 월 25 일 하오 2시부터 3시30분까지 외무부장관 회의실에서 개최된 제 27 차 주둔군지위협정 체결교섭회의에서 토의된 내용을 별첨과 같이 보고합니다.

유 첨 : 제 27 차 교섭회의 보고서 1 부, 끝.

외 무 부 장 관　　김 용 식

0250

0585

제 27 차

한미간 주둔군 지위협정 체결실무자 회의

보 고 서

1. 일 시 : 1963 년 7 월 25 일 하오 2 시부터 3시30분까지

2. 장 소 : 외무부장관 회의실

3. 참석자 : 한국측 : 신 관 섭 (재무부 세관국장)

구 충 회 (외무부 미주과장)

신 정 섭 (외무부 조약과장)

이 남 구 (국방부 군무과장)

주 문 기 (법무부 법무과장)

이 경 훈 (외무부 2등서기관)

강 석 재 (")

조 광 제 (")

정 인 용 (재무부 사무관)

미국측 : 교섭대표단 전원("푸특" 및 "루이스" 양대표 불참)

4. 토의 사항 :

(1) 보건 및 위생조치, 현지조달 그리고 외환관리 문제를 순차적으로 토의함.

(2) 보건 및 위생조치문제의 토의에 있어서 보건 및 위생에 관한 한미상호간에 관련된 문제는 합동위원회에서 양국 정부관계 당국자에 의하여 결정된다 라는 규정에 관하여 우리측은 보건 및 위생에 관한 대한민국의 관계법령의 규정이 동 위원회에서 정당히 존중되어야 한다는 것을 강조하고 또한 이러한 한국측이 강조한 점은 합동위원회에서 토의와 심의의 지침이 되어야 할

63-1-117

0251

0252

것이라는 점을 강조한데 대하여 미국측은 이를 전적으로 찬동하였으므로 미국측안을 수락하여 주었음.

(3) 미국군대의 현지조달용 물품에 대한 면세규정에 있어서 미국측은 최종적으로 미국군대에 의하여 사용케 되는 물자의 구매에 따르는 면세사항을 보통 미국군대가 사용케되는 물자의 구매에 따르는 면세사항과 일괄하여 같이 규정하자고 주장한데 대하여 우리측은 이 양자를 구별하여,

(가) 보통 미국 군대에 의하여 사용되는 물자의 구매에 따르는 면세사항으로서는 미국측이 제시한 대로 물품세, 통행세, 석유세, 전기 및 까스세 그리고 영업세 등의 세종에 대한 면세를 인정하여 줄수 있으나 (나) 최종적으로 미국군대에 의하여 사용케되는 물자의 구매에 따르는 면세사항으로서는 물품세, 및 석유세 만을 면세 세종으로서 인정해 줄수 있다고 주장하여 이 문제는 다음에 다시 토의키로 함.

(4) 현지 조달 조항의 합의 의사록에 있어서 (가) 한국 및 미국의 경제관계법률 및 상업관례의 차이로 인하여 발생되는 조달 계약에 관한 제 문제해결은 합동위원회나 또는 기타 "적절한 자"에 의하여 검토되도록 하자고 미국측은 주장한데 대하여 우리측은 "적절한 자"가 법률을 검토한다는 것은 적당치 않으니 "적절한 대표"로 하자고 주장한 점과 (나) 현지 조달물품의 수령은 미국군대의 권한있는 "대행자"에 의하여 확인되어야 한다고 미국측은 주장한데 대하여 우리측은 이러한 물품의 수령은 미국군대의 권한있는 "대표"에 의하여 확인되어야 한다고 주장한 점에 대하여 미국측은 원칙적으로 우리측 대안을 수락한다 라고 말하면서 그러나 상금 본국 정부로부터 최종 훈령을 받고 있지 않으므로 정식 확답을 할수 없다하여 이 문제는 다음에 다시 토의키로 함. 63-1-118

0253

63-1-19

미·올 1번-11

0254

(5) 외환관리 문제의 토의에 있어서 원화대 불화의 교환율에 관한 용어의 사용에 관하여 미국측은 계속하여 "최고의 환율"이라는 용어를 사용하자고 주장한데 대하여 우리측은 또한 계속하여 "유효한 공정환율"이라는 용어를 사용하자고 주장하여 이문제는 다음에 다시 토의키로 함.

5. 중요 합의 사항 :

보건 및 위생문제에 관한 조항에 완전 합의함. √

6. 기타 사항 :

(1) 차기회의일자 : 1963 년 8 월 8 일 하오 2 시

(2) 차기회의의제 : 차기회의까지 양측수석대표간에 합의된 사항.

63-1-118

0255

63-1-19 (3)

미국문 108-11 (3)

0256

Mr. Ku
chung-mo

--1--

~~Draft -- Minutes of the Twenty-Seventh ROK-US Negotiating Mtg for SOFA~~

1. Mr. ~~XXXXXXXXX Sin~~ Shin Kwan-sup opened the meeting by introducing Mr. CHUNG In-young, of the Foreign Exchange ~~Section~~ Division of the Ministry of Finance, who was to be present on the Korean side as an observer of the discussion on the subject of foreign exchange controls. Mr. Habib noted that Mr. Rodney Armstrong would replace Mr. Benjamin Fleck as ~~the Secretary of~~ rapporteur and press officer for the U.S. negotiating team during the latter's absence from Korea on home leave.

~~XXXXXXXXXXXXXXXXXXXX~~
Health and Sanitation

2. Opening substantive discussion, Mr. ~~Sin~~ Shin turned to the subject of health and ~~xxxxxxxxxx~~ sanitation. Mr. ~~Sin~~ Shin said that there had been extensive and detailed discussion of the U.S. draft article on the subject of health and sanitation at the last negotiating session, and the Korean side

0257

believed that they now understood the XX U.S. position on the XXXXXXXX subject. Mr. ~~Sin~~ Shin said that he wished to emphasize the provision of the draft U.S. article which provides that the two parties to the agreement will consult on matters in the fields of health and sanitation in the Joint Committee, where due consideration and respect would be given to the medical laws and regulations of the Republic of Korea. Mr. ~~Sin~~ Shin said that he wished to emphasize that in all matters in this area the laws and regulations of the Republic of Korea should be taken into account and duly respected. Mr. ~~Sin~~ Shin said that, with this preliminary statement, he wished to agree to the U.S. draft article on behalf of the Korean side.

3. Mr. Habib said that it was his understanding that Mr. ~~Sin~~ Shin had just offered an interpretation of the U.S. draft article to the effect that the Joint Committee, during the course of its consulatations on the subjects of health and sanitation, would take into account XXX Korean laws and regulations. Mr. Habib said that it was obvious that this would happen. ~~Mr. Habib said that he~~ He wished to reiterate that the U.S. draft article on health and sanitation merely sets forth broad principles for mutual coordination and cooperation between the U.S. and XX Korean authorities

0258

concerned with these matters, and leaves the detailed implementation of these principles to the Joint Committee. [~~Mr. Habib said that~~] It is the intention of the U.S. ~~XX~~ that the Joint Committee take into account the laws and regulations of the Republic of Korea relevant to medical matters in the course of consulatations on the subjects of health and sanitation. Mr. Habib said that the negotiating record would now show the above exchange between Mr. ~~Sin~~ Shin and himself and thus set forth the principles which should guide the Joint Committee in its ~~xxxxxxxxx~~ consultations on the subjects of health and sanitation.

4. Mr. ~~Sin~~ Shin said that ~~XXX~~ Mr. Habib's statement that the record of the meeting would ~~XXXX~~ provide guidance to the Joint Committee with respect to its consultations on the subject~~sxxxxx~~ of health and sanitation was significent and welcome ~~, and that he welcomed Mr. Habib's statement.~~

5. Mr. Habib said that he wished to point out again that ~~XXX~~ nothing in the U.S. draft article on health and sanitation obligated the U.S. medical authorities to provide any particular medical services. [~~Mr. Habib said that~~] The article merely provides that the past history of mutual ROK-US cooperation

0253

in these matters ~~will be continued into the future~~ is recognized and will be regularized. Mr. Habib said that one of the early topics for consultation in the Joint Committee should be the relationship of Republic of Korea Law No. 1035, promulgated March ~~30~~ 20, 1962, to the services currently being provided to Koreans by U.S. medical authorities. Under that law, which deals with the li~~s~~censing of medical practitioners in Korea, U.S. personnel are not liscensed to provide medical services in Korea. One of the tasks of the Joint Committee, ~~Mr. Habib said,~~ would be to ~~XXXX~~ regularize the provision of medical services to Koreans by U.S. medical authorities, taking into account the provisions of the law he had just cited.

6. Mr. ~~Sin~~ Shin said that matters concerning the provision of medical services to Koreans by U.S. medical authorities had been coordinated with the Korean Government in the past, and that the work of the Joint Committee would be to carry forward this coordination into the future with due respect for Korean Laws and regulations pertaining to medical services. ~~, xxxxxx resolving and agreeing upon matters pertaining to XXXXXXXXX legislative requirements.~~

7. Mr. Habib agreed with Mr. ~~Sin's~~ Shin's statement, and stated that the article could now be regarded as agreed. ~~He noted that another XXXXXXX milestone had been passed.~~

0260

-5-

Local Procurement

8. Turning to the draft article and agreed minutes concerning local procurement, Mr. Shin said that the Korean side desired to continue the discussion of the previous meeting with respect to the exemption from taxation of materials, supplies, equipment and services procured for the "ultimate use" of the U.S. armed forces. Mr. Shin said that at the previous discussion of this subject the Korean side had noted its objections to granting exemption from electricity and gas tax to items procured for the "ultimate use" of the U.S. forces. He said that at the present meeting the Korean side wished to mention also its objections to the granting of exemptions from the traffic and business taxes to items procured for "ultimate use", and to outline the arguments in favor of separating the exemptions for items procured directly and for items procured for "ultimate use", as is done in the Korean draft of the local procurement article.

9. Mr. Habib said that it was not the U.S. side's intention, in providing for the same exemptions for items procured directly and for those procured for "ultimate use", to seek the exemption taxes which did not constitute a readily

0261

-6-

He said that ~~xxxxxx~~ identifiable portion of the cost of the article. ~~XXXXXXXXXXXXXXXXX~~ the U.S. side's contention was simply that where taxes constituted a readily identifiable portion of the cost of an item, as they often did in the case of items procured in bulk for the ultimate use of the U.S. forces, they should be exempted. ~~Mr. Habib said that~~ The U.S. draft article should be read in close correlation with the U.S. draft ~~Agreed Minute~~ agreed minute 3 (a), which was then read aloud. Mr. Habib said that this agreed minute provided a detailed explanation of the certification process ~~XXXXXXXXXX~~ by which items for "ultimate use" would be exempted from taxation, and that certification process depended upon the taxes involved being readily identifiable. # 10. Mr. Habib said that it was not the intention of the U.S. side to create any of the problems for the Korean taxation authorities which ~~XXX~~ seemed to figure in the Korean side's thinking upon these ~~XXXXXXXX~~ matters. Mr. Habib ~~said he would cite a particular example of a case in which the electricity and gas tax upon a an item procured for the "ultimate use" of the U.S. forces should, in the U.S. side's view, be exempted:~~ cited the example of a contractor serving ~~XXXX~~ exclusively for the U.S. forces builds a structure on a U.S. facility under the

0262

terms of a contract with the U.S. forces. Obviously, Mr. Habib said, the electricity and gas being utilized on such a project can be metered, and should be exempted from Korean taxes. Mr. Habib said that, on the other hand, there would be cases where the amounts of electricity and gas going into the manufacture of a product for the "ultimate use" of the U.S. forces would not be readily identifiable and the U.S. would not request a waiver; such would be the case with the brewing of beer by a brewer who sold only part of his output to the U. S. Forces. Mr. Habib said that the effect of the Korean draft article on local procurement would be to negate the principle of exemption from Korean taxes of materials purchased locally, and to penalize the U.S. Forces for their local procurement.

11. Mr. Shin said that implementation of the procedure provided for in agreed minute 3 (a) may be technically feasible on the U.S. side, but that it seemed to be difficult from the point of view of Korean tax administration. Mr. Shin said that, for example, according to Korean law, the business tax should be levied at all stages of production and manufacture, whenever a sale of intermediate products was involved. Thus, in the brewing of beer,

0263

부 전 지

19

수 신 Lee

제 목

CONFIDENTIAL

관계부처
협 조 처
전화번호 주부

the farmer grows hops; sells the hops to a wholesaler who in turn sells them to the brewer, business tax would be levied on the sale of the hops by the farmer to the wholesaler and on the sale of the hops to the brewer. Likewise, the tax would be imposed on the sale of each component part of the beer from the original producers to the brewer.

발 신

승인양식 1—24 (1112-040-032-23) (130mm×190mm 32절지)

0264

be assessed when the hops were sold XXXXXX by the farmer to the wholesaler, a monetary transaction was involved on the part of when the wholesaler sold the hops to the brewer and when each producer or XXXXXXX middleman involved in the transmission of raw materials to the brewer. xxxxxxxxxxxxxxxxxxxxxxxxxx Mr. Shin said that, according to the U.S. draft of the article under discussion, the taxes at all of these XXX levels should be exempted if the beer went for the "ultimate use" of the U.S. forces.

12. Mr. Habib said the U.S. side recognized these problems, and that it was not the intention of the U.S. side to seek exemption of taxes which did not constitute a readily identifiable element of the cost of an item procured for "ultimate use".

13. Mr. Shin said that, where it was demonstrable that an item had been procured for the "ultimate use" of the U.S. forces, the Korean authorities would be forced, under the terms of the U.S. draft of the local procurement article, to exempt taxes levied at as many stages of the production of that article as the U.S. authorities wished to identify. Mr. Shin said that problems of the sort which he had been discussing did not arise in the case of the exemption of commodity and petroleum taxes, and that these taxes were readily identifiable at the point of "ultimate use".

0265

14. Mr. Habib asked if the Korean side would agree that, in the case of the contractor which he had outlined earlier, the contractor should be exempt from the payment of electricity and gas taxes.

15. Mr. Shin said that, in the case cited there would, in the case of business tax, be three stages at which the tax would be levied: (a) when the manufacturer of materials for the project purchased his own raw materials; (b) when the manufacturer sold his processed materials to the contractor; and (c) when the contractor sold his finished project to the U.S. forces. Mr. Shin said that the Korean side would agree that an exemption from business tax should be granted only at stage (c).

16. Mr. Habib said that it would not be the intention of the U.S. forces under the terms of the U.S. draft article to trace back the taxes upon intermediate stages in the production of articles manufactured for their "ultimate use" and claim exemptions from these taxes. He urged the Korean side to read the U.S. draft article in correlation with the U.S. draft agreed minutes, and to note that agreed minute 3 (a) provided that the U.S. forces would take delivery of items directly from the manufacturer, and certify exemptions from Korean taxation only at that point.

0266

17. Mr. Shin asked a hypothetical question: would the U.S. forces, under the terms of the U.S. draft article, issue a certificate of exemption from business tax to a wholesale dealer in cement if they purchased cement from such a dealer? Would the U.S. forces also seek to secure exemption of the business tax levied upon the sale of the cement in question to the dealer by the Korean manufacturer of the cement?

18. Mr. Habib replied that the U.S. Forces would take delivery of the cement directly from the manufacturer.

19. Mr. Shin said that, in view of the preceding discussion, the U.S. side might find that it could agree with the provisions of the Korean draft article on local procurement, which exempts items procured for "ultimate use" from commodity and petroleum tax.

20. Mr. Habib said that the preceding discussion had clarified for the U.S. the points of the U.S. draft on which the Korean side had reservations, and that the U.S. would see if there might not be ways in which the intent of that draft might be better expressed. He noted that the U.S. draft agreed minutes were the same as those attached to the Status of Forces Agreement with the procedures outlined in these

0267

--11--

Agreed Minutes had worked well in Japan. ~~Mr. Habib said that~~ The U.S. side would ~~might~~ be able at some future time to explain in detail how the problems connected with the implementation of the procedures in the Agreed minute had been solved in Japan.

21. It was agreed that, with respect to the other outstanding differences ~~disagreements~~ concerning ~~with respect to~~ the wording of the Agreed Minutes to the local procurement ~~procurement~~ article, the U.S. side agreed in principle with the Korean side's suggested changes in wording, subject to later confirmation. ~~and would seek approval from the United States Government for the suggested changes.~~ The two suggested changes in the U.S. draft Agreed Minutes are: (a) in Agreed Minute No. 2, the substitution of "representative" for "persons"; and (b) in Agreed Minute No. 3, the substitution of "representative" for "agent".

0267-1

Foreign Exchange Control

22. Mr. Sin noted that the article on foreign exchange control had been agreed, and that there remained only two differences of view concerning the wording of the Agreed Minute to the article. The first of these differences of view was part of the general disagreement over the proper term to use for the description of non-appropriated fund entities. It was agreed between the U.S. and Korean sides that a resolution of this difficulty would be sought when the article concerning these entities was again discussed. The second of the differences of view, Mr. Sin said, had to do with the wording of the last sentence of the Agreed Minute and concerned the proper discription of the rate of exchange. Mr. Sin said that the Korean position upon this point had not changed since the 17th negotiating session on March 19, 1963, and the Korean side still preferred its formulation of "the effective official exchange rate" to the U.S. formulation of "the highest rate...not unlawful". Mr. Sin noted that it had been agreed at the 17th session to have this difference of view resolved in an informal working party composed of Mr. Chae Sul, Chief of the Foreign Exchange Section of the Ministry of Finance and Mr. William Ford of the U.S.

negotiating team, but that this working party had apparently not met.

23. Mr. Habib asked Mr. Ford to state the U.S. side's position upon the question of the differing formulations of the language describing the rate of exchange. Mr. Ford reviewed the differences in draft language on this point, and said that previous discussion had shown the language proposed by the Korean side is ambiguous and subject to many interpretations. These differences in interpretation could lead to disputes in the future which should be avoided by foresight in the present negotiations. Mr. Ford said that he would like to inquire of the Korean side if the "effective official rate" is at present: won 125, won 130 (won 125 plus the certificate of won 5), won 129.5, or won 130.5 (the current selling rate).

24. Mr. Ford said that under the terms of the U.S. draft of the last sentence of the Agreed Minute no difficulty in interpretation exists. The wording suggested by the U.S. side is already incorporated in a major agreement between Korea and the United States, and for nearly two and one-half years has governed transactions running into many millions of dollars. Mr. Ford said that it would be a mistake to abandon this clear and unequivocal wording

which has already proved to be satisfactory, in favor of the language proposed by the Korea side which would be open to many interpretations and give the two governments trouble in the future. Mr. Ford said that differing terminology upon the rate of exchange in the status of forces agreement and the aid agreement would open up the possibility that two agencies of the U.S. Government might be purchasing won at different rates of exchange. Mr. Ford said that standard language in the two agreements would preclude such a situation, the consequences of which would be serious for both sides.

25. Mr. Sin said that the arguments which Mr. Ford had just advanced were the same as those made by the U.S. side at the 17th negotiating session, and that he again proposed that the difference in wording be resolved by a working party made up of Mr. Yi and Mr. Ford.

26. Mr. Habib agreed with Mr. Sin's suggestion that Mr. Ford and Mr. Yi meet together, but asked Mr. Sin to have Mr. Ford's question concerning the current "effective official rate of exchange" answered by the Korean side.

27. Mr. Sin asked Mr. Chung of the Ministry of Finance to answer the question put by Mr. Ford. Mr. Chung said that the present "effective official

0270

rate of exchange" for the won ~~xxx~~ is won 129.5 per U.S. dollar. He said that the "basic rate of exchange" for the won is now won 130 per U.S. dollar.

28. It was agreed that Mr. Ford and Mr. ~~Yi~~ Lee Chae-sul would meet in an effort to ~~resolve~~ discuss the differences in view concerning the wording of the last sentence of the ~~xgx~~ Agreed Minute.

29. It was agreed that the next negotiating session would be held on August 8, 1963, at 2:00 P.M.

****

0271

JOINT SUMMARY RECORD OF THE 27TH SESSION

August 2, 1963

I. Time and Place : 2:00 to 3:30 p.m. July 25, 1963 at the Foreign Minister's Conference Room

II. Attendants :

ROK Side:

Mr. Shin, Kwan Sup	Director Bureau of Customs Duty Ministry of Finance
Mr. Koo, Choong Whay	Chief, America Section Ministry of Foreign Affairs
Mr. Shin, Jung Sup	Chief, Treaty Section Ministry of Foreign Affairs
Col. Lee, Nam Koo	Chief, Military Affairs Section Ministry of National Defense
Mr. Chu, Mun Ki	Chief, Legal Affairs Section Ministry of Justice
Mr. Lee, Kyung Hoon	2nd Secretary Ministry of Foreign Affairs
Mr. Kang, Suk Jae	2nd Secretary Ministry of Foreign Affairs
Mr. Cho, Kwang Je	2nd Secretary Ministry of Foreign Affairs
Mr. Chung, In Young	Observer Ministry of Finance

U.S. Side :

Mr. Philip C. Habib	Counselor of the Embassy for Political Affairs
Col. G.G. O'Connor	Deputy Chief of Staff 8th Army
Col. Howard Smigelow	Deputy Chief of Staff UNC
Mr. William J. Ford	First Secretary of the Embassy
Capt. R.M. Brownlie	Assistant Chief of Staff USN/K

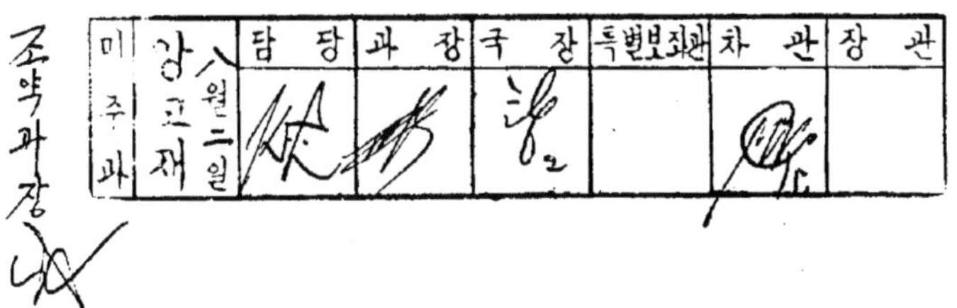

0272

Col. L.J. Fuller	Staff Judge Advocate United Nations Command
Mr. Rodney Armstrong	Economic Officer, American Embassy
Lt. Col. W.A. Burt	J-5
Major Robert D. Peckham	Staff Officer, JAG 8th Army

1. Mr. Shin Kwan Sup opened the meeting by introducing Mr. CHUNG In-young, of the Foreign Exchange Division of the Ministry of Finance, who was to be present of the Korean side as an observer of the discussion on the subject of foreign exchange controls. Mr. Habib noted that Mr. Rodney Armstrong would replace Mr. Benjamin Fleck as repporteur and press officer for the U.S. negotiating team during the latter's absence from Korea on home leave.

Health and Sanitation

2. Opening substantive discussion, Mr. Shin turned to the subject of health and sanitation. Mr. Shin said that there had been extensive and detailed discussion of the U.S. draft article on the subject of health and sanitation at the last negotiating session, and the Korean side believed that they now understood the U.S. position on the subject. Mr. Shin said that he wished to emphasize the provision of the draft U.S. article which provides that the two parties to the agreement will consult on matters in the fields of health and sanitation in the Joint Committee, where due consideration and respect would be given to the medical laws and regulations of the Republic of Korea. Mr. Shin said that he wished to emphasize that in all matters in this area the laws and regulations of the Republic of Korea should be taken into account.and duly respected. Mr. Shin said

0273

that, with this preliminary statement, he wished to agree to the U.S. draft article on behalf of the Korean side.

3. Mr. Habib said that it was his understanding that Mr.Shin had just offered an interpretation of the U.S. draft article to the effect that the Joint Committee, during the course of its consulatations on the subjects of health and sanitation, would take into account Korean laws and regulations. Mr. Habib said that it was obvious that this would happen. He wished to reiterate that the U.S. draft article on health and sanitation merely sets forth broad principles for mutual coordination and cooperation between the U.S. and Korean authorities concerned with these matters, and leaves the detailed implementation of these principles to the Joint Committee. It is the intention of the U.S. that the Joint Committee take into account the laws and regulations of the Republic of Korea relevant to medical matters in the course of consulatations on the subjects of health and sanitation. Mr. Habib said that the negotiating record would now show the above exchange between Mr. Shin and himself and thus set forth the principles which should guide the Joint Committee in its consultations on the subjects of health and sanitation.

4. Mr. Shin said that Mr. Habib's statement that the record of the meeting would provide guidance to the Joint Committee with respect to its concultations on the subject of health and sanitation was significent and welcome.

5. Mr. Habib said that he wished to point out again that nothing in the U.S. draft article on health and sanitation obligated the U.S. medical authorities to provide any particular medical services. The article merely provides that the past history of mutual ROK-US cooperation in these matters is recognized and will be regularized. Mr. Habib said that one of the early topics for consultation im the Joint Committee should be the relationship of Republic of Korea Law No. 1035, promulgated March 20,1962,

0274

to the services currently being provided to Koreans by U.S. medical authorities. Under that Law, which deals with the licensing of medical practitioners in Korea, U.S. personnel are not liscensed to provide medical services in Korea. One of the tasks of the Joint Committee would be to regularize the provision of medical services to Koreans by U.S. medical authorities, taking into account the provisions of the law he had just cited.

6. Mr. Shin said that matters concerning the provision of medical services to Koreans by U.S. medical authorities had been coordinated with the Korean Government in the past, and that the work of the Joint Committee would be to carry forward this coordination into the future with due respect for Korean Laws and regulations pertaining to medical services.

7. Mr. Habib agreed with Mr. Shin's statement, and stated that the article could now be regarded as agreed.

Local Procurement

8. Turning to the draft article and agreed minutes concerning local procurement, Mr. Shin said that the Korean side desired to continue the discussion of the previous meeting with respect to the exemption from taxation of materials, supplies, equipment and services procured for the "ultimate use" of the U.S. armed forces. Mr. Shin said that at the previous discussion of this subject the Korean side had noted its objections to granting exemption from electricity and gas tax to items procured for the "ultimate use" of the U.S. forces. He said that at the present meeting the Korean side wished to mention also its objections to the granting of exemptions from the traffic and business taxes to items procured for "ultimate use", and to outline the arguments in favor of separating the exemptions for items procured directly and for items procured for "ultimate use", as is done in the Korean draft

0275

of the local procurement article.

9. Mr. Habib said that it was not the U.S. side's intention, in providing for the same exemptions for items procured directly and for those procured for "ultimate use", to seek the exemption of taxes which did not constitute a readily identifiable portion of the cost of the article. He said that the U.S. side's contention was simply that where taxes constituted a readily identifiable portion of the cost of an item, as they often did in the case of items procured in bulk for the ultimate use of the U.S. forces, they should be exempted. The U.S. draft article should be read in close correlation with the U.S. draft agreed minute 3 (a), which was then read aloud. Mr. Habib said that this agreed minute provided a detailed explanation of the certification process by which items for "ultimate use" would be exempted from taxation, and that certification process depended upon the taxes involved being readily identifiable.

10. Mr. Habib said that it was not the intention of the U.S. side to create any of the problems for the Korean taxation authorities which seemed to figure in the Korean side's thinking upon these matters. Mr. Habib cited the example of a contractor serving exclusively for the U.S. forces builds a structure of a U.S. facility under the terms of a contract with the U.S. forces. Obviously, Mr. Habib said, the electricity and gas being utilized on such a project can be metered, and should be exempted from Korean taxes. Mr. Habib said that, on the other hand, there would be cases where the amounts of electricity and gas going into the manufacture of a product for the "ultimate use" of the U.S. forces would not be readily identifiable and the U.S. would not request a waver; such would be the case with the brewing of beer by a brewer who sold only part of his output to the U.S. Forces. Mr. Habib said that the effect of the Korean draft article on local procurement would

0276

be to negate the principle of exemption from Korean taxes, of materials purchased locally and to penalize the U.S. Forces for their local procurement.

11. Mr. Shin said that implementation of the procedure provided for in agreed minute 3 (a) may be feasible on the U.S. side, but that it seemed to be difficult from the point of view of Korean tax administration. Mr. Shin said that, for example, according to Korean law, business tax should be levied at all stages of production and manufacture, whenever a sale of intermediate products was involved. Thus, in the case of the brewing of beer, the farmer grows hops; sells the hops to a wholesaler who in turn sells them to the brewer, business tax would be levied on the sale of the hops by the farmer to the wholesaler and on the sale of the hops to the brewer. Likewise, the tax would be imposed on the sale of each component part of the beer from the original producers to the brewer. Mr. Shin said that, according to the U.S. draft of the article under discussion, the taxes at all of these levels should be exempted if the beer went for the "ultimate use" of the U.S. forces.

12. Mr. Habib said the U.S. side recognized these problems, and that it was not the intention of the U.S. side to seek exemption of taxes which did not constitute a readily identifiable element of the cost of an item procured for "ultimate use".

13. Mr. Shin said that, where it was demonstrable that an item had been procured for the "ultimate use" of the U.S. forces, the Korean authorities would be forced, under the terms of the U.S. draft of the local procurement article, to exempt taxes levied at as many stages of the production of that article as the U.S. authorities wished to identify. Mr. Shin said that problems of the sort which he had been discussing did not arise in the case

of the exemption of commodity and petroleum taxes, and that these taxes were readily identifiable at the point of "ultimate use".

14. Mr. Habib asked if the Korean side would agree that, in the case of the contractor which he had outlined earlier, the contractor should be exempt from the payment of electricity and gas tax.

15. Mr. Shin said that, in the case cited there would, in the case of business tax, be three stages at which the tax would be levied: (a) when the manufacturer of materials for the project purchased his own raw materials; (b) when the manufacturer sold his processed materials to the contractor; and (c) when the contractor sold his finished project to the U.S. forces. Mr. Shin said that the Korean side would agree that an exemption from business tax should be granted only at stage (c).

16. Mr. Habib said that it would not be the intention of the U.S. forces under the terms of the U.S. draft article to trace back the taxes upon intermediate stages in the production of articles manufactured for their "ultimate use" and claim exemptions from these taxes. He urged the Korean side to read the U.S. draft article in correlation with the U.S. draft agreed minutes, and to note that agreed minute 3 (a) provided that the U.S. forces would take delivery of items directly from the manufacturer, and certify exemptions from Korean taxation only at that point.

17. Mr. Shin asked a hypothetical question; would the U.S. forces, under the terms of the U.S. draft article, issue a certificate of exemption from business tax to a wholesale dealer in cement if they purchased cement from such a dealer? Would the U.S. forces also seek to secure exemption of the business tax levied upon the sale of the cement in question to the dealer by the Korean manufacturer of the cement?

0278

18. Mr. Habib replied that the U.S. Forces would take delivery of the cement directly from the manufacturer.

19. Mr. Shin said that, in view of the preceding discussion, the U.S. side might find that it could agree with the provisions of the Korean draft article on local procurement, which exempts items procured for "ultimate use" from commodity and petroleum tax.

20. Mr. Habib said that the preceding discussion had clarified for the U.S. the points of the U.S. draft on which the Korean side had reservations, and that the U.S. would see if there might not be ways in which the intent of that draft might be better expressed. He noted that the U.S. draft agreed minutes were the same as those attached to the Status of Forces Agreement with Japan, and that the procedures outlined in these agreed minutes had worked well in Japan. The U.S. side would be able at some future time to explain in detail how problems connected with the implementation of the procedures in the agreed minute had been solved in Japan.

21. It was agreed that, with respect to the other outstanding differences concerning the wording of the agreed minutes to the local procurement article, the U.S. side agreed in principle with the Korean side's suggested changes in wording, subject to later confirmation. The two suggested changes in the U.S. draft agreed minutes are: (a) in agreed minute No. 2, the substitution of "representative" for "persons"; and (b) in agreed minute No.3, the substitution of "representative" for "agent".

Foreign Exchange Control

22. Mr. Shin noted that the article on foreign exchange control had been ~~fully discussed~~ agreed, and that there remained only two differences of view concerning the wording of the agreed minute

0279

to the article. The first of these differences of view was part of the general disagreement over the proper term to use for the description of non-appropriated fund entities. It was agreed between the U.S. and Korean sides that a resolution of this difficulty would be sought when the article concerning these entities was again discussed. The second of the differences of view, Mr. Shin said, had to do with the wording of the last sentence of the agreed minute and concerned the proper description of the rate of exchange. Mr. Shin said that the Korean position upon this point had not changed since the 17th negotiating session on March 19, 1963, and the Korean side still preferred its formulation of "the highest rate.... not unlawful". Mr. Shin noted that it had been agreed at the 17th session to attempt to have this difference of view resolved in an informal working party composed of Mr. Lee Chae Sul, Chief of the Foreign Exchange Division of the Ministry of Finance and Mr. William Ford of the U.S. negotiating team, but that this working party had apparently not met.

23. Mr. Habib asked Mr. Ford to State the U.S. side's position upon the question of the differing formulations of the language describing the rate of exchange. Mr. Ford reviewed the differences in draft language on this point, and said that previous discussion had shown that the language proposed by the Korean side is ambiguous and subject to many interpretations. These differences in interpretation could lead to disputes in the future which should be avoided by foresight in the present negotiations. Mr. Ford said that he would like to inquire of the Korean side if the "effective official rate" is at present: won 125, won 130 (won 125 plus the certificate of won 5), won 129.5, or won 130.5 (the current selling rate).

24. Mr. Ford said that under the terms of the U.S. draft

of the last sentence of the agreed minute no difficulty in interpretation exists. The wording suggested by the U.S. side is already incorporated in a major agreement between Korea and the United States, and for nearly two and one-half years has governed transactions running into many millions of dollars. Mr. Ford said that it would be a mistake to abandon this clear and unequivocal wording which has already proved to be satisfactory, in favor of the language proposed by the Korea side which would be open to many interpretations and give the two governments trouble in the future. Mr. Ford said that differing terminolgy upon the rate of exchange in the status of forces agreement and comprehensive aid agreement would open up the possibility that two agencies of the U.S. Government might be purchasing won at different rates of exchange. Mr. Ford said that standard language in the two agreements would preclude such a situation, the consequences of which would be serious for both sides.

25. Mr. Shin said that the arguments which Mr. Ford had just advanced were the same as those made by the U.S. side at the 17th negotiating session, and that he again proposed that the difference in wording be discussed by a working party made up of Mr. Lee and Mr. Ford.

26. Mr. Habib agreed with Mr. Shin's suggestion that Mr. Ford and Mr. Lee meet together, but asked to have Mr. Ford's question concerning the current "effective official rate of exchange" answered by the Korean side.

27. Mr. Chung of the Ministry of Finance said that the present "effective official rate of exchange" for the won is won 129.5 per U.S. dollar. He said that the "basic rate of exchange" for the won is now won 130 per U.S. dollar.

28. It was agreed that Mr. Ford and Mr. Lee Chae-sul would meet in an effort to discuss the differences in view concerning

0281

the wording of the last sentence of the Agreed Minute.

29. It was agreed that the next negotiating session would be held on August 8, at 2:00 P.M.

****

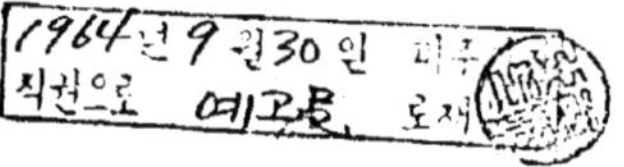

0282

정/리/보/존/문/서/목/록					
기록물종류	문서-일반공문서철	등록번호	917 9590	등록일자	2006-07-27
분류번호	741.12	국가코드	US	주제	
문서철명	한.미국 간의 상호방위조약 제4조에 의한 시설과 구역 및 한국에서의 미국군대의 지위에 관한 협정 (SOFA) 전59권. 1966.7.9 서울에서 서명 : 1967.2.9 발효 (조약 232호) *원본				
생산과	미주과/조약과	생산년도	1952 - 1967	보존기간	영구
담당과(그룹)	조약	조약	서가번호	--	
참조분류					
권차명	V.19 실무교섭회의, 제28-31차, 1963.8-9월				
내용목차	1. 제28차 회의, 8.8 (p.2~57) 2. 제29차 회의, 8.22 (p.58~113) 3. 제30차 회의, 9.5 (p.114~186) 4. 제31차 회의, 9.20 (p.187~229) * 일지 : 1953.8.7 이승만 대통령-Dulles 미국 국무장관 공동성명 - 상호방위조약 발효 후 군대지위협정 교섭 약속 1954.12.2 정부, 주한 UN군의 관세업무협정 체결 제의 1955.1월, 5월 미국, 제의 거절 1955.4.28 정부, 군대지위협정 제의 (한국측 초안 제시) 1957.9.10 Hurter 미국 국무차관 방한 시 각서 수교 (한국측 제의 수락 요구) 1957.11.13, 26 정부, 개별 협정의 단계적 체결 제의 1958.9.18 Dawling 주한미국대사, 형사재판관할권 협정 제외 조건으로 행정협정 체결 의사 전달 1960.3.10 정부, 토지, 시설협정의 우선적 체결 강력 요구 1961.4.10 장면 국무총리-McConaughy 주한미국대사 공동성명으로 교섭 개시 합의 1961.4.15, 4.25 제1, 2차 한.미국 교섭회의 (서울) 1962.3.12 정부, 교섭 재개 촉구 공한 송부 1962.5.14 Burger 주한미국대사, 최규하 장관 면담 시 형사재판관할권 문제 제기 않는 조건으로 교섭 재개 통고 1962.9.6 한.미국 간 공동성명 발표 (9월 중 교섭 재개 합의) 1962.9.20~1965.6.7 제1-81차 실무 교섭회의 (서울) 1966.7.8 제82차 실무 교섭회의 (서울) 1966.7.9 서명 1967.2.9 발효 (조약 232호)					

마/이/크/로/필/름/사/항				
촬영연도	*롤 번호	화일 번호	후레임 번호	보관함 번호
2006-11-22	I-06-0068	04	1-229	

0001

1. 제28차 회의, 8.8

0002

김, 효

협 조 전	응 신 기 일 1963. 8.6

문서번호 외정미 320 제 목 주둔군지위협정체결에 관한 문의

수 신: 조약과장 발 신: 미주과장 년 월 일 63.8.5 제1의견

1963 년 8월 8일에 개최될 제 28차 주둔군 지위협정체결 교섭회의에서는 관세 업무 및 외환관리문제가 토의되고 청구권 문제에 관한 초안이 교환될 것으로 예상되오니 동 문제에 관한 귀과의 안과 견해를 제시하여 주시기 바랍니다. 끝

미 주 과 장 구 충 회

0003

승인양식 1 — 34 11—13330—01 (195mm×265mm16절지)

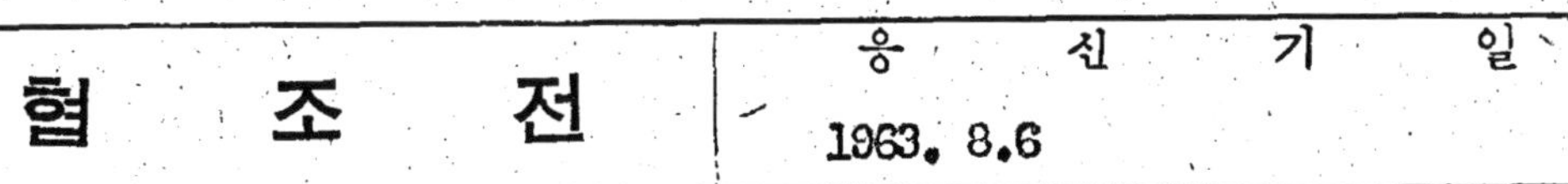

협 조 전	송 신 기 일 1963. 8.6

문서번호 외정미 340　　제 목 주둔군지위협정체결에 관한 문의

수 신: 조약과장　발 신: 미주과장　년 월 일 63.8.5　제1의견

1963년 8월 8일에 개최될 제 28차 주둔군 지위협정체결 교섭회의에서는 관세 업무 및 외환관리문제가 토의되고 청구권 문제에 관한 초안이 교환될 것으로 예상되오니 동 문제에 관한 귀과의 안과 견해를 제시하여 주시기 바랍니다. 끝

미 주 과 장　　구　충　회

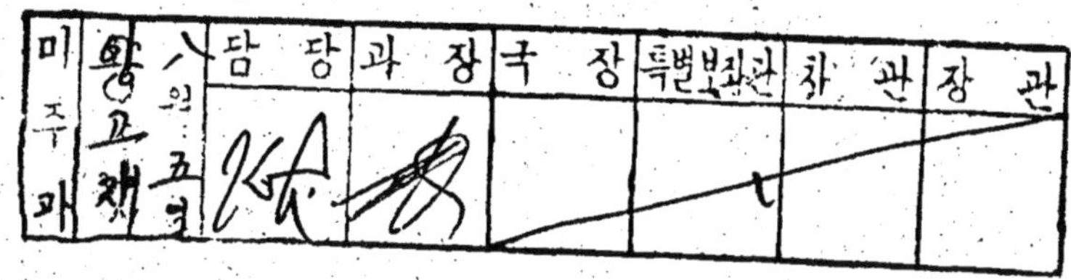

미주과	황고채	의견	담 당	과 장	국 장	특별보좌관	차 관	장 관

승인양식 1 — 34　11—13330—01　(195mm×265mm16절지)

0004

협 조 전	응 신 기 일
문서번호 방조 77	제 목 주둔군 지위협정안에 관한 의견

수 신 : 미주과장 발 신 : 조약과장 년 월 일 63.8.5. 제 1 의 견

외정미 340 으로 요청하신 한미 주둔군 지위 협정의 관세 업무 및 외환 관리 문제에 관한 당과의 초안과 견해는 관계 부처의 의견을 참작하여 당과에서 작성 발행한 "미 합중국 군대의 지위에 관한 대한 민국 정부와 미 합중국 정부 간의 협정 초안 및 설명서"(조약 집무 자료 62/2)에 수록된 내용과 다른 바 없으며, 다만 변동되는 사태에 대처하기 위하여 법무부, 재무부등 관계 부처의 의견을 다시 징함이 좋으리라 사료함을 알립니다. 끝

조 약 과 장 신 정 섭

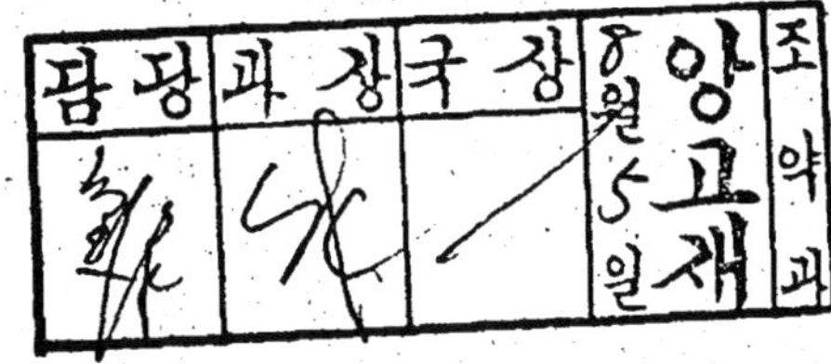

승인서식 1—34 (11—13330—01) (195mm×265mm16절지)

0005

협 조 전	응 신 기 일
문서번호 방조 77	제 목 주둔군 지위협정안에 관한 의견

수 신: 미주과장 발 신: 조약과장 년 월 일 63.8.5. 제 1 의 견

의정미 340으로 요청하신 한미 주둔군 지위 협정의 관세 업무 및 의료 관리 문제에 관한 당과의 초안과 건에는 관계 부처의 의견을 참작하여 당과에서 작성 발행한 "미 합중국 군대의 지위에 관한 대한 민국 정부와 미 합중국 정부간의 협정 초안 및 설명서"(조약 집무 자료 62/2)에 수록된 내용과 다른 바 없으며, 다만 변동되는 사태에 대처하기 위하여 법무부, 재무부등 관계 부처의 의견을 다시 징함이 좋으리라 사료함을 알립니다. 끝

신정섭

조 약 과 장 신 정 섭

승인서식 1—34 (11—13330—01) (195mm×265mm16절지)

0006 이경훈

기 안 용 지

자체 통제		기안처	미주과 이경훈	전화번호	근거서류접수일자

과장	국장	보좌관	차관	장관
(서명)	(서명) 8		(서명) 8	(서명)

관계관 서명	조약과장 (서명)						
기안 년월일	1963.8.7	시행 년월일		보존 년한		정서	기장
분류 기호	외정미	전체 통제		종결			
경유 수신 참조	건의		발신				
제목	제28차 주둔군지위협정 체결 교섭회의에 임할 우리측 입장						

8.8 에 개최될 28 차 주둔군지위협정 체결한미간 교섭회의에서는 군계약자 그리고 차량 및 운전면허에 관한 문제를 토의하고 민사청구권 문제에 관한 초안을 교환할 예정이온바, 이에 관련하여 우리측 교섭 실무자는 8.6 회합을 갖고 제 28 차 회의에서 취할 우리측 태도를 별첨과 같이 결정하였아오니 재가하여 주시기 바랍니다.

유첨: 제 28 차 주둔군지위협정 체결교섭회의에 임할 우리측 태도, 끝.

1966,12,31에 예고문에 의거 일반문서로 재분류됨

보통문서로 재분류(1966. 12. 31.)

1964년 9월 30일 직권으로 예고문 미주과장

승인양식 1-1-3 (1112-040-016-018) (190mm×260mm16절지)

0007

1. 군계약자

(1) 군계약자의 한국법에 대한 복속원칙에 관한 미국측 초안 1 항 (이는 우리측 초안 1항에 해당함)에 있어서 동 미국측 초안은 한국측 초안에 삽입되어 있는 "organized under the laws of the United States " 라는 구절과 "who are ordinarily resident in the United States " 라는 용어를 삭제하고 있는데 이는 미국측이 군계약을 체결할수 있는 사람이나 또는 그가 채용할 고용원을 미국인에 국한 시키지 않고 제 3 국인에 까지 확대시키기 위한 규정인바, 우리측은 동 구절들의 삽입을 계속 주장한다.

(2) 군계약자의 지정 및 지정철회에 관한 미국측 초안 제 2 항 (이는 우리측 초안 제 2 항에 해당함)은 우리측 초안과 실질적인 차이가 없으므로 미국측안을 수락하되 "consultation" 이라는 용어의 해석에 있어서는 대한민국 정부의 견해가 상당히 반영된다는 "협의"로서 해석된다는 양해사항을 공동 회의록에 남겨 두도록 한다.

(3) 군계약자가 향유할 이익에 관한 미국측 초안 제 3 항(이는 우리측 초안 제 3 항에 해당함)에 있어서 (가) 3(a) 및 3 (e) 항에 있어서 권리(rights)라고 규정하고 있는데 동 "권리"라는 용어는 이를 삭제토록 하자고 주장하고 (나) 3 (h) 및 3 (i) 항은 우리측 초안대로 삭제하자고 주장 한다.

(4) 증가 상구 재산에 대한 면세규정에 관한 미국측 초안 제 5 항은 이를 수락토록 한다.

(5) 군계약자에 대한 재산의 보유, 사용 및 이전에 관련한 조세 면제 규정에 관한 미국측 초안 제 6 항 (이는 우리측 초안 제5항에 해당함)에 있어서 "other business " 라는 용어는 "other business than those executing such contracts

0008

우리측 안에서 말하는 바와 같이 " other business than those executing contracts as described in paragraph 1 of this Article in the Republic of Korea " 로 대치토록 하자고 계속 주장한다.

(6) 소득세 및 법인세에 관한 미국측 초안 제 7항(이는 우리측 초안 제 6 항에 해당함)에 있어서 우리측은 우리측이 제시한 수정안을 미국측이 수락토록 계속 주장한다.

(7) 군계약자에 대한 재판관할권에 관한 규정인 우리측 초안 제7항은 미국측 초안에는 규정되어 있지 않으나 우리측은 우리측 안의 수락을 주장한다.

(8) 미국측이 제시한 합의의사록에 있어서, 우리측은 동 합의의사록의 끝에 "except paragraph 7" 이라는 용어를 삽입토록 주장한다.

2. 차량 및 운전면허

(1) 사유차량의 표식에 관한 규정에 있어서 미국측은 그의 초안 제 3 항에서 미국군대 구성원, 군속 및 그들의 가족의 개인용 차량은 미국에 의하여 부여되는 표식을 사용토록 하는 것등을 규정한데 반하여 우리측은 우리측 초안 2(b)항에서 이들의 개인용 차량은 한국이 부여한 표식을 사용토록 규정하고 있는바, 우리측은 우리측 안의 수락을 주장한다.

3. 민사 청구권

(1) 우리측은 청구권포기, 국유재산의 손해에 대한 청구, 국유선박의 정의, 군인의 부상 및 사망시의 청구, 제 3 자에 가한 손해에 대한 청구권관할, 비공무중의 불법행위로 인한 손해에 대한 청구, 군용차량의 허가 없이 사용한데서 발생하는 손해에 대한 청구, 공무, 비공무중에 관한 판단, 민사 청구권의 관할에 관한 일반원칙, 계약상의 분쟁, 비전투시의 청구권 등을 내용으로 하는 별첨과 같은 안을 제시한다.

(2) 미국측이 제시하는 안이 우리측안과 비등할 때에는 우리측안의 수락을 요구한다.

보통문서로 재분류 (1966. 12.31.)

0009

196 . . . 의거 일반문서로 재분류됨

ARTICLE

1. Each Party waives all its claims against the other party for damage to any property owned by it and used by its armed services, if such damage--
   (a) was caused by a member or an employee of the armed services of the other Party, in the execution of his official duties; or
   (b) arose from the use of any vehicle, vessel or aircraft owned by the other Party and used by its armed services, provided either that the vehicle, vessel or aircraft causing the damage was being used in the execution of its official duty or that the damage was caused to property being so used.

   Claims for maritime salvage by one Party against the other Party shall be waived, provided that the vessel or cargo salved was owned by the other Party and being used by its armed services for official purposes.

2. (a) In the case of damage caused or arising as stated in paragraph 1 to other property owned by either Party and located in the Republic of Korea, the issue of liability o of the other Party shall be determined and the amount of damage shall be assessed, unless the two Governments agree otherwise, by a sole arbitrator selected in accordance with subparagraph (b) of this paragraph. The arbitrator shall also decide any counter-claims arising out of the same incident.

0010

(b) The arbitrator referred to in subparagraph (a) above shall be selected by agreement between the two Governments from amongst the nationals of the Republic of Korea who hold or have held high judicial office.

(c) Any decision taken by the arbitrator shall be binding and conclusive upon the Parties.

(d) The amount of any compensation awarded by the arbitrator shall be distributed in accordance with the provisions of paragraph 5 (e)(i),(ii) and (iii) of this Article.

(e) The compensation of the arbitrator shall be fixed by agreement between the two Governments and shall, together with the necessary expenses incidental to the performance of his duties, be defrayed in equal propertions by them.

(f) Each Party waives its claim in any such case up to the amount equivalent to 800 United States dollars or 104,000won. In the case of considerable variation in the rate of exchange between these currencies the two Governments shall agree on the appropriate adjustments of these amounts.

3. For the purpose of paragraph 1 and 2 of this Article the expression "owned by a Party" in the case of a vessel includes a vessel on bare boat charter to that Party or requisitioned by it on bare boat terms or seized by it in

0011

prize (except to the extent that the risk of loss or liability is borne by some person other than such Party).

4. Each Party waives all its claims against the other Party for injury or death suffered by any member of its armed services while such member was engaged in the performance of his official duties.

5. Claims (other than contractual claims and those to which paragraph 6 or 7 of this Article apply) arising out of acts or omissions of members or employees of the United States armed forces, including those employees who are nationals of or ordinarily resident in the Republic of Korea, done in the performance of official duty, or out of any other act, omission or occurence for which the United States armed forces are legally responsible, and causing damage in the Republic of Korea to third Parties, other than the Government of the Republic of Korea, shall dealt with with by the Republic of Korea in accordance with the following provisions:

(a) Claims shall be filed, considered and settled or adjudicated in accordance with the laws and regulations of the Republic of Korea with respect to the claims arising from the activities of its own armed forces.

(b) The Republic of Korea may settle any such claims, and payment of the amount agreed upon or determined by adjudication shall be made by the Republic of Korea in won.

0012

(c) Such payment, whether made pursuant to a settlement or to adjudication of the case by a competent tribunal of the Republic of Korea, or the final adjudication by such a tribunal denying payment, shall be binding and conclusive upon the Parties.

(d) Every claim paid by the Republic of Korea shall be communicated to the appropriate United States authorities together with full particulars and a proposed distribution in conformity with subparagraph (e)(i) and (ii) below.

In default of a reply within two months, the proposed distribution shall be regarded as accepted.

(e) The cost incurred in satisfying claims pursuant to the preceding subparagraph and paragraph 2 of this Article shall be distributed between the Parties as follows:

(i) Where the United States alone is responsible, the amount awarded or adjudged shall be distributed in the proportion of 15 percent chargeable to the Republic of Korea and 85 per cent chargeable to the United States.

(ii) Where the Republic of Korea and the United States are responsible for the damage, the amount awarded or adjudged shall be distributed equally between them. Where the damage was caused by the armed forces of the Republic of Korea and the United States

0013

and it is not possible to attribute it specifically to one or both of those armed services, the amount awarded or adjudged shall be distributed equally between the Republic of Korea and the United States.

(iii) Every half-year, a statement of the sums paid by the Republic of Korea in the course of the half-yearly period in respect of every case regarding which the proposed distribution on a percentage basis has been accepted, shall be sent to the appropriate authorities of the United States, together with a request for reimbursement. Such reimbursement shall be made, in won, within the shortest possible time.

(f) Members or employees of the United States armed forces, excluding those employees who are nationals of or ordinarily resident in the Republic of Korea, shall not be subject to any proceedings for the enforcement any judgement given against them in the Republic of of Korea in a matter arising from the performance of their official duties.

(g) Except in so far as subparagraph (e) of this paragraph applies to claims covered by paragraph 2 of this Article, the provisions of this paragraph shall not apply to any claims arising out of or in connection with the navigation or operation of a ship or the loading, carriage, or discharge of a cargo, other than claims

0014

for death or personal injury to which paragraph 4 of this Article does not apply.

6. Claims against members or employees of the United States armed forces (except employees who are nationals of or ordinarily resident in the Republic of Korea) arising out of tortious acts or omissions in the Republic of Korea not done in the performance of official duty shall be dealt with in the following manner:

(a) The authorities of the Republic of Korea shall consider the claim and access compensation to the claimant in a fair and just manner, taking into account all the circumstances of the case, including the conduct of the injured person, and shall prepare a report on the matter.

(b) The report shall be delivered to the appropriate United States authorities, who shall then decide without delay whether they will offer an ex gratia payment, and if so, of what amount.

(c) If an offer of ex gratia payment is made, and accepted by the claimant in full satisfaction of his claim, the United States authorities shall make the payment themselves and inform the authorities of the Republic of Korea of their decision and of the sum paid.

(d) Nothing in this paragraph shall affect the jurisdiction of the courts of the Republic of Korea to entertain an action against a member or an employee of the United States armed forces unless and until there has been

0015

payment in full satisfaction of the claim.

7. Claims arising out of the unauthorized use of any vehicle of the United States forces shall be dealt with in accordance with paragraph 6 of this Article, except in so far as the United States forces are legally responsible.

8. If a dispute arises as to whether a tortious act or omission of a member or an employee of the United States armed forces was done in the performance of official duty or as to whether the use of any vehicle of the United States armed forces was unauthorized, the question shall be submitted to an arbitrator appointed in accordance with paragraph 2 (b) of this Article, whose decision on this point shall be final and conclusive.

9. (a) The United States shall not claim immunity from the jurisdiction of the courts of the Republic of Korea for members or employees of the United States armed forces in respect of the civil jurisdiction of the courts of the Republic of Korea except to the extent provided in paragraph 5 (f) of this Article.

(b) In case any private movable property, excluding that in use by the United States armed forces, which is subject to compulsory execution under the Korean law, is within the facilities and areas in use by the United States armed forces, the United States authorities shall, upon the request of the courts of the Republic of Korea, possess and turn over such property to the authorities of the Republic of Korea.

0016

(c) The authorities of the Republic of Korea and the United States shall cooperate in the procurement of evidence for a fair hearing and disposal of claims under this Article.

10. Disputes arising out of contracts concerning the procurement of materials, supplies, equipment, services by or for the United States armed forces, which are not resolved by the Parties to the contract concerned, may be submitted to the Joint Committee for conciliation, provided that the provisions of this paragraph shall not prejudice any right, which Parties to the contract may have, to file a civil suit.

11. Paragraphs 2 and 5 of this Article shall apply only to claims arising incident to non-combat activities.

보통문서로 재분류(1966.12.31.)

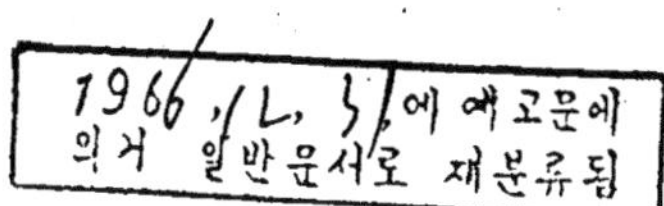

0017

기 안 용 지

자 체 통 제		기안처	미 주 과 이 경 훈	전화번호	근거서류접수일자
	과 장	국 장		차 관	장 관
관 계 관 서 명	조약과장				
기 안 년 월 일	1963.8.9	시 행 년 월 일		보존 년한	정 서 기 장
분 류 기 호	외정미 722.2	전 체 통 제	종결		
경 유 수 신 참 조	국가재건최고회의 의장 (참조 : 외무국방위원장) 내각수반		발 신	장 관	
제 목	주둔군지위 협정 체결을 위한 제28차 교섭회의 보고				

1963년 8월 8일 하오 2시부터 3시 40분까지 외무부장관 회의실에서 개최된 제 28 차 주둔군지위협정 체결 교섭회의에서 토의된 내용을 별첨과 같이 보고합니다.

유 첨 : 제 28 차 교섭회의 보고서 부, 끝.

1964년 9월 30일 미주과 직권으로 예고문 재

승인양식 1-1-3 (1112-040-016-018) (190mm×260mm16절지)

0050

제 28 차

한미간 주둔군 지위협정 체결실무자 회의

보 고 서

1. 일 시 : 1963년 8월 8일 하오 2시부터 3시 40분까지

2. 장 소 : 외무부 장관 회의실

3. 참석자 : 한국측 : 황 호 을 (외무부 정무국장)

구 충 회 (외무부 미주과장)

이 남 구 (국방부 군무과장)

주 문 기 (법무부 법무과장)

이 경 훈 (외무부 2등서기관)

강 석 재 (")

조 광 제 (")

미국측 : 교섭대표단 전원(바루이스씨 대표 불참)

4. 토의 사항

(1) 차량 및 운전면허 그리고 군계약자 문제를 순차적으로 토의하고 민사청구권 문제에 관한 조항을 교환함.

(2) 차량 및 운전면허 조항의 토의에 있어서 사유차량의 표식에 관한 규정에 관하여 미국측은 우리측이 주장한 미국군대 구성원, 군속 및 그들의 가족의 개인용 차량은 한국이 부여한 표식을 사용토록 하되 차량감찰을 이들에게 부여함에 있어서 수반되는 과세 등은 부과하지 않을 것이나 차량감찰의 실비만을 지불토록 우리측이 주장한 것과 비등한 수정안을 제시하였으므로 우리측은 이를 원측적으로 수락하여 주었음.

63-1-120

0019

13-1-20(10)

미국·을 108-10 (10)

0020

(3) 군계약자의 한국법에 대한 복속원측에 관한 규정에 있어서 우리측은 군계약자 및 이들이 채용할 고용원은 "통상 미국에 거주하는" 자료 하자고 주장한데 대하여 미국측은 제 3국인의 고용자도 필요하므로 우리측이 주장하는 "통상미국에 거주하는" 이라는 용어는 삭제하자고 주장하였으며 또한 우리측은 군계약자의 규제대상이 될 인원중 법인에 대해서는 "미국 법률하에서 조직된" 법인을 포함시키자고 주장한데 대하여 미국측은 제 3국 법인도 포함시켜야 하므로 우리측이 주장하는 "미국의 법률하에서 조직된" 이라는 구절은 삭제하자고 주장하여 이 문제는 다음에 다시 토의키로 함.

(4) 군계약자가 향유할 이익에 관한 규정에 있어서 미국측은 우리측이 주장한 것과 비등한 수정안을 제시하여 왔기 우리측은 이를 수락하여 주었으나 다만 운전면허 및 차량 등록 문제에 관하여 군계약자가 향유할 이익에 대하여는 검토후 다음에 다시 우리측 입장을 제시토록 하였음.

(5) 부동산의 과가 상구 재산에 대한 면세규정에 관한 미국측 안은 이를 수락해 주었으며 군계약자에 대한 재산의 소지, 사용 및 이전에 관련한 조세면제규정에 있어서는 우리측은 본항의 면세는 투자를 위하여 또는 "기타 사업"을 행하기 위하여 한국에 있어서 보유되는 재산 또는 한국에 있어서 등록된 무체재산에는 적용되지 않는다는 규정중 "기타 사업" 이라는 용어는 불명확한 것이니 좀더 구체적으로 "본조 제 1 항에서 기술한 대한민국내에서 이행중인 계약 이외의 기타사업"이라는 용어로 대치하자고 주장한데 대하여 미국측은 이를 고려해 보겠다고 하였음. 63-1-121

0021

63-1-20

미문 108-10

0022

(6) 소득세 및 법인세에 관한 규정에 있어서 미국측은 우리측이 제시한 수정안을 다시 검토하기로 하여 이 문제는 다음에 다시 토의키로 함.

(7) 합의 의사록에 있어서 미국측은 군계약자 조항은 군계약자가 미국군대 이외의 미국정부기관과 계약 할때에도 본 조항의 규정을 적용시키도록 하자고 주장한데 대하여 우리측은 소득세 및 법인세에 관한 규정을 제외한 군계약자 조항을 적용시키도록 하자고 주장하여 이 문제는 다음에 다시 토의키로 함.

(8) 양측은 민사청구권 문제에 관한 조문초안을 교환하고 이문제를 다음에 토의키로 함.

5. 기타 사항 :

(1) 차기회의일자 : 1963 년 8 월 22 일 하오 2 시

(2) 차기회의의제 : 차기회의까지 양측수석대표간에 합의된 사항

6. 참고 자료 :

미국측이 제의한 조문초안 (차량 및 운전면허에 관한 조문 제 3 항 수정안, 군계약자에 관한 조문 제 3 항 수정안, 그리고 민사청구권 조항) 별첨 참조.

63-1-132

0023

63-1-20

미오 108-10

0024

ARTICLE

3. The Government of the Republic of Korea will license and register those vehicles privately owned by members of the United States armed forces, the civilian component, or dependents. The names of the owners of such vehicles and such other pertinent information as is required by Korean law to effect the licensing and registration of such vehicles, shall be furnished to the Government of the Republic of Korea by officials of the United States Government through the Joint Committee. Except for the actual cost of the issuance of license plates, members of the United States armed forces, the civilian component, and their dependents shall be exempt from the payment of all fees and charges relating to the licensing, registration, or operation of vehicles in the Republic of Korea and, in accordance with the provisions of Article ____, from the payment of all taxes relating thereto. taxation

63-1-123

0025

0026

ARTICLE ______

3. Upon certification by appropriate United States authorities as to their identity, such persons shall be accorded the following benefits of this Agreement:

(a) Accession and movement, as provided for in Article ______, paragraph 2;

(b) Entry into Korea in accordance with the provisions of Article ______;

(c) The exemption from customs duties and other such charges provided for in Article ______, paragraph 3, for members of the United States armed forces, the civilian component, and their dependents;

(d) If authorized by the Government of the United States, the use of the services of the activities provided for in Article ______;

(e) Those provided in Article ______, paragraph 2, for members of the United States armed forces, the civilian component, and their dependents;

63-1-124

0027

63-1-20

미·올 108-10

0028

(f) If authorized by the Government of the United States, the use of military payment certificates, as provided in Article _______;

(g) The use of postal facilities provided for in Article ________;

(h) The use of utilities and services in accordance with those priorities, conditions, rates, or tariffs accorded the United States armed forces by Article _____, paragraph 3, relating to utilities and services;

(i) Those provided to members of the United States armed forces, the civilian component, and their dependents by Article _____, relating to driving permits and registration of vehicles;

(j) Exemption from the laws and regulations of Korea with respect to terms and conditions of employment, and licensing and registration of businesses and corporations.

63-1-175

0029

63-1-20

미.북 108-10

0030

ARTICLE ____

1. Each Party waives all its claims against the other Party for damage to any property owned by it and used by its land, sea or air armed forces, if such damage:

(a) was caused by a member or an employee of the armed forces of the other Party in the performance of his official duties; or

(b) arose from the use of any vehicle, vessel or aircraft owned by the other Party and used by its armed forces, provided either that the vehicle, vessel or aircraft causing the damage was being used for official purposes, or that the damage was caused to property being so used.

Claims by one Party against the other Party for maritime salvage shall be waived provided that the vessel or cargo salvaged was owned by a Party and being used by its armed forces for official purposes.

2. In the case of damage caused or arising as stated in paragraph 1 to other property owned by a Party:

(a) each Party waives its claim up to the amount of $1400 or its equivalent in Korean currency at the rate of exchange provided for in the Agreed Minute to Article ____ at the time the claim is filed.

63-1-12-6

(b) claims in excess of the amount stated in subparagraph (a) shall be settled by the Party against which the claim is made in

0031

63-1-20

미·울 108-10

0032

accordance with its domestic law.

3. For the purpose of paragraphs 1 and 2 of this Article, the expression "owned by a Party" in the case of a vessel includes a vessel on bare boat charter to that Party or requisitioned by it on bare boat charter terms or seized by it in prize (except to the extent that the risk of loss or liability is borne by some other person than such Party).

4. Each Party waives all its claims against the other Party for injury or death suffered by any member of its armed forces while such member was engaged in the performance of his official duties.

5. Claims (other than contractual claims) arising out of acts or omissions of members or employees of the United States armed forces done in the performance of official duty, or out of any other act, omission or occurrence for which the United States armed forces are legally responsible, and causing damage in the Republic of Korea to third parties other than the two Governments shall be processed and settled in accordance with the applicable provisions of United States law. The United States Government shall entertain other non-contractual claims against members of the United States armed forces or of the civilian component and may offer an <u>ex gratia</u> payment in such cases and in such amount as is determined by the appropriate United States authorities. 63-1-127

6. (a) A member or employee of the United States armed forces shall not be afforded immunity from the jurisdiction of the civil courts of Korea

0033

63-1-20

미문 108-10

0034

except: (1) in a matter arising out of acts or omissions done in the performance of official duty; or (2) in respect to any claim where there has been payment in full satisfaction of the claim.

(b) In the case of any private movable property, excluding that in use by the United States armed forces, which is subject to compulsory execution under Korean law, and is within the facilities and areas in use by the United States armed forces, the United States authorities shall, upon the request of the Korean courts, render all assistance within their power to see that such property is turned over to the Korean authorities.

7. The authorities of the United States and Korea shall cooperate in the procurement of evidence for a fair disposition of claims under this Article.

8. Paragraphs 2 and 5 of this Article shall apply only to claims arising incident to noncombat activities.

9. For the purposes of this Article, each Party shall have the right to determine whether a member or employee of its armed forces was engaged in the performance of official duties and whether property owned by it was being used by its armed forces for official purposes. 63-1-138

10. For the purposes of this Article, members of the Korean Augmentation to the United States Army (KATUSA) shall be considered as members of the United States armed forces, and members of the Korean

63-1-20

기-108-10.

0036

Service Corps (KSC) shall be considered as employees of the armed forces of the Republic of Korea.

11. The provisions of this Article shall not apply to any claims which arose before the entry into force of this Agreement.

63-1-129

0037

63-1-20 (10)

미국·을 108-10 (10)

0038

Status of Forces Agreement Negotiating Session

DRAFT

Minutes of the Status of Forces Agreement/Negotiating Session 28th

1. Mr. Hwang Ho-ul noted that he had been absent from the previous two negotiating sessions. He said that he was gratified that good progress had been made in the negotiations during his absence.

2. Mr. Habib said that, since members of the two negotiating teams were now a band of brothers, he knew that members of both teams would take great pleasure in noting ~~that~~ the promotion of Colonel G. G. O'Connor to the rank of Brigadier General. Mr. Hwang responded that he had been just about to mention the brilliant new star which was gracing the negotiating ~~team~~ table, and to offer the congratulations of the Korean side to its proud possessor. General O'Connor accepted the congratulations of his colleagues on the American and Korean negotiating teams, and offered to stand the house to its traditional round of ginseng tea. ~~for that session.~~

VEHICLE AND DRIVERS LICENSES

3. Opening ~~ing~~ substantive discussion, Mr. Hwang noted that there had been an exchange of views at the twenty-fourth ~~24th~~ negotiating session on the subject of the vehicle and drivers licenses article. Mr. Hwang asked if the U.S. side had any comments in response to the explanations ~~offered~~ offered by the Korean side at the twenty-fourth ~~24th~~ negotiating session.

4. Mr. Habib noted that at the twenty-fourth ~~24th~~ negotiating session there had been complete agreement ~~between the negotiators~~ on paragraph 1 and 2 of the U.S. draft article. The discussion had ~~Had~~ also revealed to the U.S. negotiators a clearer understanding of the points involved ~~by the Korean negotiators in their~~ in paragraph 2b of the Korean ~~their~~ draft article. Mr. Habib then reviewed in some detail the discussion at the twenty-fourth ~~24th~~ negotiating session on the subject of vehicle and drivers licenses. He said that the U.S. side had now developed a draft paragraph 3 which it would like to table in replacement for paragraph 3 of its original draft. He said that he ~~would~~ was confident that the new U.S. alternative draft for paragraph 3 would meet the requirements of both sides to the negotiations.

0039

5. Mr. Hwang examined the U.S. alternative paragraph 3, and stated that on first inspection he found no difficult points in it. He said that the Korean side accepted the U.S. draft in principle, and would give its definite answer at the next negotiating session.

CONTRACTORS

6. Turning to the next item on the agenda, Mr. Hwang asked if the U.S. side had comments or questions relative to the article on contractors. ~~Mr. Habib said that Colonel Fuller would make a presentation on this subject for the U.S. side.~~

7. Colonel Fuller said that in discussing the Invited Contractor Article and references to Invited Contractors in other articles, the Korean negotiators had on several occasions stated that because such persons were making a "profit" they should receive less favorable treatment than other elements to be covered by the Status of Forces Agreement. Colonel Fuller said that under the United States system of democracy, civilian control, and free enterprise, the United States Armed Forces, both in the United States and overseas, obtain a large part of their required services not by troop labor, or drafting of local labor, or even by direct-hire, but rather through contracts with private businessmen. In overseas areas most of these contracts are with local national businessmen, but it has been found in many countries that for some few highly specialized operations no local businessmen existed who were technically equipped and experienced in such operations. In these cases the United States Forces had brought in their own experienced contractors from the United States. Colonel Fuller said that he wished to emphasize that procedures he had prescribed were the American way of using private contractors instead of drafting people into the direct employment of the U.S. Forces. ~~that could possible affect employment.~~

8. Colonel Fuller said that the U.S. side had prepared a paper on this subject for distribution to the Korean side in the hope that the Korean side might see this question from the same perspective as the U.S. negotiators. Colonel

0040

Fuller said that, as to the question of profit, the paper points out that any reduction of privileges for this group, who are mostly employees anyway, would not affect the contractor's carefully calculated profit, but would instead simply increase the cost to the United States, a result which would not be beneficial to either side.

9. Colonel Fuller said that in order that both sides might see the question of invited contractors from the proper perspective in future discussions, he would distribute the prepared paper. The text of the paper distributed follows:

THE TEXT OF COLONEL FULLER'S PAPER ENTITLED "INVITED CONTRACTORS" SHALL BE REPRODUCED HERE.

10. Mr. Ku Chung-whe thanked Colonel Fuller for his explanation of the role of Invited Contractors. He said that he also had a few general remarks on the subject of contractors to offer. He said that, as Colonel Fuller had explained, it was a well-known general principle that all persons should be treated according to the principles of democracy, as human beings. He continued that the Status of Forces Agreement would be chiefly for the purpose of regulating the status of members of the United States Armed Forces, the civilian component, and their dependents, and that Invided Contractors are an exceptional category of personnel. Therefore, they are to be regulated under a separate article within the scope of the Status of Forces Agreement, and this regulation should not extend to the Invited Contractors the same privileges and immunities as granted to the members of the armed forces and the civilian component.

sonnel covered by the Status of Forces Agreement is made clear by the fact that Invited Contractors are treated in a separate article of the draft agreement. Mr. Habib noted that the first sentence of the U.S. draft article states that "except as otherwise provided in the draft paragraph below," Invited Contractors are subject to the laws and regulations of the

0041

Republic of Korea. Mr. Habib said that he hoped that there was no disagreement between the negotiators upon the legitimacy of Invited Contractors as a proper subject to be covered by the Status of Forces Agreement. Colonel Fuller's presentation and the paper he had distributed were efforts to define more clearly the U.S. position with respect to this subject.

12. Mr. Ku/said replied that the Korean negotiators knew the Invited Contractors were/in Korea solely for the purpose of serving the United States Forces and that this was the reason for the regulation of their status in the Status of Forces Agreement. Turning to the actual provisions of the Korean draft article on contractors, Mr. Ku noted that the Korean draft defines limited Invited Contractors as persons, including to corporations "organized under the laws of the United States", and their which would have employees "who are ordinarily resident in the United States".

13. Mr. Habib said that, prior to responding to Mr. Ku's statement, he would like Colonel Fuller to sum up the U.S. side's response to the Korean side's presentation at the twenty-second 22nd and twenty-third 23rd negotiating sessions on the subject of Invited Contractors.

14. Colonel Fuller said that he had one more general remarks on the subject of Invited Contractors. He said that the U.S. side said was not seeking any privileges or immunities for Invited Contractors which would be for these individuals' private benefit. He said the intent of the U.S. draft was merely to seek to PREVENT present the imposition of burdens on incurring of costs by Invited Contractors which would only be passed on to the United States Government, and which would ~~grant to them only such privileges an and immunities as would help them to assist in fulfilling~~ affect the performance of the mission of the United States Army Forces in Korea.

15. Colonel Fuller said that, turning to the provisions of the Invited Contractor article itself, the U.S. side had given further consideration to the points raised on both sides in the discussions of paragraph 3 of the draft article at the twenty-second 22nd negotiating meeting. He said that the U.S. side had been able to revise their draft of paragraph 3 to accord with the views expressed by the Korean side at the twenty-second 22nd meeting.

0042

Colonel Fuller said the U.S. side had reproduced a new draft of paragraph 3 and would now table this draft. Colonel Fuller said that the Korean negotiators would notice first that throughout the paragraph the U.S. side had, at the suggestion of the Korean negotiators, removed the word "right" or "rights" from each of the sub-paragraphs (a) through (j), so that they were all now consistent and uniform in not containing such unnecessary words. Colonel Fuller said that, secondly, at the suggestion of the Korean side, the U.S. negotiators had greatly altered sub-paragraph (h) to provide only for the use of utilities and services and had removed language that might have permitted the contractors to operate such public utilities in ways other than under contract with the U.S. Government. Colonel Fuller said that, while these changes had resulted in a new draft, it was the hope of the U.S. negotiators that, because all of the changes had been suggested by the Korean side, it would be possible to come to agreement on the draft he had just offered of paragraph 3. Colonel Fuller suggested that the negotiators adopt this paragraph.

16. Mr. Ku, after examination of the new U.S. draft paragraph 3, said he thought it would probably be agreeable to the Korean negotiators. He said the Korean negotiators would study the relationship of sub-paragraph 3 (i) to the new U.S. draft of paragraph 3 of the article on vehicle and drivers licenses.

17. Colonel Fuller, turning to paragraph 1 of the draft article on contractors, said that the U.S. side felt that the United States should retain the right to bring in whatever contractor would best advance the mission of the United States Forces in Korea. He said that this qualification would not always be possessed solely by "corporations organized under the laws of the United States" (the wording of the Korean draft paragraph 1).

18. Mr. Ku said that the wording of the Korean draft paragraph 1 would not prevent the United States Forces from bringing third country nationals to Korea to perform services for the United States Forces. He said that third country nationals could be used as contractors or employed by contractors provided that they are "ordinarily

0043

resident in the United States." He said the Korean negotiators were concerned that, under the wording of the U.S. draft paragraph 1, third country nationals employed as Invited Contractors would be treated differently from ordinary alien visitors to Korea. He said that the Korean negotiators had studied carefully the U.S.-Japan Status of Forces Agreement, and that their draft paragraph 1 had been based on the comparable article in the U.S.-Japan Agreement. Mr. Ku said that, even though in the Korean draft the dependents of the employees of Invited Contractors were not granted privileges and immunities, the Korean side would consider including these dependents if the American side would agree to the Korean draft wording of paragraph 1.

19. Colonel Fuller asked if it was the Korean side's intention that the dependents of U.S. employees of U.S. corporations be given or denied the benefits of paragraph 3?

20. Mr. Ku replied that the dependents of those employees ordinarily resident in the United States would be given such benefits.

21. Colonel Fuller [then] asked the intent of the Korean draft with respect to employees who were not ordinarily resident in the United States.

22. Mr. Ku replied that, under the terms of the Korean draft, such individuals would come to Korea, but they would not be provided for by the Status of Forces Agreement.

23. Colonel Fuller asked if the Korean side then desired that third-country national employees [of U.S invited contractors] not be paid in military payments certificates or not be authorized the use of Post Exchanges, [army post offices] or Commissaries? Colonel Fuller said that if the United States Forces could not provide these services to third-country national employees, it would be necessary to make up for the lack of these benefits by additional compensation.

24. Mr. Ku said that it was the position of the Korean side that ~~third-country national employees~~ [contractors and their employees who were not ordinarily resident in the U.S] should not be accorded the ~~full range of~~ benefits accorded U.S. [contractors and their] employees. He ~~suggested~~ [asked] the U.S. side would point out those benefits which were ~~absolute requirements, the Korean side would study the possibility of granting these benefits~~ [deemed most necessary].

25. Mr. Hwang said that he would like to supplement Mr. Ku's statement of the Korean position on this subject. He said that the Korean side had no desire to impose upon the U.S. Forces the necessity for providing additional

0044

compensation to the Invited Contractors. He said that the principal point of concern which was reflected in the Korean draft wording of paragraph 1 was that grant of the full range of privileges and immunities to third-country nationals would be agreeing to a less favorable competitive position for its own contractors in respect of contracts with the United States Forces. Mr. Hwang asked how many Invited Contractors were serving the United States Forces in Korea at the present time? Mr. Hwang also inquired in this connection whether the United States Government imposed tax on incomes derived from contracts let United States Forces within the boundaries of the continental United States?

26. Colonel Fuller said that, with respect to Mr. Hwang's concern about the competitive position of Korean contractors, the United States Forces did not have contracts with Invited Contractors when it was possible to conclude such contracts with local businessmen. He believed, therefore, that there should be no case of conflict if the U.S. wording were adopted. In this connection, Mr. Habib then read aloud to the negotiators the provisions of paragraph 2 of the United States draft, emphasizing those provisions which state that services of Invited Contractors are to be utilized only when such services are not obtainable locally.

27. Colonel Fuller, in replying to Mr. Hwang's question about the number of Invited Contractors, said he could offer only rough figures. He said there were some forty Invited Contractors serving the U.S. Forces in Korea, that these contractors have approximately 600 non-Korean employees of which 225 not ordinarily resident in the United States, and that over half of the forty odd Invited Contractors are "technical representatives", that is, one-man contracts for the supply of factory representatives of U.S. Companies who supervise the maintenance of ion with advanced weapon systems and other equipment activities. Mr. Ku said that it would be helpful for the Korean side in conducting a review of its position on the article under discussion to have a statement from the U.S. side of those privileges and immunities in paragraph 3 of the draft article which the U.S. side believes are absolutely necessary for its third country national employees of Invited Contractors.

28. Mr. Habib replied that the U.S. side considered that all of these privileges and immunities were necessary. Colonel Fuller agreed with Mr. Habib's statement that it was the thought of the U.S. negotiators that all of the privileges and immunities were necessary for third country national employees and that U.S. negotiators saw no basis for discrimination between contractors and their employees on the basis of nationality.

0046

29. Mr. Habib said that it was the U.S. side's feeling that on the basis of equitability all of these privileges should be granted to Invited Contractors and their employees without distinction on the basis of nationality. He would, however, like to reverse Mr. Ku's question to the U.S. side and ask which of the privileges and immunities granted by paragraph 3 was the Korean side most concerned about?

30. Mr. Ku replied that it had ~~originally~~ been the general position of the Korean negotiators that no privileges or immunities should be accorded to any third country nationals who are not ordinarily resident in the U.S. ~~in any of~~ the provisions of paragraph 3 of ~~the Status of Forces Agreement~~ the Article. ~~However, the Korean negotiators had made some exceptions to this principle in the negotiation of other articles of the draft agreement. He said that the Korean side would answer Mr. Habib's question at a forthcoming meeting.~~

31. Mr. Ku noted that paragraph 2 of the draft article had ~~been agreed,~~ ~~with the exception of one~~ a slight editorial difference, e.g., "Government of Korea" (U.S. draft) versus "Government of the Republic of Korea" (Korean draft). He stated that the Korean side would accept paragraph 2 of the U.S. draft Article. He ~~noted~~ said that paragraph 5 ~~had also been agreed~~ of the U.S. draft Article the Korean side accepted with the understanding that the word "consultation" be interpreted as implying that Korean views would be duly considered in the final conclusion of the process. Mr. Habib agreed to the interpretation.

32. Mr. Ku noted that the Korean draft of paragraph 6 included a phrase, the purpose of which was to make certain that the exemptions from taxation granted to Invited Contractors would apply only to their business with the United States Forces, and not to any other business they might conduct in the Republic of Korea. He said that the Korean position upon the inclusion of such a phrase had not changed.

~~Colonel Fuller asked if the Korean position on inclusion of the phrase "tangible or intangible" in paragraph 6 should be included in paragraph 6~~

33. Colonel Fuller asked if the Korean side had agreed that the phrase "tangible or intangible" should be included in paragraph 6 of the contractors article as a description of the movable property to be excluded from Korean taxation.

34. Mr. Ku said that the Korean side agreed to this inclusion. ~~He said that, however, the U.S. draft's wording of the last sentence of paragraph 6 "in Korea or to any intangible property registered in Korea," had a relationship with the U.S. draft agreed minute which the Korean side would have to~~ It was agreed that each side would give further consideration to the remaining points of difference in paragraph 6.

0047

~~study and discuss at a later time~~.

35. Turning to paragraph 7 of the U.S. draft of the article on contractors, Mr. Ku noted that the Korean side had presented an alternative draft at the twenty-third meeting. He inquired as to the U.S. side's position on this draft. Colonel Fuller responded that the U.S. side still considered it necessary to include the exemption specified in the second sentence of the U.S. draft of paragraph 7.

36. Mr. Ku noted that the Korean draft did include as a separate sentence a ~~pre~~ provision intended to fulfill the same purpose as the second clause of the second sentence of the U.S. draft. In this sentence, the Korean draft states that periods during which Invited Contractors were in Korea solely in connection with the execution of a contract with the United States Forces should not be considered as periods of residence for the purpose of Korean taxation.

37. Mr. Habib inquired why the Korean side did not care to state specifically that contractors were not liable for payment of Korean taxes on income derived from sources outside Korea?

38. It was agreed to suspend discussion upon paragraph 7 of the U.S. draft at this point, and Mr. Ku inquired if the U.S. side was prepared to table its draft of paragraph 8 of the contractors article. Mr. Habib replied that the U.S. side would table its draft of paragraph 8 at the time when it was prepared to discuss the subject of criminal jurisdiction.

39. Colonel Fuller asked if the Korean side had any comments upon the U.S. draft Agreed Minute to the Contractors Article.

40. Mr. Ku said that the Korean side had carefully studied the U.S. draft Agreed Minute. He suggested that the phrase "except paragraph 7" of the U.S. draft Article be added at the end of the Agreed Minute.

42. Mr. Ku asked which non-military agencies of the United States Government in Korea had contracts with the Invited Contractors?

43. Colonel Fuller replied that, ~~subject to later correction, he believed that only~~ the Embassy and the United States Operations Mission ~~had such contracts~~ were the non-military agencies contemplated in the proposed agreed Minute.

~~44. ... Korean side would study further the U.S. ... Minute.~~

41. Mr. Habib said that the addition of such a phrase would permit the levying of Korean income taxes on Invited Contractors [illegible] contracts with non-military U.S. government agencies. He said that the U.S. believed that the proposed Korean change would negate the entire purpose of the U.S. draft Agreed Minute.

0048

Claims

44. The negotiators exchanged draft articles dealing with the subject of claims.

Other Business

45. Mr. Habib noted that, in accordance with the instructions issued to them at the twenty-seventh negotiating session, Mr. Ford of the U.S. negotiating team and Mr. YI Chae-sul, Chief of the Foreign Exchange Division of the Ministry of Finance, had met to discuss the differences between the U.S. and Korean drafts of the last sentence of the Agreed Minute to the Foreign Exchange Controls Article. Mr. Habib said Messrs. Ford and YI required additional time for further discussion, and that they were hopeful of presenting a favorable report at the next negotiating session.

46. It was agreed that the next negotiating session would be held on August 22, 1963, at 2:00 p.m.

1966, 12.31.에 예고문에 의거 일반문서로 재분류됨

0043

JOINT SUMMARY RECORD OF THE 28TH SESSION

August 8, 1963

I. Time and Place : 2:00 to 3:40 p.m. August 8, 1963 at the Foreign Minister's Conference Room

II. Attendants:

ROK Side:

Mr. Whang, Ho Eul	Director Bureau of Political Affairs Ministry of Foreign Affairs
Mr. Shin, Kwan Sup	Director Bureau of Customs Duty Ministry of Finance
Mr. Koo, Choong Whay	Chief, America Section Ministry of Foreign Affairs
~~Mr. Shin, Jung Sup~~	~~Chief, Treaty Section~~ ~~Ministry of Foreign Affairs~~
Col. Lee, Nam Koo	Chief, Military Affairs Section Ministry of National Defense
Mr. Chu, Mun Ki	Chief, Legal Affairs Section Ministry of Justice
Mr. Lee, Kyung Hoon	2nd Secretary Ministry of Foreign Affairs
Mr. Kang, Suk Jae	2nd Secretary Ministry of Foreign Affairs
Mr. Cho, Kwang Je	2nd Secretary Ministry of Foreign Affairs
~~Mr. Chung, In Young~~	~~Observer~~ ~~Ministry of Finance~~

U.S. Side:

Mr. Philip C. Habib	Counselor of the Embassy for Political Affairs
Gen. G.G. O'Connor	Deputy Chief of Staff 8th Army
Mr. William J. Ford	First Secretary of the Embassy

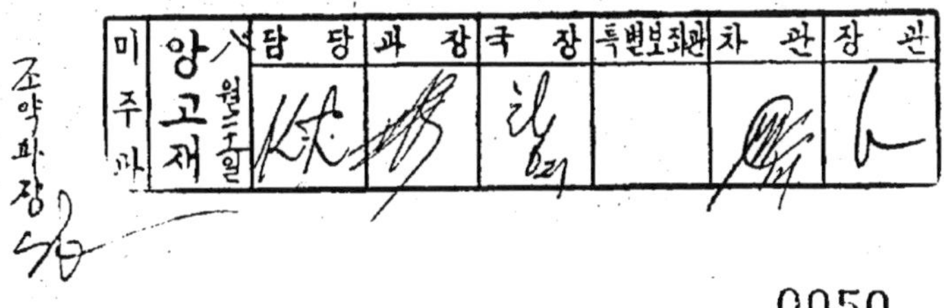

0050

Capt. R.M. Brownlie	Assistant Chief of Staff USN/K
Col. L.J. Fuller	Staff Judge Advocate United Nations Command
Mr. Rodney Armstrong	Economic Officer, American Embassy
Lt. Col. W.A. Burt	J-5
Major Robert D. Peckham	Staff Officer, JAG 8th Army
Kenneth Campen	Interpreter

1. Mr. Hwang Ho-ul noted that he had been absent from the previous two negotiating sessions. He said that he was gratified that good progress had been made in the negotiations during his absence.

2. Mr. Habib said that, since members of the two negotiating teams were now a band of brothers, he knew that members of both teams would take great pleasure in noting the promotion of Colonel G.G. O'Connor to the rank of Brigadier General. Mr. Hwang responded that he had been just about to mention the brilliant new star which was gracing the negotiating table, and to offer the congratulations of the Korean side to its proud possessor. General O'Connor accepted the congratulations of his colleagues on the American and Korean negotiating teams, and offered to stand the house to its traditional round of ginseng tea.

VEHICLE AND DRIVERS LICENSES

3. Opening substantive discussion, Mr. Hwang noted that there had been an exchange of views at the twenty-fourth negotiating session on the subject of the vehicle and drivers licenses article. Mr. Hwang asked if the U.S.

side had any comments in response to the explanations offered by the Korean side at the twenty-fourth negotiating session.

4. Mr. Habib noted that at the twenty-fourth negotiating session there had been complete agreement between the negotiators on paragraph 1 and 2 of the U.S. draft article. The discussion had also revealed to the U.S. negotiators a clearer understanding of the points involved in paragraph 2b of the Korean draft article. Mr. Habib then reviewed in some detail the discussion at the twenty-fourth negotiating session on the subject of vehicle and drivers licenses. He said that the U.S. side had now developed a draft paragraph 3 which it would like to table in replacement for paragraph 3 of its original draft. He said that he was confident that the new U.S. alternative draft for paragraph 3 would meet the requirements of both sides to the negotiations.

5. Mr. Hwang examined the U.S. alternative paragraph 3, and stated that on first inspection he found no difficult points in it. He said that the Korean side accepted the U.S. draft in principle, and would give its definite answer at the next negotiating session.

CONTRACTORS

6. Turning to the next item on the agenda, Mr. Hwang asked if the U.S. side had comments or questions relative to the article on contractors.

7. Colonel Fuller said that in discussing the Invited Contractor Article and references to Invited Contractors in other articles, the Korean negotiators had on several occasions stated that because such persons were making

0052

a"profit" they should receive less favorable treatment than other elements to be covered by the Status of Forces Agreement. Colonel Fuller said that under the United States system of democracy, civilian control, and free enterprise, the United States Armed Forces, both in the United States and overseas, obtain a large part of their required services not by troop labor, or drafting of local labor, or even by direct-hire, but rather through contracts with private business. In overseas areas most of these contracts are with local national businessmen, but it has been found in many countries that for some few highly specialized operations no local businessmen existed who were technically equipped and experienced in such operations. In these cases the United States Forces had brought in their own experienced contractors from the United States. Colonel Fuller said that he wished to emphasize that procedures he had prescribed were the American way of using private contractors instead of drafting people into the direct employment of the U.S. Forces.

8. Colonel Fuller said that the U.S. side had prepared paper on this subject for distribution to the Korean side in the hope that the Korean side might see this question from the same perspective as the U.S. negotiators. Colonel Fuller said that, as to the question of profit, the paper points out that any reduction of privileges for this group, who are mostly employees anyway, would not affect the contractors carefully calculated profit, but would instead simply increase the cost to the United States, a result which would not be beneficial to either side.

9. Colonel Fuller said that in order that both sides might see the question of invited contractors from the proper perspective in future discussions, he would distribute the prepared paper. The text of the paper distributed follows:

THE TEXT OF COLONEL FULLER'S PAPER ENTITLED "INVITED CONTRACTORS" SHALL BE REPRODUCED HERE. ※

10. Mr. Ku Chung-whe thanked Colonel Fuller for his explanation of the role of Invited Contractors. He said that he also has a few general remarks on the subject of contractors to offer. He said that, as Colonel Fuller had explained, it was a well-known general principle that all persons should be treated according to the principles of democracy, as human beings. He continued that the Status of Forces Agreement would be chiefly for the purpose of regulating the status of members of the United States Armed Forces, the civilian component, and their dependents, and that Invided Contractors are an exceptional category of personnel. Therefore, they are to be regulated under a separate article within the scope of the Status of Forces Agreement, and this regulation should not extend to the Invited Contractors the same privileges and immunities as granted to the members of the armed forces and the civilian component.

11. Mr. Habib said that he wished to make clear the feeling of the U.S. side that the status of Invited Contractors is relevant to the conclusion of a Status of Forces Agreement with the Republic of Korea. He said that the distinctions between Invited Contractors and other categories of personnel covered by the Status of Forces

0054

Agreement is made clear by the fact that Invited Contractors are treated in a separate article of the draft agreement. Mr. Habib noted that the first Sentence of the U.S. draft article states that "except as otherwise provided in the draft paragraph below", Invited Contractors are subject to the laws and regulations of the Republic of Korea. Mr. Habib said that he hoped that there was no disagreement between the negotiators upon the legitimacy of Invited Contractors as a proper subject to be covered by the Status of Forces Agreement. Colonel Fuller's presentation and the paper he had distributed were efforts to define more clearly the U.S. position with respect to this subject.

12. Mr. Ku said that the Korean negotiators knew the Invited Contractors were in Korea solely for the purpose of serving the United States Forces and that this was the reason for the regulation of their status in the Status of Forces Agreement. Turning to the actual provisions of the Korean draft article on contractors, Mr. Ku noted that the Korean draft defines Invited Contractors as persons, including corporations "organized under the laws of the United States", and their employees "who are ordinarily resident in the United States."

13. Mr. Habib said that, prior to responding to Mr. Ku's statement, he would like Colonel Fuller to sum up the U.S. side's response to the Korean side's presentation at the twenty-second and twenty-third negotiating sessions on the subject of Invited Contractors.

14. Colonel Fuller said that he had one more general remark on the subject of Invited Contractors. He said that the U.S. side was not seeking any privileges or

immunities for Invited Contractors which would be for these individuals' private benefit. He said the intent of the U.S. draft was merely to seek to prevent the imposition of burdens on by Invited Contractors which would be passed on to the United States Government, and which would affect the performance of the mission of the United States Forces in Korea.

15. Colonel Fuller said that, turning to the provisions of the Invited Contractor article itself, the U.S. side had given further consideration to the points raised on both sides in the discussions of paragraph 3 of the draft article at the twenty-second negotiating meeting. He said that the U.S. side had been able to revise their draft of paragraph 3 to accord with the views expressed by the Korean side at the twenty-second meeting. Colonel Fuller said the U.S. side had reproduced a new draft of paragraph 3 and would now table this draft. Colonel Fuller said that the Korean negotiators would notice first that throughout the paragraph the U.S. side had, at the suggestion of the Korean negotiators, removed the word "right" or "rights" from each of the sub-paragraphs (a) through (j), so that they were all now consistent and uniform in not containing such unnecessary words. Colonel Fuller said that, secondly, at the suggestion of the Korean side, the U.S. negotiators had greatly altered sub-paragraph (h) to provide only for the <u>use</u> of utilities and services and had removed language that might have permitted the contractors to <u>operate</u> such public utilities in ways other than under contract with the U.S. Government.

0056

Colonel Fuller said that, while these changes had resulted in a new draft, it was the hope of the U.S. negotiators that, because all of the changes had been suggested by the Korean side, it would be possible to come to agreement on the draft he had just offered of paragraph 3. Colonel Fuller suggested that the negotiators adopt this paragraph.

16. Mr. Ku, after examination of the new U.S. draft paragraph 3, said he thought it would probably be agreeable to the Korean negotiators. He said the Korean negotiators would study the relationship of sub-paragraph 3(i) to the new U.S. draft of paragraph 3 of the article on vehicle and drivers licenses.

17. Colonel Fuller, turning to paragraph 1 of the draft article on contractors said that the U.S. side felt that the United States should retain the right to bring in whatever contractor would best advance the mission of the United States Forces in Korea. He said that this qualification would not always be possessed solely by "corporations organized under the laws of the United States" (the wording of the Korean draft paragraph 1).

18. Mr. Ku said that the wording of the Korean draft paragraph 1 would not prevent the United States Forces from bringing third country nationals to Korea to perform services for the United States Forces. He said that third country nationals could be used as contractors or employed by contractors provided that they are "ordinarily resident in the United States."" He said the Korean negotiators were concerned that, under the wording of the U.S. draft paragraph 1, third country nationals employed as Invited Contractors would be treated differently from ordinary alien visitors to Korea. He said that the Korean

negotiators had studied carefully the U.S.-Japan Status of Forces Agreement, and that their draft paragraph 1 had been based on the comparable article in the U.S.-Japan Agreement. Mr. Ku said that, even though in the Korean draft the dependents of the employees of Invited Contractors were not granted privileges and immunities, the Korean side would consider including these dependents if the American side would agree to the Korean draft wording of paragraph 1.

19. Colonel Fuller asked if it was the Korean side's intention that the dependents of U.S. employees of U.S. corporations be given or denied the benefits of paragraph 3?

20. Mr. Ku replied that the dependents of those employees ordinarily resident in the United States would be given such benefits.

21. Colonel Fuller then asked the intent of the Korean draft with respect to employees who were not ordinarily resident in the United States.

22. Mr. Ku replied that, under the terms of the Korean draft, such individuals would come to Korea, but they would not be provided for by the Status of Forces Agreement.

23. Colonel Fuller asked if the the Korean side then desired that third-country national employees of U.S. Invited contractors not be paid in military payments certificates or not be authorized the use of Post Exchanges, Army post offices or Commissaries? Colonel Fuller said that if the United States Forces could not provide these services to third-country national employees, it would be necessary to make up for the lack of these benefits by additional compensation.

0058

24. Mr. Ku said that it was the position of the Korean side that third-country national contractors and their employees who were not ordinarily resident in the U.S. should not be accorded the benefits employees. He asked the U.S. side would point out those benefits which were deemed most necessary..

25. Mr. Whang said that he would like to supplement Mr. Ku's statement of the Korean position on this subject. He said that the Korean side had no desire to impose upon the U.S. Forces the necessity for providing additional compensation to the Invited Contractors. He said that the principal point of concern which was reflected in the Korean draft wording of paragraph 1 was that grant of the full range of privileges and immunities to third-country nationals would constitute agreement to a less favorable competitive position for its own contractors in respect of contracts with the United States Forces in Korea at the present time? Mr. Whang also inquired in this connection whether the United States Government imposed tax on incomes derived from contracts let by United States Forces within the boundaries of the continental United States?

26. Colonel Fuller said that, with respect to Mr. Hwang's concern about the competitive position of Korean contractors, the United States Forces did not have contracts with Invited Contractors when it was possible to conclude such contracts with local businessmen. He believed, therefore, that there should be no case of conflict if the U.S. wording were adopted. In this connection, Mr. Habib then read aloud to the negotiators the provisions of paragraph 2 of the United States draft, emphasizing those provisions which

state that services of Invited Contractors are to be utilized only when such services are not obtainable locally.

27. Colonel Fuller, in replying to Mr. Whang's question about the number of Invited Contractors, said he could offer only rough figures. He said there were some forty Invited Contractors serving the U.S. Forces in Korea, that these contractors have approximately 600 non-Korean employees of which 225 not ordinarily resident in the United States, and that over half of the forty odd Invited Contractors are "technical representatives", that is, one-man contracts for the supply of factory representatives of U.S. companies who supervise the maintenance of ~~with~~ advanced weapon systems and other equipment activities. Mr. Ku said that it would be helpful for the Korean side in conducting a review of its position on the article under discussion to have a statement from the U.S. side of those privileges and immunities in paragraph 3 of the draft article which the U.S. side believes are absolutely necessary for its third country national employees of Invited Contractors.

28. Mr. Habib replied that the U.S. side considered that all of these privileges and immunities were necessary. Colonel Fuller agreed with Mr. Habib's statement that it was the thought of the U.S. negotiators that all of the privileges and immunities were necessary for third country national employees and that U.S. negotiators saw no basis for discrimination between contractors and their employees on the basis of nationality.

29. Mr. Habib said that it was the U.S. side's feeling that on the basis of equitability all of these privileges should be granted to Invited Contractors and their employees

0060

without distinction on the basis of nationality. He would, however, like to reverse Mr. Ku's question to the U.S. side and aks which of the privileges and immunities granted by paragraph 3 was the Korean side most concerned about?

30. Mr. Ku replied that it had been the general position of the Korean negotiators that no privileges or immunities should be accorded to any third country nationals who are not ordinarily resident in the U.S. in the provisions of paragraph 3 of the Article.

31. Mr. Ku noted that paragraph 2 of the draft article had a slight editorial difference, e.g., "Government of Korea" (U.S. draft) versus "Government of the Republic of Korea" (Korean draft). He stated that the Korean side would accept paragraph 2 of the U.S. draft Article with the understanding that the word "consultation" be interpreted as implying that Korean reviews would be duly considered in the process of consultation. Mr. Habib agreed to this interpretation. He said that the Korean side accepted paragraph 5 of the U.S. draft Article.

32. Mr. Ku noted that the Korean draft of paragraph 6 included a final phrase, the purpose of which was to make certain that the exemptions from taxation granted to Invited Contractors would apply only to their business with the United States Forces, and not to any other business they might conduct in the Republic of Korea. He said that the Korean position upon the inclusion of such a phrase had not changed.

33. Colonel Fuller asked if the Korean side had agreed that the phrase "tangible or intangible" should be included in paragraph 6 of the contractors articles as a description of the movable property to be excluded from Korean taxation.

0061

34. Mr. Ku said that the Korean side agreed to this inclusion. It was agreed that each side would give further consideration to the remaining points of difference in paragraph 6.

35. Turning to paragraph 7 of the U.S. draft of the article on contractors, Mr. Ku noted that the Korean side had presented an alternative draft at the twenty-third meeting. He inquired as to the U.S. side's position on this draft. Colonel Fuller responded that the U.S. side still considered it necessary to include the exemption specified in the second sentence of the U.S. draft of paragraph 7.

36. Mr. Ku noted that the Korean draft did include as a separate sentence a provision intended to fulfill the same purpose as the second clause of the second sentence of the U.S. draft. In this sentence, the Korean draft states that periods during which Invited Contractors were in Korea solely in connection with the execution of a contract with the United States Forces should not be considered as periods of residence for the purpose of Korean taxation.

37. Mr. Habib inquired why the Korean side did not care to state specifically that contractors were not liable for payment of Korean taxes on income derived from sources outside Korea?

38. It was agreed to suspend discussion upon paragraph 7 of the U.S. draft at this point, and Mr. Ku inquired if the U.S. side was prepared to table its drafts of paragraph 8 of the contractors article. Mr. Habib replied that the U.S. side would table its draft of paragraph 8 at the time when it was prepared to discuss the subject of criminal jurisdiction.

0062

39. Colonel Fuller asked if the Korean side had any comments upon the U.S. draft Agreed Minute to the Contractors Article.

40. Mr. Ku said that the Korean side had carefully studied the U.S. draft Agreed Minute. He suggested that the phrase "except paragraph 7" of the U.S. draft Article be added at the end of the Agreed Minute.

41. Mr. Habib said that the addition of such a phrase would permit the leving of Korean income taxes on Invited Contractors having contracts with non-military U.S. government agencies. He said that the U.S. believed that the proposed Korean change would negate the entire purpose of the U.S. draft Agreed Minute.

42. Mr. Ku then asked which non-military agencies of the United States Government in Korea had contracts with the Invited Contractors?

43. Colonel Fuller replied that, the Embassy and the United States Operations Mission were the non-military agencies contemplated in the proposed agreed minute.

Claims

44. The negotiators exchanged draft articles dealing with the subject of claims.

Other Business

45. Mr. Habib noted that, in accordance with the instructions issued to them at the twenty-seventh negotiating session, Mr. Ford & the U.S. negotiating team and Mr. Yi Chae-sul, Chief of the Foreign Exchange Division of the Ministry of Finance, had met to discuss the differences between the U.S. and Korean drafts of the last sentence of the Agreed Minute to the Foreign Exchange Controls Article. Mr. Habib said Messrs. Ford and YI required

additional time for further discussion, and that they were hopeful of presenting a favorable report at the next negotiating session.

45. It was agreed that the next negotiating session would be held on August 22, 1963, at 2:00 p.m.

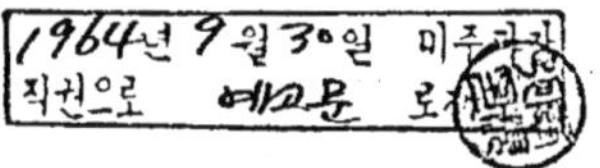

0064

On several occasions when the subject of "invited contractors" was being discussed statements have been made that because such contractors were in business for a "profit" they and their employees and their dependents should be treated less favorably than other elements contributing to the common defense effort in Korea. To put this question in its proper perspective the following points should be considered:

I. These contractors do business in Korea only for the United States forces. They are here because there is no local Korean source for the required service. They would not be here except for their US forces business. The business itself would not exist to be done by anyone if the US forces were not here.

II. The contract price paid by the United States to these contractors results from very close calculations of costs and takes into account the contract provision that purchase of materials and supplies in Korea will be free of local taxes as being made solely for US governmental purposes rather than for the contractor's benefit or profit. Under these contracts the US government pays the costs plus a small carefully calculated profit to the contractor. Any increase in the contractor's costs through taxes or otherwise would be borne by the US government and the US people, not by the contractor. Any benefit through tax or other exemption does not increase the contractor's "profit" at all; it merely continues to allow the US Government to obtain its necessary service free of local taxes.

III. The actual "contractor" is usually a United States Corporation physically located in the United States. It is represented here by its employees. These employees are not here to make a "profit" any more than the other employees of the United States, military or civilian, who are present in Korea to carry out the common defense effort. Their salaries and wages are no more a "profit" than the salaries and wages of the US Government civilian component and the pay of US soldiers. These employees and their dependents have the same need and the same justification for coverage under SOFA as the US armed forces, the civilian component, and their dependents. Any lesser coverage would simply mean that the contractor must pay them a higher wage to compensate them and that the US Government would then have to pay the contractor's increased costs.

From the foregoing it should be apparent that contractor "profit" is not a proper basis for considering these questions, that the real issue is whether the US Government should have to pay higher costs because under its system it does certain work through civilian contractors instead of by direct hire or by military labor.

0065

협 조 전	응 신 기 일
문서번호 의검미	제 목 미주둔군 지위협정 교섭진전 통보

수 신: 정보국장 발 신: 정무국장 년 월 일 63. 8. 26 제 1의 견

1963. 8. 8.일 개최되었던 미주둔군 지위협정 제28 차 회의에서 합의된 자동차 및 운전면허조항의 내용을 아래와 같이 알리나이다.

아 래

1. 제1 항:

대한민국은 미합중국 혹은 지방행정기관이 미군대 구성원 군속 및 그 가족에 대하여 발급한 운전허가증 또는 면허증 또는 군대운전면허증을 운전시험 또는 수수료없이 유효한것으로 받아 드린다.

2. 제2 항:

미합중국 군대 및 군속의 공용차량은 이를 용이하게 식별될수 있는 명확한 번호판 및 개별 표시를 부하야 한다.

3. 제3 항:

대한민국정부는 미합중국 군대 군속 및 그 가족의 사유차량의 등록을 받고 면허증을 교부한다. 대한민국법률에 따라 차량등록 및 면허교부에 필요한 소유자의 성명 및 기타사항은 합동위원회를 통하여 대한민국에 통고된다. 미합중국 군대

0066

승인서식 1—34 (11—13330—01) (195mm×265mm16절지)

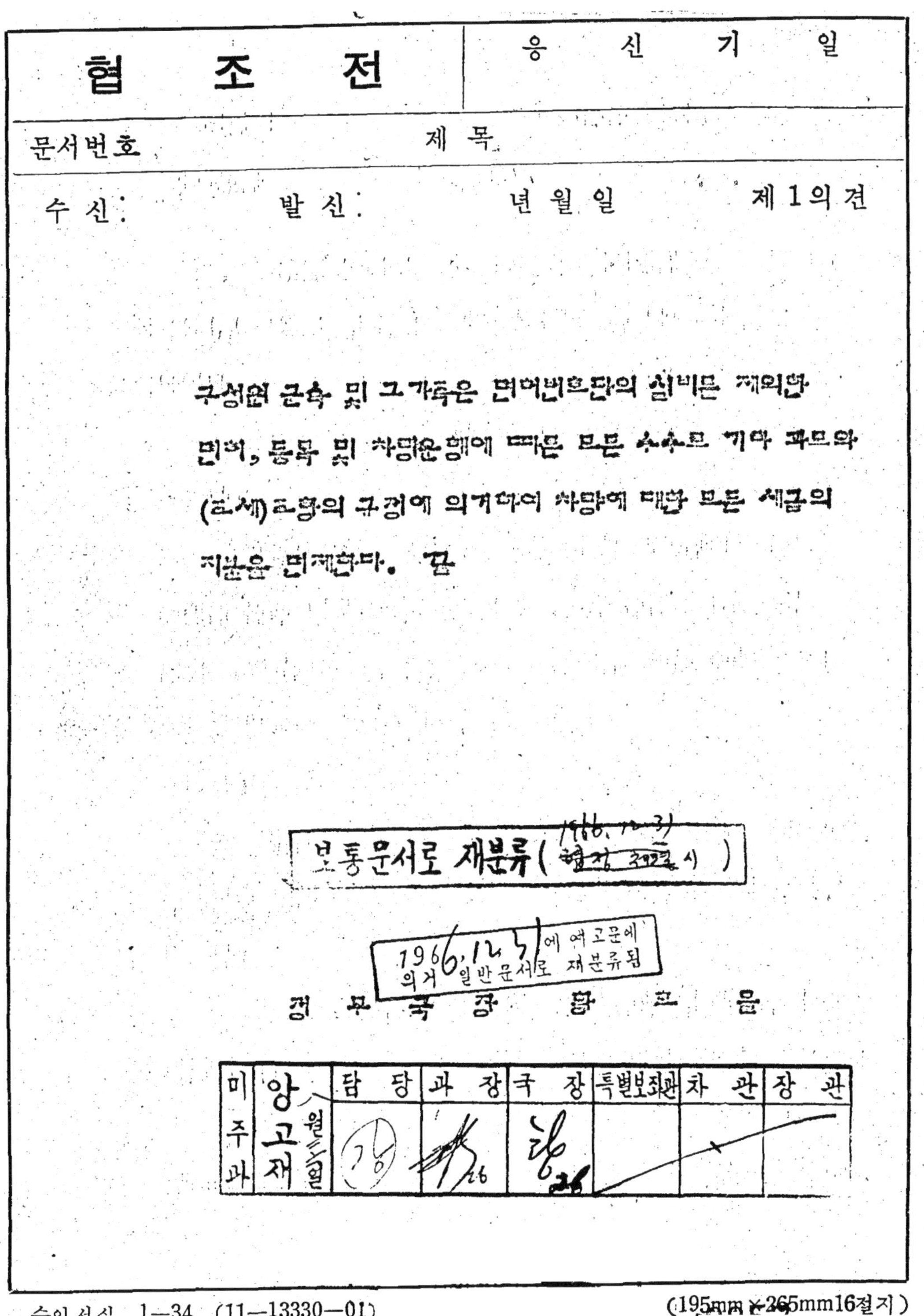

협 조 전	응 신 기 일

문서번호 　　　　　　제 목

수 신: 　　　발 신: 　　　년 월 일 　　　제 1 의 견

구성원 군속 및 그 가족은 면허번호판의 실비를 제외한 면허, 등록 및 차량운행에 따른 모든 수수료 기타 과료와 (조세)조항의 규정에 의거하여 차량에 대한 모든 세금의 지불을 면제한다. 끝

보통문서로 재분류 (1966. 12. 31)

1966, 12, 31 에 예고문에 의거 일반문서로 재분류됨

경 무 국 장 담 으 음

미주과	앙고재	담 당	과 장	국 장	특별보좌관	차 관	장 관
			26	26			

승인서식 1—34 (11—13330—01) 　　　(195mm×265mm16절지)

0067

2. 제29차 회의, 8.22

0068

법 무 부

법무법 810 11473 (2 - 4072) 1963, 8, 18.

수신 외무부장관

제목 한.미행정협정에 수반한 자료송부

한.미행정협정에 수반한 국가배상금 지급에 관한 절차의 관계자료를 송부하니 이를 영역하여 미측에 전달하여 주시기 바랍니다 (英譯)

유 첨 한.미행정협정에 수반한 자료1부 끝

법무부장관 민 복

0069

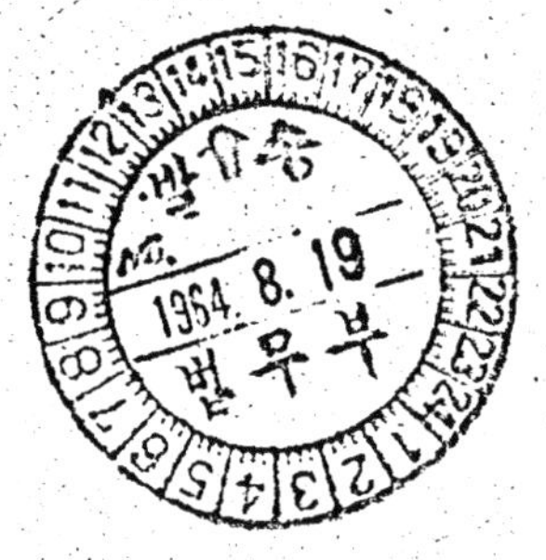

1. 關係法令
2. 職員數 (調査員, 支給担当員, 一般事務職員)
3. 職員의 俸給 또는 手当의 支給은
4. 1963年 1964年의 事件接受 및 処理件数
5. 賠償金中에는 弁護士費用도 包含되는지
6. 1963年 및 1964年의 支給予算總額
7. 申請부터 支給까지의 所要時日
8. 地方事件의 処理機構

0070

1

UNOFFICIAL TRANSLATION OF LAW NO. 1223
(PROMULGATED ON 24 DECEMBER 1962)

LAW CONCERNING PROCEDURES ON CLAIM FOR DAMAGES BY THE STATE

Article 1. (Application)

This Law shall apply to the procedures on claims for compensation for damages caused by the State (hereinafter referred to as the "compensation") unless otherwise provided in other laws.

Article 2. (Claim for Compensation)

Persons desiring to receive the compensation may submit a claim for issuance of compensation to the Minister of Justice and obtain decisions therefor.

Article 3. (Compensation Council)

Paragraph 1. A compensation council (hereinafter referred to as the "council") shall be established in the Ministry of Justice in order to have the council consider the matters concerning the decisions under the preceding article.

Paragraph 2. Matters concerning the formation, operation and other necessary matters of the council shall be determined by Cabinet decree.

Article 4. (Decisions)

Paragraph 1. In case the claim under Article 2 is made, the Minister of Justice shall make decisions as to whether he is to issue the compensation or reject the claim, through consideration of the council.

Paragraph 2. The decision of issuance under the preceding paragraph shall come into force when the consent of the claimant concerned is given.

Paragraph 3. The Minister of Justice shall make the decisions under Paragraph 1 within two months from

0071

the date of receipt of claims for issuance of compensation.

Article 5. (Service of Written Decisions)

In case the Minister of Justice has made decisions under Paragraph 1 of the preceding article, he shall serve the original copy of the written decision on the claimant concerned within one week from the date when the said decision is made.

Article 6. (Consent of Claimant)

Paragraph 1. The claimant who has received the decision of issuance of compensation shall make a claim for issuance of compensation to the Minister of Justice by attaching a written consent to the said decision within three weeks from the date he has received the original copy of the decision.

Paragraph 2. In case the claimant who has received the decision of issuance of compensation does not make the claim under the preceding paragraph, he shall be regarded not to have given consent.

Article 7. (Validity of Decisions)

The decision under Article 4, Paragraph 1, shall be regarded to be a compromise made before a court under the provisions of the Code of Civil Procedures when the claimant consents to the said decision, and the original copy of the decision shall have the same effect as the executory exemplification of a written judgement.

Article 8. (Enforcement Decree)

Matters necessary for the enforcement of this Law shall be determined by Cabinet decree.

ADDENDA

Paragraph 1. (Enforcement Day)

0072

This Law shall be effective on and after January 1, 1963.

Paragraph 2. (Interim Measures)

This Law shall not apply to the cases of claim for compensation of damages which are pending at the courts at the time of the enforcement of this Law.

0073

Number of Claims Processed in 1963 and 1964

YEAR	NUMBER OF CLAIMS RECEIVED	DISPOSITION				PENDING
		AWARDED	REJECTED	WITHDREW	TOTAL	
1963 (1 May-31 Dec.)	283	189	81	13	283	-
1964 (1 Jan.-30 June)	207	91	27	21	139	68
TOTAL	490	280	108	34	422	68

0074

2. 職員數

調査員 9名 (法務官 2名 事務官 2名 主事 5名)

支給担當員 3名

一般事務職員 2名

合 計 14名

3. 職員의 俸給 또는 手當의 支給은?

職員은 全員이 國家公務員이므로 國家公務員報酬規程에 依하여 모두 國家가 이를 支給한다.

4. 1963年. 1964年의 事件接受 및 處理件數

年度 \ 区分	接受	處理				備考
		認定	棄却	取下	合計	
1963年度	283	189	81	13	283	5月1日부터 接受處理
1964年度	207	91	27	21	139	6月30日現在 계속 68件
合計	490	280	108	34	422	

5. 賠償金中에는 弁護士費用도 包含되는지?

包含되지 않는다.

6. 1963年 및 1964年의 支給予算總額

1963年度 30,490,000원

1964年度 25,910,200원

合計 56,400,200원

공통서식 1-1 (을) 0075 (16절지)

7. 申請부터 支給까지의 所要時日
約 2月 10日이 所要됨.

※ 申請接受日로 부터 2月内에 決定하고 決定後 7日内에 申請人에게 通知하여 通知를 받은 申請人이 3週日以内에 同意하면 即時 支給됨.

8. 地方事件의 處理機構
없음.
法務部에서 一括 処理함

공통서식 1—1 (을) 0076 (16절지)

支給額 (參考).

1963年度 17,756,626원 10전
1964年度 7,850,983원 78전 (6月末現在)

공통서식 1—1 (을) (16절지)

0077

법 무 부

법무법 810 12485 1964.9.10.

수신 외무부장관

제목 한.미 행정협정에 관한 자료송부

한.미 행정협정 체결에 수반한 국가배상금 지급에 관한 참고 자료를 별첨과 같이 송부합니다

유첨 한.미 행정협정에 관한 자료 1부 끝.

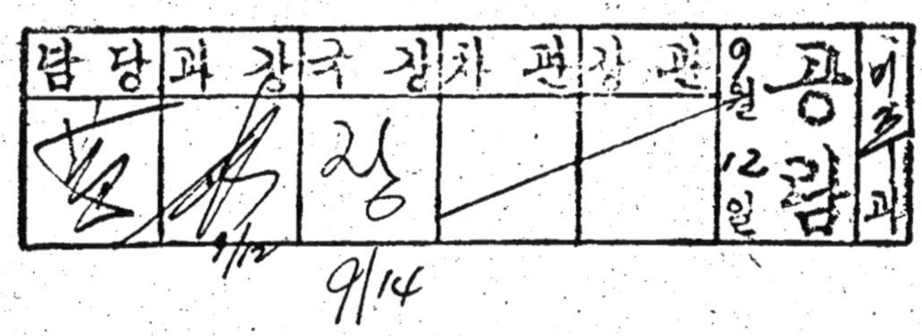

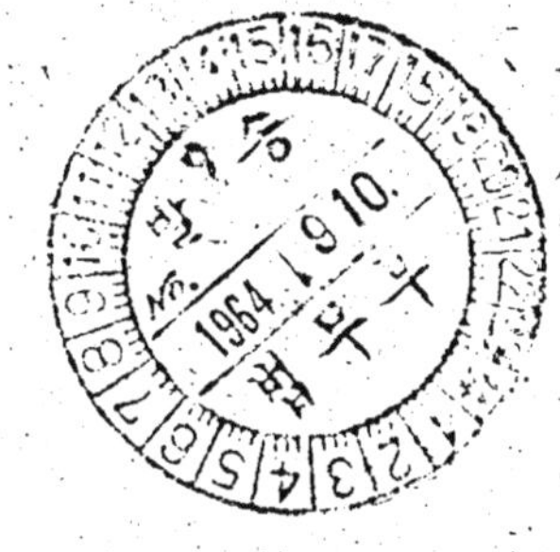

민 복

0078

2

國家賠償金 支給에 関한 参考資料

1. 最高支給 金額에 対한 事件種類 및 事件要旨

事件番号 : 64年國賠審 115号
認定金額 : 金 450,000원 整
事件要旨.
被害者인 [redacted] 은 가마니, 쌀, 고구마 장사 業을 하며 月約 10,000원의 收入이 있든者로서 1963. 11.16. 全北 裡里警察署主催 義勇消防隊 競演会에 参席하였다가 帰家中 被害者等 義勇消防隊員의 輸送을 為하여 配車된 第2訓練所 所属 2호 106号 車輛의 運転兵의 業務上 過失로 同 車輛이 轉覆되는 事故로 死亡한것인바
向後 收入 損害金으로 金 250,000원
慰藉料로 被害者의 妻에게 金 40,000원
子女 8名에게 各金 20,000원式을 認定하여
合計金 450,000원을 支給한것임

2. 最低 支給 金額에 対한 事件種類 및 事件要旨

事件番号 63年 國賠審 第109号
認定金額 金 4,006원 整

공통서식 1—1 (을) (16절지)

事件要旨

陸軍 第一 家屋設工兵団 所属 ██████가 1962. 12. 30 ████████████████ 所在 申請人 所有 家屋 前面을 同人의 業務上 過失로 運轉中인 "스리콰타"로 衝突하여 申請人에게 修理費 4,006 원의 損害를 加한 것으로 위 損害額 全部를 支給한 事件임.

3. 事件 種類別 (但 交通事故로 因한 傷害, 傷害致死) 平均賠償金額

(1) 傷害

傷害의 程度, 年令, 傷害當時의 收入等에 따라 損害發生額의 差가 甚하므로 支給額도 差가 甚하며 平均 約 80,000원 程度 支給되었음.

(2) 傷害致死

1才~20才 50,000원 ~ 80,000원

但 就業中에 있는 者인 境遇는 收入 損害金이 위 金額에 加算함.

21才 ~ 50才 200,000원 ~ 460,000원

51才 ~ 70才 100,000원 ~ 250,000원

4. 賠償金 算定의 基準에 関한 法에 根據 또는 內規가 있는지의 與否

卽 現在 賠償金 算定의 基準은 "호프만"式 計算方法에 따르고 있는데 이 "호프만"式 計算方法에 依한다는 法의 根據가 있는지? 其他 賠償金 決定에 関한 基準이나 資料

(1) 制定法에 規定은 없으나 法院 判例에 依하여 適用되고 있음.

(2) 收入損害金에 対하여는

被害当時 收入金中 被害者의 生計維持費를 除한 純收入金을 同人이 可得 可能한 年限까지 "호프만"式 計算方法에 依하여 算定한 金額을 賠償하고 다만 慰藉料는 財産上의 損害에 対한 賠償이 아니어서 賠償額 算出이 困難하므로 法院 判例에 準하여 別添 一覧表와 같이 年令別 数種의 職業別로 平均値를 算定하고 請求権者 1人에 対하여 同 算定額을 감안한 金額을 支給하고 있음.

5. 賠償金審議委員会 決定에 対하여 異議를 가지고 法院에 正式 訴를 提起한 件数와 그 結果, 審議委員会에서 決定한 金額과의 差異는 어느 程度인지?

0081

공통서식 1—1 (을) (16절지)

1件이 있으나 法院에 係屬中에 있으므로 以下 不詳임.

6. 現審議会 委員의 法官(検事, 弁護士, 経歷 包含) 経歷年数

委員長	權五柄	検事 15年 弁護士 3年 大學法律學敎授 7年 現 法務次官
委員	李坰鎬	大學法律學敎授 6年 検事 13年 現 大検 検事兼 法務局長
委員	尹斗植	検事 10年 現 大検 検事兼 検察局長
委員	李凰成	検事 10年 現 大検 検事兼 矯正局長

0082

공통서식 1—1 (을) (16절지)

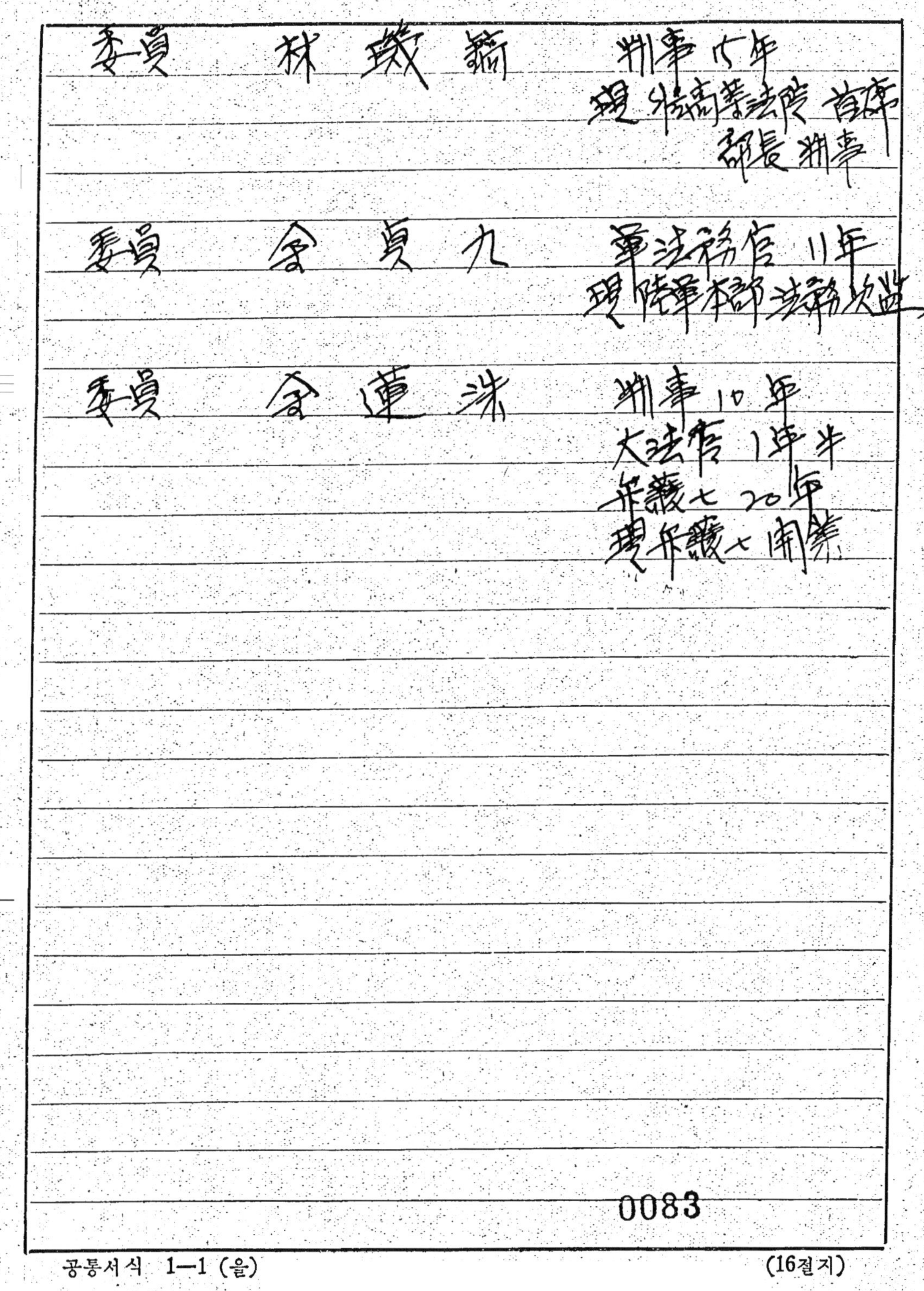

委員 林璣鎬 判事 15年
現 서울高等法院 首席部長 判事

委員 金貞九 軍法務官 11年
現 陸軍本部 法務次監

委員 金連洙 判事 10年
大法官 1年半
辯護士 20年
現 辯護士 開業

0083

공통서식 1—1 (을) (16절지)

慰藉料 支給一人當平均額一覽表

職業	性別	年令	1~5	6~10	11~15	16~20	21~25	26~30	31~35	36~40	41~45	46~50	51~55	56~60	61~65	66~70	71이상
農業	男	慰藉料				30.000	35.000	40.000	40.000	40.000	40.000	30.000	25.000	20.000	10.000	9.000	7.000
	女	〃				25.000	30.000	35.000	35.000	35.000	25.000	25.000	20.000	15.000	9.000	8.000	6.000
商業	男	〃				40.000	40.000	40.000	40.000	40.000	40.000	30.000	25.000	20.000	10.000	8.000	7.000
	女	〃				35.000	35.000	35.000	35.000	35.000	35.000	25.000	20.000	15.000	9.000	7.000	6.000
工業	男	〃				40.000	40.000	40.000	40.000	40.000	40.000	30.000	30.000	25.000	20.000	10.000	8.000
	女	〃				35.000	35.000	35.000	35.000	35.000	35.000	25.000	25.000	20.000	15.000	9.000	7.000
公務員	男	〃				40.000	45.000	50.000	45.000	45.000	45.000	40.000	35.000	30.000	25.000	20.000	16.000
	女	〃				35.000	40.000	45.000	40.000	40.000	40.000	35.000	30.000	25.000	20.000	15.000	7.000
會社員	男	〃				40.000	40.000	45.000	40.000	40.000	40.000	30.000	25.000	20.000	15.000	10.000	9.000
	女	〃				35.000	35.000	40.000	35.000	35.000	35.000	25.000	20.000	15.000	10.000	9.000	8.000
技術員	男	〃				40.000	40.000	40.000	40.000	40.000	40.000	30.000	25.000	15.000	10.000	9.000	8.000
	女	〃				35.000	35.000	35.000	35.000	35.000	35.000	25.000	20.000	10.000	9.000	8.000	7.000
雇傭員	男	〃			20.000	35.000	40.000	40.000	40.000	40.000	35.000	25.000	20.000	10.000	9.000	8.000	7.000
	女	〃				30.000	35.000	35.000	35.000	35.000	30.000	20.000	15.000	9.000	8.000	7.000	6.000
其他	男	〃	30.000	30.000	30.000	30.000	30.000	40.000	35.000	35.000	35.000	25.000	20.000	9.000	8.000	7.000	6.000
	女	〃	25.000	25.000	25.000	25.000	25.000	35.000	30.000	30.000	30.000	20.000	15.000	8.000	7.000	6.000	5.000

0084

기 안 용 지

자체 통제		기안처	미주과 이경훈	전화번호	근거서류접수일자

	과장	국장	차관	장관		
	(서명)	(서명) 22	(서명) 21	(서명)		

관계관 서명	

기안 년월일	63. 8. 21	시행 년월일		보존 년한		정서	기장
분류 기호		전체 통제		종결			
경유 수신 참조	건의			발신			

제목	제29차 주둔군지위협정 체결 교섭회의에 임할 우리측 입장

8.20.에 개최될 제29차 주둔군지위협정 체결 한미간 교섭회의에서는 민사 청구권 그리고 차량 및 운전면허에 관한 문제를 토의할 ~~민사청구권에 관한 안을 교환할~~ 예정이온바, 이에 관련하여 우리측 교섭 실무자는 8. 20. 회합을 갖고 제29차 회의에서 취할 우리측 태도를 별첨과 같이 결정하였아오니 재가하여 주시기 바랍니다.

유첨 : 제29차 주둔군지위협정 체결 교섭회의에 임할 우리측 태도, 끝

1964년 9월 30일 직권으로 예고문

1966.12.31에 예고문에 의거 일반문서로 재분류됨

승인양식 1-1-3 (1112-040-016-018) (190mm×260mm16절지)

0085

1. 민사청구권

(1) 조약 각 당사국이 소유하고 그의 군대가 사용하는 재산에대한 손해의 청구권 포기에 관한 우리측 초안 1항 (이는 미국측 초안1항에 해당함) 은 미국측 초안과 실질적인 차이가 없으므로 미국측안을 수락토록 한다.

(2) 군대가 사용하는 이외의 기타 정부재산에 대한 손해의 청구권 규정에 관한 우리측 초안 제2항 (이는 미국측 초안 제2항에 해당함)은 군대가 사용하는 재산 이외의 정부 재산에대한 손해의 청구권을 중재인에 의하여 결정되도록 하자고 주장한데 대하여 미국측은 이러한 청구권은 국내법에 의거하여 해결토록 하자고 주장하고 있는바 우리측은 우리측 안의 수락을 주장토록 한다.

(3) 국유선박의 정의에 관한 우리측 초안 제3항 (이는 미국측 초안 제3항에 해당함) 은 미국측 초안과 같으므로 상호간 합의에 이를것임.

(4) 군인의 부상 및 사망시의 청구권에 관한 규정 (우리측 초안 제4항, 미국측 초안 역시 제4항)에 있어서 양측안은 서로 같으므로 상호간 합의에 이를것임.

(5) 제3자에 가한 손해에 대한 비계약상 청구권 관할규정에 관한 우리측 초안 제5항 (이는 미국측 초안 제5항 전단에 해당함)에 있어서 우리측은 이러한 청구권은 한국에 의하여 취급되어야 한다고 규정하고 있는데 반하여 미국측은 미국법률에 의하여 해결되어야 한다고 주장하고 있는바 우리측은 우리측안의 수락을 주장토록 한다.

(6) 비공무중의 불법행위로 인한 청구권 규정에 관한 우리측 초안 제6항 (이는 미국측 초안 제5항 후단에 해당하는 것으로 사료됨)에 있어서 우리측 안은 비공무중에 행한 불법행위로 인하여 발생되는 청구권의 규정을 명백히 규정하고 있는데 반하여 미국측 초안은 극히 애매하게 규정하고 있어 우리측은 미국측 안의 설명을 요구한후 우리측안의 수락을 주장토록 한다.

(7) 차량의 무허가 사용으로부터 발생되는 청구권에 관한 우리측 초안 제7항 (이는 미국측 초안에는 명시되어 있지 않으나 미국측 초안 제5항 후단에 포함되었다고도 생각될수 있는것같음)은 이를 미국측이 수락토록 우리측은 주장한다.

0086

(8) 공무, 비공무에 관한 판단 규정인 우리측 초안 제8항 (이는 미국측 초안 제9항에 해당함)에 있어서 우리측 초안은 이러한 판단은 중재인에 의하여 결정토록 하자고 규정한데 반하여 미국측 초안은 각 당사국이 결정토록 하자고 규정하고 있는바 우리측은 우리측 안의 수락을 주장토록 한다.

(9) 민사청구권의 관할에관한 일반 원측 규정인 우리측 초안 9(a)항 (이는 미국측 초안 6(a)항에 해당함)에 있어서 우리측 초안은 미국측 초안보다 더 분명하므로 우리측은 우리측안의 수락을 주장토록 한다.

(10) 미국군대 토지 및 시설내에 있는 사유동산의 강제집행에 관한 우리측 초안 9(b)항 (이는 미국측 초안 6(b)항에 해당함)에 있어서 양측 초안은 흡사하나 우리측은 우리측안의 수락을 요구토록 한다.

(11) 청구권의 공평한 심의 및 처리를 위한 증거수집에 관한 우리측 초안 제9(c)항 (이는 미국측 초안 7항에 해당함)에 있어서 양측안은 서로 비슷하나 미국측안에는 공정한 심의라는 용어를 삭제하고 있으므로 우리측은 우리측안의 수락을 요구토록 한다.

(12) 자재, 보급품, 비품 및 용역의 조달에 관한 계약상의 분쟁문제에 관한 우리측 초안 제10항은 미국측 초안에는 규정되어 있지않는바 우리측은 동규정을 민사청구권 조항에 삽입한것은 동문제를 별도로 취급하는것 보다 이것에 포함시키는것이 편리하기 때문이였다는 의견을 진술하고 이에관한 미국측의 견해를 문의토록 한다.

(13) 비전투 행위로부터 발생되는 청구권에 대한 적응에관한 우리측 초안 제11항 (이는 미국측 초안 제8항에 해당함)에 있어서 양측안은 똑 같으므로 미국측안을 수락토록 한다.

(14) "카투사" 및 노무사단에 관한 미국측 초안 제10항은 우리측 초안에는 규정되어있지 않는바 우리측은 이에관한 미국측 안의 설명을 요구토록 한다.

2. 차량 및 운전면허

0087

(1) 사유차량의 표식 및 면세조치에 관한 규정인 미국측 수정 초안 제3항은 우리측의 주장에 응한것임으로 이를 수락토록 하며 따라서 차량 및 운전면허에 관한 조항은 한미간에 완전 합의에 도달할것임.

1966.12.31.에 예고문에 의거 일반문서로 재분류됨
일반문서로 재분류(1966.12.31.)

SOFA NEGOTIATION

Agenda for the 29th Session

15:00 August 22, 1963

1. Continuation of Discussion on:
   a. Vehicle and Driver Licenses Article
   b. Claims Article
2. Other Business
3. Agenda and Date of Next Meeting
4. Press Release

0088

기 안 용 지

자 체 통 제		기안처	미주과 이경훈	전화번호	근거서류접수일자
	과 장	국 장	~~보과관~~	차 관	장 관
	23	23		26	
관 계 관 서 명	조약과장				
기 안 년월일	1963. 8. 23.	시 행 년월일	878	보존 년한	정 서 기 장
분 류 기 호	외정미 722.2	전 체 통 제			
경 유 수 신 참 조	국가재건최고회의 의장 (참조 : 외무국방위원장) 내각수반			장 관	
제 목	주둔군지위협정 체결을 위한 제29차 교섭회의 보고				

1963년 8월22일 하오3시부터 4시35분 까지 외무부장관 회의실에서 개최된 제29차 주둔군지위협정 체결 교섭회의에서 토의된 내용을 별첨과 같이 보고합니다.

유첨 : 제 29 차 교섭회의 보고서 부.

1964 년 9 월 30 일 미주 직권으로 예고문 보재분류

0089

승인양식 1-1-3 (1112-040-016-018) (190mm×260mm16절지)

외 무 부

외정미 722.2 1963.8.26.

수 신 : 국가재건최고회의 의장

참 조 : 외무국방위원장

제 목 : 주둔군 지위 협정 체결을 위한 제 29 차 교섭회의 보고

1963년 8 월22일 하오 3시부터 4시 35분까지 외무부 장관 회의실에서 개최된 제 29 차 주둔군지위협정 체결 교섭회의에서 토의된 내용을 별첨과 같이 보고합니다.

유 첨 : 제 29차 교섭회의 보고서 2부. 끝

외 무 부 장 관 김 용 식

0090

제 29 차

한미간 주둔군지위협정 체결 실무자 회의

보 고 서

1. 일 시 : 1963. 8. 22. 하오 3시부터 4시 35분 까지

2. 장 소 : 외무부장관 회의실

3. 참석자 : 한국측 :

황 호 을	(외무부 정무국장)
신 관 섭	(재무부 세관국장)
구 충 회	(외무부 미주과장)
신 정 섭	(외무부 조약과장)
이 남 구	(국방부 군무과장)
주 문 기	(법무부 법무과장)
이 경 훈	(외무부 2 등서기관)
강 석 재	(")
조 광 제	(")
허 승	(외무부 3 등서기관)

미국측 : 교섭대표단 전원

4. 토의사항 :

(1) 차량 및 운전면허 그리고 민사 청구권 문제를 순차적으로 토의함.

(2) 차량 및 운전면허 조항의 토의에 있어서 사유 차량의 표식 및 면세조치에 관한 규정에 대하여 미국측은 우리측이 주장한대로 미국군대 구성원, 군속 및 그들의 가족의 개인용 차량은 한국이 부여한 표식을 사용토록 하되 차량감찰을 이들에게 부여함에 있어서 수반되는 과세등은 부과하지 않을것이나 차량감찰의 실비만을 지불토록 한다는 내용의 수정안을 제시하였기 우리측은 이를 수락하여 주었으며 따라서 차량 및 운전면허에 관한 조항은 한미간에 완전 합의에 도달하였음.

63-1-130

0091

63-1-21 (3)

미국:울 108-9 (3)

0092

(3) 민사 청구권 문제의 토의에 있어서 우리측은 동 조항은 형사재판 관할권 조항과 더불어 주둔군지위협정에서 중요한것 중에 하나이며 미국측 안과 우리측안은 근본적인 차이가 있다는 것을 강조하면서 우리측 안의 주요골자는

(가) 조약 각 당사국이 소유하고 그의 군대가 사용하는 재산에 대한 손해의 청구권 포기에 관한 규정은 미국측안과 같고.

(나) 군대가 사용하는 이외의 기타 정부 재산에 대한 손해의 청구권은 중재인에 의하여 결정되도록 규정하고 있고

(다) 제3자에 가한 손해에 대한 비계약상 청구권은 한국법에 의하여 취급되도록 규정되어 있으며

(라) 비공무중의 불법행위로 인하여 발생되는 청구권은 한국법에 의하여 해결되도록 규정하고 이와 관련하여 차량의 무허가 사용으로부터 발생되는 청구권도 비공무중의 불법행위로 인한 청구권의 조건과 같은 규정에 의하기 취급되도록 규정하고 있으며

(마) 공무, 비공무에 관한 판단은 중재인에 의하여 결정토록 하도록 규정하고 있고

(바) 계약상의 분쟁에 관한 규정은 편의상 민사청구권 조항에 삽입하였다고 설명하였음. 또한 우리측은 이어서 다시 우리측 안이 미국측안 보다 상세하고 구체적인 사건처리에도 신속할수 있을것이며, 이러한 우리측 초안에 의한 사건처리 방법은 종래 한국 국민이 갈망해왔던 것이라는 점을 강조하면서 이러한 점을 참작하여 미국측이 우리측 안을 전적으로 찬동해주기 바란다고 설명하면서 우리측 안대로 사건을 취급하고 처리하는 것이 한미간의 우호를 더욱더 증진할수 있을것이며 불필요한 오해를 제거 또는 야기케하지 못할 것이라는 점을 역설하고 우리측안을 토대로하여 각조항의 토의를 행할것을 제의하였음. 63-1-131

0093

63-1-21

미문 108-9

0094

(4) 미국측은 자국측안의 제안 설명에 있어서 미국측 안이나 한국측 안은 모두 청구권을 지불한다는 것에는 견해를 같이하고 있으나 미국측은 공정하고도 유효한 운영면을 고려해서 "나토" 및 미.일 간의 주둔군 지위협정의 형식에서 벗어났으며 한국에서는 이미 청구권 처리에 관한 미국군대의 기관이 설치되어 있어 오랫동안 청구권 문제의 처리를 수행하여 왔으며 동 기구는 한미 양국을 위해 가장 좋다고 역설하면서 미국이 "나토" 및 미.일 간의 주둔군지위협정으로부터 이탈한 양식은 한국에 대한 초안에서 처음 제시된것이 아니라 비률빈, 에티오피아, 리비아, 파키스탄 등과도 이러한 형식을 취했으며 현재 교섭중에 있는 중국과의 협정에도 이러한 양식을 취하고 있다고 말하였음. 이어 미국측은 설명하기를 청구권 지불은 미국의 대외 청구법에 의하여 실시되고 있으며 이는 비전투 행위에서 발생되는 손해에 대한 청구권에 관한 지불에 적용된다고 말하고 이어서 현재 한국에 있는 미국군대의 소청처의 기구를 상세하게 설명하였음. 이상과 같은 설명을 한후 미국측은 한국측은 한국측 안에 의하여 구체적으로 어떻게 청구 사무를 처리하고 (구성체의 인원, ~~한국측~~ 신속성, 장소 및 규정 등) 한국측 안은 어떠한 원칙을 지침으로 삼고 있으며 한국측 안에 의하여 어떠한 이익점이 있는가라는 점을 다음회의에서 설명 해줄것을 요구하였음.

5. 중요 합의사항 :

차량 및 운전면허 문제에 관한 조항에 완전 합의함.

6. 기타 사항 :

차기회의 일자 : 1963. 9. 5. 하오 2시 63-1-137

차기회의 의제 : 차기회의까지 양측 수석대표간에 합의된 사항

1966, 9, 30에 예고문에 의거 일반문서로 재분류됨

0095

63-1-21(3)

미국:로 108-9 (3)

0096

MINUTES OF THE 29th NEGOTIATING SESSION, SOFA NEGOTIATIONS

PARTICPANTS

Republic of Korea	United States
HWANG Ho-ul	Philip C. Habib
KU Chung-hwe	Brig. Gen. G.G. O'Connor, USA
Col. YI Nam-ku, ROKA	William J. Ford
CHU Mun-ki	Col. Howard Smigelow, USA
SIN Chung-sop	Captain R.M. Brownlie, USN
CHO Kwang-che	Col. L. J. Fuller, USA
HO	Robert A. Lewis
YI Kung-hun	Lt. Col. W.A. Burt, USA
KANG Suk-che (Interpreter)	Major Robert Peckham, USA
	Rodney E. Armstrong
	Lt. Col. Charles Nye III, USA (Observer)
	Kenneth Campen (Interpreter)

SUBJECTS: 1. Vehicle and Drivers Licenses

2. Claims

PLACE: Ministry of Foreign Affairs, Seoul

DATE: August 22, 1963

1. Mr. Hwang Ho-ul opened the meeting by introducing Mr. KIM Yun-t'aek and Mr. HO , who were joining the Korean Negotiating Team. He announced that Mr. YI Kyung-won was participating in his last negotiating session, having recently received an assignment to the Korean Mission in Japan. Mr. Habib welcomed Messrs Kim and Ho, and expressed regret at the imminent departure of Mr. Yi. He introduced Lieutenant Charles Nye III, Chief of the United States Armed Forces Claims Service, Korea, who would be present as an observer on the U.S. side during the discussions on the subject of claims.

0097

VEHICLE AND DRIVERS LICENSES

2. Opening substantive discussion, Mr. Hwang stated that the Korean

4. Mr. Chu then elaborated on the provisions of the Korean draft article on the subject of claims as follows: First, the Korean draft provided same as the U.S. draft did that each Party waives claims against the other Party for damage to any property owned by it and used by its armed forces if such damage was caused by members or employees of the armed forces or from the use of any vehicle, vessel or aircraft owned by the other Party in the execution of official duties, provided that the damage was caused to property so used. Secondly, the Korean draft provided that damage to other property owned by either party be settled by a sole arbitrator. Thirdly, it is provided that claims against damages to third Parties arising out of act or omission done in the performance of official duty shall be dealt with the Korean laws. Fourthly, the Korean draft provided that claims arising out of tortious acts or omissions not done in the performance of official duty shall also be dealt with the Korean laws and that claims arose from the use of unauthorized use of vehicle shall be handled in the same manner. Fifthly, it is provided that a dispute as to whether damage was done in the performance of official duty or as to whether the use of vehicle was unauthorized shall be submitted to an arbitrator for decision. Sixthly, in the Korean draft, the provision of contractual dispute was included in the claims article for the sake of convenience.

0038

side accepted the alternative draft of paragraph 3 of the XXXXXXXXXX article on vehicle and drivers licenses tabled at the last negotiating session. Mr. Whang noted that the first two paragraphs of the xxxxxxx xxxxx article had been agreed at previous meetings, and stated that he believed that the negotiators had now reached agreement upon the complete text of this XXXXXXX article. Mr. Habib concurred in this XXXXXXX statement.

CLAIMS

3. Mr. Whang said that Mr. CHU Mun-ki, of the Ministry of Justice would present an explanation of the Korean side's position upon the subject of claims. Mr. Chu said that it was the Korean side's belief that the claims article, together with the article on criminal jurisdiction, were the most important articles of the prospective Status of Forces XX Agreement. Mr. Chu said that in studying the draft tabled by the U. S. negotiators at the last negotiating session, the Korean side had come to the conclusion that there are fundamental fx differences in principle between the two sides' respective drafts on the subject of claims.

4. Mr. Chu then gave a brief explanation of the provisions of the Korean draft article on the subject of claims, comparing the provisions of the Korean draft with those of the U.S. draft article.

5. Mr. Chou said that the Korean draft XXXXXXX article was clearer and more xxxxx logical XXXX than its U.S. counterpart, and would result in the more speedy and XXXXXXXXXXXXXXXXXX successful settlement of claims. Mr. Chu said that the Korean draft had been

—3—

based upon the honest desire of the Korean people to encourage the ... development of processes for the resolution of common problems and misunderstandings. Mr. Chu said he wished to stress the desire of the Korean side for an appropriate reaction from the U.S. negotiators upon the Korean draft article. Mr. Chu suggested that the negotiators' discussion on the subject of claims proceed on the basis of the Korean draft article; before doing this, however, the Korean side would appreciate a general explanation by the U.S. side of its draft article.

6. Mr. Habib said that the U.S. side had studied the Korean draft article carefully. There appeared to be one common point between the two sides' drafts on the subject of claims: that claims should be paid. The U.S. side had approached the problem of providing for the payment of claims from the point of view that claims should be paid equitably and promptly, within the framework of a workable administrative system. The U.S. side in its draft had departed from the older claims formula which guided the drafting of the articles on claims in the North Atlantic Treaty Orgranization and Japanese Agreements, and which has obviously guided the Korean side in the drafting of its article. It was important to recognize why this departure had been made.

7. Mr. Habib said that the formula concept for the payment of claims, that is, the system whereby the host country bears a share of the cost of each scope-of-duty claim ... out in the NATO Agreement, The

0100

United States (at that time) had/wanted the sharing of claims costs for several reasons. There was during this period widespread inflation, particularly in Western Europe, and the United States wished to prevent sky-rocketing claims costs by the insertion of a provision which would give the host nation a financial interest in each scope-of-duty claim paid. Something of the same philosophy had been carried over into the Japanese Agreement for much the same reasons. The United States had found, however, during the course of its ten years experience with administration of the formula concept that it is time-consuming and expensive to administer, compel the host nation to establish an expensive bureaucracy, and often engenders ill-will between the host nation and the United States.

8. Mr. Habib said that in some cases administration of the formula concept for claims settlement had approached the unworkable. In Japan, the formula concept was currently being administered in a manner much different from that described in the actual Agreement. In Korea, the United States had a claims procedure in operation which had the benefit of backround and experience acquired in four years of operation. This procedure is administered by experienced Korean and American personnel who quickly and efficiently adjudicate and pay claims. The U.S. side felt that the continuation of this system would be in the best interests of Korea and the United States.

0101

9. Mr. Habib suggested that the Korean negotiators consider the advantages of the continuation of the present system of claims payment as against the disadvantages of the system proposed by the Korean side. The Korean draft article provides that proper-of-duty claims shall be paid according to the procedures and system employed by the Korean Armed Forces. The Korean Armed Forces do not have a system for the payment of claims which meets the requirements of the situation. It would, therefore, be necessary for the Korean Government to establish such a system, staffing the institutions with experienced people who have a backround in law, a knowledge of damages awards in Korea, and investigative ability. The new system would require constant recourse to the Korean courts for adjustments, for the Korean system for the payment of claims relies upon the court system.

10. Mr. Habib said that in addition to the increased costs to the Korean Government which would result from the establishment and staffing of a new claims payment system, the Korean draft article on claims would require that the Korean Government bear fifteen per cent of the cost of proper-of-duty claims. It should be noted that under the Japanese Agreement, the Government of Japan bears twenty-five per cent of the cost of such claims. The continuation of the present system of paying proper-of-duty claims would not, however, cost the Korean Government anything.

0102

11. Mr. Habib said that the claims payment procedure proposed by the Korean side would be time-consuming, and result in the delay of payments. It now requires approximately three months for the payment of a scope-of-duty claim by the U.S. Forces in Korea. In Japan, payment of a similar claim requires approximately six months, with all that such a delay implies by way of ill-will toward the United States and the host country. The U.S. side had operated a system such as is proposed in the Korean draft, and knew that this system carried with it the ever-present chance for the generation of ill-will.

12. Mr. Habib noted that the draft article on claims tabled by the U.S. in the present negotiations did not mark the first departure by U.S. negotiators from the NATO - Japan Agreements concept. The U.S. had departed from the formula concept in a number of agreements in the past, and would depart from it in other agreements to be negotiated in the future, for the reasons which had just been mentioned. It was the hope of the U.S. side that the Korean Agreement would be among those agreements which set the pace in this regard for the future. Departures from the formula concept had been made in the Philipines, Ethiopian, Pakistan, and Libyan Agreements, and a departure from the formula concept was currently being negotiated with the Government of the Republic of China.

0103

13. Mr. Habib said that the Korean side might better understand

what the U.S. negotiators were proposing, he had asked ~~XX~~ Lieutenant ~~XXXX~~ Colonel Charles Nye to come ~~XXXXXX~~ to the meeting to ~~XXXXXXX~~ explain in detail the manner in which the U.S. Forces presently pay claims in Korea, and the ~~xx~~ results of the operation of the present ~~XXXXXX~~ system. He then turned the floor over to Colonel Nye, who gave a summary of the paper which appears as an ~~enclosure~~ attachment to this ~~report~~ record.

16. Following the completion of Colonel Nye's presentation, Mr. Habib said that he wished to remind the Korean negotiators that the Colonel had presented merely the operations of his agency, and there were also hundreds of personnel who receive and process claims as they proceed through channels to Colonel Nye's office. The Korean side had proposed a system under which the Korean Government would take over the operation of the system Colonel Nye had just explained, under the terms of regulations and procedures which the U.S. side understood do not yet exist. Not only would this constitute ~~xxx~~ a tremendous administrative burden, but ~~XXXXXXXX~~ it would not in the end advance the main pronciples upon which the U.S. draft article ~~xxx~~ is based: e.g., the equitable and prompt payment of claims within the framework of a workable ~~xxxxxxxxxxxxx~~ administrative system.

17. Mr. Habib said that at this point he would like to ~~XXXXXXXXXX~~ put to the Korean negotiators certain questions, which ~~XXX~~ would not necessarily

0104

have to be answered at the present session, having to do with the manner in which the Korean side would carry out the administration of the system for the payment of claims which was set forth in its draft article. How would the Korean side staff the system contemplated in its draft? Where would the Korean side obtain the people with the experience and backround needed to administer their system? How soon would the system contemplated in ~~ix~~ the Korean draft article be ready to go into ~~XXXXX~~ operation? What advantages over the present system did the Korean negotiators see for their system, assuming that it could be put into effect? The U.S. side believed that the system it was proposing ~~XXXXXXX~~ is the best way to pay just claims, and was willing to elaborate further upon the way in which the system envisaged in the U.S. draft ~~xxxxxx~~ works. The U.S. side would be willing to take the Korean negotiators to the offices of the U.S. Armed Forces Claims Service, Korea, in order that they might better grasp the manner in which the present system operates.

16. Mr. Chu thanked the ~~XXXX~~ U.S. side for its ~~XXXXXX~~ explanation of its draft, and asked certain statistical questions which the U.S. side noted were answered in the statistical appendix to Colonel Nye's paper which had not been read in the interest of cutting short the time required for the paper's presentation. Mr. Chu then asked what ~~XXX~~ appeal procedures were open to claimants under the present U.S. Forces claims payment system?

17. Colonel Nye said that a claimant could appeal XXXXXX from the XXXXX Claims Commissions of his office XX up through to him, acting as the Chief, U.S. Armed Forces Claims Service, Korea. If not satisfied, the claimant could appeal to Headquarters, United States Armed Forces Claims Service, in the United States. XXXXXXXXXX There were, in actual practice, very few appeals lodged XXXX against the awards of the Claims Commissions. The U.S. side would provide XXXXXXXXX statistics upon the xx number of such appeals.

18. Mr. Chu said the Korean side would like to know the number of accident claims satisfied under the present U.S. ArmedXXXXXXXXXXXXX Forces claims system in Korea, and the proportion of amounts paid to the amountsxfxx of compensation requested. The U.S. side agreed to provide statistics upon these points. Mr. Chu said that the Korean negotiators would XX answer the questions put by Mr. Habib at the conclusion of the U.S. side's presentation at a later meeting.

19. Mr. Whang said that the exchange of views at the present session had given the Korean negotiators an understanding of the U.S. side's intentions. The Korean negotiators would study the XXXXX explanation given by the U.S. side, and discuss it at the next negotiating session.

20. It was agreed that the next negotiating session would be held on September 5, 1963, at 2:00 XX P.M.

0106

1966, 12 . 31 에 예고문에 의거 일반문서로 재분류됨

XXXXX Attachment: Paper Presented by the U.S. Armed Forces Claims Service,

JOINT SUMMARY RECORD OF THE 29TH SESSION

August 22, 1963

1. Time and Place : 3:00 to 4:40 p.m. August 22, 1963 at the Foreign Minister's Conference Room

II. Attendants:

ROK Side:

Mr. Whang, Ho Eul	Director Bureau of Political Affairs Ministry of Foreign Affairs
Mr. Shin, Kwan Sup	Director Bureau of Customs Dupty Ministry of Finance
Mr. Koo, Choong Whay	Chief, America Section Ministry of Foreign Affairs
Col. Lee, Nam Koo	Chief, Military Affairs Section Ministry of National Defense
Mr. Chu, Mun Ki	Chief, Legal Affairs Section Ministry of Justice
Mr. Shin, Jung Sup	Chief, Treaty Section Ministry of Foreign Affairs
Mr. Lee, Kyung Hoon	2nd Secretary Ministry of Foreign Affairs
Mr. Kang, Suk Jae	2nd Secretary Ministry of Foreign Affairs
Mr. Cho, Kwang Je	2nd Secretary Ministry of Foreign Affairs
Mr. Huh, Sung	Third Secretary Ministry of Foreign Affairs

U.S. Side:

Mr. Philip C. Habib	Counselor of the Embassy for Political Affairs
Gen. G.G. O'Connor	Deputy Chief of Staff 8th Army
Mr. William J. Ford	First Secretary of the Embassy

0107

미주과	양고재	담 당	과 장	국 장	특별보좌관	차 관	장 관

196 . 예고문에 의거 일반문서로 재분류됨

Col. Howard Smigelow, USA	Deputy Chief of Staff UNC
Capt. R.M. Brownlie	Assistant Chief of Staff USN/K
Col. L.J. Fuller	Staff Judge Advocate United Nations Command
Mr. Rodney Armstrong	Economic Officer, American Embassy
Lt. Col. W.A. Burt	J-5
Mr. Robert A. Lewis	Second Secretary and Consul of the Embassy
Major Robert D. Peckham	Staff Officer, JAG 8th Army
Lt. Col. Charles Nye III,	Chief, U.S. Armed Forces Claims Service, 8th Army (Observer)
Kenneth Campen	Interpreter

1. Mr. Whang Ho Eul opened the meeting by introducing in replacement on Mr. KIM Yun-t'aek, Mr. Huh, who was joining the Korean Negotiating Team. He announced that Mr. Lee Kyung Hoon was participating in his last negotiating session, having recently received an assignment to the Korean Mission in Japan. Mr. Habib welcomed Mr. Huh and expressed regret at the imminent departure of Mr. Lee & Mr. Kim. He introduced Lieutenant Charles Nye III, Chief of the United States Armed Forces Claims Service, Korea, who would be present as an observer on the U.S. side during the discussions on the subject of claims.

VEHICLE AND DRIVERS LICENSES

2. Opening substantive discussion, Mr. Whang stated that the Korean side accepted the alternative draft of paragraph 3 of the article on vehicle and drivers licenses tabled at the last negotiating session. Mr. Whang noted that the first two paragraphs of the article had been agreed at previous meetings, and stated that he believed that the negotiators had now reached agreement

0108

upon the complete text of this article. Mr. Habib concurred in this statement.

CLAIMS

3. Mr. Whang said that Mr. CHU Mun-ki, of the Ministry of Justice would present an explanation of the Korean side's position upon the subject of claims. Mr. Chu said that it was the Korean side's belief that the claims article, together with the article on criminal jurisdiction, were the most important articles of the prospective Status of Forces Agreement. Mr. Chu said that in studying the draft tabled by the U.S. negotiators at the last negotiating session, the Korean side had come to the conclusion that there are fundamental differences in principle between the two sides' respective drafts on the subject of claims.

4. Mr. Chu then summarized on the provisions of the Korean draft article on the subject of claims as follows:
First, the Korean draft provided in the same manner as the U.S. draft, that each Party waives claims against the other Party for damage to any property owned by it and used by its armed forces, if such damage was caused by members or employees of the armed forces or from the use of any vehicle, vessel or aircraft owned by the other Party in the execution of official duties, provided that the damage was caused to property so used. Secondly, the Korean draft provides that damage to other property owned by either party be settled by a sole arbitrator. Thirdly, it is provided that claims based upon damage to third Parties arising out of act or omission done in the performance of official duty shall be dealt with under the Korean law. Fourthly, the Korean draft provided that calims arising out of tortious acts or omissions not done in the performance of

0109

official duty shall also be dealt with under the Korean law and that claims arising from the unauthorized use of a vehicle shall be handled in the same manner. Fifthly, it is provided that a dispute as to whether damage was done in the performance of official duty or as to whether the use of vehicle was unauthorized shall be submitted to an arbitrator for decision. Sixthly, in the Korean draft, the provision of the prospective agreement governing contractual disputes was included in the claims article for the sake of convenience.

5. Mr. Chu said that the Korean draft article was clearer and more logical than its U.S. counterpart, and would result in the more speedy and successful settlement of claims. Mr. Chu said that the Korean draft had been based upon the formula concept for the settlement of scope-of-duty claims. He said the Korean people desires the inclusion of the formula concept in the claims article of the prospective Agreement, and that inclusion of formula concept would further strengthen friendly relations between Korea and the United States and permit the removal of possible misunderstanding. Mr. Chu said he hoped the full agreement upon the Korean draft article. Mr. Chu suggested that the negotiators' discussion on the subject of claims proceed on the basis of the Korean draft article; before doing this, however, the Korean side would appreciate a general explanation by the U.S. side of its draft article.

6. Mr. Habib said that the U.S. side had studied the Korean draft article carefully. There appeared to be one common point between the two sides' drafts on the subject of claims: that claims should be paid. The U.S. side had approached the problem of providing for the payment of claims from the point of view that claims should be paid equitably and promptly, within

0110

the frame-work of a workable administrative system. The U.S. side in its draft had departed from the older claims formula which guided the drafting of the articles on claims in the North Atlantic Treaty Orgznization and Japanese Agreements, and which has obviously guided the Korean side in the drafting of its article. It was important to recognize why this departure had been made.

7. Mr. Habib said that the formularconcept for the payment of claims, that is, the system whereby the host country bears a share of the cost of each scope-of-duty claim, was first worked out in the NATO Agreement, The United States had at that time wanted the sharing of claims costs for several reasons. There was during this period widespread inflation, particularly in Western Europe, and the United States wished to prevent sky-rocketing claims costs by the insertion of a provision which would give the hast nation a financial interest in each scope-of-duty claim paid. Something of the same philosophy had been carried over into the Japanese Agreement for much the same reasons. The United States had found, however, during the course of its ten years experience with administration of the formula concept that it is time consuming and expensive to administer,compel the host nation to establish an expensive bureaucracy, and often engenders ill-will between the host nation and the United States.

8. Mr. Habib said that in some cases administration of the formula concept for claims settlement had approached the unworkable. In Japan, the formula concept was currently being administered in a manner much different from that described in the actual Agreement. In Korea, the United States had a claims procedure in operation which had the benefit of backround and experience acquired in four years of operation. This procedure

0111

is administered by experienced Korean and American personnel who quickly and efficiently adjudicate and pay claims. The U.S. side felt that the continuation of this system would be in the best interests of Korea and the United States.

9. Mr. Habib suggested that the Korean negotiators consider the advantages of the continuation of the present system of claims payment as against the disadvantages of the system proposed by the Korean side. The Korean draft article provides that scope-of-duty claims shall be paid according to the procedures and system employed by the Korean Armed Forces. The Korean Armed Forces do not have a system for the payment of claims which meets the requirements of the situation. It would, therefore, be necessary for the Korean Government to establish such a system, staffing the institutions with experienced people who have a backround in law, a knowledge of damages awards in Korea, and investigative ability. The new system would require constant recourse to the Korean courts for adjustments, for the Korean system for the payment of claims relies upon the court system.

10. Mr. Habib said that in addition to the increased costs to the Korean Government which would result from the establishment and staffing of a new claims payment system, the Korean draft article on claims would require that the Korean Government bear fifteen per cent of the cost of scope-of-duty claims. It should be noted that under the Japanese Agreement, the Government of Japan bears twenty-five per cent of the cost of such claims. The continuation of the present system of paying scope-of-duty claims would not, however, cost the Korean Government anything.

0112

11. Mr. Habib said that the claims payment procedure proposed by the Korean side would be time-consuming, and result in the delay of payments. It now requires approximately three months for the payment of a scope-of-duty claim by the U.S. Forces in Korea. In Japan, payment of a similar claim requires approximately six months, with all that such a delay implies by way of ill-will toward the United States and the host country. The U.S. side had operated a system such as is proposed in the Korean draft, and knew that this system carried with it the ever-present chance for the generation of ill-will.

12. Mr. Habib noted that the draft article on claims tabled by the U.S. in the present negotiations did not mark the first departure by U.S. negotiators from the NATO -Japan Agreements formula concept. The U.S. had departed from the formula concept in a number of agreements in the past, and would depart from it in other agreements to be negotiated in the future, for the reasons which had just been mentioned. It was the hope of the U.S. side that the Korean Agreement would be among those agreements which set the pace in this regard for the future. Departures from the formula concept had been made in the philipines, Ethiopian, Pakistan, and Libyan Agreements, and a departure from the formula concept was currently being negotiated with the Government of the Republic of China.

13. Mr. Habib said that in order that the Korean side might better understand what the U.S. negotiators were proposing, he had asked Lieutenant Colonel Charles Nye to come to the meeting to explain in detail the manner in which the U.S. Forces presently pay claims in Korea, and the results of the operation of the present system. He then turned the floor over to Colonel Nye, who gave a summary of the paper which

0113

appears as an attachment to this record.

14. Following the completion of Colonel Nye's presentation, Mr. Habib said that he wished to remind the Korean negotiators that the Colonel had presented merely the operations of his agency, and there were also hundreds of personnel who receive and process claims as they proceed through channels to Colonel Nye's office. The Korean side had proposed a system under which the Korean Government would take over the operation of the system Colonel Nye had just explained, under the terms of regulations and procedures which the U.S. side understood do not yet exist. Not only would this constitute a tremendous administrative burden, but it would not in the end advance the main principles upon which the U.S. draft article is based: e.g., the equitable and prompt payment of claims within the framework of a workable administrative system.

15. Mr. Habib said that at this point he would like to put to the Korean negotiators certain questions, which would not necessarily have to be answered at the present session, having to do with the manner in which the Korean side would carry out the administration of the system for the payment of claims which was set forth in its draft article. How would the Korean side staff the system contemplated in its draft? Where would the Korean side obtain the people with the experience and backround needed to administer their system? How soon would the system contemplated in the Korean draft article be ready to go into operation? What advantages over the present system did the Korean negotiators see for their system, assuming that it could be put into effect? The U.S. side believed that the system it was proposing is the best way to pay just claims,

0114

and was willing to elaborate further upon the way in which the system envisaged in the U.S. draft works. The U.S. side would be willing to take the Korean negotiators to the offices of the U.S. Armed Forces Claims Service, Korea, in order that they might better grasp the manner in which the present system operates.

16. Mr. Chu thanked the U.S. side for its explanation of its draft, and asked certain statistical questions which the U.S. side noted were answered in the statistical appendix to Colonel Nye's paper which had not been read in the interest of cutting short the time required for the paper's presentation. Mr. Chu then asked what appeal procedures were open to claimants under the present U.S. Forces Claims payment system?

17. Colonel Nye said that a claimant could appeal from the Claims Commissions of his office up through to him, acting as the Chief, U.S. Armed Forces Claims Service, Korea, If not satisfied, the claimant could appeal to Headquarters, United States Armed Forces Claims Service, in the United States. There were, in actual practice, very few appeals lodged against the awards of the Claims Commissions. The U.S. side would provide statistics upon the number of such appeals.

18. Mr. Chu said the Korean side would like to know the number of accident claims satisfied under the present U.S. Armed Forces claims system in Korea, and the proportion of amounts paid to the amounts of compensation requested. The U.S. side agreed to provide statistics upon these points. Mr. Chu said that the Korean negotiators would answer the questions put by Mr. Habib at the conclusion of the U.S. side's presentation at a later meeting.

0115

19. Mr. Whang said that the exchange of views at the present session had given the Korean negotiators an understanding of the U.S. side's intentions. The Korean negotiators would study the explanation given by the U.S. side, and discuss it at the next negotiating session.

20. It was agreed that the next negotiating session would be held on September 5, 1963, at 2:00 P.M.

Attachment: Paper Presented by the U.S. Armed Forces Claims Service, Korea.

1966,12.31에 예고문에 의거 일반문서로 재분류됨

Attachment

U.S. ARMED FORCES CLAIMS SERVICE, KOREA
APO 301

1. General.

Payment of the claims of citizens and residents of Korea is authorized by an act of the United States Congress called the "Foreign Claims Act". This law provides for the payment of meritorious claims by the inhabitants of countries in which United States troops are stationed, based on death, personal injury, or property damage caused by noncombat activities of U.S. armed forces. This law is implemented in detail by regulations of the Army, Navy and Air Force.

2. U.S. liability.

Under the foreign claims program United States liability is established when injury, death, or property damage is caused (partially or wholly) by the careless or wrongful act of a member or U.S. civilian employee of the United States Forces Korea, or by other noncombat activities of those forces. Liability also is assumed if the damages are caused by Korean civilian employees while acting within the scope of their employment. As would be expected, the United States cannot assume responsibility for damages caused by members of the Korean Army or employees of the Korean Government, even though these persons may be engaged with U.S. forces at the time in the joint mission of maintaining military readiness against a common enemy. Cognizance is taken, however, of the unique cooperation between the military forces of the Republic of Korea and of the United States by which Korean military persons are integrated into U.S. Army units, known as the Korean Augmentation to the United States Army (KATUSA).

0117

Liability is assumed and compensation is paid for injuries and damages caused by these persons when acting within the scope of their assigned duties for U.S. Army units.

3. Investigation of claims.

An elaborate system is prescribed by U.S. Army directives for the investigation and reporting of detailed facts and circumstances involved in every incident in which a person suffers injury, death, or property damage as the result of military activities. Hundreds of investigating officers and commanders of Army units and installations are responsible for investigating the incidents and accidents in which members of the USFK are involved. Detailed reports of the investigations are forwarded to higher authority for approval, and a copy of each report is forwarded to the Claims Service. In some instances additional investigation and inquiry may be required in order to fairly evaluate a claim. This further investigation is more effectively handled by personnel specially trained in the law and procedures pertaining to the payment of claims. Consequently, the investigation at this point is normally conducted by the claims service which processes the claims against the United States.

4. The Claims Service in Korea.

a. The Department of Defense has designated the Army to settle claims arising in Korea which are caused by the activities of members and employees of the United States Forces Korea. This is accomplished through the U.S. Armed Forces Claims Service, Korea, and Claims Commissions attached to that organization, located on the Yongsan Military Reservation. The establishment of Claims Commissions are required by the "Foreign Claims Act", and their primary duty is to consider and settle claims submitted by the inhabitants of the country involved. A commissioner must be a commissioned officer and normally is a judge advocate officer of the military service concerned. One-member commissions are empowered to adjudge and pay claims for not more than $1000 (129,500 Won) and three-member commissions may pay claims for not more than $15,000 (1,942,500 Won). Claims in excess of the latter amount are transmitted to the Department of the Army for approval by the Congress before payment may be made. Commissions of any of the military services may consider and pay claims caused by the activities and members of the other services.

b. The U.S. Armed Forces Claims Service is manned by fourteen American persons and thirteen citizens of Korea. Seven of the Korean employees are specially trained claims investigators and classified among the highest paid Korean employees of the Eighth Army. Each of the three commissioned officers (including the Chief) is appointed as a one-member commission, and together they constitute a three-member commission. In addition to the Office of the Chief and the Claims Commissions, the Claims Service is organized as follows

<u>Administrative Branch</u>	<u>Investigation Branch</u>	<u>Claims Branch</u>	<u>Payment Branch</u>
5 U.S.	1 U.S.	3 U.S.	2 U.S.
3 KN	5 KN	1 KN	2 KN

c. The functions of the four branches are somewhat self-evident. Briefly:

(1) The Administration Branch maintains all records of claims, reports of investigation, and related files. When a claim initially is received in the Claims Service it is channeled to the Administration Branch for recording and indexing. A claim number is assigned by which the claim may be readily identified at all future times, and a portfolio prepared in which all documents are filed which pertain to the claim.

(2) The Investigation Branch is comprised of five (5) Korean national employees, all classified as senior investigators, and one commissioned officer as supervisor. Upon receiving a claims portfolio from the Administration Branch, the file is assigned to an investigator for translation of documents which are submitted in Korean and for development of the essential evidence required for complete adjudication of the claim. As a general principle the securing of evidence in support of a claim is the responsibility of the claimant. A large part of our investigators' duties, however, is to assist the claimant in securing the evidence and in many instances to secure the evidence for the claimant. When the Investigation Branch considers investigation is complete, the portfolio is transferred to the Claims Branch for further processing.

(a) The Investigation Branch also interviews all claimants who visit the Claims Service, assists them in preparing their claims on bi-lingual forms provided, and advises of the nature of evidence and formal documents (such as family registers, certificates of land ownership) that

4

0120

are required to support their claims. It may be noted at this point that whether a claimant desires to employ an attorney to represent him in connection with his claim is a matter solely within the discretion of the claimant. The Claims Service offers all the advice and assistance that is needed to file and establish the claim.

(3) The Claims Branch examines the claims portfolio to determine whether evidence is sufficient to support final adjudication of the claim. A resume of the claim is prepared for the benefit of the Chief and the claims commissions, including a recommendation as to the amount of compensation that should be awarded.

(4) Upon completion of the processing of a claim by the Claims Branch, the portfolio is transferred to the Chief of the Claims Service for examination and consideration. The Chief assigns claims not in excess of $1000 (129,500 Won) to the one-member commissions for final adjudication. As President of the three-member commission, he convenes the commission for consideration and adjudication of claims in excess of $1000 (129,500 Won). If the claim exceeds $15,000 (1,942,500 Won), he prepares a detailed memorandum and recommendation that is forwarded with the claim file to the Department of the Army for final action.

(5) When a commission adjudges an award in a claim, the portfolio is transferred to the Payment Branch ~~Branch~~. This Branch notifies the claimant of the amount of award and prepares a settlement agreemtn for the claimant to sign. Upon receipt of the signed settlement agreement arrangements are made for claimant to receive his compensation. Most

claimants are paid on the Yongsan Military Reservation. In many instances, however, arrangements are made for claimants to be paid at a military post near their homes. This is particularly true when claimant lives a long distance from Seoul, as in the Taegu or Pusan area. In addition, when a claimant is too old or ill to travel a representative of the Claims Service takes the compensation to him at his home. This also is done in most small claims in order that claimant may realize the full benefit of his award.

5. General criteria used in computing damages.

a. Property damage. Allowable compensation normally represents the cost of repairs to or restoration of the property damaged to its state of condition immediately prior to the time of damage. The claimant may establish these costs by receipts for amounts expended for repair, or by estimates of the cost of repair by reputable contractors or other repairmen. Compensation for lost or completely destroyed property is computed at the actual value of the property at time of loss or destruction. Value of growing crops and trees are similarly computed.

b. Compensation for personal injury and death. These computations usually are not as amenable to mathematical calculations as are costs of repair or destruction of vehicles, buildings, or other property. To obtain, however, as much consistency as may be possible standard elements are utilized in order to have a sound basis on which awards may be computed for death and in various types of personal injury. The Claims Commission is charged with the responsibility of evaluating each case in the light of these standard elements in order to arrive at fair awards. The Chief of the Claims Service supervises the activities of the Claims Commissions for the purpose of assuring that awards to claimants are fair and nondiscriminatory.

(1) Personal Injury. Standard compensable items are:

(a) Medical and hospital expenses, including immediate first aid treatment and ambulance service.

(b) Reasonable costs of Chinese medicines which are prescribed by a doctor as treatment for the injury, or resulting illness, on which claim is based.

(c) Loss of income for the period during which claimant is absent from work or occupation.

(d) Pain and suffering of the injured party.

(e) Permanent disability. A "Table of Disability Grades" is used. This table is patterned after the one provided in the Korean Labor Standard Act of 1953. The table includes four disability grades not appearing in the Korean table, and the number of days of compensation for each disability grade has been increased in recognition of the increased cost of living in Korea since 1953. If the injured party is not a wage or income earner (such as a child or housewife), emphasis is placed on the nature (rather than grade) of disability and age and pain and suffering of the injured party in order to arrive at comparable awards.

(f) Disfigurement. Scars and other disfigurements of a female are considered more serious than those suffered by a male. In addition, age, social status and occupation of both the male and female are taken into account.

(g) Cost of artificial limbs, and their repair and replacement for life expectancy of the injured party.

(h) Miscellaneous expenses attributable to the injuries sustained.

(2) Death. Standard compensable items are:

(a) Medical and hospital expenses incident to and preceding death.

(b) Funeral expenses. These include preparation of body for burial, purchase and preparation of gravesite, reasonable amounts for traditional ceremonial expenses (including food and drink).

(c) Death award. Our Korean claimants frequently refer to this element as a "solatium" or "consolation award". The amount of this award varies from case to case, being affected by the age, income and social status of the deceased, as well as his family relationship (that is, whether the father, mother, minor daughter, first son, or other). Additional amounts are computed in this award for a surviving widow and for each surviving child under age of seventeen years. Our experience indicates that average death awards range from $772.20 (100,000 Won) for young children to approximately $2702.70 (350,000 Won) for adults.

(d) Miscellaneous expenses attributable to the death on which claim is based.

6. Hospitalization of claimants.

As a general rule United States law authorizes admission to and treatment in U.S. hospitals only for U.S. persons (and some of their dependents) who are employed by the Government. Not all U.S. employees are eligible for this medical service. Exceptions may be made in emergency and unusual cases for a small number of other persons, in which event the individual is charged $37.00 (4792 Won) for each day of hospitalization and $7.00 (907 Won) for each outpatient treatment. Nevertheless special arrangements have been approved for the claims program in Korea which operates under the "Foreign Claims Act", whereunder any Korean citizen who is injured by the activities of United States Forces Korea may be admitted and treated (including all necessary surgery) in U.S. hospitals in Korea without any charge whatsoever for the medical services. In the past few years hundreds of Korean citizens have been treated under this program in Army medical facilities and furnished free hospitalization for weeks and months in our major hospitals. Several of the patients have received this hospitalization and medical service for more than one year in the 121st U.S. Hospital located near Inchon.

0125

7. Statistics.

The number of claims received by Claims Commissions and amounts of compensation paid since the Claims Service began its operations on 1 June 1959 are shown below:

	1959 (7 mos)	1960	1961	1962	1963 (6 mos)
Nr. Received:	517	2,125	1,163	979	378
Amount Paid:	$282,688.28	$727,696.22	$361,801.26	$187,633.75	$77,032.16

Total claims received since 1 June 1959: 5,162

Total compensation paid since 1 June 1959: $1,636,851.67 (12,639,775 Won)

0126

3. 제30차 회의, 9.5

0127

기 안 용 지

자체 통제		기안처	미주과 강석재	전화번호	근거서류접수일자
	과장	국장		차관	장관
	(서명)	(서명) 9.4		(서명)	(서명)
관계관 서명					
기안 년월일	1963.9.4	시행 년월일		보존 년한	정서 기장
분류 기호	외정미	전체 통제		종결	
경수참 유신조	건의		발신		
제목	제30차 주둔군지위협정 체결 교섭회의에 임할 우리측입장				

9월 5일에 개최될 제30차 주둔군지위협정 체결 한미간 교섭회의에서는 민사청구권문제를 토의할 예정이며 이에 관련하여 지난 회의에서 미국측 교섭자가 제기한 문제를 포함한 우리나라의 현행보상제도를 설명토록 되어 있는바 우리측 교섭실무자는 지난 8월 31일과 9월 3일 2차에 걸친 회합을 갖고 우리측 태도를 토의하였으며 동 토의결과 별첨과 같이 결정하였아오니 재가하여 주시기 바랍니다.

유첨: 제30차 주둔군지위협정체결 교섭회의에서 설명한 우리나라 현행보상제도 개황. 끝.

승인양식 1-1-3 (1112-040-016-018) (190mm×260mm16절지)

0128

30차

大韓民國의 國家賠償制度

1. 概要

故意 또는 過失로 因한 違法行爲로 損害를 加한 個人이 損害를 입은 個人에게 그 損害를 賠償할 責任이 있는바와 같이 國家 또는 公共団体의 公務員이 職務를 執行함에 当하여 故意 또는 過失로 法令에 違反하여 損害를 加하였거나, 道路, 河川, 其他 公共營造物의 設置 또는 管理에 瑕疵가 있어 個人에게 損害를 加하였거나 其他 民法과 其外의 法令에 違反하여 個人에게 損害를 加하였을 때, 國家 또는 公共団体는 1951.9.8. 法律第231號로 公布된 國家賠償法에 依하여 그 損害를 賠償할 責任이 있으므로 國家는 個人에게 對하여 同法에 依한 損害를 賠償하여 왔다.

2. 國家의 賠償責任

승인양식 1-1-2 (1112-040-016-017) (190mm×260mm 16절지)

0129

國家賠償法에 依하면 國家의 公務員(陸,海,空軍 및 海兵隊의 軍人,軍屬 및 雇傭員等을 包含하는 모든 公務員)이 그 職務를 執行함에 當하여 (가) 故意 또는 過失로 法令에 違反하여 個人을 死亡케 하였거나 負傷을 입혔거나 名譽를 毁損하였거나 火災 其他로 財産을 破毁하는 等 損害를 加하였을 때, (나) 또는 道路, 河川 其他 公共營造物의 設置 또는 管理에 瑕疵가 있어 個人을 死亡케 하였거나 負傷을 입혔거나 田畓等을 埋沒케하여 財産을 破毁하는 等 財産上의 損害를 加하였거나 (다) 民法 其他 法令에 違反하여 個人에게 損害를 加하였을 때에는 國家는 그 個人(相續人等을 包含한다)에게 모든 損害를 賠償할 責任이 있고, 이 境遇 外國人이 國家로부터 損害를 입었다면 ~~美國의 海外請求法과 같이 우리國民이 外國國家로부터 입은 損害를 賠償하는 것과 같이~~ 그 國家와 相互保障이 있으면 그 外國人에게도 우리 國家는

승인양식 1-1-2 (1112-040-016-017) (190mm×260mm 16절지)

0130

損害를 賠償하다.

3. 賠償機關과 그 構成員

위에서 說明한바와 같이 國家로 부터 損害를 받은 個人은 國家에 대하여 그 賠償을 請求하여 賠償金을 支給받을수 있는데 그 賠償機關과 構成員은 다음과 같다.

A. 法務部長官

1962. 12. 24 法律第1223号 國家賠償金請求에 關한 節次法이 公布施行된 后 國家賠償金을 請求하고저 하는 者는 法務部長官에게 그 支給을 申請하며 法務部長官은 이를 審議 決定하기 爲하여 法務部에 國家賠償金審議會 (法務局訟務課와 別途로)를 設置하였다.

(1) 構成

法務部에 있는 總務課는 國家賠償金

支給申請書를 接受하여 接受即時 法務部 訟務課로 送付한다.

(2) 受理 및 調査

法務部 訟務課는 國家賠償金支給關係 一般行政과 調査를 担当하며 申請書를 總務課로부터 送付받는 即時 調査官으로 하여금 調査케 하는바 調査官으로는 法官과 同一한 資格이 있는 檢事 2名, 法律專門家인 法務官 1名, 事務官 2名, 其他職員 18名으로 이들은 過去 十余年間 國家賠償關係裁判實務에 從事하여 얻은 能熟한 調査技術과 全國의 檢察庁 其他 捜査機關을 包含한 모든 行政機關과 軍機關의 積極的인 協助에 依하여 公務員의 故意, 過失과 職務執行 與否 및 그로 因한 損害發生與否와 그 証據를 蒐集하여 賠償額의 審議判斷에 必要한 모든 資料를

準備하고 調査報告書를 作成하여 申請書와 함께 審議会에

送付한다.

(3) 審議

審議会는 申請書와 調査報告書를 詳細히

検討하고 法律的인 判断을 加하여 國家賠償與否와 그 額

数를 審議議決하는데 그 構成員으로는 委員長 1名과 委員

6名 幹事 1名과 書記 若干名이 있는데 委員長은 法務部次官

委員은 法務部의 3局長, 法務官 1名, 辯護士 1名과 賠償

責任部處의 書記官 以上 職員 1名이며 이 委員들이 賠償金의

多少를 論하고 審議議決한다. 이 委員들은 모두 10年

以上 法曹経歴이 있는 분들로 大法院判事와 同一한 資格要

件을 具備한 분들이며 関係部處의 委員(例 陸軍으로 個人은

죽게 하였으면 將校한 陸軍法務將校 1名이 選任되어 当該

事件에만 関與한다)도 그部處의 高級公務員中 法律專門家(法務官)가 任命된다.

(4) 賠償額의 最終決定

審議会는 賠償金을 審議議決하여 이를 法務部長官에게 報告하며 法務部長官은 이를 根拠으로 하여 賠償額의 最終 決定을 한다.

(5) 通知 및 申請人의 同意와 賠償金 支付申請

法務部長官은 申請人에게 賠償金 決定을 通知하고 이 通知를 받은 申請人이 이에 滿足하면 同意하여 賠償金支付를 申請하며 이에 滿足하지 않으면 法院에 提訴한다.

(6) 支給依賴와 支給

法務部長官이 賠償金支付申請을 받으면

승인양식 1-1-2 (1112-040-016-017) (190mm×260mm 16절지)

0134

이를 財務部 또는 國防部長官에게 支給을 依頼하며, 이 依頼를 받으면 即時 賠償金을 支給한다.

(7) 接受日부터 賠償金支給까지의 期間

接受, 受理, 調査 및 審議議決과 法務部長官의 決定은 接受日로부터 2月以内이고 決定通知는 7日以内, 申請人의 同意與否는 3週日 以内이므로 最長期日이 3月以内이며 最短期日은 25日로 되었다.

B. 法院

法院은 最高法院인 大法院과 下級法院인 高等法院과 地方法院 및 그 支院으로 組織되어 各地에 設置되어 있고 大學을 卒業하고 資格있는 國家考試에 合格하여 2年以上 또는 이와 同等한 実務修習한 者 또는 이와 同等한 者中 優秀한 者를 抜擢 任命한 350名의 法官으로 構成되어 있다.

(1) 處理節次

國家賠償金을 받고저 하는 사람은 即時 또는 國家賠償審議会의 議決을 거쳐 法務部長官이 決定한 支給額에 不滿이 있으면 이에 不服하여 第1審法院에 提訴하여 判決을 받고, 이에 不服하면 第2審法院에 控訴하여 判決을 받고 다시 이에 不服하면 第3審法院에 上告하여 判決을 받는다. 判決에 不服이 없거나 第3審의 賠償金 支給判決이 있으면 곧 賠償金을 支給받게 된다.

승인양식 1-1-2 (1112-040-016-017) (190mm×260mm 16절지)

0136

(2) 審理期間

第1審은 5月以內, 第2審은 4月以內, 第3審은

3月以內이며, 不服申立決定期間이 2週日以內이므로,

最長期間은 1年1個月이며 最短期間은 2月이다.

4. 損害賠償額

A. 生命에 對한 損害

(1) 殘余生命年數에 따른 所得可能額; 保健

社会部統計에 依한 平均生存年數에 個人의 年純收入

額을 乘하여 「호프만」式計算法으로 中間利子를 控除

支給한다.

例, 30歲된 辯護士로 年純收入 50万원인

者가 死亡하면 殘余生命年數 35年으로 그 賠償額은

1,000万원 이며, 이를 賠償하여야 한다.

다만 收入이 없는 者는 例外이다.

(2) 死亡時까지의 治療費

即死가 아니고 負傷으로 加療中 死亡하였다면 死亡時까지의 一切의 治療費와 個人의 看護를 要하며, 나와있는 家族이 얻지 못하는 所得額 全部

(3) 慰藉料

死亡者에게 父母妻子等이 있으면 慰藉料를 支給하되 死亡者의 年令, 教育, 財產程度와 社会的 地位 및 死亡者와의 関係 및 慰藉料를 받을 사람의 諸般事情에 따라 支給하되 現在判例를 보면 大概 1人当 最高 15万원, 最下 3万원으로 1人이 死亡하면 普通 30万원 乃至 50万원이 된다.

승인양식 1-1-2 (1112-040-016-017) (190mm×260mm 16절지)

0138

(4) 葬礼費 其他費用

死亡者의 身分에 따른 葬礼費用과 其他 個人이 死亡함으로 因하여 生긴 費用一切

B. 傷害로 因한 損害

(1) 治療費

病院에서의 應急治療費, 入院費, 医薬代 等 一切

(2) 療養費

退院하여도 完治되지 아니하고 家庭 또는 転地療養이 必要한 者 및 漢, 洋藥服用이 必要한 者에 対하여 藥代 其他 療養費 一切

(3) 收入損害

負傷으로 因하여 稼動치 못하여 얻지 못하는

승인양식 1-1-2 (1112-040-016-017) (190mm×260mm 16절지)

0139

收入과 不具로 減少된 收入 또는 不具로 稼働치 못하며 完全히 없어지는 收入에 對하여 中間利子를 除한 金額

(4) 慰藉料

負傷程度와 年令, 性別等에 따라 身分에 相應한 額(未婚處女의 顔面 또는 足部負傷에 對하여는 最高額을 支給한다)

(5) 其他損害

四肢의 切斷者는 一生必要한 義肢代, 不具學生에 對하여는 通學費, 休學學生에 對하여는 學業遲延, 復旧를 爲한 學習指導費等 一切의 損害

c. 財産上의 損害

原狀回復할 수 있는 金額과 그間 그 財産을

승인양식 1-1-2 (1112-040-016-017) (190mm×260mm 16절지)

0140

使用치 못하여 입은 損害金額

例. 軍트럭의 過失로 民間택시가 損害를 입었으면

修理費, 修理期間中의 收入, 諸稅, 公課金, 人件費

一切

5. 우리나라 賠償制度의 長点

우리나라의 損害賠償審議制度는 5段階의

審議이며 迅速하고 滿足스러운 賠償을 目的으로 한다.

即 이를 例示하면, 交通事故로 因한 國家賠償은

第一段階로 自動車損害賠償保障法에 依하여 賠償의

一部로 事故即時 保險金을 받으며, 다시 法務部長官에게

나머지 損害를 請求할수 있음으로, 이에 따라 不滿足한 部分에

對한 賠償支給을 받을수 있으며, 또한 이에 不服이 있으면,

第3段階 乃至 第5段階로 3回에 亘하여 法院에 提訴

승인양식 1-1-2 (1112-040-016-017) (190mm×260mm 16절지)

0141

하고 있음으로 우리나라의 賠償制度는 거의 完璧된 制度이며

迅速한 賠償과 滿足한 賠償을 잘 認知시키고 있다.

6. 統計

A. 法務部長官 取扱事件 (1963.5.1 - 1963.8.31)

申請件數 70件

支給金額 7,622,521원

法院에 提訴 없음

B. 法院取扱事件 (1953.8.15 - 1963.8.31)

申請件數 5,235件

支給金額 100,987,679.80원

승인양식 1-1-2 (1112-040-016-017) (190mm×260mm 16절지)

0142

기 안 용 지

자 체 통 제	끝	기안처	미 주 과 공 석 재	전화번호	근거서류접수일자
	과 장	국 장		차 관	장 관
관계관 서 명	조약과장				
기 안 년월일	1963.9.9	시 행 년월일		보존 년한	정 서 / 기 장
분 류 기 호	외정미 722	전 체 통 제			
경 유 수 신 참 조	국가재건최고회의 의장 (참조: 외무국방 위원장) 내각수반	발 신	장 관		
제 목	주둔군 지위협정 체결을 위한 제 30 차 교섭회의 보고				

1963. 9. 5 일 하오 2 시부터 4시 10분까지 외무부장관 회의실에서 개최된 제30차 주둔군지위협정 체결 교섭회의에서 토의된 내용을 별첨과 같이 보고합니다.

유첨: 제30차 교섭회의보고서 7부. 끝.

1963.12.31에 예고문에 의거 일반문서로 재분류됨

승인양식 1-1-3 (1112-040-016-018) (190mm×260mm16절지)

0143

외 무 부

외정미 1963. 9. 10

수 신 : 국가재건최고회의 의장

참 조 : 외무 국방위원장

제 목 : 주둔군 지위협정 체결을 위한 제30차 교섭회의 보고

1963. 9. 5 일 하오 2시부터 4시 10분까지 외무부 장관 회의실에서 개최된 제30차 주둔군지위협정 체결 교섭회의에서 토의된 내용을 별첨과 같이 보고합니다.

유첨: 제30차 교섭회의 보고서 2부. 끝.

외 무 부 장 관 김 용 식

0144

제 30 차

한미간 주둔군 지위협정 체결실무자 회의

보 고 서

1. 일 시 : 1963. 9. 5 하오 2시부터 4시 10분까지

2. 장 소 : 외무부장관 회의실

3. 참석자 : 한국측 : 황호을 (외무부 정무국장)

신관섭 (재무부 세관국장)

구충회 (외무부 미주과장)

신정섭 (외무부 조약과장)

이남구 (국방부 군무과장)

주문기 (법무부 법무과장)

강석재 (외무부 2등서기관)

조광제 (")

허 승 (외무부 3등서기관)

미국측 : 교섭대표단 전원

("후렐" 1등서기관 대신 "암스트롱" 2등서기관이 참석하고 8군 소청책임자인 "나이" 중령이 옵서버로 참석함.)

4. 토의사항 :

(1) 의제에 따라 민사청구권문제를 토의하였으며 우리측은 제 29 차 회의에서 미국측이 질의한바 있는 우리측안에서 구상하고 있는 배상제도의 구성 인원 및 운영요령과 또한 현재 미군에서 시행하고 있는 소청사무 제도와 비교한 우리측 안이 구상하고 있는 제도의 유리점등을 포함한 답변으로서 다음과 같이 우리나라의 국가배상제도, 배상기구 및 그 조직과 배상절차를 상세히 포괄적으로 아래와 같이 설명하였으며, 설명이 끝난후 미국측은

0145

63-1-22 (…)

미국문 108-8 (8)

0146

우리의 배상제도에 대한 의문점을 질문하여 왔으며 우리측은 이에 대한 상세한 설명을 하였음.

(2) 우리측이 설명한 대한민국 국가배상제도 내용은 아래와 같다.

가. 개요

고의 또는 과실로 인한 위법행위로 손해를 가한 개인이 손해를 입은 개인에게 그 손해를 배상할 책임이 있는바와 같이 국가 또는 공공단체의 공무원이 직무를 집행함에 당하여 고의 또는 과실로 법령에 위반하여 손해를 가하였거나, 도로, 하천, 기타 공공영조물의 설치또는 관리에 하자가 있어 개인에게 손해를 가하였거나 기타 민법과 그외의 법령에 위반하여 개인에게 손해를 가하였을 때, 국가 또는 공공단체는 1951.9.8 자 법률 제 231 호로 공포된 국가배상법에 의하여 그 손해를 배상할 책임이 있으므로 국가는 개인에게 대하여 동 법에 의한 손해를 배상하여야 한다.

나. 국가의 배상책임.

국가배상법에 의하면 국가의 공무원(육,해,공군 및 해병대의 군인, 군속 및 고용원 등을 포함하는 모든 공무원)이 그 직무를 집행함에 당하여 (1) 고의 또는 과실로 법령에 위반하여 개인을 사망케 하였거나 부상을 입혔거나 명예를 훼손하였거나 화재 기타로 재산을 파손하는 등 손해를 가하였을때, (2) 또는 도로, 하천 기타 공공영조물의 설치 또는 관리에 하자가 있어 개인을 사망케하였거나 부상을 입혔거나 전답등을 매몰케하여 재산을 파손하는 등 재산상의 손해를 가하였거나 (3) 민법 기타 법령에 위반하여 개인에게 손해를 가하였을 때에는 국가는 그 개인(상속인 등을 포함한다)에게 모든 손해를 배상할 책임이 있고, 이 경우 외국인이 국가로부터 손해를 입었다면 그 국가와 상호 보장이 있으면 그 외국인에게도 우리 국가는 손해를 배상한다.

0147

03-1-22 미·오 118-8

0148

다. 배상기관과 그 구성원

위에서 설명한바와 같이 국가로부터 손해를 입은 개인은 국가에 대하여 그 배상을 청구하여 배상금을 지급 받을수 있는데 그 배상기관과 구성원은 다음과 같다.

1. 법무부장관

1962. 12. 24자 법률 제 1223호 국가 배상금 청구에 관한 절차법이 공포시행된 후 국가배상금을 청구하고저 하는 자는 법무부장관에게 그 지급을 신청하며 법무부장관은 이를 심의 결정하기 위하여 법무부에 국가 배상금 심의회와 법무국 송무과를 설치하였다.

ㄱ) 접 수

법무부에 있는 총무과는 국가배상금 지급신청서를 접수하며 접수즉시 법무국 송무과로 송부한다.

ㄴ) 수리 및 조사

법무국 송무과는 국가배상금 지급관계 일반행정과 조사를 담당하며 신청서를 총무과로 부터 송부 받는 즉시 조사관으로 하여금 조사케 하는바 조사관으로는 법관과 동일한 자격이 있는 검사 2 명, 법률전문가인 법무관 1명, 사무관 2명, 기타 직원 8 명으로 이들은 과거 십여년간 국가배상관계재판 실무에 종사하여 얻은 능숙한 조사기술과 전국의 검찰청 기타 조사기관을 포함한 모든 행정기관과 군기관의 적극적인 협조에 의하여 공무원의 고의, 과실과 직무집행여부 및 그로 인한 손해발생여부와 그 증거를 수집하여 배상액의 심의 판단에 필요한 모든 자료를 준비하고 조사보고서를 작성하여 신청서와 함께 심의회에 송부한다.

0149

63-1-22

미.문 108-8

0150

ㄷ) 심 의

심의회는 신청서와 조사보고서를 상세히 검토하고 법률적인 판단을 가하여 국가배상여부와 그 액수를 심의의결하는데 그 구성원으로는 위원장 1 명과 위원 6명, 간부 1 명과 서기 약간명이 있는데 위원장은 법무부차관, 위원은 법무부의 3국장, 법무관 1명, 변호사 1 명과 배상책임부처의 서기관 이상 직원 1명이며 이위원들이 배상금의 다소를 막론하고 심의의결한다.. 위의 위원들은 모두 10년 이상 법조경력이 있는 분들로 대법원 판사와 동일한 자격요건을 구비한 분들이며 관계부처의 위원(예, 육군 트럭이 개인을 사망케하였으면 노련한 육군법무장교 1명이 선임되어 당해 사건에만 관여한다)도 그 부처의 고급공무원중 법률전문가(법무관)가 임명된다.

ㄹ) 배상액의 최종결정

심의회는 배상금을 심의의결하여 이를 법무부장관에게 보고하며 법무부 장관은 이를 근거로 하여 배상액의 최종 결정을 한다.

ㅁ) 통지 및 신청인의 동의와 배상금 교부 신청

법무부 장관은 신청인에게 배상금 결정을 통지하고 이 통지를 받은 신청인이 이에 만족하면 동의하여 배상금교부를 신청하며 이에 만족할수 없으면 법원에 제소한다.

ㅂ) 지급의뢰와 지급

법무장관이 배상금 교부신청을 받으면 이를 재무부 또는 국방부장관에게 지급을 의뢰하며, 이 의뢰를 받으면 즉시 배상금을 지급한다.

0151

63-1.22

0152

ㅅ) 접수일부터 배상금지급 까지의 기간

접수, 수리, 조사 및 심의의결과 법무부장관의 결정은 접수일로부터 2개월이내이고 결정통지는 7일 이내, 신청인의 동의여부는 3주일이내이므로 최장기일이 3개월이내이며, 최단기일은 25일도 있었다.

2. 법 원

법원은 최고법원인 대법원과 하급법원인 고등법원과 지방법원 및 그 지원으로 조직되어 각지에 설치되어 있고 대학을 졸업하고 엄격한 국가고시에 합격하여 2 년이상 또는 이와 동등한 실무수습한 자 또는 이와 동등한 자중 우수한 자를 발탁 임명한 350명의 법관으로 구성되어 있다.

ㄱ) 처리결과

국가배상금을 받고저 하는 사람은 즉시 또는 국가배상심의회의 의결을 거쳐 법무부장관이 결정한 지급액에 불만이 있으며 이에 불복하여 제1 심 법원에 제소하여 판결을 받고, 이에 불복하면 제2심 법원에 공소하여 판결을 받고 다시 이에 불복하면 제3 심 법원에 상고하여 판결을 받으며 판결에 불복이 없거나 제 3심의 배상금 지급판결이 있으면 곧 배상금을 지급받게 된다.

ㄴ) 심리기간

제1심은 5개월 이내, 제2심은 4개월이내, 제3심은 3개월 이내이며, 불복여부결정기간이 2주일이내이므로, 최장기간은 1년1월이며, 최단기간은 2월이다.

다. 손해 배상액

1. 생명에 대한 손해

0153

ㄱ) 잔여 생명년수에 따른 소득가능액; 보건사회부 통계에 의한 평균생존년수에 동인의 년순수입액을 승하여 "호프만"식 계산법으로 중간이자를 공제지급한다.

0154

예, 30세된 변호사로 년순수입 50만원인 자가 사망하면 잔여생명년수 35년으로 그 배상액은 1,000만원이며, 이를 배상하여야 한다.

다만 수입이 없는 자는 예외이다.

ㄴ) 사망시까지의 치료비

즉사가 아니고 중상으로 가료중 사망하였다면 사망시까지의 일체의 치료비와 동인의 간호를 위하여 나와있는 가족이 얻지 못하는 소득액 전부.

ㄷ) 위자료

사망자에게 부모처자등이 있으면 위자료를 지급하되 사망자의 년령,교육,재산정도와 사회적지위 및 사망자와의 관계 및 위자료를 받을 사람의 제반사정에 따라 지급하되 현재 판례를 보면 대개 1 인당 최고 15 만원, 최하 3만원으로 1인이 사망하면 보통 30만원 내지 50 만원이 된다.

ㄹ) 장례비 기타 비용

사망자의 신분에 따른 장례비용과 기타 동인이 사망함으로 인하여 생긴 비용일체.

2. 상해로 인한 손해

ㄱ) 치료비

병원에서의 응급치료비, 입원비, 의약대 등 일체.

ㄴ) 요양비

퇴원하여도 완치되지 아니하고 가정 또는 전지 요양이 필요한 자 및 한,양약 복용이 필요한 자에 대하여 약대 기타 요양비 일체.

ㄷ) 수입손해

부상으로 인하여 가동치 못하여 얻지 못하는 수입과 불구로 감소될 수입 또는 불구로 가동치 못하여 완전히 없어지는 수입에 대하여 중간이자를 제한 전액.

0155

0156

ㄹ) 위자료

부상정도와 년령, 성별등에 따라 신분에 상응한 액(미혼처녀의 안면 또는 족부부상에 대하여는 최고액을 지급한다.)

ㅁ) 기타 손해

사지의 절단자는 일생 필요한 의지대, 불구학생에 대하여는 통학비, 휴학학생에 대하여는 학업지연, 복구를 위한 학습지도비등 일체의 손해

3. 재산상의 손해

원상회복할수 있는 전액과 그간 그 재산을 사용치 못하여 입은 손해전액.

예, 군트럭의 과실로 민간택시가 손해를 입었으면 수리비, 수리기간중의 수입, 제세, 공과금, 인건비 일체.

마. 우리나라 배상제도의 장점.

우리나라의 손해배상심의제도는 5단계의 심의이며 신속하고 만족스러운 배상을 목적으로 한다.

즉, 이를 예시하면, 교통사고로 인한 국가배상은 제1 단계로 자동차손해배상보장법에 의하여 배상의 일부로 사고즉시 보험금을 받으며, 다시 법무부장관에게 나머지 손해를 청구할수 있으므로, 이에 따라 그 불만족한 부분에 대한 배상지급을 받을수 있으며, 또한 이에 불복이 있으면, 제3단계 내지 제5단계로 3회에 긍하여 법원에 제소할수 있으므로 우리나라의 배상제도는 거의 완벽된 제도이며 신속한 배상 및 만족한 배상을 잘 조화시키고 있다.

(3) 우리측 설명이 끝난다음 미국측은 우리의 현행 배상제도 운영에 관한 소청의 접수, 국가배상심의회의 배상금 심의 결정 액의 한도 여부, 심의회 및 법원에서의 처리건수 및 그 액수, 청구액에 대한 배상비율, 배상의 결정 기준, 신청인의 배상청구액에 대한 증빙서 제출여부 및 위증에 대한 처분 여부등 의문점에 대한 질의가 있어

0157

63-1-22

미·보 108-8

0158

이에 대하여 우리측은 구체적인 설명을 하였음.

5. 중요 합의 사항:

미국측은 우리의 배상제도 및 운영에 관하여 매우 세부적인 문제는 직접 주무부인 법무부 실무자와의 비공식 회합을 통하여 확인하기를 희망하였으므로 우리는 이에 동의함.

6. 기타 사항 :

차기회의 일자 : 1963. 9. 20 하오 2 시

차기회의 의제: 차기회의까지 양측 수석대표간에 합의된 사항

1966.12.31 예고문에 의거 일반문서로 재분류됨

0159

63-1-22(8)

미각.문 108-8(8)

0160

Minutes of the 30th Negotiating Session, SOFA Negotiations

SUBJECT: Claims

PLACE: Ministry of Foreign Affairs

DATE: September 5, 1963

PARTICIPANTS

Republic of Korea

HWANG Ho-ul
SIN Kwon-sup
KU Chung-hwe
Col. YI Nam-ku, ROKA
CHU Mun-ki
SIN Chung-sop
CHO Kwang-che
HO Sung
KANG Suk-che (Interpreter)
YUN Sung-~~Nam~~ Yong, Claims Section, Ministry of Justice (Observer)

United States

Philip C. Habib
Brig. Gen. G.G. O'Conner, USA
William J. Ford
Col. Howard Smigelow, USA
Captain R.M. Brownlie, USN
~~Col. L.J. Fuller, USA~~
Robert A. Lewis
Robert A. Kinney
Major Robert Peckham, USA
Rodney E. Armstrong
Lt. Col. Charles Nye III, USA (Observer)
Lt. Col. Martin Drucker, USA (Observer)

0161

1. Mr. Hwang Ho-ul opened the meeting by introducing Mr. Yun Sung-yong, of the Claims Section of the Ministry of Justice, who was to be present on the Korean side in the capacity of Observer during the negotiators' discussion of the subject of claims. Mr. Habib welcomed Mr. Yun, introduced Lt. Col. Martin Drucker, Chief-designate of the United States Armed Forces Claims Service, Korea, who was to be present for the discussion of claims as an observer for the U.S. side, and noted that Mr. Ford was attending his last negotiating session, having been transferred to Washington. Mr. Hwang welcomed Colonel Drucker, and expressed regret at the departure of Mr. Ford.

2. Mr. Ford expressed regret at his imminent departure from the negotiations. He drew the attention of the negotiators to the fact that the letters SOFA have a double meaning in the English language: a Status of Forces Agreement, and an upholstered bench for relaxation. He said that in his experience participation in SOFA negotiations were not relaxing, and that the two meanings of the letters in English were incompatible. He said that he had, however, enjoyed his labors, and had found good friends on both sides of the negotiating table; since all of the participants in the negotiations were, in a sense, in "foreign service", it would be his hope that he might meet many of his former colleagues around the table again.

0162

-3-

CLAIMS

3. Opening substantive discussion, Mr. Hwang noted that at the preceding meeting both sides had given explanations of their draft articles on the subject of claims. He said that, in response to the requestxx of the XX U.S. side at the previous meeting, the Korean side would give an explanation of XXX the system employed by the Korean Government for the settlement of claimsXXXXXXXXXXXX . He asked Mr. CHU Mun-ki to present this explanation.

There follows the text of the Korean Presentation

0163

a1

THE STATE COMPENSATION System OF THE REPUBLIC OF KOREA

XXX

4. Under the terms of the State Compensation Law (Republic of Korea Law No. 231, promulgated September 8, 1951), the Government's liability is established for damages caused to individuals. This law provides that, in the same manner as would be the case with private individuals, the Government is liable for compensation when an official or a member of the Government or employee of a public corporation has caused damge to an individual or to property, either by intent or by fault, in contravention of the law of the Republic. The liability arises when the Government official causes damage while acting in the performance of his official duties, or when the damage arises from defects in the establishment or XXXXX maintenance of highways, rivers, public utilities, or services, or XX when the damage arises from acts done in contravention of the xxxxxxx civil code or other laws.

XXX 5. Under the provisions of the State Compensation Law, the Government and public corporations are liable for compensation:

(a) When a public official (including a member of the Army, Navy, Air Force or the Marine Corps, or the XXX civilian compenent of these forces, or xxxxxxx an employee of these entities) has caused death, injury, or disgrace x to an individual, or has caused damage to personal property by fire or otherwise, either by intention or by fault, in contravention of the laws of the Republic during the course of his performance of official duty;

0164

(b) When personal injury or death, or property damage has been caused by reason of defects in the establishment, or maintenance of highways, rivers, or other public utilities or services (an example of this type of damage would be the inudation of farmlands through improper management of irrigation facilities);

(c) When damage has been caused to personal property by an act on the part of a Government official or agency which is in contravention of the civil code or other laws.

6. An alien who sustains personal or property damage from an act by a Government official or agency falling into one of the categories described above is entitled to State Compensation only if an ageement exists between the alien's Government and the Government of the Republic of Korea providing for the mutual satisfaction of claims filed against the Governments for compensation owing to injured nationals of the other party.

7. As described above, any person who has been damaged by the act of a Government official is entitled to claim compensation from the Government, and the Government is liable for the payment of compensation for damage caused, if the claim is just. The organization of the Korean Government for the consideration of claims is ~~as follows:~~ described below.

8. Since the promulgation and effectuation of the Law Governing Procedures for Claims for State Compensation (Law No. 1223, promulgated December 24, 1962), claims against the Government have been filed with the Ministry of Justice. For the purpose of implementing the law, a

0165

—C—

State Compensation Committee was established within the Ministry. There had already existed in the Ministry a Claims Section which had examined claims (and in the past, had also decided upon the amounts payable in compensation for these claims). When claims are filed with the General Affairs Section of the Ministry, they are immediately sent to the Claims Section. Upon receipt of the claim, the Claims Section , which is in charge of administration and investigation, immediately starts the investigation of the claim. There are now 13 investigators in the Claims Section. Two of these investigators hold the rank of prosecutor and have qualifications equivalent to those of judges in the Korean judicial system. The other personnel of the Section are: one legal officer, two Class Three Public Officials, and eight other officials. The investigators of the Section develop facts bearing upon whether any official act in question was done in the performance of official duties and whether the damage which is alleged was caused by the act in question; they also collect evidence and gather information required for establishment of the amount of compensation to be offered. When their investigation is completed, the investigators prepare reports and forward them, together with the claims, to the State Compensation Committee for its consideration. The processing of claims is carried out with efficiency, and with the skills and knowledge which the investigators have gained in performing their duties for over ten years. The processing is carried out with the positive cooperation of other entities of the Korean Government: Prosecutors' Offices, the Korean Forces,

0166

—d—

and the various investigation agencies of the Korean Government.

9. The State Compensation Committee carefully examines the claims and the investigation reports attached to them in the light of applicable laws. The Committee decides whether the Government is liable for compensation, and, if xxxx so, in what amount compensation shall be offered. The Committee is composed of a Chairman and six Committee Members. The Committee has a Secretary and a few clerks assigned to it for the performance of xdmimx administrative tasks. At present, the Vice-Minister of Justice holds the appointment as Chairman of the Committee, and three Bureau Directors of the Ministry of Justice, one judge, and one attorney at law hold appointments as Members of the Committee. In addition, one representative (of the rank of xxxxxxxxxxxxx Section Chief or above) from the Ministry concerned with the claim being considered sits as an ad hoc Member of the Committee during its sessions. The Committee is empowered to consider and decide upon claims regardless of the amounts involved. The Members of the Committee are all in possession of legal experience extending over ten years, and have qualifications comparable with those possessed by xx XXXXXXX Judges of the Supreme Court of Korea. The Ministry involved is allowed to take part in the consideration of a claim in which it is involved; for example, in a Committee session called to consider the case of a death caused by an Army truck, one of the senior judge advocates of the ROKA would probably be nominated as XXXXXXX the representative of the Ministry of National Defense. The representative from the concerned Ministry is usually a legal specialist, such as a XXX legal ~~XXXXXXX~~ counsel, selected from among the XXXXX high-ranking officers of the ~~Ministry~~ involved.

0167

10. After having considered XXX a claim and XXXX decided upon the amount of compensation, the State Compensation Committee reports to the Minister of Justice. The Minister makes the final decision on the amount of compensation, based upon the report prepared by the Committee.

11. The Claimant is XXXXXX notified of the amount of compensation decided upon by the Ministry of XXXXXX Justice. He may then apply, if the decision is satisfactory to him, for the XXXXXXX payment of the compensation. If the Claimant is not fully satisfied, however, he may bring a suit against the decision XXX in the courts.

12. When an XXX application for claims payment is received from the Claimant, the Ministry of Justice requests the Ministry of Finance or the Ministry of National Defense to effect payment without delay.

13. It is imperative that the final decision of the Minister of Justice, and all the processing upon which this decision is based, must be effected within two months from the date of the receipt of the XXXXX claim. The notification of the Minister's decision and the Claimant's acceptance or rejection of the award have to be made within seven days and three weeks, respectively. Therefore, the maximum length of time required for the XXXX settlement of a claim is less than three months. XXXXXXXXXXXXXX As for the minimum length of time required, however, there has been a case which was settled within 25 days from the date of the receipt of the XX claim.

14. ~~It going to discuss the role of~~ the Korean courts also have a role in the setttlement of claims. The Korean court system consists of the Supreme Court as the

0168

highest court and the courts of appeal, district courts and their branches as the lower courts. These courts are established in various parts of the country, and are manned by 350 judges appointed from among those individuals who have graduated from a university, xxxhave passed a strict national examination for the judiciary, and have finished a period of probation in excess of two yr years.

15. Any claimant may bring a suit at a XXXXXXX District Court (or to one of its branches) directly, without recourse to the Committee, or when he XXX has a complaint against the amount of compensation decided upon by the Minister of Justice on the basis of processing by the State Compensation Committee. If the claimant is not satisfied with the adjudication of the District Court, he may appeal to the court of XXX second instance, which in XXX this case would be the Court of Appeal. If the claimant xx is still unsatisfied, he may appeal to the Supreme Court. When the claimant is either satisfied with the judgement of a lower court or a final adjudication of the matter xxx has been made by the Supreme Court, the payment of compensation will be made immediately to the claimant.

16. It is imperative that the judgements of the XXXXXXXXXXXXX three levels of courts which may be involved in the settlement of a claims case be delivered within a period of five months, four months, and three months respectively. The decision upon the part of the claimant as to whether the judgement of a lower court is acceptable should be made within a period of two weeks from the date of the judgement in question. The maximum pxxxx period of time necessary for the settlement of a claim through the courts is, therefore, one year and ~~one month~~. ~~In~~ The Ministry Of Justice's experience,

0163

however, claims have been settled through the courts in as little as two months.

17. Turning to the subject of the determination of the amount of compensation XXXXX to claimants, the sub-topic of compensation for death will be discussed first. The factors upon which compensation for death XXX is based are listed below.

(a) The amount of income based on life XXXXX expectancy. In judgingxx the weight to be given this factor, the Hoffmann formula and schedule is utilized. Under the terms of this formula, the amount of award is given by the deduction of interest from the amount that is given by the multiplication of the XXXXXXX deceased person's life expectancy (as given by the mortality tables of the Ministry of Health and Social Affairs) by the amount of the yearly income of the deaceased. For example, in the case of the death of an attorney at law aged 30, with a yearly income of won 500,000 (US $ 3,846 at the official rate of exchange), the amount of compensation, based upon this individual's life expectancy of 65, will amount to won 10 million (US $ 76, 923). There are, however, exceptional cases in which the deceased has no earnings.

(b) Medical and hospital expenses incident to a death. When a XXXXXXXX claim is based upon the death of a person after serious injury, the amount compensable will include, in addition to the amount based upon the XXXXXXX XXXXX deceased person's predictable earnings, all of the medical and hospital expenses incident to mdecial treatment preceding death, plus the xx full amount which might otherwise have been earned by the family of the deceased person during the period they were obliged to be in attendence upon the deceased.

0170

(c) Ex gratia payments. These payments are provided to XXX the surviving parents, widow or children, if any, of a deceased person. The amounts of xxxxxx awards xxxxxxxxxxxxxxxxx of this nature are varied, being affected by such factors as the age, education, income and social status of the deceased, as well as by the family relationship and circumstances of the person who will receive the award. Until the present, xx the Ministry of Justice's experience has been that when the death of one person is involved, the award generally ranges from won 300,000 (US $ 2,308 at the official rate of exchange) to won 500,000 (US $3,846), with a maximum of won 150,000 and a minimum of won 30,000 distributed to each surviving family member entitled to an award.

(d) Funeral expenses. Funeral expenses are paid, including all expenses incurred for the interment. The amount paid in this category are related to the income and social status of the deceased.

18. In XXXXXXXXXXXXXXXXX determining the amount of compensation for personal injuries, the following factors are relevent:

(a) Medical and hospital expenses, including all expenses of first aid xxx treatment, and of hospital and medical care.

(b) Other XXXXXXXXXXXXXXXXXX treatment expenses, including all of the costs of medicine and recreation, when the injured person is not fully recovered, and requires XXXXXXXXXXXX continuous treatment or recreation, XXXXXXXX XXXXXXXXXXXXXXX even after leaving the hospital, at home or at resorts, or xxxx needs the continuous application of Chinese or other medicines prescribed by a doctor.

0171

—i—

(c) Loss of income during the period in which the claimant is absent from work, and the amount of income foregone (whether only a partial XXXXXXX or complete loss of earning power) because of physical incapacity, minus interest.

(d) *Ex gratia* amounts in compensation for injuries, varied according to the degree of injury, age, sex and social status of the injured. The maximum amount is paid for scars and other dixfi disfigurements sustained by an unmarried female, particularly when these injurx injuries are sustained on the legs.

(e) Awards for miscellaneous expenses are also made to injured persons. For example, compensation is paid for the cost of obtaining artificial limbs and for the cost of maintaining these limbs during the expected life of their wearer. Awards are made for travel expenses inxxxxxx incurred by an injured person in going to and from school. XXXXXXXXXXXXXXX Awards are also made for expenses incurred in arranging for special tuition to make up for time lost from educational activities XXXXXX because of injuries.

19. In determining the amounts of allowable compensation for xx property damage, allowable compensation includes the cost of repairs XX necessary to retore the property to its condition xx prior to the damage. Awards of this nature also include compensation for the loss of income to the owner of the property resulting from XXXXXX his inability to utilize the property while damaged. For example, when a civilian taxi is damaged by the wrongful act of a vehicle of the Korean Armed Forces, compensation will include the cost

0172

of repairs to the taxi, ~~an amount in lieu of~~ the loss of income to the owner

—j—

while the taxi was under repair, XXX as well as amount reimbursing the taxi owner for his payment of taxes and XXXXXXXXXXXX driver's wages during the period the taxi was inoperable.

20. The compensation system now in operation in the Republic of Korea consists of five different stages of consideration and adjudication designed to XXXXXXX ensure a speedy as well as satisfactory XXXXXXX settlement of claims. For example, compensation for personal injury or death, XXXXXXXX or for damage to individual property, arising out a traffic accident can be ~~settled~~ made, at its first stage, throughxx the xxxxx payment of insurance as xxxx part of compensation immediately following the accident, ~~as provided for in~~ by the Motor Vehicle ~~Compensation Law~~ Insurance Company. XX As a next step, it is possible for the Claimant to file a claim with the Ministry of Justice for full compensation if he is not satisfied with the above mentioned payment of insurance. ~~Thus~~ ~~and~~ Claimant is assured of equitable and just compensation. Furthermore, the Claimant, if not fully xxxx satisfied, ~~and~~ can procede in the Korean court system up through three levels of xx judgement. Therefore, the claims compensation system of the Republic of Korea is deemed XXX to be efficiently and soundly instituted, and is well harmonized to effect speedy and satisfactory compensation.

0173

A

21. Mr. Habib thanked Mr. Chu for his presentation. There followed an extended exchange of questions and answers in which additional information concerning the Korean system for the settlement of claims was developed. This information is summarized in the paragraphs below.

22. At the present time, there are no local offices to which a Korean claimant can present a claim ~~against his Government~~, and the claim may ~~must~~ be mailed or directly submitted to the General Affairs Section of the Ministry of Justice in Seoul. There is, however, under consideration the formation of a network of local offices which might handle certain civil affairs such as claims at the local level. ~~There is no standard form~~ For the transmission of a claim to the Ministry of Justice, the claimant is required to furnish such information as his personal references (name, address, age & occupation) amount of compensation requested and the facts involved in the accident. ~~principally because the information required is believed by the Ministry to be of such a simple nature that the facts to be set down are self-evident.~~

0174

B

23. The State Compensation Committee is empowered to settle all claims against the Korean Government arising out of acts or omissions of employees of the Korean Government acting within the scope of their official duties, as well as any claims arising out of an act or omission which constitutes a violation of the civil or other special codes. Claims arising from the expropriation of property by the Korean Government, or from the exercise by the Korean Government of the right of eminent domain are not within the purview of the State Compensation Committtee. The State Compensation Committee, in arriving at its judgement, takes into account the general principles of Korean law: for example, the doctrine of contributory negligence. The State Compensation Committee follows precedents established by the Korean courts in detrmining the amounts allowable as part of its awards for the payment of court costs and attorneys' fees.

__. Under the Ministry of Justice's interpretation of Article 24 of the Korean Constitution, any Korean citizen may litigate any problem he might have with his Government in the courts. The Ministry of Justice, therefore, interprets that this provision as permitting any claimant to take up his claim directly to the courts without recourse to the State compensation Committee. The utilization of the claims procedure described above is, therefore, entirely voluntary on the part of the claimant, and the claimant may discontinue the procedings at any point if he is dissatified, and seek redress in the Korean courts. The Ministry of Justice hopes, however, for an increasing reliance by claimants upon the procedures developed under the terms of the State Compensation Law, and is undertaking efforts to publicize nationally these procedures. At present, roughly 70 per cent of the claims filed against the Government

0175

C

being pressed under the terms of the procedures available under the State Compensation Law, and number of claims taken up with the courts is gradually decreasing.

25. If an unsatisfied claimant rejects the decision of the State Compensation Committee, and takes his claim to the courts, the judge hearing the case is, under the terms of the Korean Constitution, bound only by the provisions of Korean law and by his conscience. The proceedings and determinations of the State Compensation Committee, while available to him for review, are not dispositive of the issue when it comes before the court. There have been cases in which dissatisfied claimants have gone from the State Compensation Committee to the courts; one such case now in the courts involves a claim arising out of a maritime accident which was disallowed by the State Compensation Committee because of the difficulty of finding reliable evidence due to the place where the accident took place.

26. The State Compensation Committee operates under the terms of generalized regulations which however do not apply to each claim on special basis because each claim presents its own somewhat unique aspects which require different modes and procedures for settlement. For example, the Korean regulations do not set forth in detail the types of evidence required by the State Compensation Committee to support a claim for giving awards because in each case the relevent material evidence will be different, e.g., hospital bill receipts, family registration papers, etc. The State Compensation Committee does, however, in practice require the submission of all the relevent material evidence which it considers necessary. ~~For much the same reasons, the regulations~~

0176

If false evidence is submitted by the claimant, he is subject to punishment under the terms of the criminal code and other Korean laws.

27. The factors used by the State Compensation Committee in fixing each award are related to the individual requirements of the claim being satisfied, and may include such matters as the occupation, income, age, sex, social status and/role of the family injured party, etc. In making lump sum awards in lieu of prospective earnings, the State Compensation Committee relies upon the Hofmann formula described in the Korean presentation above. In determining its award the Committee does not take into account the amounts paid the injured party under the terms of pension and workmen's compensation programs, or amounts paid to the injured party from any private insurance policies he might hold because such payments are fundamentally different in nature from an award made in compensation for injury and damage.

28. The State Compensation Committee relies upon the Claims Section of the Ministry of Justice (as well as, of course, the claimant) for the development of evidence with respect to each claim which it handles. The Claims Section does not, however, have the authority to disallow claims for lack of evidence or for any other reason; disallowment is the perogative of the Committee itself.

29. The State Compensation Committee commenced operation in December, 1962. Claims to be acted upon did not, however, come in any quantities until In the three months previous to this meeting, more than 80 claims have been filed, of which more than 70

0177

have been settled. The total compensation paid thus far ~~XXX~~ by the Committee~~xx~~ to claimants is approximately won ~~9~~ 6 million (US ~~$53,846~~ 46,154 at the official rate of exchange). ~~No precise figures are available, but~~ The Ministry of Justice estimates that the State Compensation Committee is paying awards which are approximately 45 per cent of the amount requested by claimants. No ~~XXXXXX~~ ~~statistics are available concerning the number of claims which have been settled by the Korean courts in the past three months.~~

OTHER BUSINESS

~~1~~ 3. It was agreed that the next negotiating session would be held on September 20, 1963, at ~~XXX~~ 2:00 P.M.

The Korean negotiators offered to provide the U.S. side with statistics covering the exact number of claims settled by the courts and by the Committee, and the awards of compensation paid claimants utilizing both systems, in the past three months.

(3) It was agreed that, if it is felt desirable, Korean and American claims specialists would meet to continue discussions on the subject of Korean claims procedures outside the formal negotiating sessions.

0178

The State Compensation System of the Republic of Korea

1. Outline

Under the State Compensation Law promulgated as the Republic of Korea Law No. 231 on September 8, 1951, the Government's liability is established when ~~the~~ damage~~s~~ ~~are~~ is caused upon an individual. This law provides that in the same manner as any person who, either by intention or by fault, has caused ~~the~~ damage~~s~~ upon ~~the~~ an other ~~party~~ person is liable for compensation, the Government shall be liable for compensation when an official or a member of the Government or public corporations has caused ~~the~~ damage~~s~~ upon an individual or property either by intention or by fault in contravention of laws in the performance of official duties or when such damage~~s~~ ~~have~~ has been arisen due to defects in the establishment and maintenance of highways, rivers and public utilities and services or due to ~~the wrongful~~ act~~s~~ done in contravention of the civil code or other laws.

2. State Liability for Compensation

Under the provisions of the State Compensation Law the Government and public corporations are liable for compensation;

(a) when a public official including a member of Army, Navy, Air forces and Marine Corps, and civilian component and their employee has caused death, injury or disgrace upon an individual or caused damage~~s~~ to

0179

personal property by causing fire or otherwise either by intention or by fault in contravention of laws during the execution of official duties; and

(b) when personal injury or death or property damage has been caused by reason of defects in the establishment and maintenance of highways, rivers and other public utilities and services; or (c) when such damage has been caused in contravention of the civil code or other laws.

In these cases as described above, any alien who sustains damages upon himself or upon his property will be entitled to the State Compensation if there has been an agreement on reciprocal assurance of compensating the damage caused upon the individual of the other party between the Government of the Republic of Korea and the Gov't such alien belongs to.

3. Organization of compensation and its structure

As described above, any person who has been damaged by a Government official is entitled to claim for compensation against the Government and the Government is lible to compensate for the damage. The organization of compensation and its structure are as follows:

(a) Minister of Justice:

Since the Law Governing Procedures of Claim for State Compensation (ROK Law No. 1223) was promulgated and put into effect as of December 24, 1962, claims against

0180

the Government have been filed with the Minister of Justice. For the purpose of implementing the law, the State Compensation Committee in the Ministry of Justice, in addition to the Claims Section, were newly established that had been in operation to examine and decide on the claims.

(i) Filing of Claims

When the claims are filed with the General Section of the Ministry of Justice, they are immediately sent to the Claims Section

(ii) Receipt and Investigation

Upon the receipt of the claims from the General Affairs section, the Claims Section which is in charge of the administrative work and investigation immediately starts investigating cases with investigators. There are now 13 investigators out of which 2 are prosecutors who hold qualifications equivalent to those of judges, 1 legal officer, 2 "samukwan" and 8 other officials. These investigators conduct investigations as to whether the act of a government official is intentional or faulty or done in the performance of official duties and as to whether the damage is caused as a result of such act, and they collect evidences and gather information required for considering

0181

and deciding the amount of compensation. Finally they prepare investigation reports and forward them together with the claims to the State Compensation Committee for its consideration. These processes are carried out all the way with efficient investigating skills and knowledge the investigators have acquired through their past experience dealing with the State Compensation business over 10 years and in positive cooperation with the Prosecutors' Offices, Government agencies and the armed services including various investigation agencies throughout Korea.

(iii) Consideration of Claims

The State Compensation Committee carefully examines the claims and investigation reports thereof in the light of applicable laws, and consider and decide on whether the Government is liable for compensation as well as its amount. The Committee is composed of 1 chairman, 6 committee members, and there are 1 secretary and a few clerks assigned for its administrative work. At present, the Vice-Minister of Justice is appointed as Chairman and 3 Bureau

0182

Directors of the Ministry of Justice, 1 judge and 1 attorney at law and 1 representative above the rank of a section chief from the Ministry concerned are assigned as ~~commissioner~~ committee members. This Committee is empowered to consider and decide the claims regardless of the amount to be compensated. These ~~Commissioners~~ committee members are in possession of legal background and experience over 10 years and have ~~bad~~ qualifications ~~equivalent to~~ competent with ~~those of~~ judges of the Supreme Court.

The Ministry concerned is allowed to take part in the consideration of ~~the~~ a claim in which it is involved, e.g., when an Army truck has killed a person, one of senior judge advocates may be selected and represented at the Committee. Thus, a representative from the Ministry concerned is usually a legal specialist such as legal officer selected from among the high ranking officials of the Ministry involved.

(iv) Final decision on compensation amount

After having considered the claims and decided the amount of compensation, the State Compensation Committee reports to the Minister of Justice. Then the Minister makes ~~the~~ a final

0183

decision on the amount of compensation on the basis of the report prepared by the Committee.

(v) Notification of decision, ~~the~~ claimant's consent and application for payment

The claimant is notified of the decision of the amount of compensation by the Ministry of Justice. He then may apply, if the decision is satisfactory, for the payment of ~~the~~ compensation. However, when the claimant is not fully satisfied he may bring a suit against the decision to a court.

(vi) Payment

When an application for the claim payment is received from the claimant, the Ministry of Justice requests the Ministry of Finance or the Ministry of National Defense to pay ~~the~~ compensation to the claimant without delay.

(vii) Necessary legth of time for the settlement

It is imperative that the final decision of the Minister of Justice with all the processes such as the receipt of a claim, investigation and consideration and decision by the Committee must be made within two months from the date of receipt of the claim and the notification of the decision and the claimant's

0184

consent or disconset to the decision have to be also within 7 days and 3 weeks respectively. Therefore, the maximum length of time required for the settlement is less than three months. However, as for minimum length of time required, there has been a case which was settled within 25 days from the date of receipt of the claim.

b. Courts

The Korean courts are consisted of the Supreme Court as the highest court and the courts of appeal, district courts and their branches as lower courts. They are established at various parts of the country and manned with 350 judges appointed from among those who have graduated from universities, passed a strict national examination for the judiciary and then finished probation over two years.

(i) Procedures

Any calimant may bring a suit to a District Court or its branches directly or when he has complaint against the amount of compensation decided by the Minister of Justice through the consideration of the claim at the Committee. If he is not satisfied with the adjudication made by the court, he may appeal his claim to the court of second instance, in this case, the Court of Appeal. Again if the claimant is still not satisfied with the adjudication made at this court, it is open for

0185

him to further appeal to the Supreme Court.

When either he is satisfied with the judgement of a court or the final adjudication is made by the Supreme Court, the payment of compensation will be immediately made to the claimant.

(ii) Necessary length of time for adjudications

Since it is imperative that the adjudications of the claims at various courts must be made within the period of 5 months, 4 months and 3 months respectively and decision as to whether or not to accept adjudication by the claimant within 2 weeks, the maximum length of time necessary for the settlement of the claim is considered one year and 1 month. However, our experience indicates that the case which took the minimum length of time was the one which was settled within 2 months.

4. Determination of the amount of compensation

a. Compensation for death: The compensable items are:

(1) Amount of foreseeable income based on life expectancy

The amount of compensation for death is computed on the basis of the Hopmann's calculation method, according to which the amount of award may be obtained by subtracting interest from the amount that is arrived at by multiplying the life expectancy based on statistics of the Ministry of Social Welfare by the

0186

amount of the yearly income of the deceased. For example, in case of the death of a attorney at law who has the age of 30 years and the yearly income of ₩500,000 (US $3,846.15), the amount compensable, taking into account his life expectancy as 35 years, will amount to ₩10,000,000 (US$76,923.00) for which the governemnt is responsible to compensate. However, the case of the death of a person who does not earn is exceptional.

(2) Medical and hospital expenses incident to and preceding death

When a person is dead during hospitalization due to a serious injury, the amount of compensation will include, in addition to the above, all the medical and hospital expenses incident to and preceding death plus the full amount of income the family might otherwise earn for the period during which the family had attended upon the deceased.

(3) Ex gratia

Ex gratia is awarded for surviving parent, widow and children of the deceased if there are. However, the amount of this award may be varied being effected by elements such as age, education, income and social status of the deceased as well as his family relationship and

0187

the circumstances of a person who will receive the award. Up to the present, our experience shows that when the death of one person is involved, the award generally amounts W300,000 (US $2,307.70) up to W500,000 (US$3,846,15) with W150,000 at maximum and W30,000 at minimum for each entitled surviving family.

(4) Funeral and other expenses

These include funeral expenses as are effected by social status of the deceased and all other expenses incurred due to such death.

b. Compensation for personal injury: The compensable items are:

(1) Medical and hospital expenses

These include all the expenses such as first aid treatment, hospital and medical expenses

(2) Other treatment expenses

These include all the costs of medicines and recreation, when the injured person is not fully recovered and needs the continuous treatment or recreation, even after leaving the hospital, at home or at resort places, or needs the treatment of medicines chinese or otherwise which are prescribed by a doctor.

(3) Loss of income 0188

Loss of income for the period during which

the claimant is absent from work, the amount of income which may be depreciated due to physical disability or the total loss of income owing to permanent physical disability minus interest.

(4) Ex gratia

Reasonable amount of ex gratia according to the degree of injury, age, sex and social status etc., of the injured. However, the maximum amount is paid specially for scars and other disfigurements of a female and injury on legs.

(5) Miscellaneous compensation

The cost of artificial limbs and their maintenance for life expectancy of the injured person, travel expenses to and from school for a disabled student and all the expenses necessary for catching up with schooling for the period during which the student is absent from school.

c. Property damage

Allowable compensation includes the cost of repairs to or restoration of the property damaged to its state of condition prior to the time of damage and the loss of income for the period during which the property damaged is not able to use. For instance, when a civilian taxi is damaged arising out of the wrongful use of a vehicle owned by the armed forces, the amount compensable will include the cost of repairs, the loss of income and various taxes and charges during the period of its repair and labor expenses.

0189

5. Advantages of the Korean compensation system

The compensation system now in operation in the Republic of Korea is consisted of five different stages of consideration and adjudication in order to ensure the most speedy as well as satisfactory settlement of the claims payment. For example, the compensation for personal injury or death, or ~~the~~ damage to an individual property arising out of a traffic accident can be settled, at its first stage, through the payment of insurance as a part of compensation immediately following the accident as provided for in the Motor Vehicle Compensation Law. and, for the next step, it is also possible for the claimant to file his claim with the Ministry of Justice for full compensation. Thus, any claimant is assured of equitable and just compensation. Furthermore, the claimant, if not fully satisfied, can further procede the case to the Korean courts up to three times. Therefore, the compensation system of the Republic of Korea is deemed most efficiently and soundly instituted and is well harmonized to effect speedy and satisfactory compensation.

0190

JOINT SUMMARY RECORD OF THE 30TH SESSION

September 5, 1963

1. Time and Place : 2:00 to 4:10 p.m. September 5, 1963 at the Foreign Minister's Conference Room

2. Attendants:

ROK side:

Mr. Whang, Ho Eul	Director Bureau of Political Affairs Ministry of Foreign Affairs
Mr. Shin, Kwan Sup	Director Bureau of Customs Duty Ministry of Finance
Mr. Koo, Choong Whay	Chief, America Section Ministry of Foreign Affairs
Col. Lee, Nam Koo	Chief, Military Affairs Section Ministry of National Defense
Mr. Chu, Mun Ki	Chief, Legal Affairs Section Ministry of Justice
Mr. Shin, Jung Sup	Chief, Treaty Section Ministry of Foreign Affairs
Mr. Kang, Suk Jae	2nd Secretary Ministry of Foreign Affairs
Mr. Cho, Kwang Je	2nd Secretary Ministry of Foreign Affairs
Mr. Huh, Sung	3rd Secretary Ministry of Foreign Affairs
Mr. Yun, Song Yong	Prosecutor Ministry of Justice (Observer)

U.S. side:

Mr. Philip C. Habib	Counselor of the Embassy for Political Affairs American Embassy
Gen. G. G. O'Connor	Deputy Chief of Staff 8th U.S. Army
Mr. William J. Ford	1st Secretary American Embassy

미주과	양고재 九월 일	담 당	과 장	국 장	특별보좌관	차 관	장 관
				21			

0191

Col. Howard Smigelor	Deputy Chief of Staff UNC
Capt. R. M. Brownlie	Assistant Chief of Staff USN/K
Mr. Rodney E. Armstrong	2nd Secretary American Embassy
Mr. Robert A. Lewis	2nd Secretary and Consul American Embassy
Mr. Robert A. Kinney	J-5 8th U.S. Army
Maj. Robert D. Peckham	Staff Officer, JAG 8th U.S. Army
Lt. Col. Charles Nye III	Chief, U.S. Armed Forces Claims Service, 8th U.S. Army (Observer)
Lt. Col. Martin Drucker	Claims Service, 8th U.S. Army (Observer)

1. Mr. Hwang Ho Eul opened the meeting by introducing Mr. Yun, Sung Yong of the Claims Section of the Ministry of Justice, who was to be present on the Korean side in the capacity of Observer during the negotiator's discussion of the subject of claims. Mr. Habib welcomed Mr. Yun, introduced Lt. Col. Martin Drucker, Chief-designate of the United States Armed Forces Claims Service, Korea, who was to be present for the discussion of claims as an observer for the U.S. side, and noted that Mr. Ford was attending his last negotiating session, having been transferred to Washington. Mr. Whang welcomed Colonel Drucker, and expressed regret at the departure of Mr. Ford.

2. Mr. Ford expressed regret at his imminent departure from the negotiations. He drew the attention of the negotiators to the fact that the letters SOFA have a double meaning in the English language: a Status of Forces Agreement, and an upholstered bench for relaxation. He said that in his experience participation in SOFA negotiations were not relaxing, and that the two meanings of the letters in

0192

English were incompatible. He said that he had, however, enjoyed his labors, and had found good friends on both sides of the negotiating table; since all of the participants in the negotiations were, in a sense, in "foreign service", it would be his hope that he might meet many of his former colleagues around the table again.

CLAIMS

3. Opening substantive discussion, Mr. Hwang noted that at the preceding meeting both sides had given explanations of their draft articles on the subject of claims. He said that, in response to the request of the U.S. side at the previous meeting, the Korean side would give an explanation of the system employed by the Korean Government for the settlement of claims. He asked Mr. Chu Mun Ki to present this explanation.

THE STATE COMPENSATION SYSTEM OF THE REPUBLIC OF KOREA

4. Under the terms of the State Compensation Law (Republic of Korea Law No. 231, promulgated September 8, 1951), the Government's liability is established for damage caused to individuals. This law provides that, in the same manner as would be the case with private individuals, the Government is liable for compensation when an official or a member of the Government or employee of a public corporation has caused damage to an individual or to property, either by intent or by fault, in contravention of the laws of the Republic. The liability arises when the Government official causes damage while acting in the performance of his official duties, or when the damage arises from defects in the establishment or maintenance of highways, rivers, public utilities, or services, or when the damage arises from acts done in contravention of the civil code or other laws.

0193

5. Under the provisions of the State Compensation Law, the Government and public oorporations are liable for compensation:

(a) When a public official (including a member of the Army, Navy, Air Force or the Marine Corps, or the civilian compenent of these forces, or an employee of these entities) has caused death, injury, or disgrace to an individual, or has caused damage to personal property by fire or otherwise, either by intention or by fault, in contravention of the laws of the Republic during the course of his performance of official duty;

(b) When personal injury or death, or property damage has been cuased by reason of defects in the establishment, or maintenance of highways, rivers, or other public utilities or services (an example of this type of damage would be the inudation of farmlands through improper management of irrigation facilities);

(c) When damage has been caused to personal property by an act on the part of a Government official or agency which is in contravention of the civil code or other laws.

6. An alien who sustains personal or property damage from an act by a Government official or agency falling into one of the categories descrived above is entitled to State Compensation only if an agreement exists between the alien's Government and the Government of the Republic of Korea providing for the mutual satisfaction of claims

0194

filed against the Governments for compensation owing to injured nationals of the other party.

7. As described above, any person who has been damaged by the act of a Government official is entitled to claim compensation from the Government, and the Government is liable for the payment of compensation for damage caused, if the claim is just. The organization of the Korean Government for the consideration of claims is ~~derived~~ described below.

8. Since the promulgation and effectuation of the Law Governing Procedures for Claims for State Compensation (Law No. 1223, promulgated December 24, 1962), claims against the Government have been filed with the Ministry of Justice. For the purpose of implementing the law, a State Compensation Committee was established within the Ministry. There had already existed in the Ministry a Claims Section which had examined claims (and in the past, had also decided upon the amounts payable in compensation for these claims). When claims are filed with the General Affairs Section of the Ministry, they are immediately sent to the Claims Section. Upon receipt of the claim, the Claims Section, which is in charge of administration and investigation, immediately starts the investigation of the claim. There are now 13 investigators in the Claims Section. Two of these investigators hold the rank of prosecutor and have qualifications equivalent to those of judges in the Korean judicial system. The other personnel of the Section are: one legal officer, two Class Three Public Officials, and eight other officials. The investigators of the Section develop facts bearing upon whether any official act in question was done in

0195

the performance of official duties, and whether the damage which is alleged was caused by the act in question; they also collect evidence and gather information required for establishment of the amount of compensation to be offered. When their investigation is completed, the investigators prepare reports and forward them, together with the claims, to the State Compensation Committee for its consideration. The processing of claims is carried out with efficiency, and with the skills and knowledge which the investigators have gained in performing their duties for over ten years. The processing is carried out with the positive cooperation of other entities of the Korean Government: Prosecutors' Offices, the Korean Armed Forces, and the various investigation agencies of the Korean Government.

9. The State Compensation Committee carefully examines the claims and the investigation reports attached to them in the light of applicable laws. The Committee decides whether the Government is liable for compensation, and, if so, in what amount compensation shall be offered. The Committee is composed of a Chairman and six Committee Members. The Committee has a Secretary and a few clerks assigned to it for the performance of administrative tasks. At present, the Vice-Minister of Justice holds the appointment as Chairman of the Committee, and three Bureau Directors of the Ministry of Justice, one judge, and one attorney at law hold appointments as Members of the Committee. In addition, one representative (of the rank of Section Chief or above) from the Ministry concerned with the claim being considered sits as an ad hoc Member of the Committee during its sessions. The Committee is empowered to consider and decide upon claims regardless

0196

of the amounts involved. The Members of the Committee are all in possession of legal experience extending over ten years, and have qualifications comparable with those possessed by Judges of the Supreme Court of Korea. The Ministry involved is allowed to take part in the consideration of a claim in which it is involved; for example, in a Committee session called to consider the case of a death caused by an Army truck, one of the senior judge advocates of the ROKA would probably be nominated as the representative of the Ministry of National Defense. The representative from the concerned Ministry is usually a legal specialist, such as a legal counsel, selected from among the high-ranking officers of the Ministry involved.

10. After having considered a claim and decided upon the amount of compensation, the State Compensation Committee reports to the Minister of Justice. The Minister makes the final decision on the amount of compensation, based upon the report prepared by the Committee.

11. The claimant is notified of the amount of compensation decided upon by the Ministry of Justice. He may then apply, if the decision is satisfactory to him, for the payment of the compensation. If the claimant is not fully satisfied, however, he may bring a suit against the decision in the courts.

12. When an application for claims payment is received from the claimant, the Ministry of Justice requests the Ministry of Finance or the Ministry of National Defense to effect payment without delay.

13. It is imperative that the final decision of the Minister of Justice, and all the processing upon which this decision is based, must be effected within two months from the date of the receipt of the claim. The notifiєation of the Minister's decision and the claimant's acceptance or rejection of the award have to be made within seven days and three weeks, respectively. Therefore, the maximum length of time required for the settlement of a claim is less than three months. As for the minimum length of time required, however, there has been a case which was settled within 25 days from the date of the receipt of the claim.

14. The Korean courts also have a role in the settlement of claims. The Korean court system consists of the Supreme Court as the highest court and the courts of appeal, district courts and their branches as the lower courts. These courts are established in various parts of the country, and are manned by 350 judges appointed from among those individuals who have graduated from a university, have passed a strict national examination for the judiciary, and have finished a period of probation in excess of two years.

15. Any claimant may bring a suit at a District Court (or to one of its branches) directly, without recourse to the Committee, or when he has a complaint against the amount of compensation decided upon by the Minister of Justice on the basis of processing by the State Compensation Committee. If the claimant is not satisfied with the adjudication of the District Court, he may appeal to the court of second instance, which in this case would be the court of Appeal. If the claimant

0198

is still unsatisfied, he may appeal to the Supreme Court. When the claimant is either satisfied with the judgement of a lower court or a final adjudication of the matter has been made by the Supreme Court, the payment of compensation will be made immediately to the claimant.

16. It is imperative that the judgements of the three levels of courts which may be involved in the settlement of a claims case be delivered within a period of five months, four months, and three months respectively. The decision upon the part of the claimant as to whether the judgement of a lower court is acceptable should be made within a period of two weeks from the date of the judgement in question. The maximum period of time necessary for the settlement of a claim through the courts is, therefore, one year and one month. In the Ministry of Justice's experience, however, claims have been settled through the courts in as little as two months.

17. Turning to the subject of the determination of the amount of compensation to claimants, the sub-topic of compensation for death will be discussed first. The factors upon which compensation for death is based are listed below.

(a) The amount of income based on life expectancy. In judging the weight to be given this factor, the Hofmann formula and schedule is utilized. Under the terms of this formula, the amount of award is given by the deduction of interest from the amount that is given by the multiplication of the deceased person's life expectancy (as given by the mortality tables of the Ministry of Health and Social Affairs) by the amount of the yearly income of the deceased. For example, in the case of the death of an attorney at law aged 30, with a yearly income of won 500,000 (US $3,846 at the official rate of exchange), the amount of compensation, based upon this individual's life expectancy of 35, will amount to won 10million (US $76,923). There are, however, exceptional cases in which the deceased has no earnings.

(b) Medical and hospital expenses incident to a death. When a claim is based upon the death of a person after serious injury, the amount compensable will include, in addition to the amount based upon the deceased person's predictable earnings, all of the medical and hospital expenses incident to medical treatment preceding death, plus the full amount which might otherwise have been earned by the family of the deceased person during the period they were obliged to be in attendance upon the deceased.

(c) Ex gratia payments. These payments are provided to the surviving parents, widow or children, if any, of a deceased person. The amounts of awards of this nature are varied, being effected by such factors as the age, education, income and social status of the deceased, as well as by the family relationship and circumstances of the person who will receive the award. Until the present, the Ministry of Justice's experience has been that when the death of one person is involved, the award generally ranges from won 300,000

0200

(US $2,308 at the official rate of exchange) to won 500,000 (US $3,846), with a maximum of won 150,000 and a minimum of won 30,000 distributed to each surviving family member entitled to an award.

(d) Funeral expenses. Funeral expenses are paid, including all expenses incurred for the interment. The amount paid in this category are related to the income and social status of the deceased.

18. In determining the amount of compensation for personal injuries, the following factors are relevant:

(a) Medical and hospital expenses, including all expenses of first aid treatment, and of hospital and medical care.

(b) Other treatment expenses, including all of the costs of medicine and recreation, when the injured person is not fully recovered, and requires continuous treatment or recreation, even after leaving the hospital, at home or at resorts, or needs the continous application of Chinese or other medicines prescribed by a doctor.

(c) Loss of income during the period in which the claimant is absent from work, and the amount of income foregone (whether only a partial or complete loss of earning power) because of physical incapacity, minus interest.

(d) *Ex gratia* amounts in compensation for injuries, varied according to the degree of injury, age, sex and social status of the injured. The maximum amount is paid for scars and other disfigurements sustained by an unmarried female, particularly when these injuries are sustained on the legs.

0201

(e) Awards for miscellaneous expenses are also made to injured persons. For example, compensation is paid for the cost of obtaining artificial limbs and for the cost of maintaining these limbs during the expected life of their wearer. Awards are made for travel expenses incurred by an injured person in going to and from school. Awards are also made for expenses incurred in arranging for special tuition to make up for time lost from educational acitivities because of injuries.

19. In determining the amounts of allowable compensation for property damage, allowable compensation includes the cost of repairs necessary to restore the property to its condition prior to the damage. Awards of this nature also include compensation for the loss of income to the owner of the property resulting from his inability to utilize the property while damaged. For example, when a civilian taxi is damaged by the wrongful act of a vehicle of the Korean Armed Forces, compensation will include the cost of repairs to the taxi, an amount in lieu of the loss of income to the owner while the taxi was under repair, as well as amount reimbursing the taxi owner for his payment of taxes and driver's wages during the period the taxi was inoperable.

20. The compensation system now in operation in the Republic of Korea consists of five different stages of consideration and adjudication designed to ensure a speedy as well as satisfactory settlement of claims. Thus, an claimant is assured of equitable and just compensation. Furthermore, the claimant, if not fully satisfied, can procede in the Korean court system up

0202

through three levels of judgement. Therefore, the claims compensation system of the Republic of Korea is deemed to be efficiently and soundly instituted, and is well harmonized to effect speedy and satisfactory compensation.

21. Mr. Habib thanked Mr. Chu for his presentation. There followed an extended exchange of questions and answers in which additional information concerning the Korean system for the settlement of claims was developed. This information is summarized in the paragraphs below.

22. At the present time, there are no local offices to which a Korean claimant can present a claim against his Government, and the claim may be mailed or directly submitted to the General Affairs Section of the Ministry of Justice in Seoul. There is, however, under consideration the formation of a network of local offices which might handle certain civil affairs such as claims at the local level. For the transmission of a claim to the Ministry of Justice, the claimant is required to furnish such information as his personal references (name, address, age and occupation), amount of compensation requested and the facts involved in the accident.

23. The State Compensation Committee is empowered to settle all claims against the Korean Government arising out of acts or omissions of employees of the Korean Government acting within the scope of their official duties, as well as any claims arising out of an act or omission which constitutes a violation of the civil or other special codes. Claims arising from the expropriation of property by the Korean Government, or from the exercise by the Korean Government of the

0203

right of eminent domain are not within the purview of the State Compensation Committee. The State Compensation Committee, in arriving at its judgement, takes into account the general principles of Korean law: for example, the doctrine of contributory negligence. The State Compensation Committee follows precedents established by the Korean courts in determining the amounts allowable as part of its awards for the payment of court costs and attorneys' fees.

24. Under the Ministry of Justice's interpretation of Article 24 of the Korean Constitution, any Korean citizen may litigate any problem he might have with his Government in the courts. The Ministry of Justice, therefore, interprets that this provision as permitting any claimant to take up his claim diredtly with the courts without recourse to the State Compensation Committee. The utilization of the claims procedure descrived above is, therefore, entirely voluntary on the part of the claimant, and the claimant may discontinue the procedings at any point if he is dissatisfied, and seek redress in the Korean courts. The Ministry of Justice hopes, however, for an increasing reliance by claimants upon the procedures developed under the terms of the State Compensation Law, and is undertaking efforts to publicize nationally these procedures. At present, roughly 70 per cent of the claims filed against the Government are being pressed under the terms of the procedures available under the State Compensation Law, and number of claims taken up with the courts is gradually decreasing.

25. If an unsatisfied claimant rejects the decision of the State Compensation Committee, and takes his claim

0204

to the courts, the judge hearing the case is, under the terms of the Korean Constitution, bound only by the provisions of Korean law and by his conscience. The proceedings and determinations of the State Compensation Committee, while available to him for review, are not dispositive of the issue when it comes before the court. There have been cases in which dissatisfied claimants have gone from the State Compensation Committee to the courts; one such case now in the courts involves a claim arising out of a maritime accident which was disallowed by the State Compensation Committee because of difficulty of finding reliable evidence due to the place where the accident took place.

26. The State Compensation Committee operates under the terms of generalized regulations which do not, however, apply to each claim on an equal basis because each claim presents its own somewhat unique aspects which require different modes and procedures for settlement. For example, the Korean regulations do not set forth in detail the types of evidence required by the State Compensation Committee to support a claim for a giving awards because in each case the relevant material evidence will be different, e.g., hospital bill receipts, family registration papers, etc. The State Compensation Committee does, however, in practice require the submission of all the relevant material evidence which it considers necessary. If false evidence is submitted by the claimant, he is subject to punishment under the terms of the criminal code and other Korean laws.

27. The factors used by the State Compensation Committee in fixing each award are related to the individual requirements of the claim being satisfied, and

0205

may include such matters as occupation, income, age, sex, the social status and family role of the injured party, etc. In making lump sum awards in lieu of prospective earnings, the State Compensation Committee relies upon the Hofmann formula described in the Korean presentation above. In determing its award the Committee does not take into account the amounts paid the injured party under the terms of pension and workmen's compensation programs, or amounts paid to the injured party from any private insurance policies he might hold because such payments are fundamentally different in nature from an award made in compensation for a wrongful injury and damage.

28. The State Compensation Committee relies upon the Claims Section of the Ministry of Justice (as well as, of course, the claimant) for the development of evidence with respect to each claim which it handles. The Claims Section does not, however, have the authority to disallow claims for lack of evidence or for any other reason; disallowment is the prerogative of the Committee itself.

29. The State Compensation Committee commenced operation in December, 1962. Claims to be acted upon did not, however, come in any quantities until May of 1963. In the three months previous to this meeting, more than 80 claims have been filed, of which more than 70 have been settled. The total compensation paid thus far by the Committee to claimants is approximately won 6 million (US $46,154)at the official rate of exchange). The Ministry of Justice estimates that the State Compensation Committee is paying awards which are

0206

approximately 45 per cent of the amount requested by claimants. The Korean negotiators offered to provide the U.S. side with statistics concerning the exact number of claims settled by the courts and by the Committee,and the awards of compensation paid claimant utilizing both systems, in the past three months.

30. It was agreed that, if it is felt desirable, Korean and American claims specialists would meet to continue discussions on the subject of Korean claims procedures outside the formal negotiating sessions.

OTHER BUSINESS

31. It was agreed that the next negotiating session would be held on September 20, 1963, at 2:00 p.m.

1966,12,31에 예고문에 의거 일반문서로 재분류됨

4. 제31차 회의, 9.20

0208

기 안 용 지

자체 통제		기안처	미주과 강석재	전화번호	근거서류접수일자

	과장	국장		차관	장관
	(서명)	(서명) 13		출장중 (서명)	(서명)

관계관 서명	

기안 년월일	1963. 9. 12	시행 년월일		보존 년한		정서	기장
분류 기호		전체 통제		종결			
경유 수신 참조	건 의			발신			

제목	미주둔군 지위협정체결 교섭 실무자 만찬회 개최

미 주둔군 지위협정 체결을 위한 한미간 실무자 교섭회의 개최 1주년 기념일인 9월 20일을 맞이하고 아울러 미국측 대표 ~~하트~~ 드씨 1등서기관의 이한 환송을 겸하여 한미 실무교섭자간의 친목을 도모하기 위하여 아래와 같이 만찬회를 갖고저 건의하오니 재가하여 주시기 바랍니다.

아 래

1. 일 시: 1963. 9. 20 하오 7시
2. 장 소: 청운각
3. 참 석 자: 별첨 명단 참조 (미국측 13명 한국측 7명 계20명)
4. 경 비: ₩2,500 × 20명 = ₩50,000 끝

0209

승인서식 1-1-3 (11-00900-03) (195mm×265mm16절지)

만찬회 참석자 명단

미국측

1. Mr. Philip C. Habib
   주한미대사관 참사관
2. Gen. G. G. O'Connor
   8군 참모차장
3. Mr. William J. Ford
   주한미대사관 1등서기관
4. Col. Howard Smigelow
   극동사령부 참모차장
5. Capt. R. M. Brownlie
   주한미해군 참모부장
6. Col. L. J. Fuller
   극동사령부 법무참모
7. Mr. Rodney Armstrong
   주한미대사관 2등서기관
8. Lt. Col. W. A. Burt
   8군 민사장교
9. Mr. Robert A. Lewis
   주한미대사관 2등서기관 겸 영사
10. Mr. Robert A. Kinney
    8군 민사부
11. Maj. Robert D. Peckham
    8군 법무장교
12. Lt.Col. Charles Nye III
    8군 소청장교
13. Mr. Kenneth Campen

한국측

1. 황 호 을
   정무국장
2. 신 관 섭
   재무부 세관국장
3. 구 충 회
   미주과장
4. 이 남 구 대령
   국방부 군무과 장
5. 주 문 기
   법무부 법무과장
6. 신 정 섭
   조약과장
7. 박 도 준 중령
   국방부 군무과

0210

기 안 용 지

자체 통제	3등서기관 강상황	기안처	미주과 강석재	전화번호	근거서류접수일자
		과장	국장	차관	장관
		19	19		
관계관 서명					
기안 년월일	1963. 9.18.	시행 년월일		보존 년한	정서기장
분류 기호	외정미	전체 통제		종결	
경유 수신 참조	건의			발신	
제목	제31차 주둔군지위협정 체결교섭회의에 임할 우리측 입장				

9.20일에 개최될 제31차 주둔군지위협정체결 한미간 교섭회의에서는 토지시설(B 및 C 조항), 계약자, 군표 및 현지 조달에 관한 문제를 토의할 예정인바, 이에 관련하여 우리측 교섭실무자는 9월17일 회합을 갖고 제31차 회의에서 취할 우리측 태도를 별첨과 같이 결정하였아오니 재가하여 주시기 바랍니다.

유첨: 제31차 주둔군지위협정체결교섭회의에 임할 우리측 태도, 끝.

보통문서로 재분류(1966. 12. 31)

1966.12.31에 예고문에 의거 일반문서로 재분류됨

승인양식 1-1-3 (1112-040-016-018) (190mm×260mm16절지)

0211

1. 토지시설(B 및 C 조항)

가. 미국측은 토지 및 시설에 대한 B 조 1항에 있어서 "비상시에 토지시설부근에 있어서 필요한 조치를 취한다" 라는 규정을 두고 있는바 우리측은 지난번 회의에서 주장한바와 같이 미국측이 "한국인의 생명 및 재산이 부당하게 저해되지 않는 범위 내에서" 라는 조건을 수락하고 이를 합의 의사록에 삽입하는데 동의한다면 받아드리도록 한다.

나. 미국측 B 조 1항에 있어서의 " at the request of the United States armed forces "라는 용어는 '합동위원회를 통한 양국정부간의 협의를 통해서, 라는 단서가 있기 때문에 미국측 용어를 수락하기로 한다.

다. 원상회복문제에 관한 미국측 초안 C 조1항(우리측 초안 13항에 해당)에 있어서 우리측은 원측적으로 미군의 원상회복의무를 면제하고 단지 미군의 사용으로 막심한 파손을 입은 사유재산에 대해서만 우리정부요청에 의하여 원상회복 또는 이에 대한 보상에 관하여 충분한 고려를 하도록 규정하고 있는데 미국측 초안에서는 이에 관한 규정을 두고 있지 않으므로 우리측 안에 대한 미국측의 입장을 계속 묻기로 한다.

라. 가동설비 소유권 및 처분문제에 관한 미국측 초안 C 조2항은 우리측 초안에 규정되어 있지 않는바 이러한 설비가 미국정부의 재산이며 따라서 한국외로 철거할수 있다함은 당연한 것으로서 우리측은 조약에서 규정할 필요가 없으므로 삭제할 것을 주장한다. 만약 미국측이 이를 삽입할 것을 계속 요구할 경우에는 체제상 합의 의사록에 넣도록 제의한다.

마. 토지시설 개량에 대한 우리정부의 보상의무면제에 관한 미국측이 제시한 추가조항(우리측 조항14항에 해당)은 "for the building or structure "대신에 " for the building, structure, supplies or any other materials "로 하도록 계속 주장하며 이에 대한 미국측 의견을 듣도록 한다. 만약 합의되지

0212

않을 경우에는 " supplies or any other materials "만을 빼고 우리측 안대로 수락할 것을 요구한다.

2. 군계약자

가. 군계약자의 한국법에 대한 복속원칙에 관한 미국측 초안 1항 (우리측 초안 1항에 해당)에 있어서 미국측 초안은 우리측 초안에 삽입되어 있는 " organized under the laws of the United States "라는 구절과 " who are ordinarily resident in the United States "라는 용어를 삭제하고 계약을 체결할수 있는 법인이나 군계약자 및 그 고용원을 제3국인까지 확대시킬수 있도록 규정하고 있는바 우리측은 동 구절의 삽입을 계속 주장하고 미국측의 입장을 듣기로 한다.

나. 군계약자에 대한 재산의 보유,사용 및 이전에 관련한 조세 면제 규정인 미국측 초안 6 항(우리측 초안 5항에 해당)에 있는 " other business in Korea "라는 용어는 "제1절에서 말하고 있는 계약 수행이외의 기타 영업행위"라는 양해 밑에서 수락하기로 한다.

다. 소득세 및 법인세에 관한 미국측 초안 7항(우리측 초안 6항에 해당)에 관해서는 우리측 초안 6항에 대한 추가대안에 미국측 초안대로 " Persons in Korea in connection with the execution of such a contract with the United States shall not be liable to pay any Korean taxes to the Government of Korea or to any taxing agency in Korean on income derived from sources outside of Korea ".

라는 구절은 삽입토록 수락하되 우리측의 대안대로 합의할 것을 주장한다.

0213

라. 미국측이 제의한 군계약자 조항에 대한 합의 의사록은 군계약자가 군대 이외의 미국기관(예, 미대사관 및 유솜)과의 계약을 수행하는 경우에도 본 계약자 조항의 적용에서 제외되지 않음을 규정하고 있는바 우리측은 소득세의 면제를 배제하고저 " except paragraph 7 "이라는 구절을 삽입토록 계속 주장한다.

3. 군 표

가. 미국측 조안 1항 a 절 (우리측 조안 1항 a 절에 해당)에 있어서는 인가된자 상호간의 군표 거래는 장소에 제한없이 허용토록 규정하고 있는바 (ㄱ) 인가된 자간의 거래인 점과 (ㄴ) 장차 환전업무의 확대 가능성을 고려하여 우리측은 " within the facilities and areas in use by the United States forces "라는 제한적 구절을 삭제하는데 동의한다.

나. 미국측 조안 1항 d 절(우리측 조안 1항d절에 해당)에서는 비인가자에게 군표를 사용한 자에 대한 체포 및 처벌규정과 아울러 군표불법사용으로 인한 비인가자나 한국정부에 대한 책임을 면제하는 규정을 두고 있으며 우리측 안은 합의 의사록에서 협정체결당시 한국정부가 보관하고 있는 군표는 양국 정부간에 합의된바에 따라 처분한다는 규정과 부합시키기 위하여 " after the date of coming into force of this Agreement "라는 추가적 구절을 삽입하고 있는바 우리정부가 보관중인 군표를 교환하기 위하여 미국 정부와 앞으로 별도 교섭하는데 있어서 하등 불리한 영향을 주지 않을 것이라는 양해하에 동 구절 삭제에 합의한다.

4. 현지조달

가. 미국군대의 현지 조달용 물품에 대한 면세규정인 미국측 조안 제3항(우리측조안 제3항에 해당)에 있어서 최종적으로 미국군대에

0214

의하여 사용케되는 물자의 구매에 대한 면세는 사실상 전기세, 영업세 등을 소급하여 면세함이 복잡하고 곤란함으로 물품세 및 석유세만을 면세토록 규정한 우리의 주장을 계속 한다.

나. 합의 의사록 제2항에 있어서 미국측은 경제상의 법률의 차이로부터 발생하는 구매계약에 관한 문제해결을 합동위원회나 또는 " other appropriate persons "에 의하여 심의하도록 규정하고 있는데 우리측은 적절한 자가 법률을 심의한다는 것은 부적당하므로 기타 적절한 대표(other appropriate representative)로 대치하도록 계속 주장하고 미국측의 의견을 듣기로 한다.

(1966.12.31)

1966.12.31.에 예고문에 의거 일반문서로 재분류됨

0215

기 안 용 지

자체 통제		기안처	미주과 강석재	전화번호	근거서류접수일자
	과장	국장		차관	장관
	23	전결			23

관계관 서명	조약과장
기안 년월일	1963.9.23
시행 년월일	
보존 년한	
분류 기호	외정미 722.2
전체 통제	
종결	
경유 수신 참조	국가재건 최고회의 의장 (참조: 외무국방 위원장) 내각 수반
발신	장관
제목	주둔군 지위협정 체결을 위한 제31차 교섭회의 보고

1963. 9. 20일 하오 2시부터 4시20분까지 외무부 장관 회의실에서 개최된 제31차 주둔군 지위협정 체결 교섭회의에서 토의된 내용을 별첨과 같이 보고합니다.

유첨: 제31차 교섭회의 보고서 1부 끝

196 . . 에 예고문에 의거 일반문서로 재분류됨

승인서식 1-1-3 (11 00900-03) (195mm×265mm16절지)

0216

외 무 부

외정미 722.2 1963.9.24

수 신: 국가재건최고회의 의장

참 조: 외무 국방위원장

제 목: 주둔군 지위협정 체결을 위한 제31차 교섭회의 보고

1963. 9. 20일 하오 3시부터 4시 20분까지 외무부 장관 회의실에서 개최된 제 31차 주둔 군 지위협정 체결 교섭 회의에서 토의된 내용을 별첨과 같이 보고합니다.

유첨: 제31차 교섭회의 보고서 2부 끝

외무부장관 김 용 식

0217

외 무 부

외정미 722.2　　　　　　　　　　　　　1963.9.24

수 신 : 내각 수반

제목 : 주둔군 지위협정 체결을 위한 제31차 교섭회의 보고

1963. 9. 20일 하오 3시부터 4시 20분까지 외무부 장관회의실에서 개최된 제31차 주둔 군 지위협정 체결 교섭 회의에서 토의된 내용을 별첨과 같이 보고합니다.

유첨 : 제31차 교섭회의 보고서 1부　　　끝

외무부장관　　　김　용　식

0218

제 31 차

한미간 주둔군 지위협정 체결실무자 회의

보 고 서

1. 일 시 : 1963. 9. 20 하오 2시부터 4시 20분까지

2. 장 소 : 외무부 장관 회의실

3. 참석자 : 한국측 : 황 호 을 (외무부 정무국장)

신 관 섭 (재무부 세관국장)

구 충 회 (외무부 미주과장)

신 정 섭 (외무부 조약과장)

이 남 구 (국방부 군무과장)

주 문 기 (법무부 법무과장)

강 석 재 (외무부 2등서기관)

조 광 제 (외무부 2등서기관)

미국측 : 교섭대표단 전원

("호드" 1등서기관 후임으로 "제임스, A, 사토리오스 2등서기관이 참석함)

4. 토의사항 :

(1) 양측 수석대표는 주둔군지위 협정 체결교섭이 개시된 일주년을 맞이하여 그간 여러 어려운 문제를 해결하고 많은 진전을 보았음을 회고하고 앞으로 계속 성의있는 교섭을 통하여 남은 문제를 해결하자고 서로 다짐하였음.

(2) 의제에 따라 토지 및 시설, 군표 및 현지조달에 관한 조항을 순차적으로 토의함.

63-1-147

192

0213

63-1-24(1)

미국문 108-7(3)

0220

(3) 토지 및 시설

가) 미국측은 A 조 1 (b)항 (우리측 초안 3항에 해당)에 대하여 본 협정발효시 미군이 사용하는 토지 및 시설로서 재사용권을 보유하고 한국정부에 반환한 토지시설도 포함시키도록 규정하고 또한 우리측 안을 참작하여 그러한 토지 및 시설의 기록을 합동위원회가 유지한다는 별첨 1 과 같은 대안을 제시하였으며 우리측은 이를 검토후 다음회의에서 논의키로 하였음.

나) 미국측 안 (B)조 1항중 "비상시에는 토지 및 시설 부근에 있어서 필요한 조치를 취할수 있다"라는 규정에 대하여 우리측은 미국측 의견을 문의하였던바 미국측은 우리의 요구에 따라 합의 의사록에 넣는데 동의하였으나 별첨 2와 같이 새로운 대안을 수교하였다. 우리측은 "필요한 조치"는 "한국인의 생명과 재산을 부당하게 저해하지 않는 범위내에서"라는 어구를 계속 삽입하도록 요구하였으며 미국측은 비상시에 취하는 조치는 항상 최소한도로 필요한 조치에만 한 한다고 답변하였으며 다음 회의에서 계속 토의키로 하였음.

다) 우리측은 미국측 (B)조 1항의 "미군의 요청이 있을시" 라는 어구에 대하여 "합동위원회를 통한 양국정부간에 협의를 통해서"라는 설명적인 어구가 있음을 고려하여 미국측 용어를 수락하였음. 63-1-148

마) 우리측 초안 13항은 미군의 토지시설에 대한 원상회복 의무를 면제하고 예외적으로 막심한 파손을 입은 사유 재산에 대해서만 우리정부의 요청에 의하여 원상회복 또는 보상에 관하여 미국측이 충분한 고려를 하도록

0221

-3-1-24

기.울108-7

0222

규정하고 있는데 미국측은 이러한 보상문제를 고려할 수 없다는 종래의 태도에 변함이 없다고 답변하였음.

마) 우리측은 가동설비 소유권 및 처분문제에 관한 미국측 초안 (C)조 2항은 그러한 설비, 비품 및 보급품은 미국의 재산이며 따라서 한국외로 철거할수 있다함은 당연한 것으로서 조약에서 규정할 필요가 없음으로 삭제할 것을 주장하고 만약 미국측이 이를 삽입할 것을 요구한다면 합의 의사록에 넣도록 제의하였던바 미국측은 우리의 주장을 고려하겠다 함.

바) 미군이 한국정부에 반환하는 토지 및 시설에 가한 개량에 대하여 우리정부의 보상의무 면제를 규정한 미국측 대안에 대하여 우리측은 "보급품 혹은 기타 자재"를 삭제하고 우리측 초안대로 수락할 것을 요구하였던바 미국측은 이를 고려하겠다고 답변하였음.

(4) 군 표

가) 인가된 자 상호간의 군표거래에 관하여 우리측은 (1) 인가된 자간의 거래 인정과 (2) 장차 환전업무확대 가능성을 고려하여 "미군이 사용하고 있는 시설 및 토지 내에 있어서"라는 제한적 구절을 우리측 초안에서 삭제키로 하여 원칙적인 합의를 보았음.

나) 군표 비인가 사용자에 대한 체포 및 처벌규정과 아울러 군표 불법사용의 결과에 대한 한국인 또는 한국정부의 책임면제에 관한 규정에 대하여 우리측은 우리정부가 보관중인 군표를 교환하기 위하여 앞으로 미국정부와 별도 교섭하는데 있어서 하등 불리한 영향을 주지않을 것이라는 양해하에 "본협정 발효일자후"라는 구절을 삭제할 것을 제의하였던바 미국측은 동

63-1-14

0223

63-1-24

기.문 108-1

0224

구절의 삭제가 또한 미국의 교섭입장을 방해할수 없다고 주장하여 왔음. 이에 대하여 우리측은 한국정부가 보관하고 있는 군표는 과거 한국국민들이 의식적이든 혹은 불의식적이든 간에 부득이한 환경하에서 용역 혹은 물자의 제공 대가로서 받은 것이기 때문에 선의의 이들 피해자에 대한 보상을 해주어야 한다는 것은 양국 정부의 도의적인 의무라는 점을 재삼 강력히 주장하였음. 이에 관하여 미국측은 한국정부가 현재 혹은 장차 가지게 될 군표를 보상없이 신속히 미군당국에 반환해야 한다는 별첨 3 과 같은 합의 의사록을 제시하였음. 우리측은 이 문제에 관한 토의를 중단하고 "본 협정 발효일자후"라는 용어의 삭제를 당분간 보류하였음.

(5) 현지 조달

가) 미국군대의 현지조달 물품에 대한 면세규정중 최종적으로 미국군대에 의하여 사용되는 물자의 구매에 대한 면세 문제에 관하여 미국측은 계속 전기세, 영업세도 면제할 것을 주장하였으나 우리측은 그러한 물품에 대한 면세를 허용한다면 그 절차가 복잡하고 세액보다 오히려 더 많은 경비가 소요되며 징세비가 세액보다 많으면 조세가 불가하다는 조세 원칙에도 부합되지 않는다고 설명하였다. 우리측은 이 문제가 복잡한 만큼 이문제를 다루는 양측 교섭실무자가 별도 비공식 회합에서 논의키로 제의하여 합의를 보았음.

5. 중요합의 사항 :

무

6. 기타 사항 :

차기회의 일자 : 1963. 10. 4 하오 2 시

차기회의의제 : 차기회의까지 양측수석대표간에 합의된 사항

1966, 12, 31에 예고문에 의거 일반문서로 재분류됨

63-1-1/70

0225

보관 1-3

63-1-24

미호108-7

0226

별첨 1.

Article II - Facilities and Areas (Grant of and Return)

1. .....

(b) The facilities and areas of which the United States armed forces have the use at the effective date of this agreement together with those areas and facilities which the United States armed forces have returned to the Republic of Korea with the reserved right of re-entry, when these facilities and areas have been re-entered by U.S. forces, shall be considered as the facilities and areas agreed upon between the two Governments in accordance with subparagraph (a) above. Records of facilities and areas of which the United States armed forces have the use or right of re-entry shall be maintained through the Joint Committee after this Agreement comes into force.

63-1-151

0227

63-1-24

비문 108-4

0228

별첨 2.

<u>Article III - Facilities and Areas</u>

(Security Measures In)

AGREED MINUTE

It is agreed that in the event of an emergency, the United States armed forces shall be authorized to take such measures in the vicinity of the areas and facilities as may be necessary to provide for their safeguarding and control.

63-1-15

0229

0230

별첨 3

ARTICLE XIX - Military Payment Certificates

AGREED MINUTE

Inasmuch as United States Military Payment Certificates are property of the United States Government, any Military Payment Certificates which are in, or come into, the possession of the Government of the Republic of Korea shall be returned without compensation to the authorities of the United States armed forces as expeditiously as practicable.

63-1-153

178

1966,12,31,에 예고문에 의거 일반문서로 재분류됨

0231

0232

DRAFT

MINUTES OF THE THIRTY-FIRST NEGOTIATING SESSION FOR ROK-US SOFA

Time & Place: Ministry of Foreign Affairs, September 20, 1963

Agenda: 1 Facilities and Areas

2 Military Paymentxx Certificates

3 Local Procurement

PARTICIPANTS:

Republic of Korea	United States
HWANG ~~XXX~~ Ho-ul	Philip C. Habib
SIN Kwon-sup	Brig. Gen. G.G. O'Conner, USA
KU Chung-hwe	Col. Howard G. Smigelow, USA
Colonel YI Nam-ku, ROKA	Captain R.M. Brownlie, USN
CHU Mun-ki	Robert A. Lewis
SIN Chung-sop	Robert A. Kinney
~~HO Sung~~	James Sartorius
KANG Suk-che (Interpreter)	Major Robert D. Peckham, USA
CHO KWANG JAE	Rodney E. Armstrong
	Kenneth Campen (Interpreter)

0233

1. Mr. HWANG Ho-ul opened the meeting by saying that he wished to note that the thirty-first session marked the first anniversary of the reopening of the negotiations for a ROK-US Status of Forces Agreement on September 20, 1962. Many difficult problems have been tackled cooperatively and with sincerity. The complexities of the negotiations are now understood more thoroughly. The Korean side hopes that the negotiations will be carried forward with continued sincerity and good intent, and that the negotiations will be successfully completed at the earliest possible date.

2. Mr. Habib responded that the negotiators on both sides of the table know better than anyone else that the discussions deal with a complex instrument. The U.S. side considers that the discussions have made exceptional progress and is pleased with the spirit in which this progress has been made. As intimated in some of the early public statements by the U.S. side, the negotiators have taken up some of the less complex topics first, and have now gotten these subjects pretty much out of the way. In the discussion of some of the more difficult articles and clauses which still remain for negotiation, the U.S. side pledges a continuation of the sincerity which has thus far characterized its approach to the negotiations. Mr. Habib then introduced James Sartorius, Second Secretary of Embassy, who replaces Mr. William Ford on the U.S. negotiating team.

0234

his confidence

3. Mr. Hwang welcomed Mr. Sartorius, and expressed that Mr. Sartorius would continue Mr. Ford's contribution to the progress of the negotiations.

FACILITIES AND AREAS - Grant of and Return

4. Opening substantive discussion, Mr. Hwang asked if the U.S. side had any new thoughts on the draft article dealing with the grant of and return of facilities and areas(US draft Article I, or "A").

5. Mr. Habib recalled that the negotiators have reached agreement upon paragraphs 2,3, and 4 of the U.S. draft article, and that the remaining points of difference all have to do with those points covered in paragraph 1 of the US. draft article. The U.S. side had considered the points made by the Korean side in previous discussions of this paragraph. First, the Korean draft provided in paragraph 3 for a new survey of the facilities and areas used by the U.S. Forces after the coming into force of the Agreement; as an alternative, the Korean side had suggested that language embodying the substance of paragraph 3 of their draft article might be added at the end of paragraph 1 b. of the U.S. draft. The U.S. side wished to point out that the U.S. Forces in Korea had under way a comprehensive survey of the facilities and areas in use by them. This survey was begun in 1959 and is scheduled to be completed by 10 October, 1964. The results are being transmitted to the Korean Government as they become available, and information on 95% of the areas and facilities surveyed thus far have been supplied the Korean Government. ~~This survey is 95 per cent completed as of the present time, and the information concerning this proportion of the facilities and areas is, therefore, in the hands of the Korean Government. It is estimated that this survey will be completed~~

0235

~~by October, 1964.~~ The U.S. side ~~cXXXXXXX~~ sees no good reason to include language in the prospective Agreement requiring that a new survey ~~xxx~~ be made at great expense of time and money to do essentially what has already been done and to replace information which is already or will shortly be in the hands of the proper Korean authorities.

6. Continuing his review of the points of difference in paragraph 1 of the U.S. draft, Mr. Habib said that the U.S. ~~XXX~~ side had been able to take into account the desire of the Korean negotiators expressed in an earlier meeting that the Joint Committee be given a role ~~XX~~ as the custodian of the records concerning the facilities and areas in use by the U.S. Forces. In ~~XXXXX~~ considering this point, the U.S. side ~~xxxxxxx~~ discovered ~~XX~~ a gap in its draft which it would like to remedy. This gap concerns the lack of any provision in the prospective agreement concerning those areas and facilities, mostly airfields, which the U.S. has returned to Korea with the reserved right of re-entry. There exist mutual understandings between the U.S. and Korea concerning these facilities and areas where the U.S. has a reserved right of re-entry (~~XXX~~ Mr. Habib quoted one such agreement with respect to the Suwon Auxiliary Air Field), but such agreements do not specify that the ~~XXXXXXXXXXXXXXXXXX~~ facilities and areas, once re-entered, shall be considered as ~~XXXXXXXXXX~~ part of the facilities and areas specified in the ~~XXXXX~~ prospective ~~XXXXXXXX~~ Status of Forces Agreement.

7. Mr. Habib thereupon tabled a ~~XXXXXXXXXXXXXXXXXXXXXXXXXXXXXXXXXXXXX~~ new paragraph 1b. of the draft U.S. article on the grant of and return of facilities and areas. He said that this ~~draft~~

0236

revision sought to accomplish two purposes: take into account Korean desires concerning the role of the Joint Committee in the maintenance of records concerning the facilities and areas utilized by the U.S Forces, and regularize the relationship of the existing re-entry agreements between the two Governments to the prospective Status of Forces Agreement.

8. Mr. Hwang said the Korean side would study the new draft language taking into account the explanation just offered by Mr. Habib, and would give its views at a forthcoming meeting. It was agreed to pass on to a review of the draft article on measures which may be taken in facilities and areas (U.S. draft Article III, or "B").

FACILITIES AND AREAS - Measures which May be Taken in

9. Mr. Habib recalled that in the course of previous discussions of this article the Korean side suggested that the second sentence of the first paragraph of the U.S. draft article might more appropriately be handled as an agreed minute to the article. The U.S. side accepted this suggestion and now tabled a draft agreed minute embodying the substance of the second sentence of paragraph 1 of the U.S. draft article.

10. Mr. Hwang recalled that at a previous meeting the Korean negotiators had suggested that the phrase "within the extent that Korean nationals and their property are not unduly impaired" be added at the end of the sentence in the Agreement dealing with emergency measures. At the time this suggestion was

0237

made, the U.S. side had responded that there was no intent to take measures which would have any of the effects contemplated by the suggested Korean language. Mr. Hwang suggested that this understanding be supplemented by an agreed minute to the article under consideration.

11. Mr. Habib objected that the phrase proposed by the Korean side is indefinable. The problem to be met by the language dealing with this matter is obvious; since by definition the language deals with emergency situations, it should set forth a clear principle and not one incapable of definition with precision. The emergency doctrine of the U.S. Forces, as set forth in their regulations, is to take only such actions as are necessary for the resolution of a given emergency. The Korean language would disregard the only real measure of actions to be taken in any emergency situation: necessity. The Korean side would agree that it is most essential that in an emergency should the U.S. Forces be given the necessary scope of action to fulfill their mission. Mr. Habib asked that the Korean side consider the U.S. draft, bearing in mind the emergency doctrine of the U.S. Forces.

12. Mr. Hwang said that the Korean side would study the U.S. draft and would give its views at a forthcoming meeting. He recalled that in the course of previous discussions of this article the Korean side was uncertain that the language of the U.S. draft paragraph 1 adequately set forth Government-to-Government nature of requests

0238

for Korean measures to provide access to facilities and areas. The Korean negotiators had, however, studied the article thoroughly, and now considered that, given the language XXXXXXXXX of the U.S. draft concerning "consultation between the two Governments in the Joint XXXXXXX Committee", the requests made under the paragraph 1 of the U.S. draft article could be considered as requests by the Government of the United States. The Korean side therefore wished to withdraw its objections to this XXXXXXXX aspect of the U.S. draft article.

13. Mr. Habib said that the understanding just set forth by Mr. Hwang was shared by the XXXXXX U.S. side. He noted that XXXXXXXX paragraphs 2 and 3 of the XXXXXX U.S. draft article had previously been agreed upon.

FACILITIES AND AREAS — Return of

14. Turning to the draft article on the return of facilities (U.S. draft article IV, or "C"), Mr. Hwang suggested a discussion of paragraph 1 of the U.S. draft article. Mr. Habib responded that the U.S. position upon the matters covered in paragraph 1 is unchanged, and that the U.S. side still considers that the XXXXXXXX question of compensation for the use of facilities and areas is outside the scope of an agreement such as the prospective Status of Forces Agreement.

15. Mr. Hwang recalled that the U.S. side at a previous meeting had tabled a new paragraph to be added to the article on return of facilities and areas, specifying the fact that Korea has no obligation to pay for the residual value of improvements made to facilities and areas returned to Korea by the U.S. In the course of the discussion following the tabling of this

0239

new paragraph, the Korean side suggested the inclusion XXXXXXXXXX in the paragraph of a phrase which provided that "supplies or other materials" were among the objects for which XXX Korea would not XXX be required to XXX compensate the U.S. The Korean side felt that the topic of XXXXXXXXXXXX XXXXXX non-liability for residual value should be covered ~~in an agreed minute and not~~ in the text of the article dealing with the return of facilities and areas. The Korean side therefore XXXXXX proposed that the U.S. side agree to ~~an~~ drop its paragraph 2 in favor of ~~agreed minute which would consist of~~ the text of paragraph 14 of the Korean draft article, minus the language concerning "supplies XXX or other materials" which the U.S. negotiators had previously found objectionable. The proposed ~~agreed~~ paragraph 2 (following the U.S. side's rewording) ~~minute~~ would read: "The Government of the Republic of Korea is not obliged to make any compensation to the Government of the United States for any improvements made in facilities and areas or for the buildingsx or structures left thereon on the expiration of this Agreement or the earlier return of the facilities and areas."

16. Mr. Hwang went on to say that the topics XXXXXXX covered in paragraph 2 of the U.S. darft article on the return of facilities and areas seemed to the Korean XXXXXX negotiators to be matters of common sense. It was common sense that the items specified in this draft paragraph, if XXXX the property of the U.S., could be removed at will from the XXX Republic of Korea. The Korean side therefore suggested the deletion of this paragraph or XXXXXXXXX alternatively XXX its relegation to an agreed minute.

0240

17. Mr. Habib said that the U.S. side would study the Korean proposal with respect to the arrangement of the provisions concerning residual value. As for the Korean suggestion with respect to paragraph 2 of the U.S. draft article, however, it was the feeling of the U.S. side that it was necessary to have language covering the right of re-export of the items specified in the draft paragraph included in the text of the prospective Agreement. It was agreed at this point to suspend discussion of the topic of facilities and areas and to pass on to the draft article on Military Payment Certificates.

MILITARY PAYMENT CERTIFICATES

18. Mr. Hwang said the Korean negotiators had restudied the text of the U.S. draft article on Military Payment Certificates (MPC) and were willing to withdraw their suggestion that the words "within the facilities and areas in use by the United States Forces" be attached to the end of the first sentence of the article. The Korean side agreed to the deletion of this phrase because MPC transactions were internal transactions among authorized users and the additional limiting language is believed to be unnecessary. Mr. Habib welcomed this statement.

19. Mr. Hwang continued that the Korean side had also reviewed its position on the language in the Korean draft article which states that the lack of obligation on the part of the U.S. to redeem MPC held by unauthorized persons is recognized only "after the date of coming into force of this agreement". The Korean side would delete this language if there is an understanding

0241

that the deletion would not affect adversely XXX negotiations with U.S. authorities for the exchange of MPC now held by the Korean XXXXXXX Government for XXXXXXX U.S. dollars.

20. Mr. Hwang said tXXX the Korean Government now has a certain amount of MPC in its custody. At some future time, the Korean Government may enter into negotiations with the U.S. Government for the exchange of these MPC into U.S. dollars. It was with this xx possibility in mind that the Korean draft article on MPC XX was drafted, and that the phrase quoted earlier was inserted. By agreeing to deletion of this phrase, the Korean negotiators would not wish to have their position in the prospective negotiations adversely XXXXX affected.

20. Mr. Hwang continued that, while in law unauthorized persons XXXXXXX are not supposed to utilize MPC, in practical xx terms XX MPC were often handed over in the past to Koreans by authorized users in payment for goods and services provided to the authorized user. The Koreans had no choice; it was a question of either accepting the MPC, possibly without knowledge of the illegality of the transaction, or receiving no payment at all. In the future, the Korean Government intended to XXXXXXX publicize the illegality of such transactions, but in the meantime large quantities of MPC had come into the hands of Koreans, some of which was turned XXX over to the Korean Government in response to its call for a declaration of holdings of foreign currency. A way should be found to redeem this MPC in usable foreign exchange, in order to make up the loss now outstanding to the original recipi[illegible] to repair the loss of good will which

0242

will otherwise accrue to the U.S.

21. Mr. Habib inquired what amount of MPC the Korean Government is currently holding in custody. Mr. Hwang replied that he had no exact figures on XXXX the Government's holdings.

22. Mr. Habib asked whether the Korean side would XXXXXX agree to deletion of the phrase quoted by Mr. Hwang if the understanding with respect to non-prejudice to any future negotiations were made reciprocal; that is, if the negotiating record also included a statement that the US has no obligation to redeem any amounts of MPC held by the Korean Government. Each side to the present negotiations would, under the terms of such an understanding, retain its independence with respect to a matter which should properly be discussed outside the present negotiations.

23. Mr. Hwang said that the answer to Mr. Habib's proposal was complex and difficult, and that he wished to withdraw his offer of the deletion of the phrase under discussion. The Korean side would stand on its original draft language.

24. Mr Habib said he regretted Mr. Hwang's retreat from a proposal which seemed to offer a solution by which the interests of both sides to the present negotiations could be preserved and the negotiation of a Status of Forces Agreement advanced. The U.S. is, of course, not prepared to agree to compensation for MPC illegally acquired and was not willing to assist in the ex post facto legalization of illegal transactions just because they had taken place on a broad scale.

0243

—12—

Mr. Hwang had, unfortunately, in the preceding discussion made clear that the Korean side wished to impose an obligation upon the U.S. side to agree at some time in the future to exchange the Korean Government's holdings of illegally acquired MPC for dollars. In these circumstances, he was compelled to table a draft agreed minute which rules out the possibility of any future negotiations for the conversion of Korean Government holdings of illegally acquired MPC. Mr. Habib tabled the draft agreed minute he had just described, and it was agreed to turn to the topic of local procurement.

LOCAL PROCUREMENT

25. Major Peckham presented a detailed explanation of the manner in which the U.S. side envisaged that the exemptions from Korean taxation specified in the U.S. draft article on local procurement would be granted. He stressed that the key to a proper understanding of the U.S. draft article is a close reading of U.S. draft agreed minute number 3 to the U.S. draft article, which sets forth in detail the procedures by which the U.S. Forces would obtain the exemptions specified in the article above. Examples of the manner in which these procedures would be implemented were set forth. Major Peckham also emphasized that the U.S. Forces in Korea are already receiving exemptions, for both direct and "ultimate use" procurement, from most of the taxes specified in the U.S. draft article under the terms of existing Korean legislation. The implementation of the U.S. draft article would require only a broadening and formalizing of the existing procedures, and not the development of any new procedures. 0244

26. Mr. SIN XXXXXXX Kwon-sup, replying to Major Peckham's presentation on behalf of the Korean side, expressed certain reservations about certain points, and said that a broadening of the present system for the exemption of U.S. Forces procurement from Korean taxation would increase the cost of tax administration appreciably. He suggested that the matters touched upon in Major Peckham's presentation be discussed between specialists from the two negotiating teams outside the formal negotiating sessions. The U.S. negotiators agreed to this suggestion.

OTHER BUSINESS

27. It was agreed that the next negotiating session would be held on October 4, 1963, at 2:00 PM. The negotiators having remained in session almost three hours, the meeting was thereupon adjourned.

1966, 12.31 예 예고문에 의거 일반문서로 재분류됨

JOINT SUMMARY RECORD OF THE 31ST SESSION

September 20, 1963

1. Time and Place: 2:00 to 4:20 p.m. September 20, 1963 at the Foreign Minister's Conference Room

2. Attendants:

ROK Side:

Mr. Whang, Ho Eul	Director Bureau of Political Affairs Ministry of Foreign Affairs
Mr. Shin, Kwan Sup	Director Bureau of Customs Duty Ministry of Finance
Mr. Koo, Choong Whay	Chief, America Section Ministry of Foreign Affairs
Col. Lee, Nam Koo	Chief, Military Affairs Section Ministry of National Defense
Mr. Chu, Mun Ki	Chief, Legal Affairs Section Ministry of Justice
Mr. Shin, Jung Sup	Chief, Treaty Section Ministry of Foreign Affairs
Mr. Kang, Suk Jae	2nd Secretary Ministry of Foreign Affairs
Mr. Cho, Kwang Jae	2nd Secretary Ministry of Foreign Affairs

U. S. Side:

Mr. Philip C. Habib	Counselor for Political Affairs American Embassy
Brig. Gen. G.G. O'Connor	Deputy Chief of Staff 8th U. S. Army
Col. Howard Smigelor	Deputy Chief of Staff UNC
Capt. R. M. Brownlie	Assistant Chief of Staff USN/K
Mr. Robert A. Lewis	2nd Secretary and Consul American Embassy
Mr. James Sartorius	2nd Secretary American Embassy
Mr. Rodney E. Armstrong	2nd Secretary American Embassy

0246

미주과	양고재 7월 20일	담당	과장	국장	국방보좌관	차관	장관

Mr. Robert A. Kinney	J-5 8th U.S. Army
Maj. Robert D. Peckham	Staff Officer, JAG 8th U.S. Army

1. Mr. Whang Ho Eul opened the meeting by saying that he wished to note that the thirty-first session marked the first anniversery of the reopening of the negotiations for a ROK-US Status of Forces Agreement on September 20, 1962. Many difficult problems have been tackled cooperatively and with sincerity. The complexities of the negotiations are now understood more thoroughly. The Korean side hopes that the negotiations will be carried forward with continued sincerity and good intent, and that the negotiations will be successfully completed at the earliest possible date.

2. Mr. Habib responded that the negotiators on both sides of the table know better than anyone else that the discussions deal with a complex instrument. The U.S. side considers that the discussions have made exceptional progress and is pleased with the spirit in which this progress has been made. As intimated in some of the early public statements by the U.S. side, the negotiators have taken up some of the less complex topics first, and have now gotten these subjects pretty much out of the way. In the discussion of some of the more difficult articles and clauses which still remain for negotiation, the U.S. side pledges a continuation of the sincerity which has thus far characterized its approach to the negotiations. Mr. Habib then introduced James Sartorius, Second Secretary of Embassy, who replaces Mr. William Ford on the U.S. negotiating team.

3. Mr. Whang welcomed Mr. Sartorius, and expressed his confidence that Mr. Sartorius would continue Mr.

0247

Ford's contribution to the progress of the negotiations.

FACILITIES AND AREAS - Grant of and Return

4. Opening substantive discussion, Mr. Hwang asked if the U.S. side had any new thoughts on the draft article dealing with the grant of and return of facilities and areas (US draft Article I, or "A").

5. Mr. Habib recalled that the negotiators have reached agreement upon paragraphs 2,3, and 4 of the U.S. draft article, and that the remaining points of difference all have to do with those points covered in paragraph 1 of the US draft article. The U.S. side had considered the points made by the Korean side in previous discussions of this paragraph. First, the Korean draft provided in paragraph 3 for a new survey of the facilities and areas used by the U.S. Forces after the coming into force of the Agreement as an alternative; the Korean side had suggested that language embodying the substance of paragraph 3 of their draft article might be added at the end of paragraph 1b. of the U.S. draft. The U.S. side wished to point out that the U.S. Forces in Korea had under way a comprehensive survey of the facilities and areas in use by them (This survey was begun in 1959) and is scheduled to be completed by 10 October, 1964. The results are being transmitted to the Korean Government as they become available, and it is estimated information on 95% of the areas and facilities surveyed thus far has been supplied the Korean Government. The U.S. side sees no good reason to include language in the prospective Agreement requiring that a new survey be made at great expense of time and money to do essentially what has already been done and to replace information which is already or will shortly be in the hands of the proper Korean authorities.

0248

6. Continuing his review of the points of difference in paragraph 1 of the U.S. draft, Mr. Habib said that the U.S. side had been able to take into account the desire of the Korean negotiators expressed in an earlier meeting that the Joint Committee be given a role as the custodian of the records concerning the facilities and areas in use by the U.S. Forces. In considering this point, the U.S. side discovered a gap in its draft which it would like to remedy. This gap concerns the lack of any provision in the prospective agreement concerning those areas and facilities, mostly airfields, which the U.S. has returned to Korea with the reserved right of re-entry. There exist mutual understandings between the U.S. and Korea concerning these facilities and areas where the U.S. has a reserved right of re-entry (Mr. Habib quoted one such agreement with respect to the Suwon Auxiliary Air Field), but such agreements do not specify that the facilities and areas, once re-entered, shall be considered as part of the facilities and areas specified in the prospective Status of Forces Agreement.

7. Mr. Habib thereupon tabled a new paragraph 1b. of the draft U.S. article on the grant of and return of facilities and areas. He said that this revision sought to accomplish two purposes: take into account Korean desires concerning the role of the Joint Committee in the maintenance of records concerning the facilities and areas utilized by the U.S. Forces, and regularize the relationship of the existing re-entry agreements between the two Governments to the prospective Status of Forces Agreement.

8. Mr. Whang said the Korean side would study the new draft language taking into account the explanation just offered by Mr. Habib, and would give its views at a forthcoming meeting. It was agreed to pass on to a review of the draft article on measures which may be taken in facilities and areas (U.S. draft article III or "B").

FACILITIES AND AREAS -Measures Which May be Taken in

9. Mr. Habib recalled that in the course of previous discussions of this article the Korean side suggested that the second sentence of the first paragraph of the U.S. draft article might more appropriately be handled as an agreed minute to the article. The U.S. side accepted this suggestion and now table a draft agreed minute embodying the substance of the second sentence of paragraph 1 of the U.S. draft article.

10. Mr. Whang recalled that at a previous meeting the Korean negotiators had suggested that the phrase "within the extent that Korean nationals and their property are not unduly impaired" be added at the end of the sentence in the Agreement dealing with emergency measures. At the time this suggestion was made, the U.S. side had responded that there was no intent to take measures which would have any of the effects contemplated by the suggested Korean language. Mr. Whang suggested that this understanding be supplemented by an agreed minute to the article under consideration.

11. Mr. Habib objected that the phrase proposed by the Korean side is indefinable. The problem to be met by the language dealing with this matter is obvious; since by definition the language deals with emergency

0250

situations, it should set forth a clear principle and not one incapable of definition with precision. The embrgency doctrine of the U.S. Forces, as set forth in their regulations, is to take only such actions as are necessary for the resolution of a given emergency. The Korean language would disregard the only real measure of actions to be taken in any emergency situation: necessity. The Korean side would agree that it is most essential that in an emergency the U.S. Forces should be given the necessary scope of action to fulfill their mission. Mr. Habib asked that the Korean side consider the U.S. draft, bearing in mind the emergency doctrine of the U.S. Forces.

12. Mr. Whang said that the Korean side would study the U.S. draft and would give its views at a forthcoming meeting. He recalled that in the course of previous discussions of this article the Korean side was uncertain that the language of the U.S. draft paragraph 1 adequately set forth the Government-to-Government nature of requests for Korean measures to provide access to facilities and areas. The Korean negotiators had, however, studied the article thoroughly, and now considered that, given the language of the U.S. draft conerning "consultation between the two Governments in the Joint Committee", the requests made under the terms of paragraph 1 of the U.S. draft article could be considered as requests by the Government of the United States. The Korean side therefore wished to withdraw its objections to this aspect of the U.S. draft article.

13. Mr. Habib said that the understanding just set

0251

forth by Mr. Whang was shared by the U.S. side. He noted that paragraphs 2 and 3 of the U.S. draft article had previously been agreed upon.

FACILITIES AND AREAS -Return of

14. Turning to the draft article on the return of facilities (U.S. draft article IV, or "C"), Mr. Whang suggested a discussion of paragraph 1 of the U.S. draft article. Mr. Habib responded that the U.S. position upon the matters covered in paragraph 1 is unchanged, and that the U.S. side still considers that the question of compensation for the use of facilities and areas is outside the scope of an agreement such as the prospective Status of Forces Agreement.

15. Mr. Whang recalled that the U.S. side at a previous meeting had tabled a new paragraph to be added to the article on return of facilities and areas, specifying the fact that Korea has no obligation to pay for the residual value of improvements made to facilities and areas returned to Korea by the U.S. In the course of the discussion following the tabling of this new paragraph, the Korean side suggested the inclusion in the paragraph of a phrase which provided that "supplies or other materials" were among the objects for which Korea would not be required to compensate the U.S. The Korean side felt that the topic of non-liability for residual value should be covered in the text of the article dealing with the return of facilities and areas. The Korean side therefore proposed that the U.S. side agree to drop its paragraph 2 in favor of the text of paragraph 14 of the Korean draft article, minus the language concerning "supplies or other materials" which the U.S. negotiators had pr

0252

previously found objectionable. The proposed paragraph 2 (following the U.S. side's numbering) would read: "The Government of the Republic of Korea is not obliged to make any compensation to the Government of the United States for any improvements made in facilities and areas or for the buildings or structures left thereon on the expiration of this Agreement or the earlier return of the facilities and areas."

16. Mr. Whang went on to say that the topics covered in paragraph 2 of the U.S. draft article on the return of facilities and areas seemed to the Korean negotiators to be matters of common sense. It was common sense that the items specified in this draft paragraph, if the property of the U.S., could be removed at will from the Republic of Korea. The Korean side therefore suggested the deletion of this paragraph or alternatively its relegation to an agreed minute.

17. Mr. Habib said that the U.S. side would study the Korean proposal with respect to the arrangement of the provisions concerning residual value. As for the Korean suggestion with respect to paragraph 2 of the U.S. draft article, however, it was the feeling of the U.S. side that it was necessary to have language covering the right of re-export of the items specified in the draft paragraph included in the text of the prospective Agreement. It was agreed at this point to suspend discussion of the topic of facilities and areas and to pass on to the draft article on Military Payment Certificates.

MILITARY PAYMENT CERTIFICATES

18. Mr. Whang said the Korean negotiators had restudied the text of the U.S. draft article on Military Payment

0253

Certificates (MPC), and were willing to withdraw their suggestion that the words "within the facilities and areas in use by the United States Forces" be attached to the end of the first sentence of the article. The Korean side agreed to the deletion of this phrase because MPC transactions were internal transactions among authorized users and the additional limiting language is believed to be unnecessary. Mr. Habib welcomed this statement.

19. Mr. Whang continued that the Korean side had also reviewed its position on the language in the Korean draft article which states that the lack of obligation on the part of the U.S. to redeem MPC held by unauthorized persons is recognized only "after the date of coming into force of this agreement". The Korean side would delete this language if there is an understanding that the deletion would not affect adversely negotiations with U.S. authorities for the exchange of MPC now held by the Korean Government for U.S. dollars.

20. Mr. Whang said the Korean Government now has a certain amount of MPC in its custody. At some future time, the Korean Government may enter into negotiations with the U.S. Government for the exchange of these MPC into U.S. dollars. It was with this possibility in mind that the Korean draft article on MPC was drafted, and that the phrase quoted earlier was inserted. By agreeing to deletion of this phrase, the Korean negotiators would not wish to have their position in the prospective negotiations adversely affected. Mr. Whang continued that, while in law unauthorized persons are not supposed to utilize MPC, in practical terms MPC were often handed over in the past to Koreans by authorized users in payment for goods and services provided to the authorized user. The Koreans had no choice; it was a question of either

0254

accepting the MPC, possibly without knowledge of the illegality of the transaction, or receiving no payment at all. In the future, the Korean Government intended to publicize the illegality of such transactions, but in the meantime large quantities of MPC had come into the hands of Koreans, some of which was turned over to the Korean Government in response to its call for a declaration of holdings of foreign currency. A way should be found to redeem this MPC in usable foreign exchange, in order to make up the loss now outstanding to the original recipients, and in order to repair the loss of good will which will otherwise accrue to the U.S.

21. Mr. Habib inquired what amount of MPC the Korean Government is currently holding in custody. Mr. Whang replied that he had no exact figures on the Government's holdings.

22. Mr. Habib asked whether the Korean side would agree to deletion of the phrase quoted by Mr. Whang if the understanding with respect to non-prejudice to any future negotiations were made reciprocal; that is, if the negotiating record also included a statement that the US has no obligation to redeem any amounts of MPC held by the Korean Government. Each side to the present negotiations would, under the terms of such an understanding, retain its independence with respect to a matter which should properly be discussed outside the present negotiations.

23. Mr. Whang said that the answer to Mr. Habib's proposal was complex and difficult, and that he wished to withdraw his offer of the deletion of the phrase under discussion. The Korean side would stand on its original draft language.

0255

24. Mr. Habib said he regretted Mr. Whang's retreat from a proposal which seemed to offer a solution by which the interests of both sides to the present negotiations could be preserved and the negotiation of a Status of Forces Agreement advanced. The U.S. is, of course, not prepared to agree to compensation for MPC illegally acquired and was not willing to assist in the ex post facto legalization of illegal transactions just because they had taken place on a broad scale. Mr. Whang had, unfortunately, in the preceding discussion made clear that the Korean side wished to impose an obligation upon the U.S. side to agree at some time in the future to exchange the Korean Government's holdings of illegally acquired MPC for dollars. In these circumstances, he was compelled to table a draft agreed minute which rules out the possibility of any future negotiations for the conversion of Korean Government holdings of illegally acquired MPC. Mr. Habib tabled the draft agreed minute he had just described, and it was agreed to turn to the topic of local procurement.

LOCAL PROCUREMENT

25. Major Peckham presented a detailed explanation of the manner in which the U.S. side envisaged that the exemptions from Korean taxation specified in the U.S. draft article on local procurement would be granted. He stressed that the key to a proper understanding of the U.S. draft article is a close reading of U.S. draft agreed minute number 3 to the U.S. draft article, which sets forth in detail the procedures by which the U.S. Forces would obtain the exemptions specified in the article above. Examples of the manner in which these procedures would be implemented were set forth. Major Peckham also emphasized

0256

that the U.S. Forces in Korea are already receiving exemptions, for both direct and "ultimate use" procurement, from most of the taxes specified in the U.S. draft article under the terms of existing Korean legislation. The implementation of the U.S. draft article would require only a broadening and formalizing of the existing procedures, and not the development of any new procedures.

26. Mr. Sin Kwan-sup, replying to Major Peckham's presentation on behalf of the Korean side, expressed certain reservations about certain points, and said that a broadening of the present system for the exemption of U.S. Forces procurement from Korean taxation would increase the cost of tax administration appreciably. He suggested that the matters touched upon in Major Peckham's presentation be discussed between specialists from the two negotiating teams outside the formal negotiating sessions. The U.S. negotiators agreed to this suggestion.

OTHER BUSINESS

27. It was agreed that the next negotiating session would be held on October 4, 1963, at 2:00 P.M. The negotiators having remained in session almost three hours, the meeting was thereupon adjourned.

1966.12.31에 예고문에 의거 일반문서로 재분류됨

외교문서 비밀해제: 주한미군지위협정(SOFA) 6
주한미군지위협정(SOFA) 서명 및 발효 6

초판인쇄 2024년 03월 15일
초판발행 2024년 03월 15일

지은이 한국학술정보(주)
펴낸이 채종준
펴낸곳 한국학술정보(주)
주 소 경기도 파주시 회동길 230(문발동)
전 화 031-908-3181(대표)
팩 스 031-908-3189
홈페이지 http://ebook.kstudy.com
E-mail 출판사업부 publish@kstudy.com
등 록 제일산-115호(2000. 6. 19)

ISBN 979-11-7217-017-2 94340
979-11-7217-011-0 94340 (set)

이 책은 한국학술정보(주)와 저작자의 지적 재산으로서 무단 전재와 복제를 금합니다.
책에 대한 더 나은 생각, 끊임없는 고민, 독자를 생각하는 마음으로 보다 좋은 책을 만들어갑니다.